Chinese Houses

The Architectural Heritage of a Nation

Ronald G. Knapp

Foreword by Jonathan Spence
Photography by A. Chester Ong

TUTTLE

Published in 2005 by Tuttle Publishing, an imprint of Periplus Editions (HK) Ltd, with editorial offices at 364 Innovation Drive, North Clarendon, Vermont 05759, USA, and 130 Joo Seng Road #06-01/03, Singapore 368357.

Text © Ronald G. Knapp
Photographs © A. Chester Ong and Periplus Editions (HK) Ltd

All rights reserved. No part of this publication may be reproduced, stored in a retrieval system or transmitted in any form or by any means, electronic, mechanical, photocopying, recording or otherwise without prior permission of the publisher.

Library of Congress Control Number 2004114425
ISBN 0 8048 3537 3

Design: Holger Jacobs, Gennett Agbenu and Wiesia Power at Mind Design

Printed in Singapore

Distributed by:
Japan
Tuttle Publishing, Yaekari Building, 3F,
5-4-12 Osaki, Shinagawa-ku, Tokyo 141-0032
Tel: (813) 5437 0171; Fax: (813) 5437 0755
E-mail: tuttle-sales@gol.com

North America, Latin America and Europe
Tuttle Publishing, 364 Innovation Drive,
North Clarendon, VT 05759-9436, USA
Tel: (802) 773 8930; Fax: (802) 773 6993
E-mail: info@tuttlepublishing.com
http://www.tuttlepublishing.com

Asia Pacific
Berkeley Books Pte Ltd, 130 Joo Seng
Road #06-01/03, Singapore 368357
Tel: (65) 6280 1330; Fax: (65) 6280 6290
E-mail: inquiries@periplus.com.sg
http://www.periplus.com

08 07 06 05
6 5 4 3 2 1

TUTTLE PUBLISHING® is a registered trademark of Tuttle Publishing

Page 1:
Feng family residence, Sichuan (page 232).

Page 2:
Cheng Zhi Tang, Hongcun village, Anhui (page 73).

Pages 4–5:
A contemporary painting by Robert Powell, showing the abundant use of structural and ornamental wood in Laowu Ge, heralded as the earliest Ming period private residence in China, perhaps dating from the 1470s. Xixinan village, Anhui.

Page 6:
Xu Wei's Green Vine Studio, Shaoxing, Zhejiang (page 140).

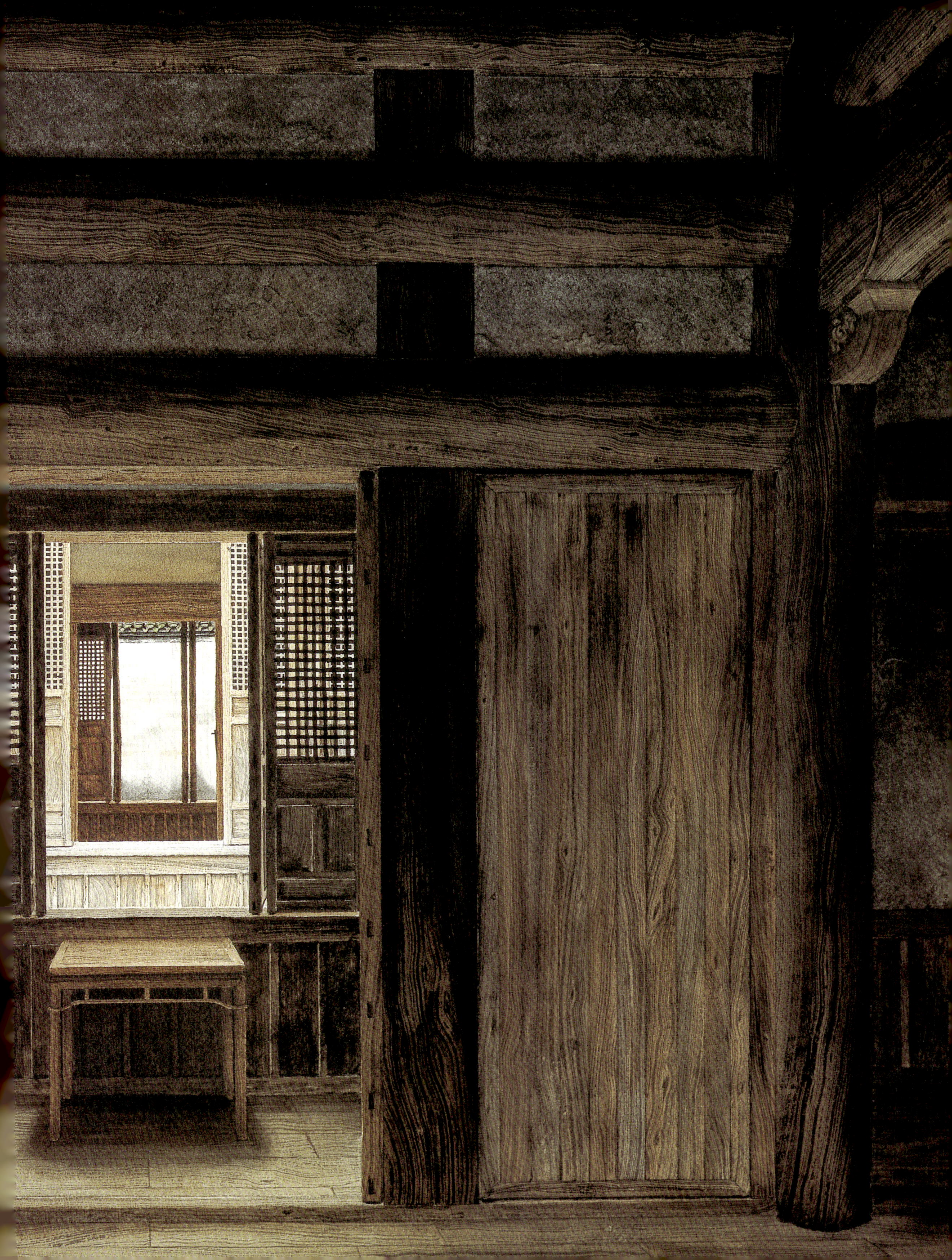

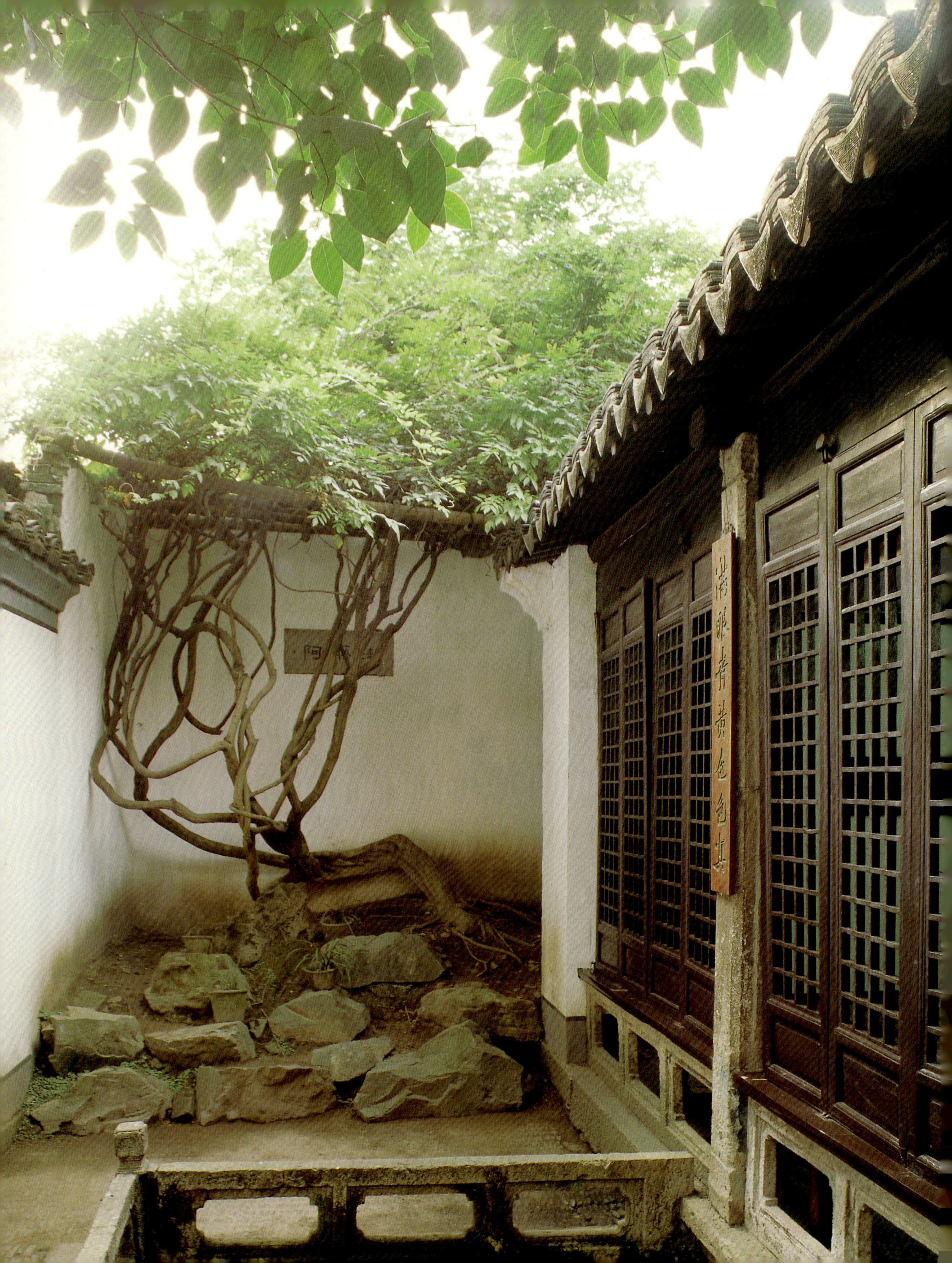
满眼青黄色色真

CONTENTS

8	**Foreword** by Jonathan Spence

10 **Part One**
THE ARCHITECTURE OF THE CHINESE HOUSE

52 **Part Two**
THE CHINESE HOUSE AS LIVING SPACE

98 **Part Three**
CHINA'S FINE HERITAGE HOUSES

100 **A Beijing Courtyard House**
Mei Lanfang's Siheyuan
Beijing

112 **Northern Mountain Houses**
Chuandixia Village
Mentougou, Beijing

120 **Jiangnan Canal Houses**
Homes in Yangzi Delta Watertowns
Jiangnan

132 **An Educator's Residence**
Shen Family Home
Luzhi, Jiangsu Province

140 **A Scholar's Study**
Xu Wei's Green Vine Studio
Shaoxing, Zhejiang Province

146 **A Millionaire's Home**
Kang Family Manor
Henan Province

156 **A Three-Story Ming Dynasty House**
Wang Ganchen's "Swallow's Wing Hall"
Chengkan, Anhui Province

166 **A Merchant's Residence**
Wang Dinggui's "Hall of Inheriting Ambition"
Anhui Province

176 **The Five Phoenix Mansion**
Lin Family's "Fortune in Abundance Tower"
Fujian Province

184 **Round Fortress Ramparts in Fujian**
"Inspiring Success Tower" and "Like a Sheng Tower"
Fujian Province

192 **Hakka Encircling Dragons**
De Xing Tang and Ning'an Lu Weilongwu
Guangdong Province

202 **A Mandarin's Mansion in Hong Kong**
Man Chung-luen's Residence
Hong Kong, SAR

210 **A Country Farmhouse**
Mao Zedong's Boyhood Home
Hunan Province

220 **A Landlord's Village Home**
Liu Shaoqi's Boyhood Home
Hunan Province

228 **Urban Dwellings in Northern Sichuan**
Ma and Feng Family Residences
Langzhong, Sichuan Province

240 **A U-Shaped Farmhouse**
Deng Xiaoping's Boyhood Home
Sichuan Province

248 **A Grand Qing Manor and a Simple Ming Courtyard House**
Qiao Family Manor and Ding Family Village
Shanxi Province

256 **The Manor of a Bean Curd Maker**
Wang Family Manor
Jingsheng, Shanxi Province

264 **Walled City Residences**
Fan Family Courtyard
Pingyao, Shanxi Province

274 **Cave Dwellings of the North**
Subterranean Adaptations
Henan, Shaanxi, and Shanxi Provinces

282 Bibliography
284 Index
287 Acknowledgments

FOREWORD

For a good many years now, thanks to the ambitious and sensitive researches of Ronald Knapp, historians of China have learned to be more aware of the beauty and complexity of the spaces in which the Chinese live and have lived.

I still remember when I first got my own real sense of this. It was on a sunny day several years ago as I was driving with some recently made friends through southeastern Hunan. Acting on a whim, we parked by the side of a road and set off to look at a nearby valley. After strolling a short while, we found ourselves in a village, navigating a maze of narrow lanes between mud or adobe walls. The walls grew steadily higher, until suddenly we came out into an open space full of sunshine. The view, as we had hoped, was breathtaking: in the foreground, a long expanse of beaten earth, clearly a threshing floor; beyond that, the slender but sturdy lines of stone-paved dikes that served as dividers and paths between the paddy fields of shimmering rice plants; and across the fields, wooded hills below distant mountains.

But the real surprise came when I turned around, to look back at the narrow alleys from which our little group had come. For now I could see that in the very front of the village through which we had been walking stood three stone houses, side by side. They were tall, with massive doors, smooth walls, and curving black roofs. The framings around the windows were decorated with dark wood lattice and wooden carvings of intricate elegance. One of the doors stood ajar: from the threshold one could look into a lofty entrance hall, cool and spacious. Straight ahead, clearly visible despite the shadows, was a space for ancestral portraits and tablets; to left and right, openings led to side courts, and what appeared to be rows of smaller rooms. The place seemed deserted, perhaps abandoned.

As Knapp would have told me had he been there, the house I was peering into represented the four basic norms for traditional Chinese dwellings: "bilateral symmetry, axiality, hierarchy, and enclosure" (Knapp, page 195). The strong stone structure defined a flow of specialized and functional spaces that in the past would have "mediated behavior and helped mold the actions of family members" (page 68). And the positioning of the house, its relationship to the landscape and to its neighbors, were all conditioned by the rigorous yet fluid demands of *fengshui*, which Knapp helpfully defines as a "topographic configuration" for the village as a whole, an "orderly arrangement" of space and warmth for those living within (page 166).

Amongst the twenty case studies of specific houses—from Shaanxi to Fujian, from Sichuan to Jiangsu—that Knapp presents in this splendid and comprehensive new book, I found many depictions that enriched my understanding of that Hunan house I saw in earlier years. But more than that, he has also made me reflect on wider issues of Chinese economics and politics. Knapp's houses are often parts of networks of power and money, which he painstakingly dissects for us, whereas there is no indication that the little community I stumbled upon had any political or financial history of note. The valley was a long distance from any township, let alone a larger central hub of gentry living, or élite and wealthy merchant culture. The architectural beauty and the craftsmanship I chanced upon may have been diffused local variants of a dominant Hunanese urban center, but if so I could not find the link. And if mine was just a random encounter, as I believe it was, how many such chance encounters must be waiting others, in sites of equal beauty where the turbulence of wars and revolutions has still left the architectural fabric intact? I had always thought it was too late to save China's architectural legacy from the iron laws of development. But perhaps that is not so, after all.

Jonathan Spence
Yale University

This painting by Daoji, also known as Shitao (1642–1707), illustrates Tao Yuanming's poem "The Peach Blossom Spring," that tells of a lost fisherman who comes across a bucolic, utopian community of farmers living in simple dwellings. Freer Gallery of Art, Smithsonian Institution, Washington, DC.

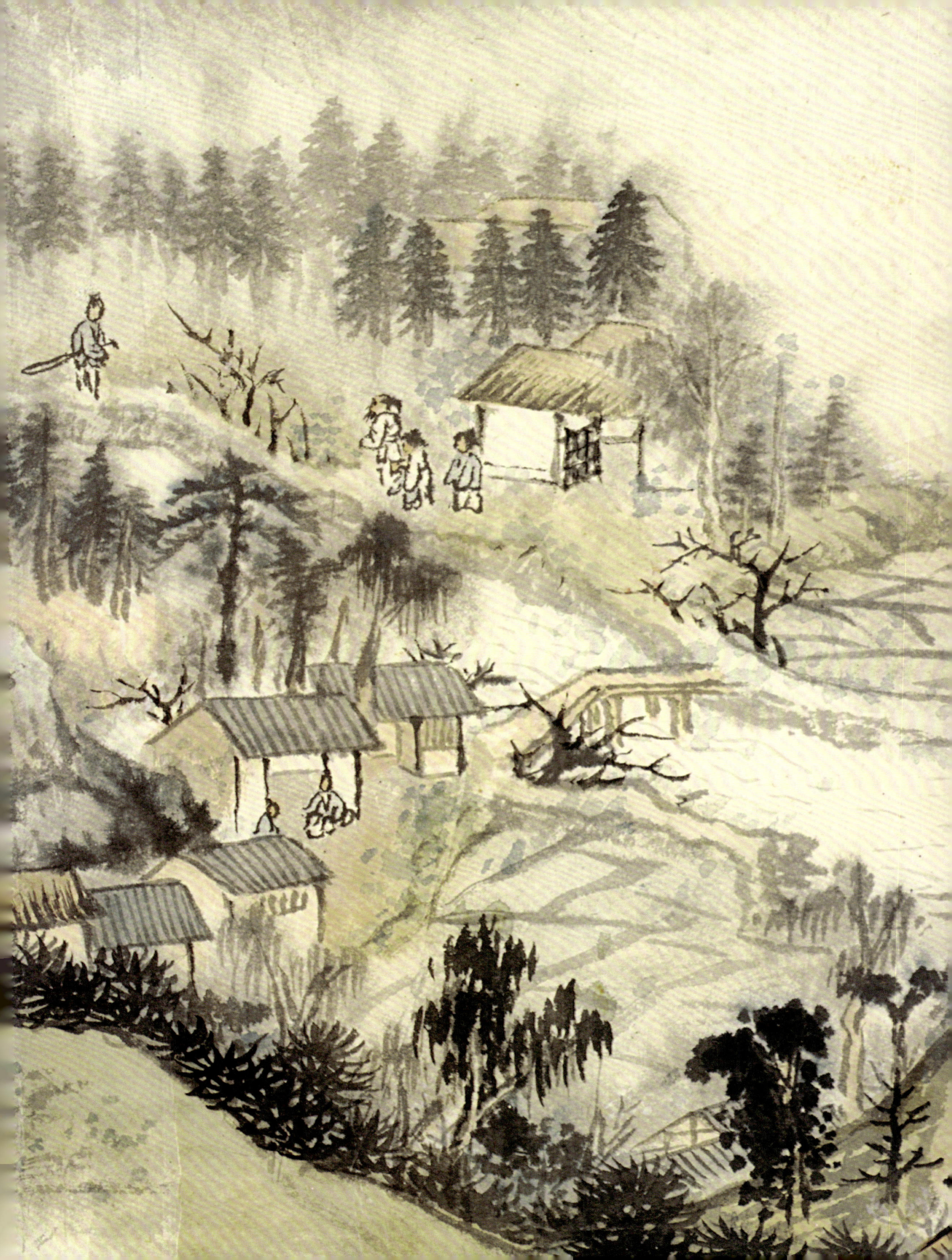

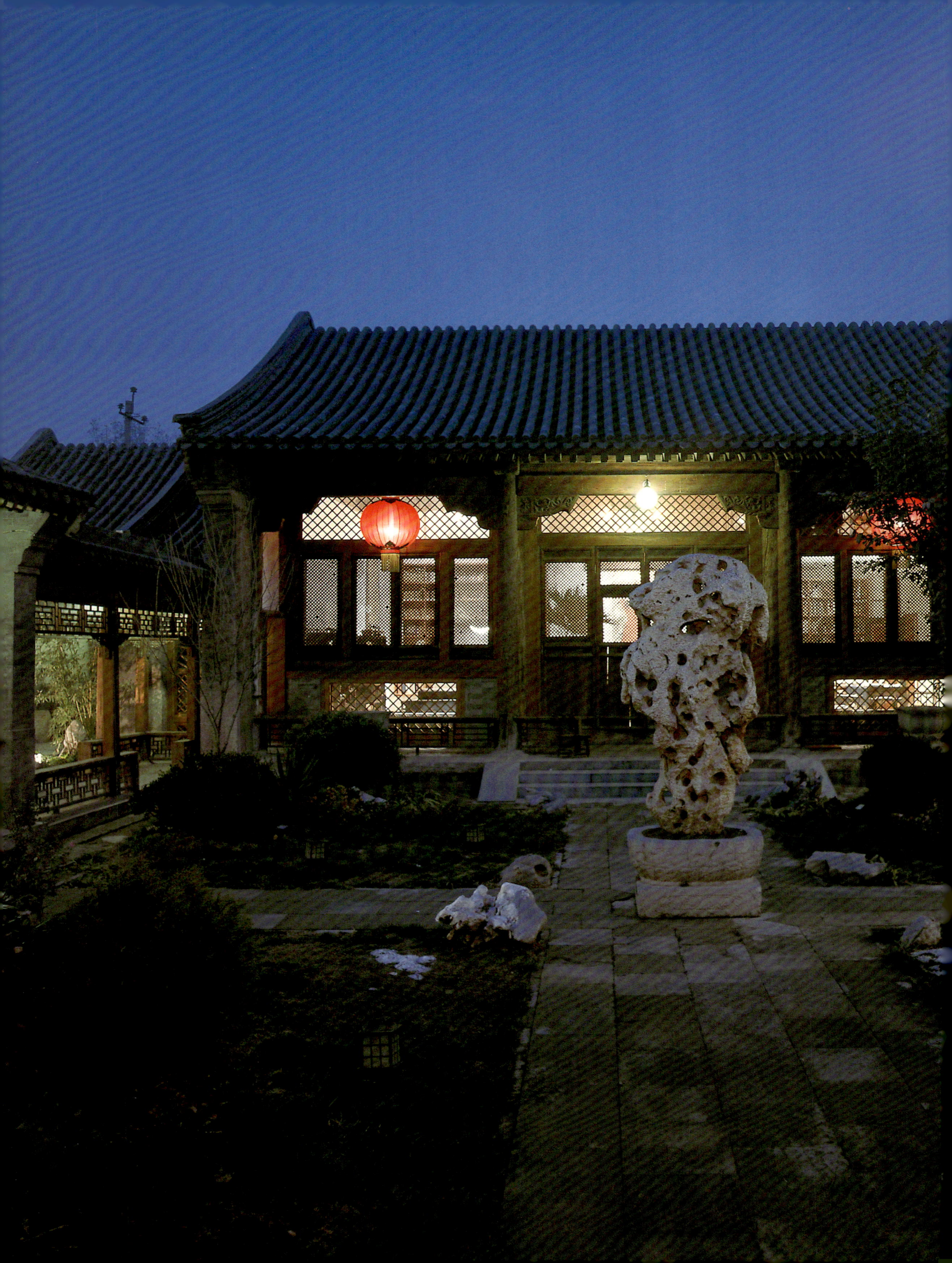

Part One

THE ARCHITECTURE OF THE CHINESE HOUSE

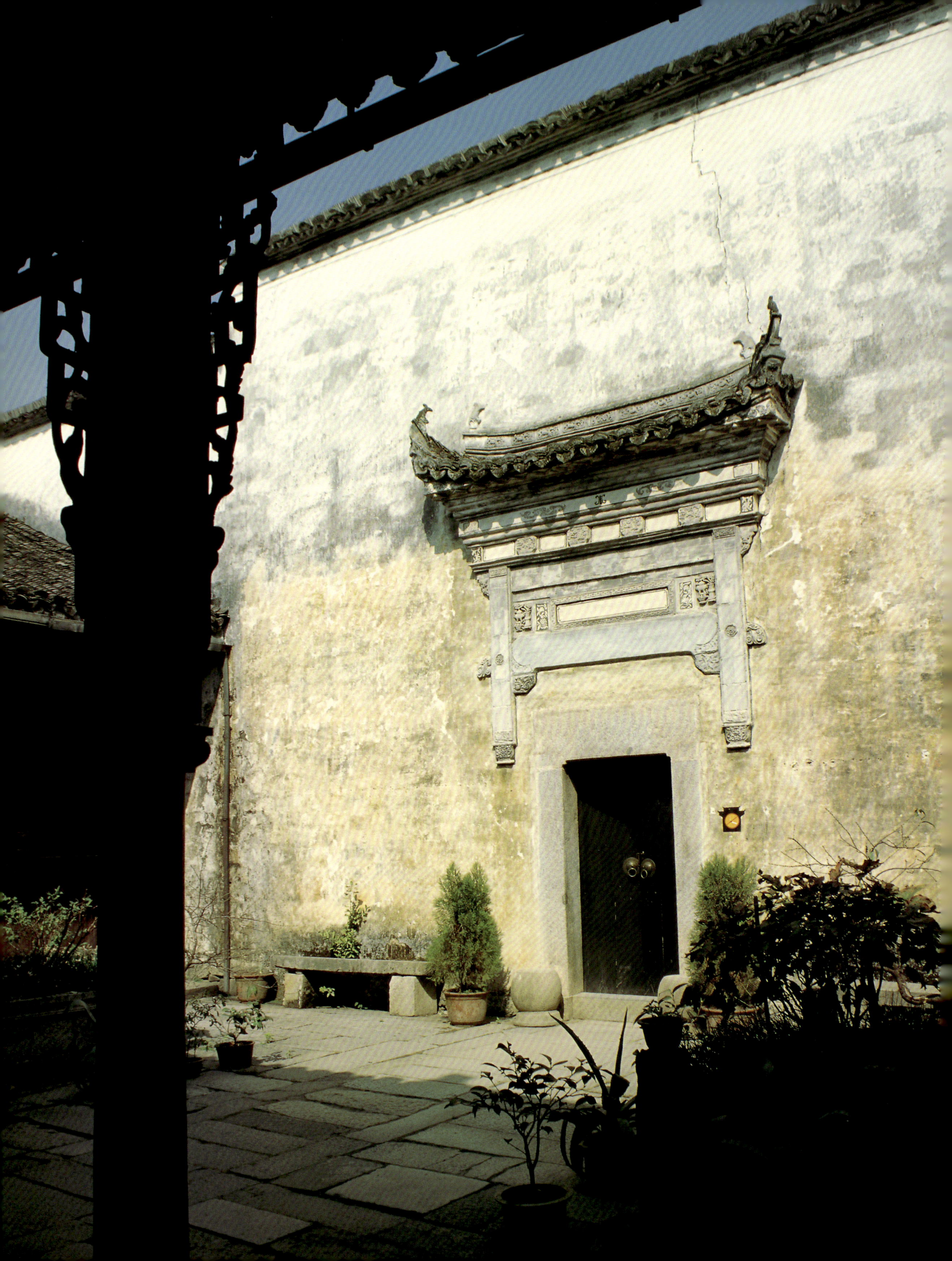

A COMPLEX MOSAIC OF ARCHITECTURAL STYLES

The houses within which Chinese families live their lives encompass a remarkable variety of styles. Until recent years, most Chinese dwellings were small, rather ordinary rectangular cottages, many mere huts, but there always have been significant numbers of expansive courtyard residences, as well as sometimes-grand manor complexes, and even sumptuous palaces, that are all in one way or other Chinese houses. While there is no single building style that can be called "Chinese," thus no "typical Chinese house," Chinese dwellings generally share a number of conventional features. Some of these architectural features—once thought to be universal and unchanging—have ceased to exist over the past quarter century as new ideas and new building materials have brought a striking transformation of housing throughout urban *and* rural China. While the predominance of traditional dwellings and local styles has been eclipsed in many ways by new housing styles, there is still much to be learned by looking at and appreciating examples of fine Chinese houses built in the past that even now are still found all over the country. Today, housing forms that break with tradition are common throughout China, yet dwellings continue to be built as they have for centuries by those without the means or inclination to build a "modern" dwelling.

Many, perhaps even most, old Chinese houses still seen today in villages, towns, and cities are rather unexceptional, nondescript, and thus ordinary, reflecting in part the fact that they were built of impermanent, easily accessible materials such as soil and plant materials that deteriorated over time. Many old houses remain standing, however often in dilapidated condition, among larger numbers of newer villa-style houses built of modern materials such as cement and tile. Yet, throughout China many old houses can still be visited that are grand in scale, sometimes even exquisite in terms of their proportions, constructed as they are of durable building materials, including fired bricks, rare timbers, and cut stone. Many of these are graced with skillfully crafted ornamentation—carved wood, stone, and clay—most of which evoke rich meanings that are sadly lost on most contemporary viewers. It is a selection of these fine examples of Chinese houses built over the past 500 years that are featured in this book. Together, they represent a personal and limited selection of *some* of my favorite Chinese houses culled from visits to literally thousands of Chinese dwellings over the past forty years. To do justice to China's domestic architectural patrimony would lead to a book many times larger than this one.

Although it is possible to note similarities and differences regarding Chinese houses, it is not possible to understand variations and changes clearly over the sweep of Chinese history because of insufficient textual, archaeological, and visual evidence. Specialists, unfortunately, are not yet able to determine, for example, how a particular building form, floor plan, or structural element evolved historically or how any particular aspect came to be spread across China's vast territory. Yet, it is certain that the weight of precedence and pragmatism arising from practical experience as well as the widespread use of conventionalized building elements all contributed to a conservative Chinese building tradition. Indeed, building forms that took shape thousands of years ago have had a remarkable resilience down to the

Opposite:
This view from a covered area used to store sedan chairs is across an open courtyard to the formal entry into the Main Hall of Cheng Zhi Tang, the residence of Wang Dinggui in Hongcun village, Anhui.

Left:
In the Kang family manor in Henan province, some rooms are dug as caves into the loessial hill slope. This room serves as the shrine for the Three Living Gods of Wealth.

Pages 10–11:
Glowing in the early evening, this newly renovated *siheyuan* in the Beijing area reveals the very active life of the family living within.

Key
1 Mei Lanfang's Siheyuan
2 Mountain Houses
3 Qiao Family Manor
4 Fan Family Courtyard
5 Wang Family Manor
6 Ding Family Village
7 Houwang Village cave dwellings
8 Kangdian Village cave dwellings
9 Kang Family Manor
10 Shen Family Home
11 Jiangnan Canal Houses
12 Xu Wei's Green Vine Studio
13 Wang Ganchen's "Swallow's Wing Hall"
14 Wang Dinggui's "Hall of Inheriting Ambition"
15 Liu Shaoqi's Boyhood Home
16 Mao Zedong's Boyhood Home
17 Lin Family's "Fortune in Abundance Tower"; "Inspiring Success Tower" and "Like a Sheng Tower"
18 Hakka Encircling Dragons
19 Man Chung-luen's Residence
20 Deng Xiaoping's Boyhood Home
21 Ma and Feng Family Residences

present. On the other hand, there is significant visual evidence, observable today, of striking variations in architectural styles that are geographical—that is, varying over space—rather than the more elusive historical, varying over time. These geographical disparities reflect often practical responses to differing regional environmental conditions, underscoring the adaptability of traditional building forms and building practices under varying conditions.

Strong local or regional idioms are characteristic of houses throughout China, so that it is proper to view Chinese dwellings as "vernacular architecture," common forms whose variations are as diverse as vernacular languages and other aspects of everyday culture. Houses, indeed, are among the most lasting of all cultural artifacts, even though the materials of which they are made may decay or disintegrate, and the circumstances leading to their creation have passed. Dwellings take shape over time, sometimes growing and at others retrenching, but at all times suggestive of the internal as well as external dynamics giving them shape. Houses sometimes take shape over a long period of time, reflecting the ideas of successive generations and their changing abilities to shoulder the substantial costs associated with ongoing construction and the maintenance of what has been completed.

Old houses in China are not the product of a motionless traditional culture in which building forms were stagnant. Indeed, the rather simple terms "tradition" and "traditional" are in reality loaded with the ambiguities of agelessness, monotony, and permanence, and must be used carefully when describing old Chinese houses. The geographer Yi-Fu Tuan invites readers to ponder: "When we say of a building that it is traditional, do we intend approval or, on the contrary, criticism? Why is it that the word 'traditional' can evoke, on the one hand, a feeling of the real and the authentic and hence some quality to be desired, but, on the other hand, a sense of limitation—of a deficiency in boldness and originality?" (1989: 27). In fact, the notion of "tradition" is rooted in the literal meaning of "that which is handed down," an often robustly dynamic process whatever its pace, that has bequeathed buildings which are often original and bold while sometimes displaying deficiencies and incongruities as well as utilitarian and attractive formulaic elements.

No purpose is served in searching for a simple, single explanation about why Chinese houses generally were as they were in the past or even why one house in one place differs from another in another place. While it is oftentimes facile to see common patterns that only differ in details, it is important to recognize as well a significant heterogeneity of forms and explanations relating to houses as well as the settlements within which they are found (Ho, 2001).

Many of us who study Chinese houses have moved away from looking at dwellings with mere buildings as the units of analysis. Each house is a home for a family that exists in both time and space, a dynamic entity that manifests not only the family within it in its varying evolving forms, but as well is a constituent part of the place in which it is located.

A Complex Mosaic of Architectural Styles   15

Like any building, a house protects those inside from the vagaries of weather—heat and cold, rain and snow, humidity, and wind—yet "sheltering" is only one of the factors contributing to house form. Every dwelling is constructed within a broader environmental context—climate, that is, the long-term conditions of weather, as well as soils, rock, and available vegetation—that is often well understood by local inhabitants, who—because of pragmatic habits and environmental sensibilities—build their dwellings in order to provide a level of physical comfort, a habitable internal microclimate. In China and nearby areas of East Asia, this attentiveness to environmental conditions is significantly amplified because of the application of *fengshui* ("wind and water"), or geomancy, which has at its base a sensitivity to recurring patterns of nature and a generally heightened level of environmental awareness.

As compelling as are the varying responses to environmental conditions, dwellings, however, are more than mere refuges from the extremes of weather, havens from the changing forces of nature. Chinese housing forms may have similarities, but each is created under local conditions. Whether small or large, it seems that any Chinese house is in a continuous state of alteration in order to meet the ongoing life cycle changes and often irregular requirements of a family: a marriage of a son brings a new woman into the house and the formation of a conjugal unit; a marriage of a daughter leads to her abandoning her old room and attenuating long-held family relationships as she leaves her parents' home; new family members are born and others die; relatives come for lengthy stays; and rooms are sometimes rented out to others as a family's needs require. New cooking stoves are added to accommodate some of these changes, even as doors are sealed or opened and ritual spaces redefined.

Rural as well as urban houses serve as the essential stages for each household's production and consumption activities and reflect elements of their religious and cosmological beliefs, in addition to expressing at least some aspects of the often complicated patterns of personal relationships of the household in terms of age, gender, and generational status. Examples of these dynamic elements are portrayed in many of the examples discussed and illustrated in the pages that follow.

Chinese Houses: Similarities and Differences

With land area approximately the same as that of the United States and twice that of Europe, as well as widely varying climatic conditions, China includes fifty-six disparate nationalities and a remarkable diversity even among its dominant Han ethnic majority. It is thus not surprising that Chinese houses are at least as varied as those found in multinational Europe and are more diverse than those in the United States. Rather straightforward and simple I-shaped houses, often with peculiar local characteristics, are ubiquitous throughout China. Less well known, however, are the many larger, quite distinctive housing types of remarkable complexity that complement the relatively uncomplicated rectangular houses, and underscore the richness of China's housing traditions. These larger structures include hierarchically organized quadrangular courtyard residences in the Beijing area, unique below-ground cave-like dwellings in the north and northwest, expansive manor-complexes in the north, extraordinarily beautiful two- and three-story merchant dwellings in central China, massive multistoried fortresses in the hilly south, portable tents and cantilevered pile-dwellings occupied by ethnic minority populations, as well as boats of many types along the coast and embayed rivers. Each of these will be represented in the sections that follow.

While there is no single style that can be called "a Chinese house" across time and space, it is possible to point to a set of remarkably similar elements shared by many—if not most—houses, whether simple or grand. Chinese builders throughout the country historically favored a number of conventional building plans and structural principles. In addition, special attention was paid to the environmental conditions of specific building sites and to manipulating building parts in order to acquire some control of natural conditions, including access to sunlight and prevailing winds in addition to blocking cold winds and collecting rainwater. Rooted deeply in Chinese building traditions, these fundamental building rudiments have influenced as well the building traditions found in Japan, Korea, and to some degree Vietnam (Balderstone and Logan, 2003; Ho, 2003; Lee, 2003; Matsuda, 2003; Ruan, 2003; Steinhardt et al., 2002).

"Su Shi's Second Poem on the Red Cliff" (ink on paper), completed by Qiao Zhongchang during the Northern Song dynasty (1123), depicts Su Shi's experience while jaunting with friends in the wild landscape surrounding his place of exile, as recounted in his poem. In the scene reproduced above, Su says goodbye to his wife before setting off from his farmstead, which the painting shows as a compact courtyard dwelling wrapped with an outer wall. Nelson-Atkins Museum of Art, Kansas City, Missouri.

A Complex Mosaic of Architectural Styles

Published in 1911, this is among the first photographs of a round "clan house" rampart on a hilltop in southwestern Fujian. Strangely, unique structures of this type were not further photographed or even noted for nearly a half century after.

18   The Architecture of the Chinese House

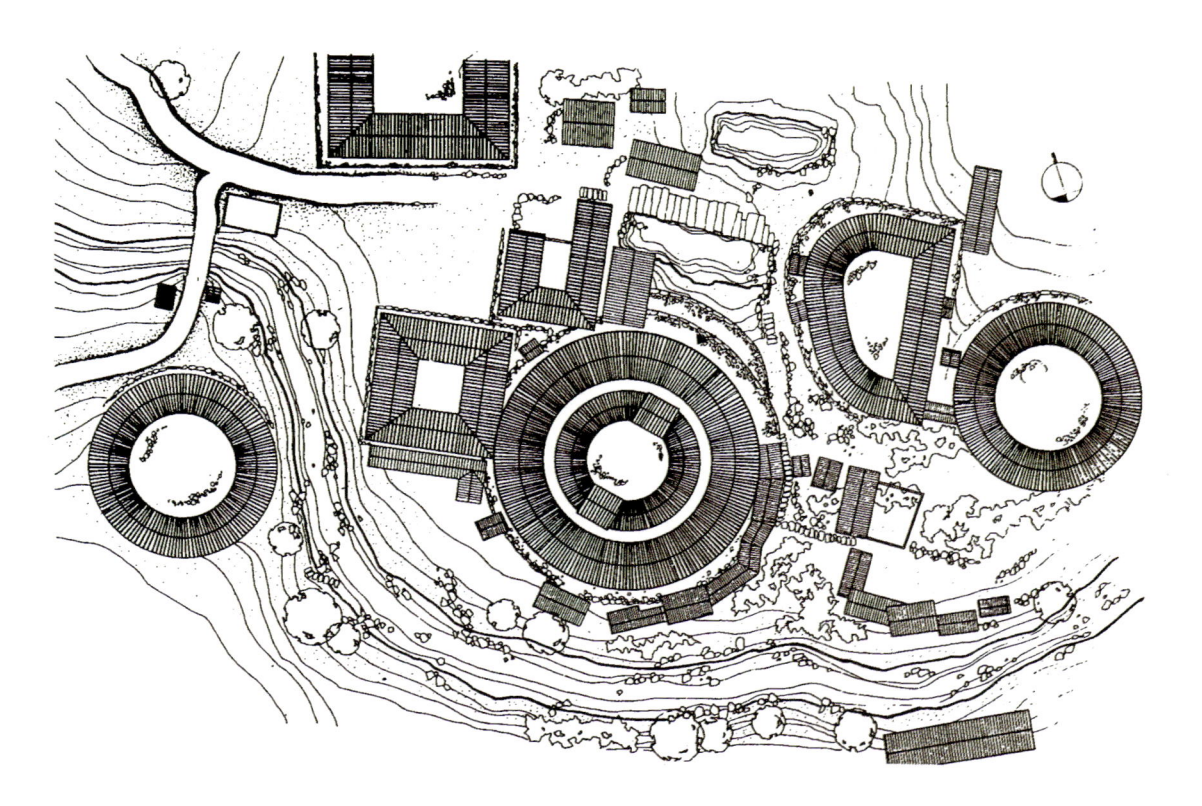

Left:
Mixed among structures of various shapes in a village in southwestern Fujian province, the large circular structures appear like landed UFOs.

Below:
Zhen Cheng Lou, a massive structure built in 1912 in Hongkeng village, Fujian, is a four-story circular fortified structure with windows only on two levels of the upper wall.

A Complex Mosaic of Architectural Styles

Open Spaces: Courtyards and Skywells

Chinese builders not only create structures—space that is enclosed with walls and a roof—but also recognize the need to create exposed spaces for living, work, and leisure. Open spaces, often loosely referred to as "courtyards," are an important category in the spatial layout of any fully formed Chinese house. They are found in seemingly endless variations, in relatively tiny houses as well as in complicated, expansive ones in which enclosed open spaces even include within them other buildings surrounding open spaces. Archaeological evidence shows that courtyards, a negative space, were elements of Chinese structures as early as 3000 years ago, and continued to be a fundamental design principle of temples and palaces, in addition to houses, down through the ages.

In "composing a house," to use Nelson Wu's apt phrase, open spaces are part of a "house–yard" complex. "The student of Chinese architecture," he continues, "will miss the point if he does not focus his attention on the space and the impalpable relationships between members of this complex, but, rather, fixes his eyes on the solids of the building alone" (Wu, 1963: 32). It is important, of course, to recall that the "solids of the building" themselves are spaces, created by the structure. The *Dao De Jing*, a fourth-century BCE work attributed to Laozi, anticipated the significance of voids, of apparent emptiness: "We put thirty spokes together and call it a wheel; But it is on the space where there is nothing that the usefulness of the wheel depends. We turn clay to make a vessel; But it is on the space where there is nothing that the usefulness of the vessel depends. We pierce doors and windows to make a house; And it is on these spaces where there is nothing that the usefulness of the house depends. Therefore just as we take advantage of what is, we should recognize the usefulness of what is not" (Waley, 1958: 155).

At least one open space is an important element of any Chinese house, even when the space is merely the outdoors immediately in front of a rectangular structure and without surrounding structures. Adjacent to most courtyards on at least two and often four sides are the buildings, positive constructed spaces. Full enclosure with buildings on three sides—an inverted U-shape—is quite common throughout China. Sometimes the fourth side is defined by a wall, which from the outside may make it appear as if the dwelling is wrapped by structures on four sides when this is not, in fact, the case.

Below:
Compact *siheyuan* or quadrangular courtyard houses of this type are found in villages, such as Chuandixia, in the mountainous areas around Beijing municipality.

Shown in this rubbing is an upper-class residence built some 2000 years ago. The complex comprises multiple courtyards surrounded by flanking structures and watchtowers. Yinan county, Shandong.

The common English term "courtyard" itself, or even its many Chinese language equivalents, is insufficient in differentiating the many types of open spaces seen from place to place in China. Still, there are a number of principles even if there is inconsistency in how terms are used. In general, the proportion of open space to enclosed space is significantly less in southeast and southwest China as compared to the north and northeast. In northeastern and northern China, courtyards are comparatively broad while in southern China they are usually condensed in size, sometimes becoming a mere shaft of open space. The Chinese term *tianjing*, translated as "skywell," catches well the meaning of constricted southern "courtyards," especially in two- or three-story dwellings where their verticality accentuates their diminished horizontal dimensions. Yet, in some parts of southern China, these small openings are still referred to as "courtyards."

Climatic variables play critical roles in differentiating the proportions of enclosed structures, transitional spaces, and open spaces. In the dry, colder areas of north and northeastern China, open spaces are generous portions of the house–courtyard complex, with the ratio decreasing as one moves south. Attention is paid to blocking cold winter winds and increasing the receipt of winter sunshine by eliminating windows and doors on back and side walls. Throughout central China, where winters are mild and summers hot, transitional spaces, such as verandahs and rooms with open-faced lattice door panels, increase in extent, while open spaces generally decrease in proportion to enclosed spaces. In the hot and humid areas of southeastern China, open spaces—here usually only skywells—shrink in size while transitional "gray" spaces increase significantly. Special attention is paid to ventilation of interior spaces and to blocking sunlight from penetrating the buildings. Local microclimates in any of these areas allow deviations from normal patterns.

The classic design of a fully developed Chinese courtyard is the Beijing *siheyuan*, a quadrangle of low buildings enclosing a courtyard, whose origins go back to the eleventh century BCE. *Siheyuan* are distinguished by being enclosed within gray brick walls with only a single entry—back and side walls lack both windows and doors; orientation to the cardinal directions with main halls generally facing south or southeast; balanced side-to-side symmetry in terms of layout; and a well-defined axis with an implied hierarchical organization of space. Each *siheyuan* has at least one courtyard at its center, covering about 40 percent of the total area of the dwelling complex, while many have a sequential series of subsidiary courtyards to the front and/or rear. Privacy and security are provided in residential sanctuaries of this sort, with public spaces towards the front and with increasing levels of personal spaces as one moves from outside to inside. In Beijing, *siheyuan* are the basic components of a checkerboard pattern of low-rise neighborhoods tightly packed along narrow lanes called *hutong*.

Modularized quadrangular dwellings show striking regional differences that reveal the versatility and flexibility of a basic form even as they all are called by the common name *siheyuan*. Mountain dwellings in northern China often have what appear to be miniature courtyards embraced by similarly small buildings. In the northeast region beyond the Great Wall, for example, *siheyuan* courtyards are

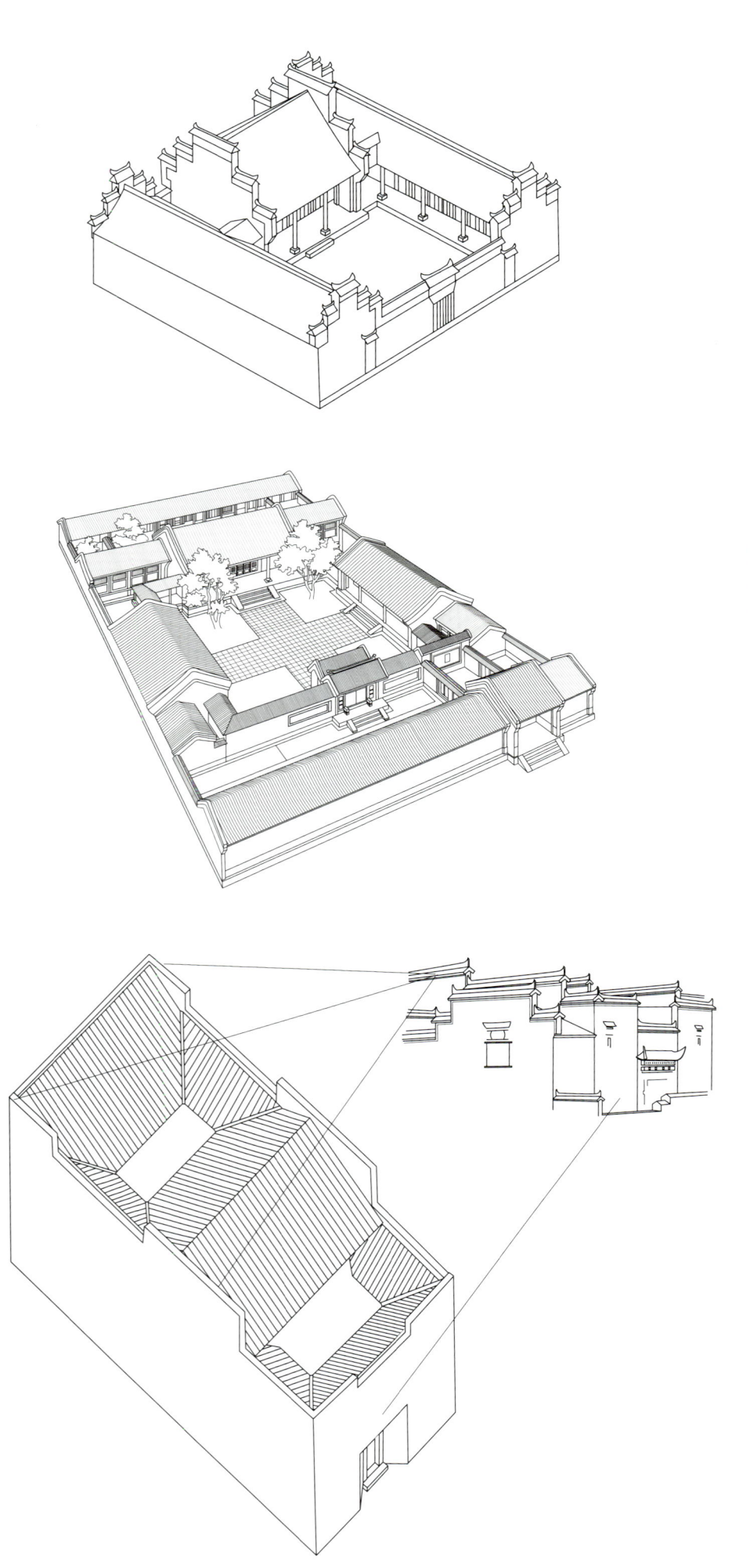

Left:
While differing in details, the dwelling types shown here all include the fundamental elements of Chinese architecture: enclosure, axiality, hierarchy, and symmetry. The central image is that of a classic Beijing *siheyuan* or quadrangular courtyard house.

Below:
Side rooms come in many shapes, including this arcuate—cave-like—form in the Fan family residence, Pingyao, Shanxi.

quite broad; in Shanxi and Shaanxi provinces, on the other hand, *siheyuan* courtyards are elongated and narrow. Because of very hot summers and severe winters, buildings in central Shanxi are placed closer together than is the case in the Beijing area so that direct and intense sunlight is blocked during the summer from entering rooms except in the early morning and late afternoon, while the surrounding tight structures with high walls reduce the intrusion of cold winds in winter. In Fujian, as can be seen in the eighteenth-century Wu family dwelling in Quanzhou, small courtyards can be linked in a series of adjacent house–yard complexes.

While the typical courtyard of a *siheyuan* emerges in the void or open space formed by the buildings that enclose it, sunken courtyards are carved into the earth in northern Henan and southern Shanxi provinces. Here, a courtyard for an underground or subterranean dwelling, sometimes called a cave dwelling, is in fact formed first, the initial "constructed" component of the dwelling complex whose "walls" provide the exposed surfaces into which the adjacent residential "structures" are then dug. A sunken courtyard of this type thus becomes a "walled" compound with a core outdoor living space open to the sky, just as with any courtyard built directly on the surface. Elsewhere in China, circular, elliptical, trapezoidal, rectangular, even octagonal courtyards are found within surrounding walls.

Throughout southern China, as mentioned above, dwellings are often punctuated with abbreviated rectangular open spaces or cavities that local people refer to as "courtyards" but which in fact are skywells or *tianjing*. Although usually quite small

22   The Architecture of the Chinese House

Left:
Close-up of the lattice doors of a side hall under the narrow eaves of a renovated courtyard dwelling in Beijing.

Below:
From northeast to southeast in four regions of China, open spaces decrease in proportion to enclosed built spaces so that broad courtyards become increasingly smaller, eventually being mere skywells. Transitional gray spaces increase in significance from north to south.

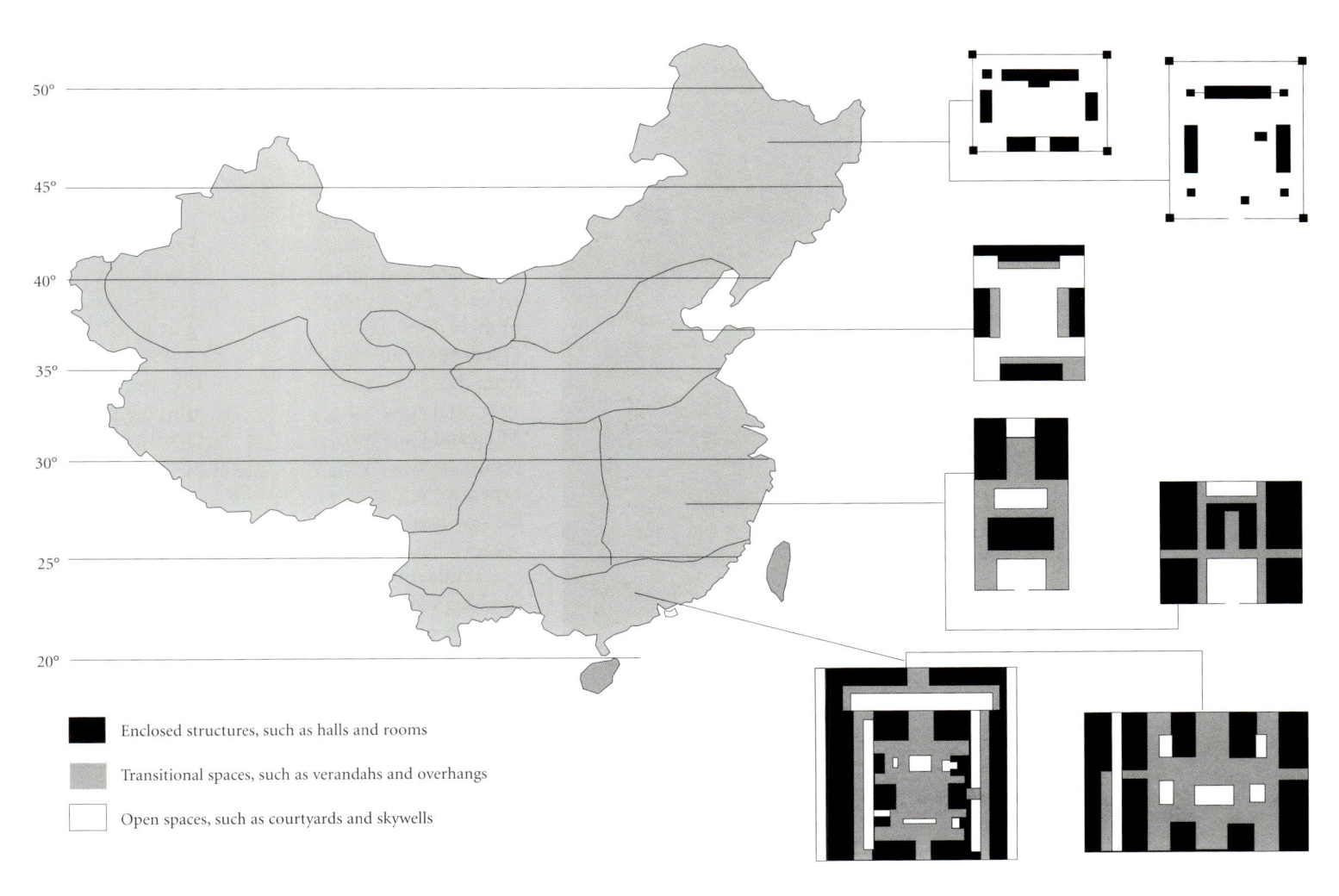

■ Enclosed structures, such as halls and rooms
▨ Transitional spaces, such as verandahs and overhangs
□ Open spaces, such as courtyards and skywells

A Complex Mosaic of Architectural Styles   23

Right:
Much of imperial Beijing in the past was laid out like a chessboard with well-defined neighborhoods developed along parallel lanes. Called *hutong*, these narrow lanes were said to be "like ox hair" in that their number was beyond calculation.

Below:
In Langzhong, Sichuan, low buildings—residences-cum-shops—are arranged along narrow parallel lanes.

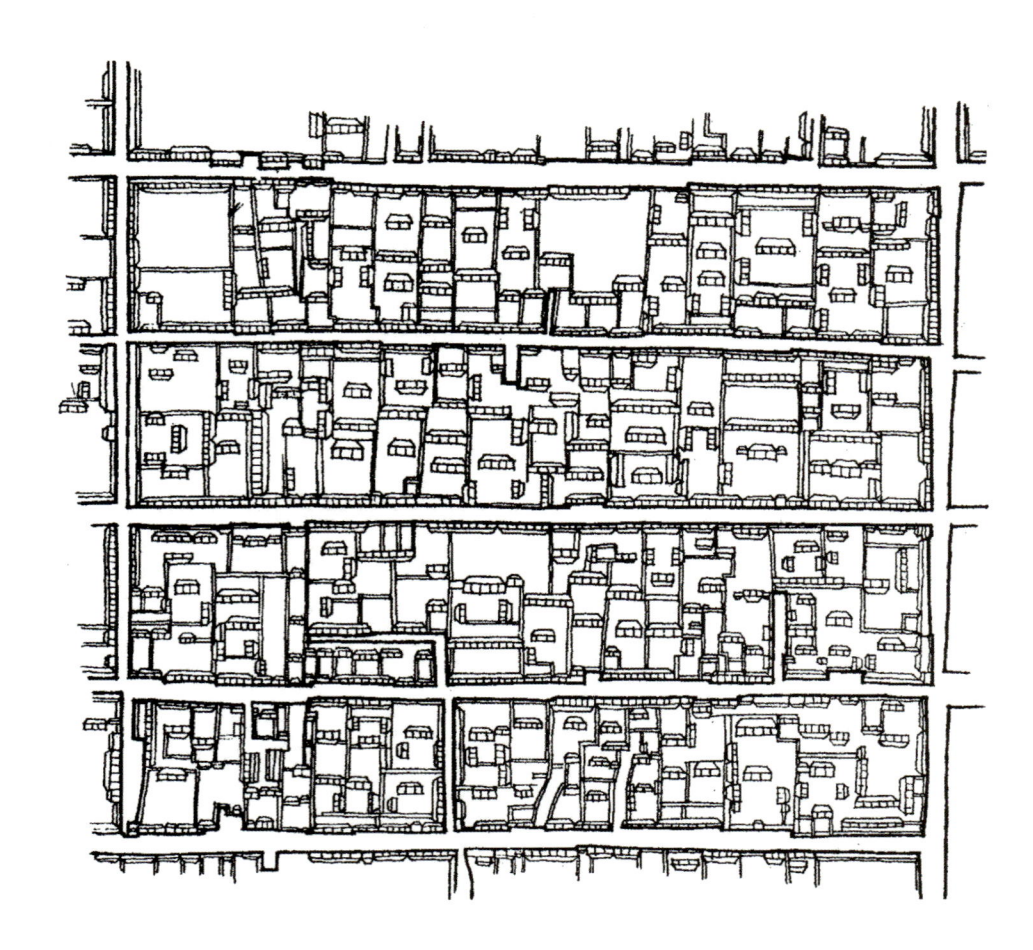

and compact, with a restricted openness to the broad sky above, skywells respond well to the hot and humid conditions characteristic of southern China where they catch passing breezes, evacuate interior heat, and lead rainwater into dwellings. The most distinctive *tianjing*-style dwellings are found in multistoried merchant dwellings in Anhui, Jiangxi, and Zhejiang provinces, centered on an area historically known as Huizhou, which appear like squat boxes or elongated loafs with solid walls and limited windows on the exterior walls. On the inside of these compact structures, there are usually several skywells, each an atrium-like enclosed vertical space whose size, shape, and number vary according to the overall scale of the dwelling. Some of the best examples of these dwellings survive from the Ming dynasty (1368–1644) but significantly larger numbers exist from the Qing dynasty (1644–1911). There are structural and aesthetic differences when comparing Ming and Qing dwellings in this area, with Qing residences usually having a greater profusion of expensive woods as well as carved stone and brick that are used structurally and ornamentally in the spaces adjacent to the *tianjing*.

While some open spaces are designed into a dwelling's plan and immediately "built" as part of it, others emerge over time as a house becomes more complicated in terms of its layout. An I-shaped rectangular house in northern and in some parts of coastal southern China becomes L-shaped with the addition of a perpendicular wing, then a U-shape with a facing perpendicular wing—in the process embracing a well-defined open courtyard. Enclosing the fourth side leads to a true quadrangular dwelling with a courtyard at its core. In southern China, a

Right:
Framed by a pair of wing buildings, the narrow and elongated courtyard—even here divided into "inner" and "outer" portions—is only as wide as the central bay of the main structure on the left. Xi'an area, Shaanxi.

Below and bottom:
The inward-sloping roofs of the wing structures lead water into the slender courtyard of the Fan family house, Pingyao, Shanxi. Viewed from a high vantage point, the small spaces, called *tianjing* or "skywells," which are integral parts of dwellings in southern and southwestern China, help ventilate the interiors while providing some light and water to the interior. Langzhong, Sichuan.

Below right:
Over a period of time as a family's circumstances improve, dwellings tend to grow from a three-bay rectangle, shown here on the left, to more complex shapes. The top drawing shows the common pattern in northern China where, first, an L-shape emerges and then an inverted U-shape, before full enclosure of a courtyard within a rectangle. In southern China, as the bottom drawing reveals, additions are sometimes added to the front or back with small "skywells" situated within the growing mass.

Northern China

Southern China

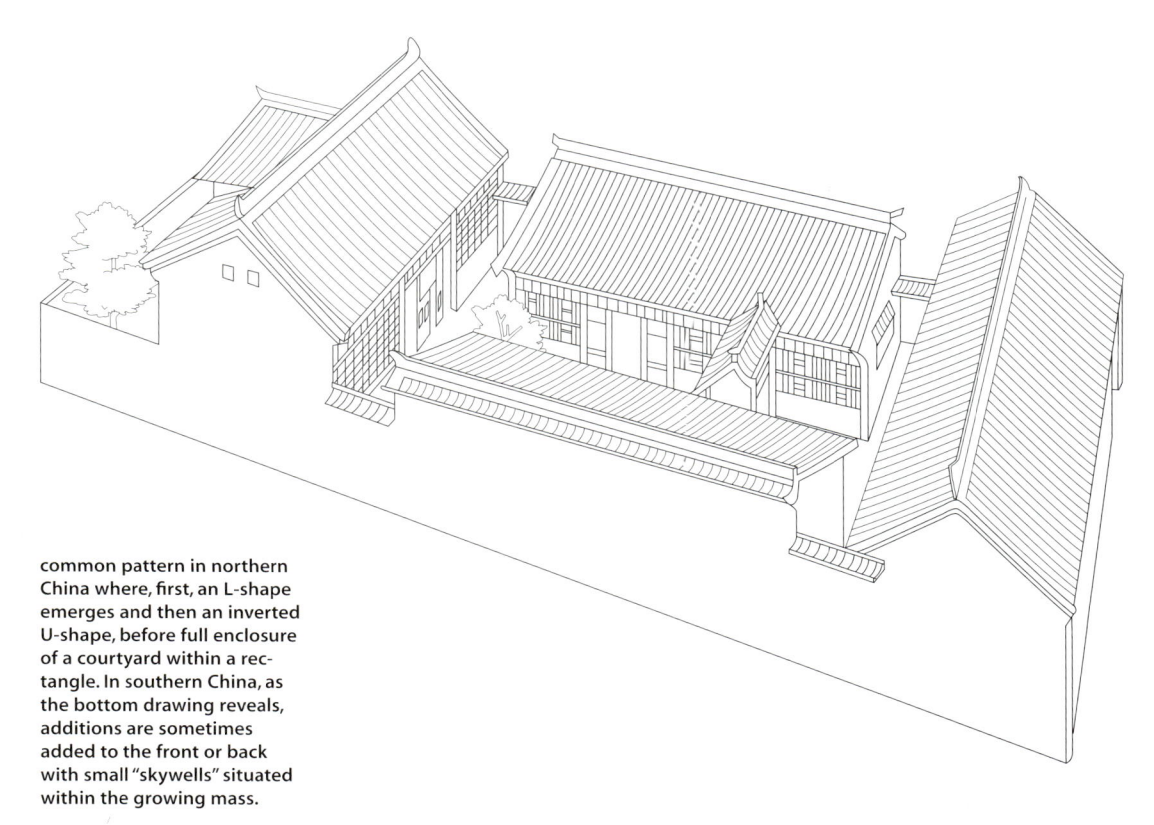

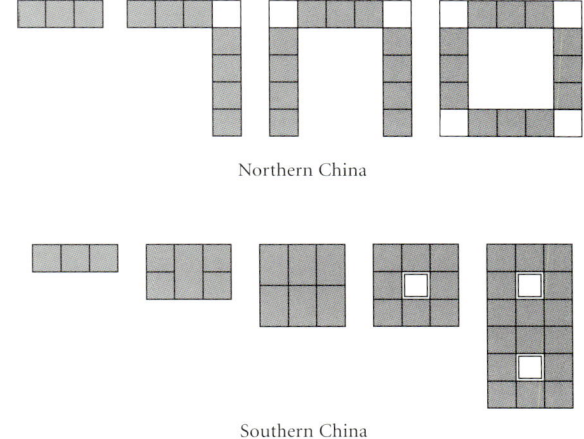

rectangular structure is more likely to expand towards the front or the back as enclosed space is doubled with open spaces—skywells—emerging in the interior of the building's mass as the house grows. Whether in the north or the south, perimeter walls and the surrounding structures effectively block out sounds from the outside, leaving the interior open spaces relatively quiet and quite private.

Whether compact or spread out, many Chinese houses exhibit a clear spatial hierarchy that mirrors the relationships among the family living within it and their interaction with visitors. Adjacent open and closed spaces help define this spatial hierarchy, aided in fundamental ways by the purposeful use of gates, screen walls, and steps. Casual visitors, for example, in the past were only invited into the front part of the house, perhaps only the entry vestibule near the main gate or into the first slender courtyard. The larger courtyard and the Main Hall were accessible

26 The Architecture of the Chinese House

Framed with a cracked ice lattice pattern, this moon gate leads from one courtyard to another. Wang family manor, Jingsheng village, Lingshi county, Shanxi.

only to family members. In addition, privileged spaces for women in the family were placed deeper in northern houses and in upper stories of southern houses, far from places where non-family visitors would see them. Separate passageways and doors sometimes helped enforce segregation. In some extensive residential complexes, moreover, a barely noticeable increase in elevation from the exterior to the interior, with each structure a few steps higher than the preceding courtyard, was employed to accentuate status differences from the outside deep into the interior. For women, the bed was a space for more than sleeping, whether it was a simple platform or an elevated brick surface heated from a nearby stove. A woman's bed often was a rectangular structure with its own architecture, raised on a dais with doors and screen walls that made it a veritable room within a room.

Indeed, whenever possible, open spaces—whatever the dimensions and however enclosed by buildings—are nearly obligatory elements of traditional Chinese houses. Open spaces offer abundant advantages in terms of providing enhanced ventilation and sunlight, a place to gather and work, and privacy and safety. Buildings are typically arranged symmetrically, facing each other around courtyards, with the principal building, usually where the main ceremonial hall is located, orientated towards the south or southeast. In many areas of northern China, this principal building is referred to as "northern building" or "upper building," both indicating a superior position. Side halls then can easily be designated "east hall" and "west hall" using descriptions that are both tied to the cardinal directions and hierarchy.

Many houses, especially those in Beijing, are meant to be viewed from the south, with the observer looking *up* towards the main structure with its striking façade. Balanced side-to-side symmetry is revealed in the floor plans of virtually all larger fully developed Chinese houses. The mansion of the Kong family, descendants of Confucius, in Qufu, Shandong province, is a fine example of an extensive *siheyuan* for an official of the first rank. It occupies some 4.6 hectares, including *yamen* or offices in front where the Duke of Yansheng administered the town, inner quarters for women, an eastern study, a western study, and gardens. Walls, gates, halls, side halls, and courtyards were all laid out in a plan that made hierarchy and status explicit.

Left:
The inner courtyard of the second residential courtyard in the Kang family manor, Henan province, is proportionally quite narrow even as the surrounding structures are tall.

Right:
This view across the courtyard of the Wang family manor in Shanxi shows a single-story main building with one of a pair of perpendicular two-story side buildings.

Below:
This schematic floor plan of a Beijing-style *siheyuan* portrays the complementary patterns of open courtyards and enclosed structures.

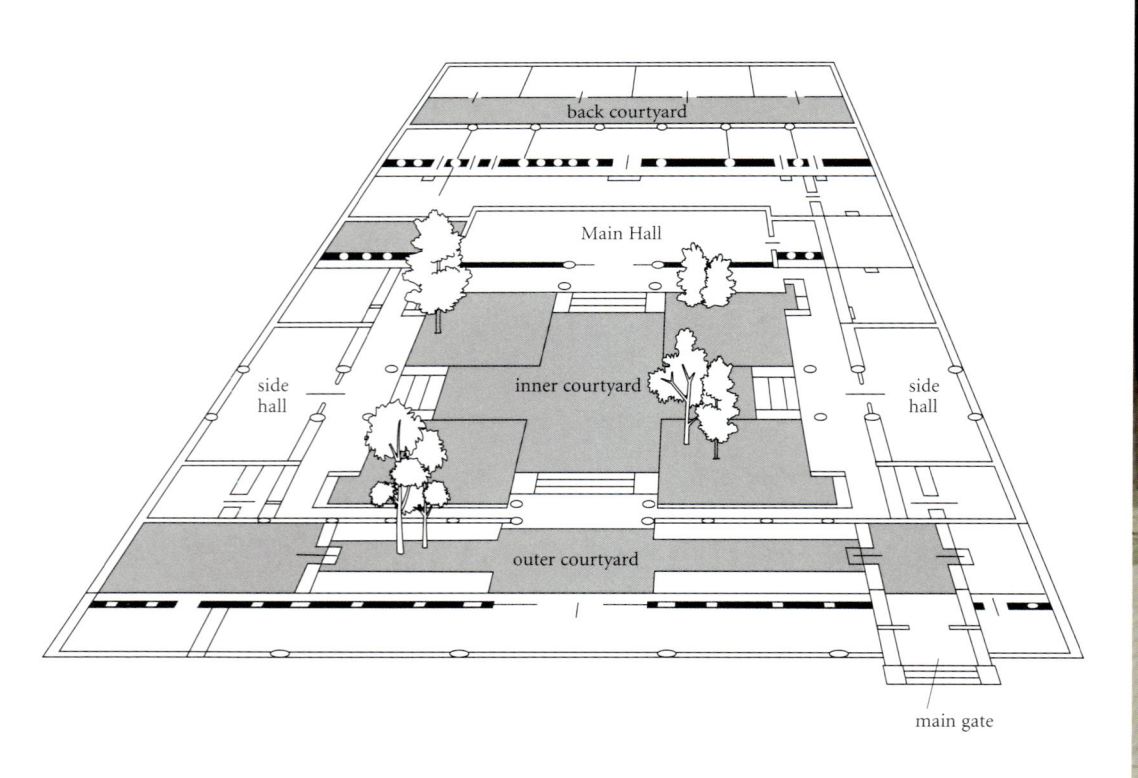

back courtyard

Main Hall

side hall — inner courtyard — side hall

outer courtyard

main gate

28 The Architecture of the Chinese House

A Complex Mosaic of Architectural Styles 29

Enclosing Spaces: Building Structure and Materials

Whether found in an opulent palace or a humble home, the common denominator of any Chinese structure is a modular building unit known as a *jian*. A *jian* is not only a fundamental measure of width, the span between two lateral columns that constitutes a bay, but it also represents the two-dimensional floor space bounded between four columns, as well as the volumetric measure of the void defined by the floor and the walls. Sometimes a *jian* forms "a room" although often a room is made up of several structural *jian*. In Chinese dwellings, it is rare for any effort to be made to hide structural columns that give shape to a *jian*, thus each stands not only as a marker of space but as a natural aesthetic element as well.

Jian: Building Module

Most rural Chinese dwellings are relatively simple I-shaped structures comprising at least three *jian*. Regional variations in the height, width, and depth of the *jian* naturally lead to differences in appearance from one area of China to another. In northern China, *jian* range in width between 3.3 and 3.6 meters while they are typically wider, between 3.6 and 3.9 meters, in southern China. The depth of a bay—often as much as 6.6 meters—in southern China is also usually greater than the 4.8-meter depth common in the north. Throughout the country, *jian* are usually found in odd-numbered units—three or five—as this is believed by many Chinese to afford balance and symmetry, a configuration seen sometimes in the façades of gravesites constructed to look like a dwelling as well as in even greater odd multiples in imperial palaces. As I-shaped dwellings evolve into L-shaped or U-shaped structures, *jian* serve as easily multiplied modular units for the expansion of a house.

During the Ming dynasty, especially, sumptuary regulations ordered the dimensions of timber that could be used by princes, ranked individuals, merchants, and commoners, contributing in the process to the standardization and modularization of Chinese houses. The central *jian* of a three- or five-bay rectangular dwelling, moreover, is generally wider than flanking *jian* since it often serves as the principal ceremonial or utility "room" of the house, an auspiciously located space that is symbolic of a family's unity and continuity. Here, a standard set of furniture would be symmetrically arranged: along the back wall, and facing the entryway is the place for a long table to hold the ancestral tablets, images of gods and goddesses, family mementos, and ceremonial paraphernalia. It was here that a family gathered for ancestral rituals, enjoyed festive family meals, including those that were part of weddings and funerals, entertained important guests, and carried out day-to-day activities. Whether open and apparent or enclosed and hidden, the use of *jian* as a building module is a basic element in the design of most Chinese houses.

Chinese houses and other buildings generally take shape from a conventional set of elementary parts—foundation, wooden framework, and roof—using readily available building materials such as earth, timber, and stone. Many old dwellings throughout the country lack a wooden framework, so that load-bearing walls directly support the roof system, a condition that is almost universal with contemporary Chinese houses. Basements are rare in Chinese dwellings and most houses traditionally were built directly on compacted earth that had been leveled or slightly raised on a solid podium of tamped earth or layered stone. In some cases, a shallow trench was dug, filled with pebble stone and then earth, which was tamped firm with a rammer operated by two men. Stone foundations can be

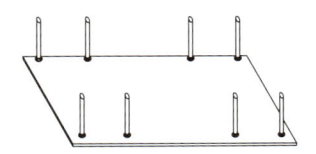

A *jian* or bay is a building module representing the distance between two columns, as well as four columns in addition to the volume bounded by four columns—literally representing a room.

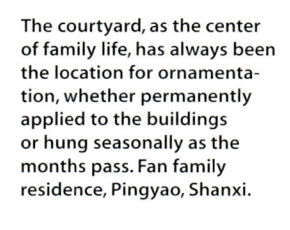

The courtyard, as the center of family life, has always been the location for ornamentation, whether permanently applied to the buildings or hung seasonally as the months pass. Fan family residence, Pingyao, Shanxi.

seen supporting the walls of small and large dwellings all over China in order to create a dry and secure base. Some extend a meter or two above the tamped earth podium and are composed of rocks of various shapes and sizes, which are laid with or without mortar. Foundations of this sort are stable enough to support a tamped earth, adobe, or fired brick wall above, which then either supports the roof structure directly or merely serves as a curtain wall around a timber framework.

Timber Framework Types

Load-bearing walls, that is, walls that directly support a roof structure, have a long history of use in common houses throughout China, whether the walls are of adobe brick, fired brick, or tamped earth. With higher quality dwellings seen throughout this book, however, walls do not support the weight of the roof above but are merely curtain walls set between complicated structural wooden frameworks that lift the roof rather than using the walls themselves for this purpose. Independent of the walls, which are thus nonload-bearing, the timber framework is a kind of "osseous" structure analogous to the human skeleton. Liang Sicheng, China's revered architectural historian, claimed that the use of a timber framework "permits complete freedom in walling and fenestration and, by the simple adjustment of the proportion between walls and openings, renders a house practical and comfortable in any climate from that of tropical Indochina to that of subarctic Manchuria. Due to this extreme flexibility and adaptability, this method of construction could be employed wherever Chinese civilization spread and would effectively shelter occupants from the elements, however diverse they might be. Perhaps nothing analogous is found in Western architecture … until the invention of reinforced concrete and the steel framing systems of the twentieth century" (Liang, 1984: 8).

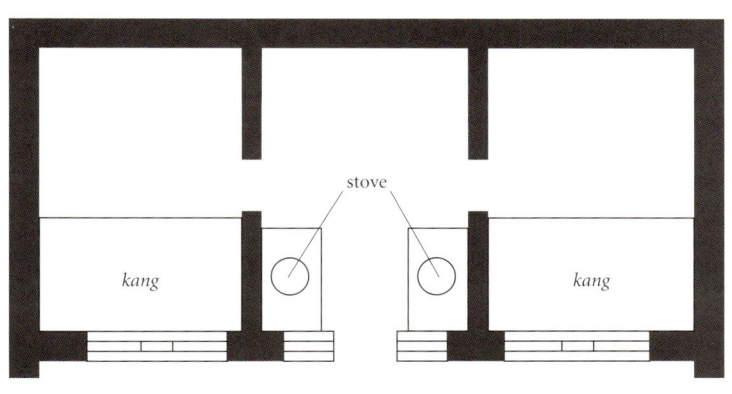

Above:
While common dwellings throughout China are usually three bays in width, those in northern China (left) are not as deep as those in southern China (right). Northern dwellings also rarely have windows on their back walls while in the south they are more common. In northern China, *kang* or brick beds, connected to stoves in the kitchen, are common features.

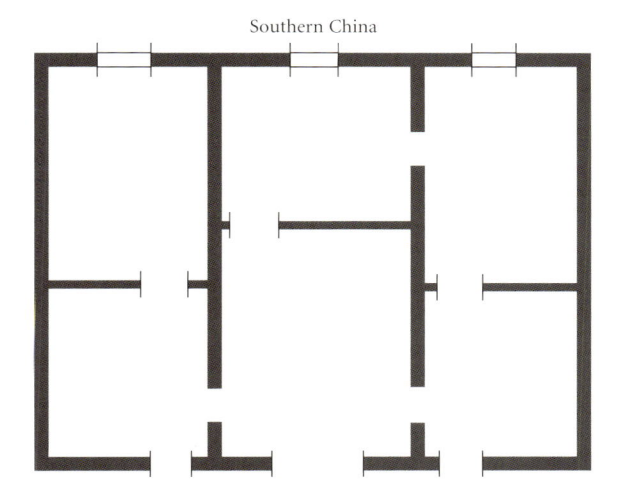

Top:
Photographed early in the twentieth century in either Shaanxi or Shanxi province in northern China, these workmen are hefting a heavy rammer in order to tamp the foundation for a building.

Center:
The façade of this omega-shaped tomb includes a three-bay structure similar to that of a dwelling. Here, the space is used for periodic ritual purposes.

A Complex Mosaic of Architectural Styles

Now fitted with the furniture and ornamental objects typical of the late nineteenth century, the Main Hall of Wang Dinggui's Hall of Inheriting Ambition, Anhui, expresses both the formality and taste of a wealthy merchant.

A Complex Mosaic of Architectural Styles   33

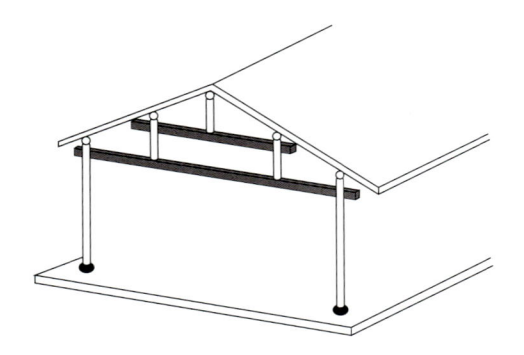

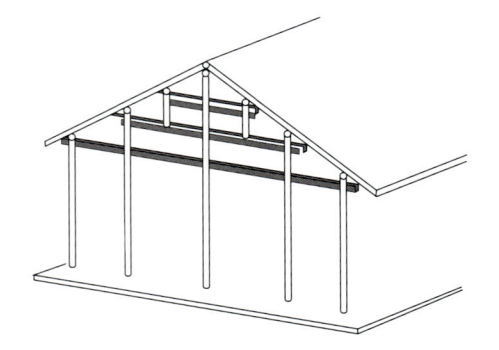

On the left is a columns-and-beams wooden framework, most common in northern China. With larger diameter corner columns and heavy beams, this type differs from the pillars-and-transverse tie beams (right), with multiple pillars and thin beams that are either mortised directly into or tenoned through the slender pillars.

All embedded into the wall, corner columns and short stocky queen posts lift three tiers of massive beams that support a heavy roof. Beijing.

Wooden structural frameworks lifting the roof were universally used in the construction of Chinese temples and palaces as well as the houses of those with the means to purchase expensive timber parts for the pillars and beams. The houses built by ordinary Chinese, on the other hand, almost always utilized limited amounts of timber because of cost and other factors, and thus generally were built with load-bearing walls. Timber framework structures can be essentially assembled from standard modular parts rather than being "constructed" using building materials. In no other feature of traditional Chinese housing was the prosperity of the owner so clearly expressed than that of the wooden frame since the cost of timber always far exceeded that of the earth required to compose the walls, even when fired bricks were used.

Two basic wood framework systems—columns-and-beams and pillars-and-transverse-tie beams—are common throughout the country, with some being rather simple while others are elaborate. Columns-and-beams construction is widespread in northern China but is employed only in grander houses in southern China where slender pillars-and-transverse-tie beam frameworks are more common. Both of these framing systems are illustrated in Qing dynasty woodblock prints that contrast a variety of types, including common three-column framing systems with lighter seven-pillar frames. Although the term "column" and "pillar" are usually described in Chinese using the same term, they are differentiated here in English in terms of "columns" being thicker than slender "pillars." A pair of columns typically is able to directly support a heavy beam without bowing under the weight while the rigidity of a set of parallel pillars and its ability to support a heavy load is only made possible because of the use of transverse tie beams mortised and tenoned into the pillars.

Columns-and-beams construction, referred to in Chinese as the *tailiang* framing system, may be as simple as a pair of columns situated as corner posts and used to support a single beam, which is either laid atop and perpendicular to the columns or slightly inclined to create a flat- or shed-like roof. Even in small northern dwellings, *tailiang* structures are often more complicated, involving a stacking of building parts in order for there to be a rise to a central peak so as to produce a double sloping roof. First, two squat queen posts, or struts, are set symmetrically upon the horizontal beam. On top of the pair of queen posts another beam is set. Then a culminating short post is placed. A matching pair of columns and beams is situated at the opposite end of the house. A longitudinal ridgepole, which defines the peak of a triangular roof, as well as parallel purlins, which are the longitudinal timbers that are seated directly on the beams, connect the pair of end column-and-beam sets which are piled perpendicular to the ridgepole and purlins. Together, they provide support for roof rafters bearing the weight of roof tiles and carrying the massive load to the ground.

Variations in framing sometimes occur in order to accommodate available timber, some of which may not be straight or the same length as corresponding members. The upper cross section of a *tailiang* structure is made up of only vertical and horizontal elements, which may be positioned in such a way as to introduce a degree of curvature into the roofline by creating at least one break in the slope of the roof. This is quite different from what is possible with the rigid roof truss system based upon triangularly positioned segments that is common in the West. Chinese builders and homeowners traditionally held the belief that placing great weight on the roof insured a building's sturdiness. Indeed, in northern China, wooden timbers are often massive in size, far beyond what is actually necessary to support the roof.

The pillars-and-transverse-tie beams wooden framework, also called the *chuandou* framing system, is common throughout southern China. It differs from the *tailiang* system in three important ways: the number of vertical components is greater, yet the pillars all have a smaller diameter; each of the slender pillars is notched at the top to directly support a longitudinal roof purlin; and horizontal tie beam members, called *chuanfang*, are mortised directly into or tenoned through the pillars in order to inhibit skewing of what would otherwise be a relatively flexible frame. Smaller diameter *chuandou* pillars, often only 20 to 30 centimeters, are less expensive than the larger timbers required in a *tailiang* frame. Trees as young as five years can be used for purlins, *chuandou* pillars, and tie beams, while it takes at least a generation for columns and beams to mature to sufficient size for use in a *tailiang* structure. Sometimes in southern China, the lower wall of a two-story dwelling may be solid masonry or it may utilize a columns-and-beams structure while the upper story supporting the roof uses a lighter *chuandou* wooden framework.

The positions of purlins in terms of the spacing of the pillars supporting them and the elevation of each define the slope of the roof, which varies significantly from place to place. Where the relative position of the purlins remains fixed, there is a constant downward slope to the roofline, without a break. If a curved roofline is desired, the pitch is then varied from one purlin to another in a regular mathematical relationship. Carpenters' manuals provided guidance for builders of palaces and temples, whose wooden frameworks are quite complex, but carpenters engaged in building houses typically

Left:
This pillars-and-transverse-tie beams wooden framework, comprised of timbers of relatively modest diameter, was raised first and was covered with a roof even before the infilling of the curtain walls was begun. Emeishan area, western Sichuan.

Below:
Viewed from inside the kitchen, both the pillars and the transverse tie beams are visible. The space between pillars and beams was filled with nonload-bearing panels of woven bamboo that were then covered with mud plaster before being whitewashed. Nanchong, Sichuan.

A Complex Mosaic of Architectural Styles 35

Right:
Horizontal and vertical carved wooden members, including supporting brackets, serve more decorative than functional purposes at an entry to the Ning'an Lu residence, Nankou township, Meixian, Guangdong.

Far right:
Close-up of wooden ornamentation attached to the pillars and beams using mortise-and-tenon joinery. Fan family residence, Pingyao, Shanxi.

Below:
These drawings show complex mortise-and-tenon wooden joinery found at the Hemudu Neolithic archaeological site in Zhejiang province, clear evidence of such practices in China 7000 years ago.

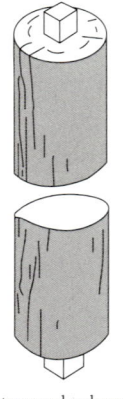

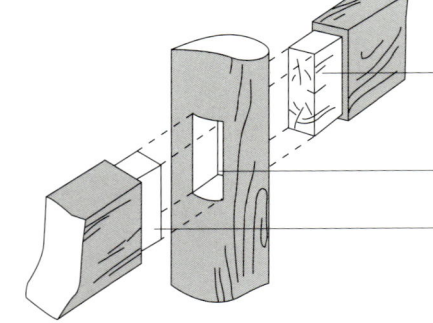

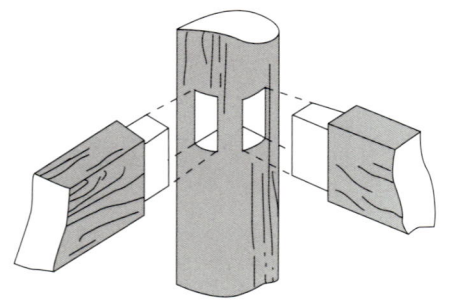

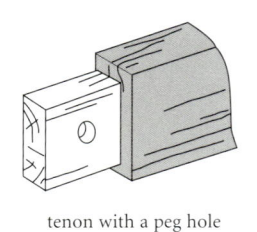

tenoned column

butt-joined mortise and tenon
- tenon
- mortise
- tenon

mortise-and-tenon corner

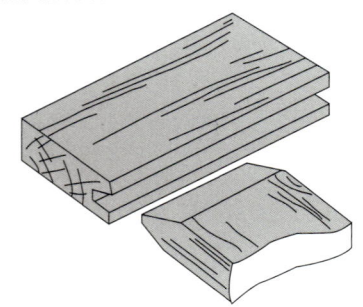

tenon with a peg hole

tongue-and-groove joinery

drew from their experience rather than the written word. In rural China today, it is still possible to encounter carpenters who depend upon mnemonic verses committed to memory in order to recall the necessary formulas for required sizes and shapes. In the past, mnemonic verses also were the means used to transmit this specialized knowledge to apprentices, but young carpenters now can find the same information in readily available manuals.

The wooden framework of a new house in western Sichuan, as seen on the previous page, employs an interconnected pillars-and-transverse-tie beam skeleton. Its various components provide connections needed to link one modular unit with another. Of seven interlocked pillars that directly support the purlins, only five reach to the ground. A transverse tie beam halfway up the frame serves as a base for two additional pillars while also locking the pillars together. Mortised, tenoned, and notched joinery is apparent.

Carpenters wielding a simple adze dress each timber on a trestle sawhorse, marking locations for every mortise and tenon before each is chiseled to shape. Elements of the framework are assembled into a unit on the ground before being raised to a perpendicular location, where they are then propped and secured to adjacent segments by longitudinal cross members. The raising of the ridgepole as well as some of the columns is an especially important action in Chinese house-building, a subject discussed later. Wooden or bamboo roof rafters are laid crosswise between the purlins to serve as the base for layers of roof tiles. Lifted by the wooden framework, the mass of the heavy roof helps anchor the structure even before the wall infilling is put into place.

Mortise-and-Tenon Joinery

Tailiang wooden frames depend principally on the dead weight of beams as well as dowels and wedges to insure a snug fit. On the other hand, until the twentieth century, *chuandou* frames relied only on ingenuous joinery systems, sometimes assisted by wooden pegs, to interlock the wooden structural components. The basic elements of *chuandou* mortise-and-tenon joinery include tenons, which are shaped to fit into cut-out mortised openings in order to create a strong joint capable of expanding according to changing temperature and humidity conditions. (Joinery of this type is used for both Chinese buildings and Chinese furniture, and draws on practices that can be traced back 7000 years via archaeological evidence at the Hemudu site in Zhejiang province during the Neolithic period.) "Mortises," Rudolf Hommel observed more than sixty years ago, "are an infatuation of the Chinese carpenter" (1937: 299). Metal fittings such as nails and clamps until recently have had only limited use in Chinese timber frame construction because of suitable alternatives, cost, and the fact that they sometimes disintegrate and lead to structural failure. The clever use of mortise-and-tenon as well as other joinery techniques makes it possible to assemble even pieces of timber of different sizes together into an interlocked frame. *Chuandou* wooden frameworks are especially adaptable for construction on hill slopes and river banks where the lengths of timbers vary according to the specific needs of the sites.

In most cases, the various components making up a timber frame—whether *tailiang* or *chuandou*—are left fully exposed although sometimes they are embedded within the wall. Their natural outline can be enjoyed as an aesthetic element as can often be seen in the interplay of columns and beams and the displays of intricate carpentry used in fashioning brackets that support overhanging eaves.

Both columns and pillars are usually set on stone or brick bases in order to retard the transmission of moisture and make difficult the movement of termites from the ground below into the vulnerable wooden uprights above. Bases, also called pedestals, are often roughly hewn stone blocks, either chamfered along the top or edges or gently rounded, but in large dwellings are usually carved into elaborate shapes—drums, octagons, and lotuses, among many others—and ornamented with auspicious symbols. Bases themselves frequently are set on a stabilizing slab of stone sunk into the ground or floor.

Nonload-Bearing Curtain Walls

In order to protect interior space given shape by the timber framing system, many types of exterior walling are employed: tamped earth, adobe brick, fired brick, stone, wooden logs or planks, bamboo, wattle, and daub. Walls that enclose and surround space also protect and divide it, and it is common to see a variety of wall materials used in a single house. In southern China, nonload-bearing walling is sometimes of vegetative origin, utilizing grasses, grain stalks, and even cob walls mixed with sand

Left:
One of a pair of carved stone drums with characters for "longevity" and "good fortune" found at the entrance of a doorway. Wang family manor, Shanxi.

Below:
Ornamented stone column bases or pedestals are common features of Chinese houses, appearing in a large variety. Top left: Fan family residence, Pingyao, Shanxi. Top right: De Xing Tang, Meixian, Guangdong, which includes a stone column; Bottom right: Ning'an Lu residence, Meixian, Guangdong; Bottom left: Deng family residence, Guang'an, Sichuan.

and straw that are not even capable of supporting any mass other than their own. Sawn timber and bamboo are also used.

Sturdy load-bearing walls—far more common in the construction of Chinese dwellings than is generally acknowledged—are made of a variety of natural materials that are tamped, formed, or hewn. These same substantial materials are used to form nonload-bearing curtain walls, either completely encircling the wooden skeleton or simply filling the gaps between the columns or pillars. Tamped walls, described in greater detail below, are composed of mixtures of clay-textured soils as well as composite amalgamations of other substances. Blocks of clay are molded into bricks that can be either sun-dried or kiln-fired. Chinese builders generally show a decided preference for earthen structures, so that stone and rock are not used in housing construction to the degree that matches their availability. Hewn stone, particularly granite, is a common material in coastal areas of southern China, where it is employed in laying up the lower courses of walls, for floors, and as columns. Collected from riverbeds and gathered from hill slopes, stones of various sizes are laid up as low walls in many parts of the country. Both load-bearing and nonload-bearing walls are sometimes made of a mixture of locally available building materials, arising out of availability and/or cost factors.

Tamped Earth

Tamping or pounding clay soil or other materials—called the *hangtu* method of construction—has been used for much of Chinese history to create solid walls for houses and other buildings, including imperial palaces. In addition, this method was widely used to fortify villages and cities with high protective walls and enclose compounds and open areas as well, an economical and low-tech practice that can still be seen throughout much of rural China. The emperor of Qin in the third century BCE supervised the construction of an immense range of tamped earthen walls to demarcate borders, precursor forms of what today is China's legendary Great Wall. The firing of bricks also was common by the third century BCE but did not become economical and widely available for housing construction until the fourteenth century, so tamped earth and adobe bricks continued to be preferred walling until at least the Ming dynasty; even today, tamped earthen walls continue to be raised all over China for utilitarian and economic reasons.

Throughout China, the use of *hangtu* construction arises out of the ubiquity of accessible clay soils, generally found immediately adjacent to building sites and thus requiring no transport of heavy materials over any distance, as well as the scarcity and cost of alternative building materials. In spite of being a remarkably durable building material, tamped earth, however, has some fundamental limitations, especially weaknesses in supporting heavy loads and relative inflexibility in the placement of windows and doors. Yet, even large structures, such as the multistoried fortifications in Fujian and Guangdong, have been built using this simple technique.

Known in the West as rammed or tamped earth, the *hangtu* method involves piling freshly dug earth into a slightly battered frame where it is pounded firmly with a rammer. Local formulas often include sand as well as lime with the earth in order to create a material that is mortar-like in composition. A common mixture in central China is 60 percent fine sand, 30 percent lime (ground limestone or shells), and 10 percent earth mixed with a small amount of water.

In northern China, the basic frame consists of a confining shutter mold with a pair of H-shaped supports reaching perhaps four meters in height that are framed on their long sides by movable wooden poles lashed together with thin rope or held by dowels.

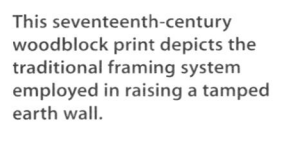

This seventeenth-century woodblock print depicts the traditional framing system employed in raising a tamped earth wall.

The thin poles can be quickly and easily raised up the sloping supports, level by level, as the ramming takes place. Each of the poles must be periodically removed and cleaned of clinging earth. Shuttering boards are used instead of timber poles in southern China as a three-sided box frame formwork, without either a cover or bottom, and these vary in size from place to place. An end board with projecting tenons secured by wooden pegs holds the flanking boards together on one end while the other is held by an easily manipulated crosspiece that grips the bottom flanks of the frame and which passes through the rising wall. An end clamp or a set of braces tightens the frame. A plumb line weighted with a stone serves as a simple level. Freshly dug earth or a composite material—perhaps 10 centimeters thick at a time— is mixed with a small amount of broken grain stalks, paper, lime, and sometimes water or oil, and then pounded with a stone or wooden rammer until it is uniformly compacted. A typical rammer is made of a heavy stone head, perhaps 25 centimeters wide, which is rounded on the bottom and attached to a projecting wooden rod. In some areas, rammers consist of a single piece of hardwood with a large wooden block carved into one end and a smaller one chiseled on the other end, a configuration that is reminiscent of the pestles used to husk rice. Smaller tools of various sizes are used to insure that the soil mixture is firmly packed. In some areas, a thin layer of bamboo strips or stone rubble may be laid to encourage drying of the earthen core before the movable shutters of the frame are raised, leveled, and clamped into place, to begin the process anew. The sequence is repeated until the desired height is met.

Spaces for the frames of windows and doors can be set into the rising tamped earth wall using wooden or stone lintels, but it is necessary to carve out the opening in the compacted soil within the frames once the wall is completed. Because of the weakening of the wall with such openings, care is taken to limit their number and size so as not to diminish the wall's ability to carry the weight of the rising mass and eventually the roof as well. With multistoried dwellings in Fujian province, windows in the walls are narrower near the base and increase in width on upper floors. The full drying of the exterior surface may take months, depending on rainfall and humidity levels. Once the wall cures completely, a soil-and-lime based slurry plaster may be spread over the wall.

Left:
As this old photograph shows, a box frame with a small block on one end and a larger block on the other— held together with cross bars and secured with dowels— can be filled with earth or an earthen mixture before being tamped firm with wooden rammers. Guling, northern Jiangxi. Similar practices are still observable in south central China.

Below:
Captured in 1984 in Shaanxi province, this photograph reveals the continuing use of the centuries-old method of tamping walls using stone rammers and a frame made of shuttered logs.

Far left:
Tiangong kaiwu (The Creations of Nature and Man), a seventeenth-century work on technological topics, depicts the use of a shallow wooden frame into which soft mud was placed to form a brick. A wire-strung bow was used to cut off excess mud once the mud had been tamped firmly. Formed bricks are shown being carried by an assistant to a nearby area for drying.

Left:
The use of kilns to fire thin bricks and roof tiles, shown here stacked in the rear, became popular during the Ming dynasty (1368–1644). In this depiction from the *Tiangong kaiwu*, water is poured into the top of the kiln in order to create a superficial glazing on the surfaces of the bricks being fired within.

Sun-dried Bricks

Sun-dried bricks or adobe bricks retain many of the economic characteristics of tamped earth but allow greater flexibility in building form. The earliest use of adobe bricks in China appears to have simply supplemented *hangtu* construction in that bricks were used to build stairs, frame gateways, form interior partition walls, and make the heatable beds, known as *kang*, that are found throughout northern China. Even today, new houses in many villages throughout rural China are being built at relatively low cost of adobe bricks as well as tamped earth even as news reports tell of the vulnerability of earthen buildings in China because of natural disasters such as floods and earthquakes. If compacted well and dried completely, adobe bricks become stone-like, but, if improperly cured, become friable.

Bricks, whether sun- or kiln-dried are made using relatively common techniques applied to locally available soils near a building site, just as is the case with *hangtu* walls. The seventeenth-century manual *Tiangong kaiwu* (The Creations of Nature and Man) depicts techniques of brick manufacture still encountered throughout China today. First, moistened clay soil dug from nearby is formed by hand in double non-releasable molds, trimmed with a bow-shaped wire cutter, before two uniform bricks are dumped from the frame and left to cure. In other cases, earth is packed into a mold, shaped by hand, and then pounded with the feet or a stone pestle to firmly compact the soil. Bricks made from moistened soil are usually thicker and broader but shorter than those made from completely dry earth. However they are made, the bricks are stacked for drying and usually capped with a sloping cover of straw to keep them from getting wet from passing showers.

Adobe bricks, as thick rectangular slices, are sometimes simply cut from the bottom of rice fields, not only to produce a necessary building material but also to correct for the natural siltation of fields. In parts of southern China, this is usually done every ten years or so during the fall after the field has been plowed, harrowed, and compressed with a stone roller. Once the fields have been puddled from a heavy rain and evaporation has reduced the moisture content of the soil to a dense yet viscous consistency, brick-size sections of earth, each approximately 15 centimeters thick, are sliced and lifted from the floor of the field with a spade. In some areas, rough-cut bricks are simply stacked to dry, but in Guangxi each segment of paddy floor is placed in a simple wooden and bamboo frame where the soil is then tamped with the feet to a common shape. Once the brick is molded, the bamboo handle of the shaping frame is lifted and the brick is allowed to dry for days *in situ* adjacent to other bricks. Later stacked and left to cure for several weeks under a straw cap, the adobe bricks are ready for use.

Kiln-dried Bricks

Although it was not until the Ming dynasty in the fourteenth century that fired bricks became relatively inexpensive and widely used, the practice of using fired bricks in residences gained currency by the Han dynasty in the third century BCE. Kiln-dried bricks are a qualitative improvement over inferior adobe bricks in terms of durability, imperviousness to water, and fire resistance, but they have always been significantly more costly because of the extraordinary amounts of fuel necessary to bake them. The firing of bricks at temperatures that reach 1150° C essentially changes the raw soil that constitutes them as sintering and partial vitrification take place, to the degree that baked bricks cannot be pulverized, reconstituted, and then reused as is the case with adobe bricks. Throughout China, fired bricks vary significantly in color as a consequence of the different types of soils utilized in making them as well as the techniques employed in firing and cooling them.

Only about 20 percent of all rural dwellings surveyed in China in the early 1930s had kiln-dried brick walls, with most of them being found in prosperous areas, such as in the fertile rice-growing valleys and lowlands of central and southern China. Over the past quarter century, as China's house-building boom has led to increasing numbers of boxy adobe and fired brick houses, it has been possible to observe traditional production and construction practices throughout the country. From preparation of the soil to forming to firing, the making of baked bricks is a specialized process that demands higher levels of skill and technological know-how than is the case in making adobe bricks, in addition to consuming substantial amounts of fuel. Many Chinese also prefer the texture and color of fired brick to walls made of gray cement.

The use of adobe bricks or fired bricks is a tangible statement of a household's general wealth. Poorer households primarily use tamped earth and adobe bricks while those who can afford them prefer kiln-dried bricks. Chinese peasants in the past were known to replace portions of a tamped earth wall with adobe bricks and then later substitute fired bricks for adobe piece by piece in their search for strength, durability, and resistance to water. This level of resourcefulness can still be observed today as farmers attempt to stretch their financial resources. Some modern dwellings employ fired bricks in visible locations while utilizing cement or stone in less obvious places. Brick bonds, the patterned arrangement of individual bricks across a wall surface, vary from place to place in China. Most bonds are similar to those seen in the West.

Above:
In some areas of southern China, bricks are cut from paddy fields, producing not only a needed building material but also providing a means to correct the natural siltation of the fields by removing the excess earth. Lipu county, Guangxi Zhuang Autonomous Region.

Below left:
Near the end of the twentieth century in China's countryside, bricks continued to be made using similar techniques to those shown in the seventeenth-century drawing on the previous page. Just as in the print, the worker stands in a depression to ease the tamping of the mud and his use of the wire bow. Zhejiang.

A Complex Mosaic of Architectural Styles 41

Above left and center:
Adobe bricks vary in size from place to place. The walls of the Mao family farmhouse in northern Hunan province—viewed from both the inside and the outside—show the use of large 34 by 11.5 cm adobe bricks. Bricks of this sort were made in molds and then left to dry before being used. Over time, the bricks continued to harden as they were exposed to the sun and warm air.

Above right:
Fired bricks are employed in the interior party walls of this building even though the exterior walls are constructed of tamped earth. Fu Yu Lou residence, Hongkeng village, Fujian.

Right:
Producing a composite wall surface, the red brick exterior walls along this narrow lane have within them readily available blocks of granite. Quanzhou, Fujian.

42   The Architecture of the Chinese House

Bamboo
This is among the most versatile of all plant materials used in building Chinese houses. Its use is especially common from Sichuan through Hunan and Hebei in the middle reaches of the Yangzi River as well as in Yunnan and Guizhou provinces where it is used widely in house-building by members of ethnic minority groups. Bamboo, a multipurpose grass that grows rapidly and in many forms, has many structural qualities—strong yet light, rigid yet pliant— but also has certain shortcomings—difficult to join as well as vulnerable to splitting, rotting, and burning. Because the cylindrical shells of bamboo come in different sizes and can be easily cut, split, and worked with simple tools, it is an all-purpose building material. Bamboo is used for framing members and floor joists, for roof components such as rafters, purlins, and ridgepoles, as well as a variety of walling forms. When split and with their inner diaphragms scooped out, half rounds of bamboo can be laid as a roof covering, either side by side with the open face up or overlapping as roof "tiles."

For walling, bamboo culms are split into thin flexible splines that are interlaced at a 90-degree angle to form a kind of woven lattice or lathing matting that can be used for all or part of the wall. Bamboo plaited curtain walls are often sealed with a mud or mud-and-lime plaster on both sides to make the wall tight to air and water. Those seen in Sichuan and Jiangxi provinces remind some Westerners of simple vernacular half-timbered dwellings seen in England and Germany. According to surveys done in the 1930s, nearly 30 percent of houses countrywide had walls of woven plant materials while in southwestern China the percentage reached nearly two-thirds. Even in moderately prosperous Taiwan, as recently as 1958, dwellings that included substantial amounts of bamboo, rather than adobe or fired brick, represented 40 percent of rural dwellings.

Despite its ubiquity, versatility, and long history of use, bamboo nonetheless has significant shortcomings. Compared to wood, for example, bamboo rots easily, especially when in contact with damp soil. It is vulnerable to insects such as termites and is also highly inflammable. As a result, bamboo paneling is usually found in higher locations on a wall rather than nearer the ground. Today, it is rare to find much bamboo used structurally in Chinese houses. Even ethnic minority groups, such as the Dai in Yunnan province who were known in the past for their *zhulou* or "stilt bamboo storied-houses," which are elaborate structures with multiple roof pitches, today usually construct their houses of wooden poles with wooden walling. Peculiarly, they continue to refer to the structures as *zhulou*. Even as bamboo has declined as a building component, it remains an important quick-growing, versatile raw material as the extensive hillside stands and ubiquitous thickets of bamboo suggest. Some architects interested in promoting sustainable building practices have called for increasing the use of structural bamboo by substituting fast-growing bamboo for timber, which increasingly is costly and sometimes in short supply. Used in making furniture, mats, artwork, fences, baskets, ornaments, cables, stakes, umbrellas, baby carriages, cooking vessels, boxes, needles, shoulder poles, and baskets, among many items, bamboo continues to rival more modern materials in Chinese daily life.

Above:
Itinerant workers are splitting bamboo into thin splines that are then interlaced to form wall panels. Zhejiang.

Left:
The interlaced bamboo wall panels are sealed first with a mud or mud-and-lime plaster before being whitewashed. Langzhong, Sichuan.

Sorghum and Corn Stalks
Although commonly used by poor peasants in northern and northeastern China up until the middle of the twentieth century, sorghum, also called kaoliang, and corn stalks are rarely seen today used in the walls of houses. In the past, grain stalks were packed together, stood on end against an unfinished wall frame before being crudely plastered with mud as a kind of daub. Sometimes a second layer of stalks was placed inside the house that, after being plastered, would leave a dead air space between itself and the outside wall to serve as insulation.

Stone
This is not used in China as a building material to the degree that matches its availability except in relatively barren mountainous and coastal areas where soil suitable for tamping or making bricks is limited. On the other hand, stone is widely used for foundations, in lower walls, for making steps and pavements, and is sometimes hewn for columns and windows.

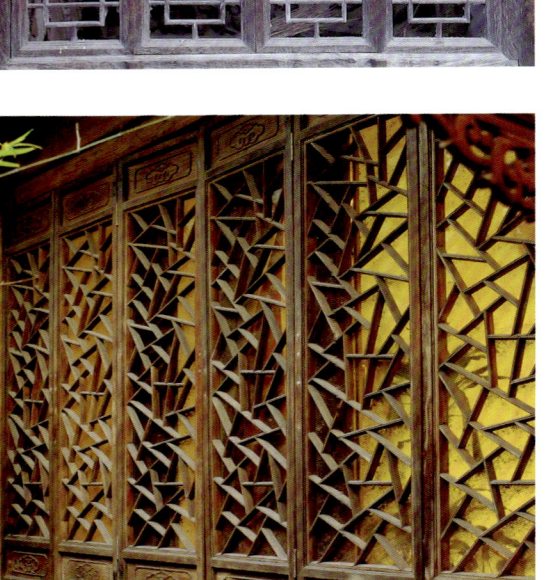

Above left:
Close-up of simple wooden lattice window frames showing the tattered paper on the inside. Chuandixia village, Beijing.

Above right:
Wooden timbers are used here as columns, beams, and eaves brackets—all embedded within the wall—that lift the roof purlins supporting the rafters. Quanzhou, Fujian.

Below left:
This intricate "cracked ice" lattice pattern is found on a door panel of a renovated *siheyuan* in Beijing.

Below right:
Lattice window panels provide variable amounts of light, air, and privacy to interior spaces. Kang family manor, Henan.

Bottom:
In wealthier homes, hardwoods and softwoods are used functionally and ornamentally. Fu Yu Lou Lin family residence, Hongkeng village, Fujian.

Timber

Where forests are extensive in some areas of northwest, southwest, and northeast China, load-bearing walls of roughly hewn logs are built and finished with a mud-plaster. Log cabin-type dwellings have been built and used principally by ethnic minorities in upland areas on China's periphery. Often log dwellings are built of only simply dressed tree trunks that are placed horizontally one on top of the other so that they overlap to form the corners of the structure. The unhewn logs normally project from the corners but are notched above and below in order to "lock" each of the levels in place in a relatively tight joint.

Sawn wood has never been widely used to form exterior walls in humble dwellings yet it continues to be utilized in houses throughout many of the mountainous areas of central and southern China where timber is readily available. Within the houses of the wealthy, sawn wood was fashioned by carpenters into exquisite wooden latticework as part of door and window panels that complemented carved beams and brackets, serving in the process as flexible fittings for connecting interior and exterior spaces. With most any type of light curtain walls, no attempt is made to conceal the wooden framework so that the natural lines of the wooden pillars and beams beautify the house.

Roof Shapes and Profiles

Although a roof is principally a functional canopy sheltering a structure and its interior living space from the elements, it may also be an expressive feature with sometimes powerful symbolism attached to it. The materials used to cover a roof, its degree of slope, as well as its profile are strongly influenced by both climatic and economic factors. In areas of substantial rainfall, the major concern is quickly moving falling water to the eaves in order to minimize the infiltration of moisture into the building. Pitched roofs—with surfaces that operate to disperse water like the scales of fish or the feathers of birds—are most common on Chinese dwellings. Roofs also contribute to insulating the inside of the dwelling, shielding the inhabitants from either heat or cold. Probably most Chinese roofs are merely utilitarian, providing crude water shedding and waterproofing. The profiles of many, however, exhibit a powerful elegance in terms of their curvature and covering, conditions that are more common in the residences of those with greater means than those who live in humble dwellings. Some scholars have claimed that Chinese pay as much attention to the appearance of the roof as Westerners do to the façade.

In addition to uncomplicated flat and shed types, there are four major Chinese roof styles. For the most part, Chinese roof profiles are symmetrical in side and front elevation, the first emphasizing the gable end of a dwelling and the second the ridgeline. Throughout rural and urban north China, the *yingshanding* ("firm mountain") type roof profile exhibits a flush gable with no overhang, a type that is suited to areas of limited rainfall where there is no critical need for shielding the gable end of a dwelling from weathering. Flush gables are also found on houses in southern China where rainfall is plentiful in the coastal areas but the lack of eaves overhang is seen as an advantage to counter strong winds that accompany frequent typhoons. Simple decorative brickwork is sometimes added at the top of the gable or along the ridgeline. There is no record of *yingshanding* roof profiles prior to the Ming period, the use of which appears to have increased with the expanded availability of fired bricks. Many *shanqiang* gable walls indeed are load-bearing, directly carrying the purlins and the substantial weight of a tile roof.

Matouqiang ("horses' head wall"), although not properly a "hard mountain type," is discussed here because it also does not have a gable overhang even as the gable wall rises above the adjacent slope of the roof. A type common in Anhui, Jiangxi, Zhejiang, and southern Jiangsu provinces, where the gable walls rise in dramatic steps above the roofline, *matouqiang* probably began as firewalls.

The flush gable of this fired brick dwelling is richly ornamented with cloud patterns surrounding a stylized "longevity" character. Kang family manor, Henan.

A variety of rooflines are seen along the canals in Wuzhen in northern Zhejiang province. On the right, the rather simple *matouqiang* style also serves as important firewalls.

A Complex Mosaic of Architectural Styles 45

Above left:
These stepped gables rising above the slope of the roof of the Main Hall are also called *matouqiang*, said by some to represent raised "horses' heads." Shen family residence, Luzhi, Jiangsu.

Above right:
The layered rooflines of Fu Yu Lou in Hongkeng village, Fujian, are said to suggest a phoenix taking flight.

Forming party or common walls between two structures, *matouqiang* rise high above the general roofline in order to retard the spread of sweeping roof fires in adjacent dwellings, temples, clan halls, and other buildings in towns and compact villages. Their use increased during the Ming dynasty as fired bricks became relatively inexpensive. Usually symmetrical in their upper profile, they nonetheless vary significantly. Serving very much like *matouqiang* are *qiaoji* ("upward-turning spine"), the sweeping undulation of end walls found in southeastern China. Aesthetically pleasing, stepped *matouqiang* and soaring *qiaoji* end walls, which are usually accentuated with dark tile copings that contrast with the white walls below, are distinctive features of Chinese domestic architecture.

A roof type in which the purlins extend out beyond the end walls, thus creating a substantial eaves overhang that offers some protection of the gable walls, is called "overhanging gables" (*xuanshanding* or *tiaoshanding*). Found throughout the country, it is peculiar nonetheless that they are not common in some areas of substantial rainfall such as Taiwan and Fujian. Archaeological evidence shows that "overhanging gables" were used during the Eastern Han period but they did not enter the architectural mainstream until more than a half century later, in the Tang period.

Hipped types, called *sizhuding* or *sihuding*, utilize four sloping surfaces on the roof, the hip representing the exterior angle where any two slopes come together. They are most commonly seen today on Ming and Qing period palaces, temples, and large residences, presenting a profile that is quite graceful. Involving intricate carpentry of radiating woodwork, they are found nonetheless on some common houses as well and, perhaps surprisingly, even covering quite modest thatched dwellings such as those of the Korean minority nationality. With hipped roofs, sloping eaves similarly overhang the side walls just as they normally overhang the front and back. A complex variant type that is a challenge even to a skilled carpenter is the combined hipped and gable type (*xieshanding*). Its construction involves the foreshortening of two hipped slopes on the ends of the roof in order to form a gablet, a small triangular gable that fits beneath the peak. This structural type is known in the West as a gambrel roof. The hipped style was widely employed for dwellings prior to the Song dynasty, as can be seen in paintings of many periods. During the subsequent Ming and Qing periods, however, its use became restricted because of the imposition of sumptuary regulations that limited hipped roofs to palace construction. In areas remote from imperial control and occupied by minority groups such as the Dai, Jingpo, De'ang,

46   The Architecture of the Chinese House

Blang, and Jino in Yunnan province, many simple dwellings made of bamboo and thatch have rather complex roof profiles, such as the *xieshanding*, a combined hipped and gable roof.

Embellishments along the ridges and at the eaves enhance the silhouettes of many Chinese houses. Seams along any of the junctures between different roof slopes demand particular attention because it is in these places that seepage of water from outside and loss of heat from inside are most likely to occur.

V-shaped and inverted U-shaped capping tiles have a long history of use to seal vulnerable seams, serving critical functional purposes. In addition, these locations also often have rooftop, eave, or gable end ornamentation that suggests other than mere functional explanations.

Concerning the upturned ends of a roof's ridge, Chinese architectural historians speculate that it resulted from a need to increase protection of an area that might be lifted by the wind, thus exposing

Above left:
Believed by some to be a totem as protection against fire, creatures of this type are found on palaces as well as upon dwellings. Kang family manor, Henan.

Above right:
Along the ridgeline, a simple ornamental treatment results from using stacked flat roof tiles, here embellished with a coin-like design also made of thin roof tiles. Nanchong, Sichuan.

Center left:
Adjacent layers of concave and convex tiles across the slope of a roof usually terminate in ornamental end tiles. Yongding, Fujian.

Below left:
Close-up of two types of ornamental *wadang* or end tiles, here shown with the patina of mold. The triangular dripping tiles are said to facilitate the movement of water off the roof. Nanchong, Sichuan.

Below right:
Close-up of molded ornamentation along a tin gutter that utilizes the Chinese character for "purity." Located in an area visible only to women in their *neifang* or inner quarters, the character served as a didactic admonition. Hongcun, Anhui.

A Complex Mosaic of Architectural Styles 47

Left and right:
The making of roof tiles is shown clearly in these drawings from the seventeenth-century manual *Tiangong kaiwu* (The Creations of Nature and Man). The worker in the center is using a wire bow to slice a thin slab of clay from an oblong block of compacted earth. This slab is wrapped around the side of a flexible cylindrical mold where it is smoothed and shaped by another craftsman. On the right, the cylindrical shape is broken into concave tiles, which are shown stacked in the rear.

the interior to wind and water damage. Over time, areas near the ends of ridgelines acquired heavy, finial-like ornamentation known as *chiwei* ("owl's tail") or *zhengwen* ("animal's mouth") that came to serve also as totems guarding against fire. At each end of the ridgeline on many houses in northern China, a brick molding runs along the length of the ridge. Sometimes with a slightly raised extension, even a projection, the raised molding is freely carved with line patterns and even occasionally has ornamentation added atop it. In southern Shaanxi, prefabricated, fired roof ornaments are generically called "ridge mouths" (*jiwen*) after the traditional "animal mouths," and are said to have a magical power against the possibility of fire.

Even simple concave roof tiles are arranged in interesting ornamental patterns, including some with auspicious meanings. In Fujian and Taiwan, for example, there are three basic ridge style profiles: the so-called "swallowtail" style, the "horseback" or "saddle" style, and the "tile weighing" style. Graceful "swallowtail" rooflines traditionally were given shape with bricks cantilevered out from the ridge and supported by a metal rod, but today they are more likely to be molded from reinforced concrete. "Horseback" or "saddle" style ridges, while maintaining a low-slung curved ridgeline like the "swallowtail" style, lack the "swallowtail's" upward sweep at the end of the roof ridge. Gable end profiles known as the "tile weighing" style are found on Hakka dwellings in southern Taiwan, as well as in scattered parts of northern Taiwan. But the meaning of the term goes beyond functionality to describe a guarding or protective purpose for the house.

Roofing Materials

Early roofs on Chinese houses were nothing more than saplings and branches laid on a slope, perhaps supplemented with a mud coating to shed rain and break the wind, while baked roof tiles began to be used as early as the eleventh century BCE. Plants and mud continue to be used as roof covering in some parts of the country, yet tile roofs of many types are ubiquitous throughout China today.

Mud Compositions

Roofs made of multilayered compositions of vegetable and mineral matter vary from place to place in north and northeastern China, areas where semi-aridity and extreme cold help govern the nature of roofs. Throughout this region, roofs take various shapes: flat, slightly pitched, single-slope, double-slope, and even barrel-like convex curved profiles. With densely packed exterior back and side walls of earth or brick as well as a thick mud roof, the interiors of northern houses are well insulated from the bitter cold outside and are able to hinder whatever heat is generated on the inside from escaping.

Multilayered composition roofs traditionally began first with the laying of either a roof board or reed mat, sometimes both, over the rafters, atop which reeds or sorghum stalks would be spread as an insulating barrier. Two or three layers of a mud and straw composition were then placed over the plant layer, which would be tamped down until smooth, before finally being covered with one or two layers of a mixture of common white lime and gray lime, which included some graphite and water. Crushed coal cinders as well as alkalized soils were

Left and right:
The tile-making practices still observed in many parts of rural China differ little from those of centuries past.

sometimes substituted for mud where they were easily available. The use of calcium oxide or lime—a white, lumpy caustic powder—is an old practice in China. Besides being used as a waterproofing adhesive in the layered composition roofs of north China, lime serves also as the basic bonding component for plasters that harden after application to walls, floors, and ceilings. Wherever sedimentary rocks, which contain more than 50 percent carbonate materials, or seashells can be found, there are lime kilns, often side by side with kilns for the firing of bricks.

Thatch
This is a sturdy, durable, and relatively inexpensive roofing material, which was traditionally used on the houses of the poor as well as on the residences and studios of literati who sought inspiration from simple rural life. Containing natural chemicals that contribute to water-repellent and insulating properties, thatch—grass, reeds, and straw of various species—differs from place to place. Wheat and rice straw, sorghum/kaoliang stalks, millet stalks, and reeds traditionally were used throughout north and northeastern China. Thatch, a relatively light material, is gathered, dried, bundled, and secured to a framework on top of a building in thick, overlain layers but does not normally require a massive structural framework to support it. However, when there is insufficient attention to slope and compaction, thatched roofs can gain substantial weight when they are soaked during heavy summer rains, and consequently may break down. Original thatch roofs are usually relatively thin, but bulk up over time as thatching accumulates as a result of needed repairs.

Throughout southern China, bundled rice straw and wild grasses are used for thatching. In the early 1930s, thatching covered a majority (55 percent) of common roofs in the large winter wheat-kaoliang region that included parts of Hebei, Henan, Anhui, and northern Jiangsu, and was extensively used even in the more prosperous Sichuan rice (44 percent) and Yangzi rice-wheat (41 percent) areas. Countrywide, however, thatched roofs accounted for only 28 percent of all roofing materials, exceeding only slightly those covered by packed mud and mud-lime (24 percent), and far behind the 48 percent with tile roofs. Today, it is rather rare to encounter a thatched roof on a house, yet thatching continues to be used atop farm structures such as large sheds used for housing ducks and other animals.

Clay Tiles
Unlike covering large areas of a roof with mud compositions and thatching, employing tiles involves the use of individual units of relatively small pieces of clay laid so that they overlap from side to side and also from top to bottom. Both the methods of making tiles and the skill required in laying them are not particularly simple. The use of roof tiles is described in documents from the Xia dynasty about 1561 BCE, continuing to develop over the centuries as styles multiplied to include plate, arcuate, and cylindrical tiles as well as special-use tiles such as eaves tiles. Advances in pottery-making appear to have influenced the development of both tile- and brick-making technology, with major advances made first during the Han dynasty and then later during the Ming dynasty. The resourcefulness of potters led

to the production of tiles of many shapes and uses, unglazed and glazed, gray and colored. Over time, improvements in technique brought forth thinner yet less brittle tiles and those less given to slippage.

Flat, plate-like roof tiles, laid in an overlapping fashion, probably came first. With technical innovations in the production of cylindrical shapes, resulting in reductions in cost, their use became more widespread. The manner of laying roof tiles varies, as does the appearance of a tile roof and its ability to shed water. Throughout southern China, it is often only the weight of the tiles themselves, rather than a bonding layer, that holds them in place. This is done in order to allow the house to breathe and to evacuate warm air that would build up otherwise in the interior, since ventilation is more important than insulation in subtropical areas.

In general, roof tiles are able to shed water more quickly than either thatch- or mud-surfaced roofs. Innovative changes in production and tile-laying further helped to enhance their superior performance. Among the most useful innovations was the introduction of eaves tiles or *wadang* that are found in many shapes—semicircular, circular, and somewhat triangular. Most eaves tiles are prominently molded or carved on their exposed surfaces, and are thus viewed only as decorative additions along the projecting eaves. However, architectural historians have determined that circular eaves tiles drain water much faster along their circumference than is the case with truncated semicircular end tiles. Some suggest that this enhancement, rather than aesthetic considerations, fostered their eventually eclipsing semicircular shapes. Triangular dripping tiles similarly draw water rapidly from a sloping roof and hasten its dropping to the ground below. Because Chinese roofs are typically steeper near the ridgeline than at the eaves, attention is paid to ways of increasing water flow along the eaves line. The use of certain shapes over others is a pragmatic solution for shedding water.

In the 1930s, nearly half of all farm buildings throughout China had tile roofs, although regional differences were striking. More than two-thirds of dwellings in the rice region of the south had tile roofs, while only a quarter of farmhouses in the northern wheat region did. In the prosperous double-cropping rice region along China's southeastern coast, 98 percent of dwellings used baked roof tiles. Small and medium-sized farms were less likely than large farms to have tile roofs on dwellings.

The seventeenth-century *Tiangong kaiwu* illustrates the traditional methods of tile manufacturing, actually labor-intensive handicraft, that can still be observed in many areas of China today. The making of roof tiles usually occurs where raw materials are found, rather than at a fixed production site, because it is easier to transport the simple tools and even build a kiln than it is to transport large amounts of soil as necessary raw materials. In order to make tiles, clay is taken from nearby fields or mud from nearby river bottoms, which is then worked with small amounts of water into a suitable consistency, either through the action of workmen kneading it with their feet or large animals treading over the puddled soil. Out of this mixture, a rectangular block of tightly kneaded clay, perhaps a meter high and sized according to the intended tile dimensions, is given shape.

Using a wire bow fashioned from wood or bamboo, a tile-maker slices from the block a slab of clay to the intended thickness and height of the tile. Since multiple tiles typically are produced from a single slice, its length will vary depending not only on the expected size of the tile but also that of the potter's wheel. Lifted with the lower arms and hands, the pliable slice is draped around a collapsible cylindrical mold that is tapered towards the top. While most cylindrical molds seen today rotate like a potter's wheel so the workman can remain at a fixed position, it appears that the seventeenth-century frame was stationary and the workman had to move about the cylinder. Made like a flexible shutter composed of multiple joints, which are sheathed in a cheese-type cloth, the rotating tile-maker's mold typically has four raised vertical strips of wood or bamboo that leave indentations on the molded slab. These shallow notches in due course enable breaking the cylindrical clay form easily into four evenly shaped tiles. With only several turns of the wheel, the tile-maker smoothes the clay, first with his hand and then with a shaping tool held between the fingers and the palm, in order to fuse the ends of the strip into a truncated conical shape. A simple wire-cutting tool is used to even the clay at the top of the mold. Then the wooden frame with the clay cylinder attached to its outside is carried to the drying yard where, with a twist of the wrist, the two are disengaged as the wooden frame collapses. The clay cylinders are left to air-dry either in the sun or in the shade, depending on the temperature and the day's humidity. After a day or so, the tubular shapes can be stacked to save space. Once dry, each clay cylinder is then broken by hand along the inside indentations that were formed by the ridges of the collapsible mold while it was being turned. Four concave segments, each forming an individual gutter-shaped tile, result and are ready for firing in a kiln that normally turns them from light brown to gray.

Wood and Stone Shingles

Wood and slab stone have a long history of use in some mountain areas of northeast and southwest China, where soil is thin. Wooden shingles, made by splitting them from sections of logs, are usually laid without bonding in a pattern in which approximately two-thirds are overlapped and only a third exposed. As a result, wooden shingles are prone to being lifted during periods of heavy winds, but it is relatively easy to rearrange them afterwards. Stones are sometimes set on the tiles to help secure them but they too are likely to be moved by wind and rain.

Both slate, a dense rock that splits into relatively thin sheets, and shale, a softer sedimentary rock, are employed locally as durable roof covering in several parts of China. Both are impervious to water and both are long-lasting, fireproof, and resistant to being uplifted by the wind.

Environmental Awareness

China is a vast country, similar in size to the United States and occupying similar latitudes. As a result, its inhabitants live in environments with quite different climates, ranging from the hot-humid subtropics to cold-dry temperate climates. It should not be surprising then that Chinese dwellings differ in terms of fenestration, orientation, building materials, depth of eaves overhang, and roof pitch. In northern China, the orientation of many dwellings is such that the façade faces south or southeast. To many observers, this reveals a clear awareness of the ability to gain heat from the low angles of winter sunshine even as the high sun angles of summer are restricted from penetrating the dwelling and warming it excessively. At the same time, side and back walls are usually without windows or doors, thus providing important barriers against the intrusion of the predictably steady, relentless, and cold northwest winds in winter. Together with a thick roof—flat, concave, or pitched with a single or double slope—northern dwellings generally provide substantial protection for enduring the bitter cold and powerful winds of northern winters and early springs. As discussed earlier, the shape and size of courtyards differ from place to place in northern China as a response to local climatic conditions, with some being slender while others are broad. It is common for deciduous trees to be planted within courtyards in order to disperse heat in the summer and allow it to reach the ground in winter. Along the relatively open façade, sheets of paper traditionally were pasted on the inside of window frames and along cracks in the upper wall in order to lessen the seepage of cold air and contain some of the heat generated within. With the natural deterioration of the paper over the course of the year, it was renewed seasonally but only after the period during which the gaping holes welcomed the breezes of spring, summer, and fall. Because of the tightness of these paper linings, it was sometimes necessary during winter to poke a hole into one of the paper sheets covering a window in order to vent poisonous gases, with the mouth of the vent hole usually reinforced with a decorative papercut. Houses built into the hill or underground in the loessial region of China are a particularly ingenious response to climate in that the interior is cool during the day and warm at night. In arid regions, houses might be built with mud brick or pounded earth in order for the thermal properties of the earthen walls to mediate the extreme diurnal temperature changes in such a climate.

Varying topographic conditions in southern China have provided opportunities for villagers to take advantage of sunny slopes, local microclimates, limited arable land, and available water as they build their dwellings. Here, they are able to modify the interior ambient conditions by utilizing the ingenious *tianjing* or skywell, open to the sky above to allow light, air, and water to enter the dwelling, as well as using shaded transitional arcades with broad eaves overhangs in order to mediate hot and humid conditions. Ventilation not only removes heat and offers some cooling breezes but plays an important role in reducing humidity levels by flushing out moist air before it can condense on interior surfaces. Along the southeast coast, choosing building sites that capture steady winds is as important as creating openings and corridors in a house that lead prevailing winds directly and indirectly through even a complex building. Rooftop transom windows, openings placed high on gable walls, lattice windows, and the careful placement of doors—some of which have ingenious designs that allow a door to be open yet secure—all facilitate the thorough ventilation of southern houses, not only cooling the air but also reducing sultry humidities by moving the moist air. Intense sunlight and long periods of daylight are countered by whitewashing walls so they become reflective surfaces, and by massing structures.

Chinese craftsmen employ standard measurements, locally available building materials, experience and skill, and an acute awareness of environmental conditions in order to build Chinese houses. Structural and spatial variations throughout China reflect pragmatism and a conspicuous empiricism as builders act in response to local conditions, even as they are guided by building traditions from elsewhere. Whether built of earth, wood, stone, or some combination of these materials, Chinese houses are relatively easy and economical to repair or modify. Parts that are damaged by water or fire, because of the modularity of Chinese construction techniques, can be swapped out and replaced. The recycling of old materials and the adaptable reuse of old spaces are fundamental traditional practices. Evolving over thousands of years to meet changing environmental and social conditions, the courtyard in its extensive and condensed forms continues to unfold as an appropriate component in the spatial composition of Chinese residences throughout the country.

No other area of the world has such a dense and extensive network of canals, ponds, and rivers as the Jiangnan area, called by Chinese "the land of fish and rice." Dwellings, agriculture, and commerce—life in general—in the Jiangnan region in the floodplain of the Yangzi River are well adjusted to the ubiquity of water. Photographed at the end of the nineteenth century, the low skyline of dwellings along a canal in Suzhou, Jiangsu province, is punctuated in the distance by the spire of a Christian church.

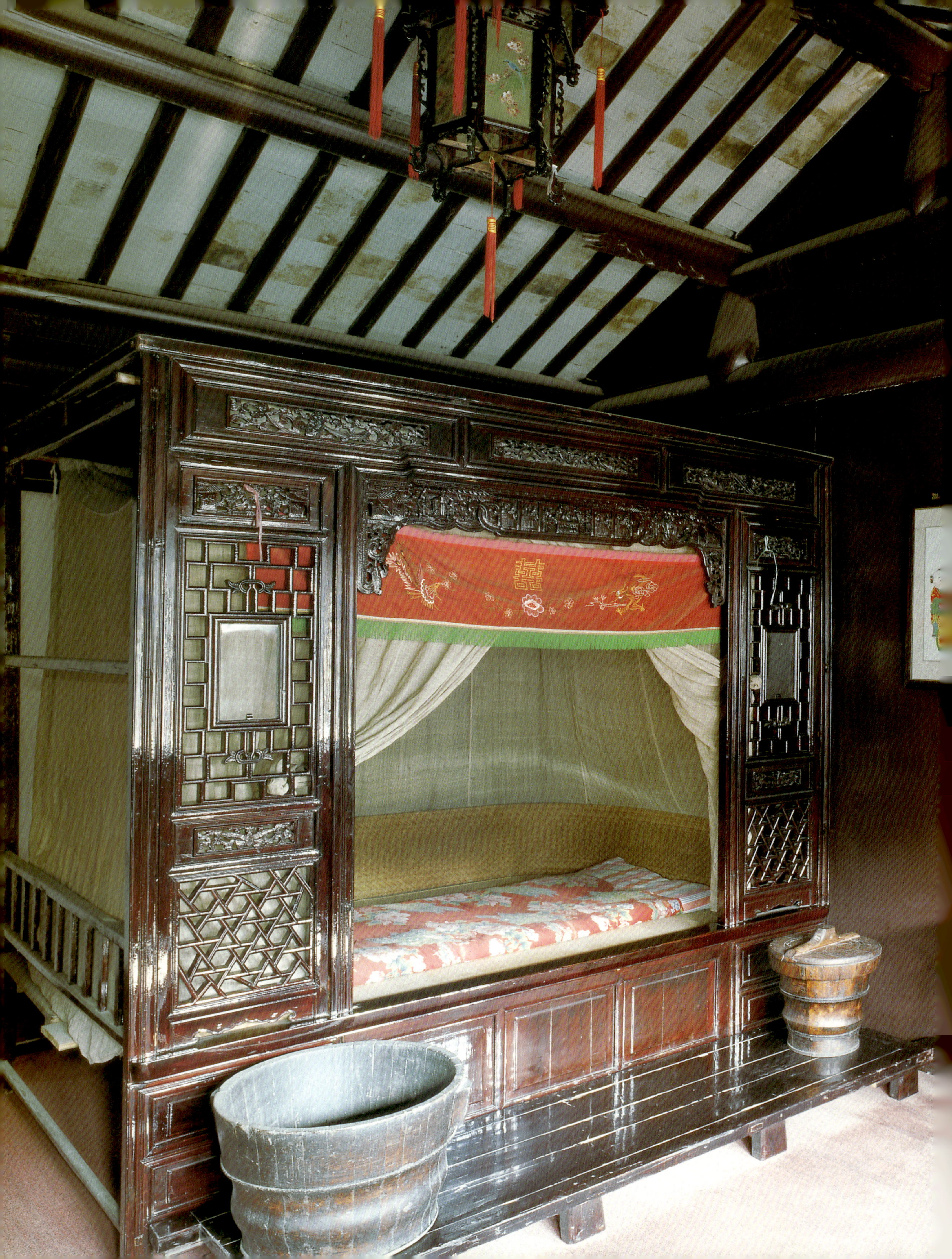

Part Two

THE CHINESE HOUSE AS LIVING SPACE

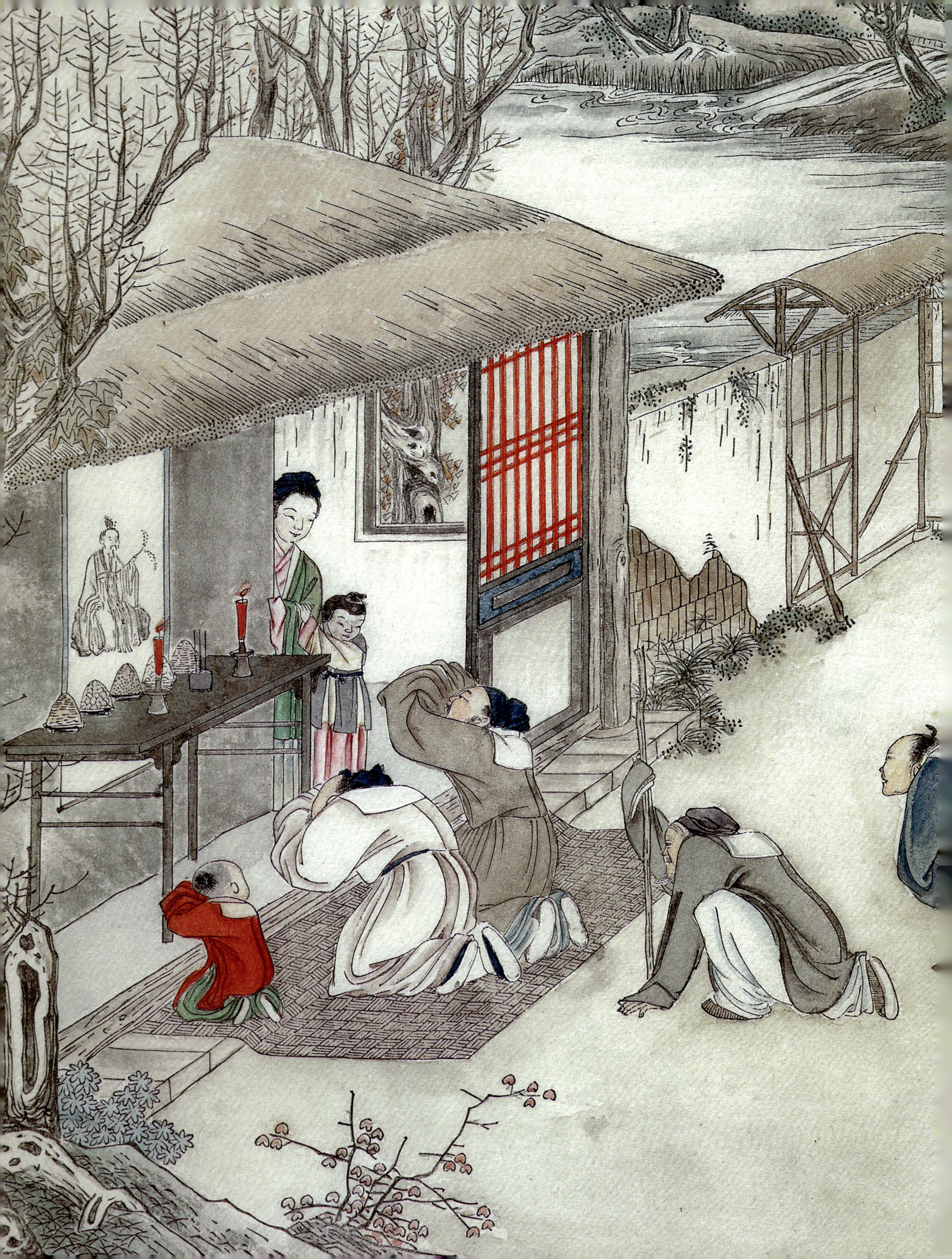

THE HOUSE AS HOME

Even though it may appear that craft and function are the overriding concerns when building a Chinese house, it is rare when the senses are not able to appreciate some of the other qualities of a house, especially when the structure is viewed as a home. Relatively unadorned cottages, however simple, often blend materials and forms that have charm even as the house itself may be rudimentary and appear uncomfortable. Larger dwellings—many surviving ones indeed are impressively grand in scale as the examples later will show—are often extravagantly ornamented, well sited within a larger context, and flush with the accoutrements of a family's life within it.

Many features worth appreciating are introduced as a house is built or expanded, intimately related to the choice of a building site as well as modification and beautification of structural components as a family occupies its spaces. Other features emerge later as financial resources permit and aesthetic sensibilities evolve. Some are obvious, appearing and reappearing as the seasons change. Others are masked because the conditions that created them are forgotten or lay latent because they are overlain with newer elements.

The evolutionary process by which a raw house is transformed into a home through the routine of daily life and requirements of periodical ritual is not easy to understand. This is because the process is usually ongoing and additive, sometimes taking decades, if not longer, and includes not only ornamentation but also the installation of furniture and fittings. Indeed, at any point in time, a house is just its most recent manifestation, a transitory artifact, encompassing and abridging the dynamics of its evolution over time.

Houses, of course, cannot be separated from the families that translate them into homes. Nancy Berliner's recent study of Yin Yu Tang, a merchant house in Anhui province that was moved to Massachusetts, comes close to being an architectural biography of a Chinese house and its residents over eight generations of occupancy and change. The book documents the development of the house and the changing fortunes of those living within it. More portraits of individual Chinese houses over time are needed to fully understand these dynamic relationships. Occupying as it does both space and time, a house typically outlasts its inhabitants—especially successive generations of residents—and provides an evocative medium for immortalizing the intertwined relationships linking families and their home. While the expansive manor complexes discussed later embody these dynamics, even relatively simple farmhouses, such as those preserved as the boyhood homes of famous personages, reveal the changing fortunes of families.

Chinese houses over time come to transcend the materials out of which they are constructed and the defined spaces that give them shape. Self-conscious actions taken when a building site is selected, as construction proceeds, and as the house is "stabilized" set the stage for occupancy. Patterns of daily life as well as periodic rituals and celebrations of individual families then operate to transform the house into a home. As a family occupies its dwelling, the built form becomes their abode, a living house, and the theater for their lives. This section will attempt to give some sense of the interrelatedness of both the artifactual and experiential elements of Chinese houses, as background for the specific examples of Chinese houses treated in the section that follows.

Opposite:
Gengzhi tu (Illustrations of Tilling and Weaving) includes a depiction of a family making offerings to the God of Agriculture in a shrine adjacent to their country dwelling.

Below:
With encircling hills protecting it to the rear and a crescent pool to its front, this building site for a dwelling is judged optimal in terms of good *fengshui*.

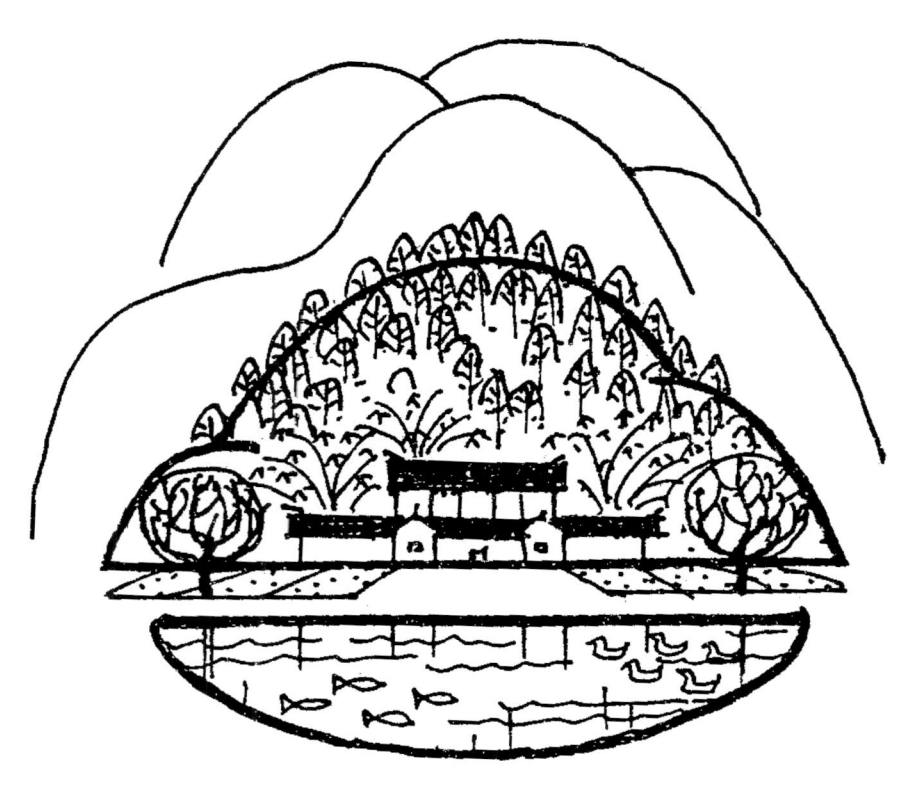

Fengshui: Siting and Situating a House

Although there are intimations of *fengshui* across the course of Chinese history and its roots are deep in the historical consciousness of the Chinese people, popular concern for *fengshui* when building a house has been widespread only since the Ming dynasty. *Fengshui* is but one of a broader set of approaches and practices that have had a powerful hold on Chinese and others. Throughout East Asia, *fengshui* continues to be applied in the search for appropriate settings for houses, graves, gardens, and temples in the developing countryside as well as in dynamically modern cities. When coupled with house-building rituals and protective amulets, as well as actions and items that summon good fortune, *fengshui* is believed by many to provide a means for influencing—even controlling—a family's fate and other aspects of its future. In recent decades, *fengshui* has become a globalized phenomenon.

Fengshui is fundamentally rooted in the conscious action of choosing an auspicious location—a spatial setting involving two fundamental geographic attributes: a "site"—the actual space occupied by the structure—and its "situation"—the location of the site in relation to its broader surroundings. Even centuries ago, when China's countryside was relatively unpopulated, the search for a suitable—some sought an ideal—spatial setting for a house or grave often took a good deal of time as even illiterate peasants wanted to insure their share of whatever benefits would come because of *fengshui* considerations and decision making.

Fengshui is a modern colloquial expression, literally meaning "wind and water," usually translated in English as "geomancy." Its complexity, however, is nuanced, with additional notions suggested by alternative translations such as "topomancy," "astro-ecology," "topographical siting," "ecomancy," "mystical ecology," and "natural science of the landscape."

Although abstruse principles and esoteric terms abound in *fengshui*, its essence can be distilled into several essential elements. These involve the interaction of *yin* and *yang* in which an ethereal property known as *qi*, translated as "life breath" or "cosmic energy," gives character and meaning to a place. At an elementary level, each place exemplifies either *yin* or *yang* characteristics, yet in actuality places usually exhibit both traits simultaneously. Falling away from the sun to the north or northwest, *yin* sites, which are optimal for burial, are said to exemplify the female aspect, passivity and darkness, as well as the Earth and moon. *Yinzhai* or "abode for the dead" is a common expression for a grave or tomb.

Divining a suitable gravesite is carried out to "comfort" those who will occupy the *yinzhai*, but also to insure good fortune to those descendants who continue to live. Locating a building site for a house for the living, a *yangzhai* or "abode for the living," is also itself a quest for benefits and "comfort." Indeed, there are sometimes remarkable resemblances in the outward appearance of *yangzhai* and *yinzhai*

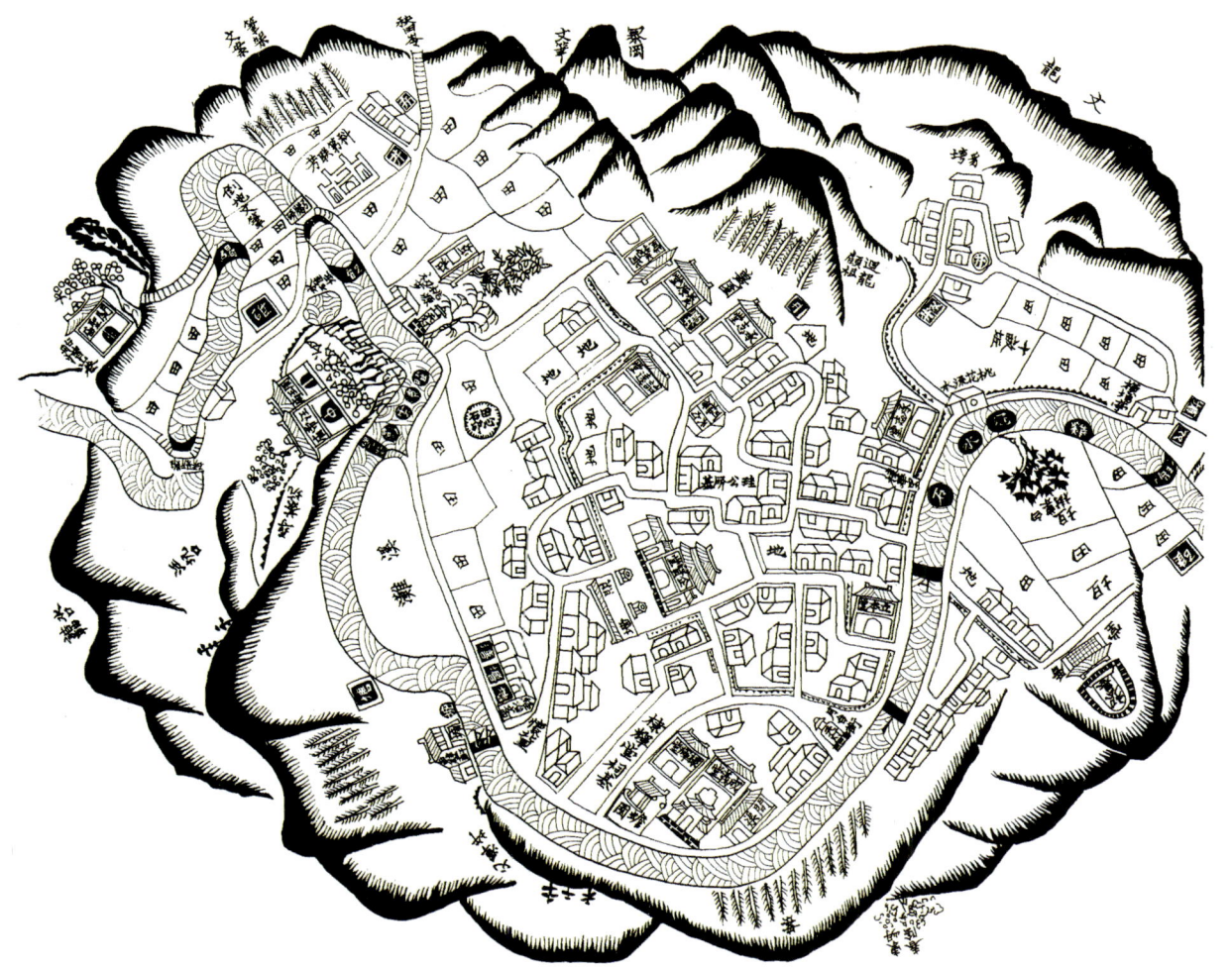

Above:
With ridges of mountains behind it and ponded water towards the front, the layout of Hongcun, a village in southern Anhui province, is said to have very favorable *fengshui*.

Left:
On this *fengshui* drawing for Zhifeng village, Jiangxi province, each of the mountains, water bodies, graves, and important structures is named as part of an auspicious composition. The embracing ranges on the sides are considered analogous to a protecting Azure Dragon on the east and a White Tiger on the west.

The House as Home

Left:
A *fengshui* master and his assistants are shown here ascertaining the attributes of a building site by consulting a dish-like apparatus, called in English a "compass," and a manual, while also using measuring rods.

Below:
This *yinzhai*—a "residence of the dead"—is an omega-shaped gravesite with felicitous ornamentation that speaks of longevity and filial piety, themes also found in and about common homes. Fuzhou, Fujian.

in terms of layout and structure. In addition, the arrangement of "rooms" in larger tombs is often similar to those of spaces in houses and stone is used to imitate wood for columns and decorative features (Steinhardt, 2005).

Understood by common people as popular lore, the tenets of *fengshui* are harbored as well by "wind and water interpreters," whose prognostic faculties depend upon knowledge transmitted from master to apprentice or gleaned from written texts, manuals whose contents are obscure to laypersons. There are two basic approaches to *fengshui*, which once were quite distinct but today are entangled. One stresses cosmic patterns and esoteric principles while the other focuses on the topography of an area: an Analytical School, which utilizes complicated calculations and an intricate compass, and a Configurations School, which visually and intuitively assesses the lay of the land. *Fengshui* practices often appear idiosyncratic and lacking in consistency but always focus on a search for equilibrium and harmony in order to avert misfortune and insure good fortune.

Some *fengshui* practitioners arm themselves with a dish-like apparatus, called in English a "compass." In actuality, this compass is more than a device for finding directions since it is, in fact, an analytical tool for making judgments about a range of cosmic variables that constitute Chinese metaphysical thinking. By manipulating cosmological correspondences, including numerical and correlative associations, the suitability of a house-building site is said to be both determinable and necessary.

The Configurations School, with its focus on landscape features such as mountains and waters, is less abstruse than the Analytical School. Indeed, there often is an aesthetic logic to building sites chosen by *fengshui* practitioners in that good, auspicious sites are felt to be "comfortable" and "suitable," sometimes delightful and expressive, even sublime and picturesque: "At a true site … there is a touch of magic light…. The hills are fair, the waters fine, the sun handsome, the breeze mild; and the sky has a new light: another world. Amid confusion, peace; amid peace, a festive air. Upon coming into its presence, one's eyes are opened; if one sits or lies, one's heart is joyful. Here the breath gathers, and the essence collects" (March, 1968: 159).

Vivid imagery, metaphorical expressions, and correlative thinking abound in *fengshui*, especially those relating to topographic features and cardinal directions. Undulating ridges and hills as well as meandering streams are necessary components of a favorable house site. Observations all over China reveal that individual dwellings as well as an assemblage of dwellings in a village often face south or southeast following the principles of *fengshui*. In cases where buildings face north, for example, north is usually treated as "conceptual south" using a symbolic vocabulary that reorients the actual compass direction to an abstract direction.

Proper siting clearly goes well beyond mere compass readings. It is not surprising that a good site for a Chinese house, according to *fengshui* prescriptions, is one that is well-drained, well-watered, and reasonably sheltered from cold winds and intrusive heat. *Fengshui* principles, in this regard, have led to construction on building sites where flooding and erosion are minimized, restraining reckless environmental damage, and helping to limit building on cultivable land. Still, one must be careful not to romanticize *fengshui* either in the past or present since rural Chinese continue to make decisions that also contradict sound ecological practices (Bruun, 2003). Some still regard *fengshui* with disdain.

58 The Chinese House as Living Space

House Construction: Craft and Ritual

With a site chosen for a house, the actual building process then becomes an activity that significantly surpasses the gathering together of raw materials and their working by carpenters and masons. Timing, ritual, and the use of amulets continue to be viewed by some as necessary in order to overcome intrinsic "antagonisms" among the household itself, the *fengshui* master, as well as tradesmen such as masons and carpenters. Almanacs, purchasable in the market, as well as secret manuals passed down from generation to generation, traditionally were available for consultation in order to navigate through the potentially perilous construction stages. Bookstores and websites today continue to offer updated advice that is rooted in customary practices of the past.

In the past, attention was paid to the dates and hours that trees could be felled, when the building lot could be leveled and the ground broken, and the propitious time when the stone foundation could be set. Careful thought was given to how the carpenter's trestle was placed as well as how wood was shaped on it. Special ritual attended several critical junctures in house-building, each of which was judged especially consequential and demanding of attention as the dwelling took shape: raising the columns and beams, hoisting the ridgepole, determining the slope of the roof, laying the surrounding brick or tamped earth wall, tiling the roof, paving the floors, plastering the walls, installing the door, building a kitchen stove, sweeping the floors, digging the well, creating a cow shed, stable, pigsty or privy, as well as the actual moving in.

It is still possible to encounter evidence of such house-building practices in China even in the twenty-first century, although they are certainly much less common than in the past.

Breaking ground and leveling the foundation especially demanded the choice of an auspicious date since it had the potential of upsetting natural forces. The lighting of firecrackers and often the sprinkling of chicken blood as a means of expelling malevolent forces stirred up by the breaking of the ground accompanied ritual offerings of incense and fruit to tutelary deities, such as the Earth God Tudi Gong and the spirits of the five directions. The locations of column bases get special ritual attention from both masons and carpenters since these spots must be firmly tamped in order to support the weight of the columns, the wooden frame, as well as a heavy roof. In some parts of northern China, old coins continue to be buried at the location where the main door is to be positioned. Although with significantly less ubiquity than in the past, it is still possible to see these rituals, which also include the use of calligraphic charms written on peach wood slips that appeal to the guardians of each of the directions affected by the ground-breaking.

The work of carpenters traditionally went beyond selecting, measuring, marking, cutting, carving, and fitting a complex repertoire of wooden parts for the timber frame of the house. Carpenters, too, had to be aware of the prescriptions set by calendars.

According to common belief, breaking the ground in order to start construction unleashes hostile forces. In order to propitiate these negative forces, calligraphic charms addressed to the four directions are still sometimes written on wooden slips. Rui'an county, Zhejiang.

Carpenters and masons also were known to insert offerings, charms, and talismans in order to summon good fortune or prevent adversity, in addition to amulets to avenge slights against them.

On an auspicious day, chosen from a calendar and sanctioned by the *fengshui* master, the carpenters would set up their sawhorses, the wooden racks to be used to hold timbers as they were worked with an adze. The actual first day of work would begin with a feast of auspicious foods provided by the head of the household, including noodles for longevity and watermelon for fecundity. It was traditionally believed that this feast was an appropriate time and place for generosity in order to insure good quality work.

Carpenters also paid special attention to fixing favorable measurements and avoiding unfavorable ones for the length, width, and height of the dwelling as well as non-structural carpentry for building parts, such as doors, windows, and interior partition walls.

Once all the columns, beams or tie beams, brackets, as well as the manifold wooden parts needed for the roof were crafted and clearly marked with words describing how they were to fit together, it was time to assemble the components into a bent. The bent, which is a transverse framing unit comprised of columns and beams, becomes then a fabricated modular frame that can be lifted into place. While ritual guides many of these steps, the most critical ritual was associated with the hoisting of the ridgepole, the most costly building component, whose strength was critical in supporting the weight of a massive roof. Again, a banquet had to be prepared for the carpenters as part of a series of rituals associated with *shang liang*, "raising the ridgepole."

Shang liang rituals and festivities have been recorded all over China, differing only in minor details, and are still observable in some rural areas of China although much simpler than those in the past. The basic elements include a table holding several carpenter's tools, incense, and two candles, which is set beneath the roof trusses and just in front of the resting ridgepole, itself draped with an auspicious red cloth, red paper, or auspicious words written directly on it. Among the auspicious features seen in recent years are a combined *taiji* (yin–yang diagram) and *bagua* (Eight Trigrams) sign used as antispectral charms, couplets such as "(Jiang) Taigong is here" (*Taigong zai ci*) and "All the spirits abdicate in his favor" (*zhushen tuiwei*). Sometimes old copper octagonal coins, called *bagua qian*, are nailed to the

Below:
Like other shrines to the Earth God, this one is at a numinous location under a gnarled tree. Offerings are still made here every day by villagers. Hongkeng village, Yongding county, Fujian.

Far left:
Viewed from below, this very old ridgepole still shows evidence of an auspicious crimson band, within which is visible a powerful Eight Trigrams amulet with the characters *taiji*, meaning "Great Ultimate." Fu Yu Lou, Hongkeng village, Yongding county, Fujian.

Left:
Even today, the ridgepole of a new dwelling sometimes receives special attention in terms of auspicious calligraphy and protective amulets, such as the Eight Trigrams or *bagua* shown here. The timing of raising the ridgepole is carefully calculated so that it occurs at a "lucky" time.

ridgepole as protective amulets. After tribute is made to Lu Ban, the patron of carpenters, and accompanied by the sound of firecrackers, the ridgepole is hoisted atop the wooden framework as the household head proclaims "the auspicious time has come!" while the carpenter follows with "raise the ridgepole!" (*shang liang!*). As the actual raising takes place accompanied by the sound of firecrackers, there is chanting of rhymed "luck bringing" verses that praise the quality of the raw materials, the skill of the carpenters, and summon good fortune to the family who will occupy the house. Wine is then poured from a wine pot from one end of the ridgepole to the other as a set of rhymes calls for noble positions. As specified in the *Lu Ban jing*, after the third libation the following words are spoken: "We humbly wish that after the pious gentleman/official so-and-so has built his house and raised the ridgepole, his household will be magnificent and his work will be prosperous. May he have a thousand granaries, may he have ten thousand chests. First comes wealth, then comes long life. Private and public affairs will both be profitable. The family will enjoy great fame, the house will prosper. Fire and robbery need not be feared, everything will go favorably. In all four seasons, floods and thunder will not pose a threat; during the eight half seasons, the bounties of heaven and earth will be received" (Ruitenbeek, 1993: 166).

To complete the ritual, the master carpenter casts out the five grains, a handful at a time, hurling each handful towards the five directions as he alludes to each of the five elements using a metered chant of subjugation that will "vanquish the demons" (*da sha*). Countless variations play on these associations, differing in detail from place to place. Although it is sometimes only a chance encounter that allows someone to witness the *shang liang* ceremony itself, it is not at all uncommon for the careful observer to spot the red cloths with their potent messages and associated amulets hanging in the dim recesses of the upper roof structure of a house. Some are darkened by soot while others are frayed by weather.

Even today in some areas of coastal southern China, invocations for fertility and prosperity are made by suspending a bamboo lantern, bamboo sieve, grains of rice in small sacks, bundles of red chopsticks, or trousers from the ridgepole or from the eaves overhang of a dwelling in order to bring forth good fortune. These assorted items are employed because they have homophonous associations in the local dialects, even if not apparent in standard Chinese. A hanging lantern, for example, invokes a desire for sons and grandsons since "adding a lantern" has the same sound as "adding a son."

Similar wordplay is said to work with small silver nails, called *yinding*, that are pounded into the ridgepole. The square openings in a red bamboo sieve are said to represent the "mouths" or *kou* in a large family while chopsticks, pronounced *kuaizi*, has a punning relationship with "sons coming quickly," also *kuai zi*. The word for men's trousers in some southern dialects sounds close enough to that of the auspicious Chinese character *fu*, meaning "riches," that they also are sometimes wrapped around a ridgepole.

Painted red, this massive ridgepole has several auspicious objects suspended from it, including a threadbare bamboo lantern. In Hong Kong and adjacent areas of Guangdong, the word for "lantern" is homophonous with the word for "sons." "A hundred sons, a thousand grandsons" and "Good fortune with the raising of the ridgepole" are two of the phrases written on the red cloth wrapped around the ridgepole. Sheung Wo Hang village, Hong Kong.

The House as Home 61

This contemporary all-purpose protective amulet, printed on a thin sheet of plastic, contains not only the Eight Trigrams symbol and esoteric writing but also the image of Zhang Daoling (Zhang Tianshi), the Daoist Heavenly Master, who is said to be an effective dispeller of demons and ghosts. Zhejiang.

Stabilizing and Defending a Home

Having completed rituals and shown concern for workers, the head of the household still must worry about the possibility that carpenters and masons might have employed "building sorcery." Craftsmen have been known to secrete objects during the process of building in an attempt to exact vengeance over slights, stinginess, loss of face, and general mistreatment. On the other hand, carpenters and masons also had the ability to "reward" a family for kindnesses, and often did so by secreting positive amulets as they carried out their work.

The *Lu Ban jing* or Lu Ban Manual illustrates various types of charm-based actions that craftsmen might take: three-quarters of the charms avenge slights while a far smaller number speak of rewards, such as promising wealth, long life, high position, and general happiness to household members.

For example, a broken rice bowl with a single chopstick hidden in the door frame was said to bring destitution and hardship to both sons and grandsons. On the other hand, a cassia leaf, whose name *gui* in Chinese is synonymous with "honorable" and "of high rank," was said to insure a first degree in the civil service examination system if it was placed on top of a column. Two copper coins placed face down on each end of the main beam or rice grains placed on the roof brackets were said to insure wealth for the family. Placing a white tiger on the lintel above the door, facing inward, was meant to assure much family quarreling, sickness for womenfolk, and death for the wife.

Neutralizing amulets continue to be viewed as necessary in order to "stabilize the dwelling" or *zhenzhai*, making it inviolable and thus protecting the family. Precautionary dos and don'ts as well as various charms are found in *fengshui* manuals that help shield a house and home from danger. Zhang Daoling (Zhang Tianshi), the Daoist "Heavenly Master," is sometimes featured on these esoteric charms because of his reputation for vanquishing demons. One can readily see today in rural China indecipherable charms using misshapened Chinese characters that serve as all-purpose calligraphic amulets said to be able to break a multitude of spells. Almanacs, still found in rural and urban markets, also reproduce calligraphic charms said "to stabilize" or *zhen* the bed, stove, well, chicken coop, and other parts of a house.

Because shortcomings and imperfections are likely to be manifested in any chosen building, it has always been felt necessary to rebalance a site by making modifications. A protective line of trees or a dense stand of bamboo might be used to simulate a needed ridgeline, in the process overcoming a terrain deficiency. At a broader scale, a prominent *fengshui* pagoda might be raised to counter unsatisfactory or ominous terrain characteristics, thus improving the propitious elements of an overall village's geomantic character. In the hilly areas of southern China, special attention was paid to *shuikou*, the location of water inlets and outlets where a stream coursed through a village and near houses. In addition, odd-shaped rocks as well as enormous camphor or banyan trees have always been viewed as numinous locations, preferred sites for small shrines and village temples.

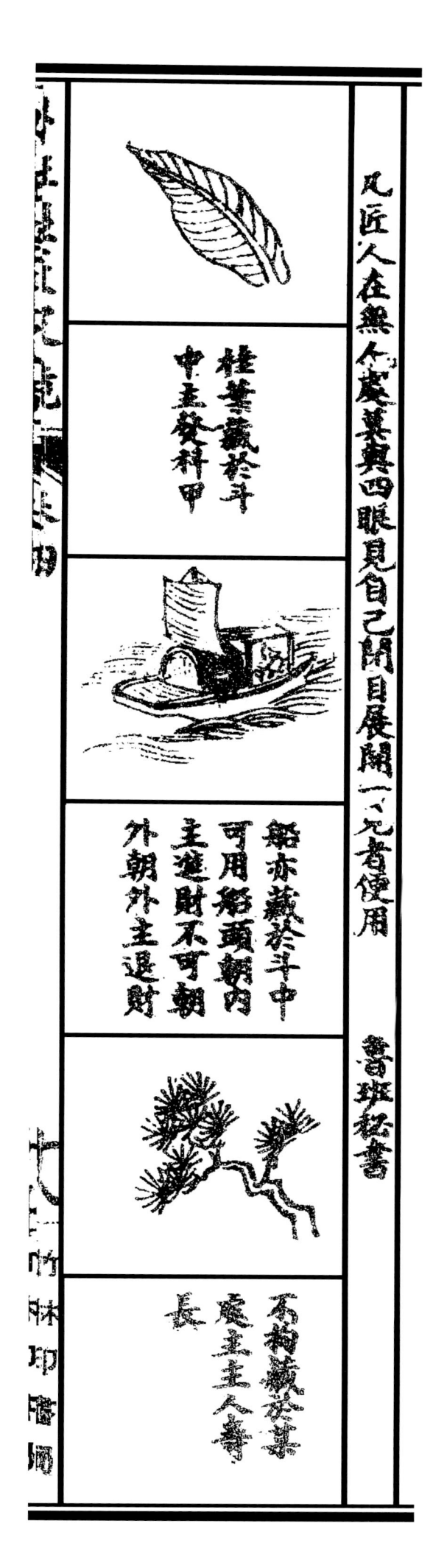

As a family occupies its house, further efforts are required to overcome new threats that might lead to the possible destabilization of the household's wishes for harmony. Whenever a new gate is installed, a building is to rise taller than surrounding structures, or when a lane or driveway will lead directly to a doorway, vigilance must be heightened in order to counter the potentially antagonistic building situations that might affect a household. In order to counteract, neutralize, or exorcise potentially malignant forces, new forms of protection, called "dominating" (*yasheng*) or "exorcising" (*bixie*) objects, should be employed defensively. Throughout China and even in the Chinese diaspora throughout the world, these concerns continue to be well documented even if appropriate traditional devices are not employed.

While walking on village paths or on lanes in towns, a careful observer is able today to spot these shielding objects along the ridgeline, in a courtyard, as well as above, in front of, or on the door or gate, and even at some distance from the dwelling. Taken collectively, they represent a kind of concentric spatial defense system utilizing calligraphic or non-calligraphic charms, printed on paper, carved on tablets, or represented by actual objects. The *Lu Ban jing* recommends a unique type of mirror called an "inverting mirror" (*daojing*), shaped like a concave plate with a higher rim and a depressed middle, that is said to be capable of overturning whatever antagonistic feature is reflected in it just as the image itself is turned on its head. An ordinary mirror, said to radiate *yang*, hung above a doorway, however, is generally believed to be sufficiently efficacious as a deflector of malevolent influences. Just as the *bagua* or Eight Trigrams sign, usually with the *taiji* or

Above:
Placed high above a door, this "inverting mirror" is said by the *Lu Ban jing* to be capable of overturning any malevolent element reflected in it.

Left:
Found in the manual of Lu Ban, the patron of carpenters, are twenty-seven charms that can be used to bless or curse a family. From top to bottom, the instructions state: a cassia leaf, if placed in the column bracket, is to insure that descendants of the household head will achieve scholarly success and thus riches; hiding a boat in a column bracket will guarantee prosperity for the household if the bow is pointed in, but poverty if it is pointed out; if a sprig of pine is hidden anywhere in the house, longevity will be insured for the household.

The House as Home

Far left:
As a protective amulet, the Chinese characters *Taishan zai ci* (Taishan is here) are shown here written in crude calligraphy on a vulnerable corner of two lanes. Cangpo village, Gangtou township, Yongjia county, Zhejiang.

Left:
Framed within a formal niche, the characters *Taishan shi gandang* (the stone of Taishan dares to resist evil/danger/catastrophe). Wang family manor, Shanxi.

Below:
This all-purpose calligraphic charm to "stabilize a dwelling," according to the Lu Ban manual, is to be written in cinnabar and pasted on the ridgepole in order to counter any untoward efforts by carpenters or masons. The surname of the family is to be written in the circle.

yin–yang symbols incorporated into it, is affixed to the ridgepole when it is raised, *bagua* are commonly found attached above the lintel of the main gate or frequently placed directly on the leaves of the gate. A three-pronged trident, a pair of scissors, or a head of a wild animal, growling viciously while baring its teeth, when hung on a window, from the lintel of a door, low beneath the eaves, or even fashioned into a door knocker are also to forestall misfortune by serving as a prophylactic defense.

"Resisting stones" are strategically placed at the foot of a wall, along a corner, beside a doorway, at the head of a bridge, or at a juncture in villages all over China. Most only employ inscribed Chinese characters but others have a lion or tiger's head carved atop the stone. Sometimes the animal holds a knife in its mouth. Most are rectangular shaped stone stele with only the three characters *shi gandang* or "this stone dares to resist" etched into it. Some have an additional two characters—*Taishan*—atop *shi gandang* to form an idiom meaning "The stone of Taishan dares to resist evil/danger/catastrophe." The power of Taishan "resisting stones" is a metonymic representation of the "legal" authority of heaven to repel, restrain, and dispatch errant ghosts who threaten the living. Taishan stones ideally should have been hewn from the rocky mountain itself in order to be effective, but it is likely that most such stones found in villages are bogus, spurious imitations whose calligraphic declaration alone is held to be powerful enough to provide defense. In fact, sometimes simply the five-character phrase *Taishan shi gandang* or *Taishan zai ci* (Taishan is here) written on a wall or on a plaque is believed to be sufficient as an efficacious amulet.

Particularly significant for the security of a family is protection of the main gate to a house. Such a gate is thought to be like the mouth and nostrils of a human body, a conduit for happiness and good fortune or an entry for bad elements. The use of protective screens called *yingbi* or *zhaobi*, seen in association with several of the houses described later, is widely employed as barriers inside the gate to mask the view into a courtyard and effectively block any human or spectral intrusion. Pictorial representations of Door Gods or Guardians of the Gate, known as *Menshen* in Chinese, are frequently affixed to double-leaf gates at the entry of homes throughout China. Gate guardians, foreboding enough to repel malevolence yet benign enough to welcome visitors, are believed capable of banishing pestilential demons, punishing ghosts, slaying wild animals, and keeping generalized malevolent and demonic forces at bay. Guardians of secondary gates, back gates, gates into wing rooms, and adjacent courtyards sometimes were also deployed at critical transition points inside a rambling house.

While not a door god, an image of Zhong Kui, a formidable demon-queller and exorcist, is placed on a gate at the time of the summer solstice, an especially inauspicious day since it begins a six-month cycle of ever-shortening days. On this day, the fifth day of the fifth month, *yang* elements reach their peak and negative *yin* elements, including "ghosts" that are responsible for disease, accidental death, and financial disaster, begin to emerge. This also is a time when the so-called five noxious or poisonous creatures or *wudu*—the snake, centipede, scorpion, gecko, and toad or spider—are said to multiply, clearly a time for added protection.

Above left:
Conforming to the trapezoidal shape specified in the Lu Ban manual, this amulet includes a protective tiger as well as the Eight Trigrams. Shengxian, Zhejiang.

Above right:
One of a pair of doorknockers at the entry of a house, the growling image of a fierce animal is said to offer a layer of protection. Wang family manor, Shanxi.

Below left:
This plaque announces the "Hall of the Earth God." The Earth God is viewed as a guardian deity of a specific area, in this case a family compound. Wang family manor, Shanxi.

Below right:
Arrayed around a reflecting mirror, these three sets of pointed tridents are said to keep hostile influences at bay. Shexian, Anhui.

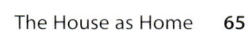

The House as Home

Above left:
Even though a full year has passed since this flanking pair of Door Gods was pasted on the panels, they remain colorful. Beijing.

Above right:
In full martial regalia, Yu Chigong, one of a pair of well-known Door Gods, guards this family home from malevolent demons and wandering ghosts, among other evils. Beijing.

Left:
With a movable protective screen ahead and a pair of Door Gods, this entryway into a courtyard of a large dwelling offers a full level of defense. Fu Yu Lou, Fujian.

Right:
In a room divided into two parts, a learned scholar served as both tutor for the family's sons in the front space and as keeper of medicines in the alcove in the rear. Sitting on the low benches on the right, boys would practice calligraphy on their slates while reciting classic texts from memory. Kang family manor, Henan.

66 The Chinese House as Living Space

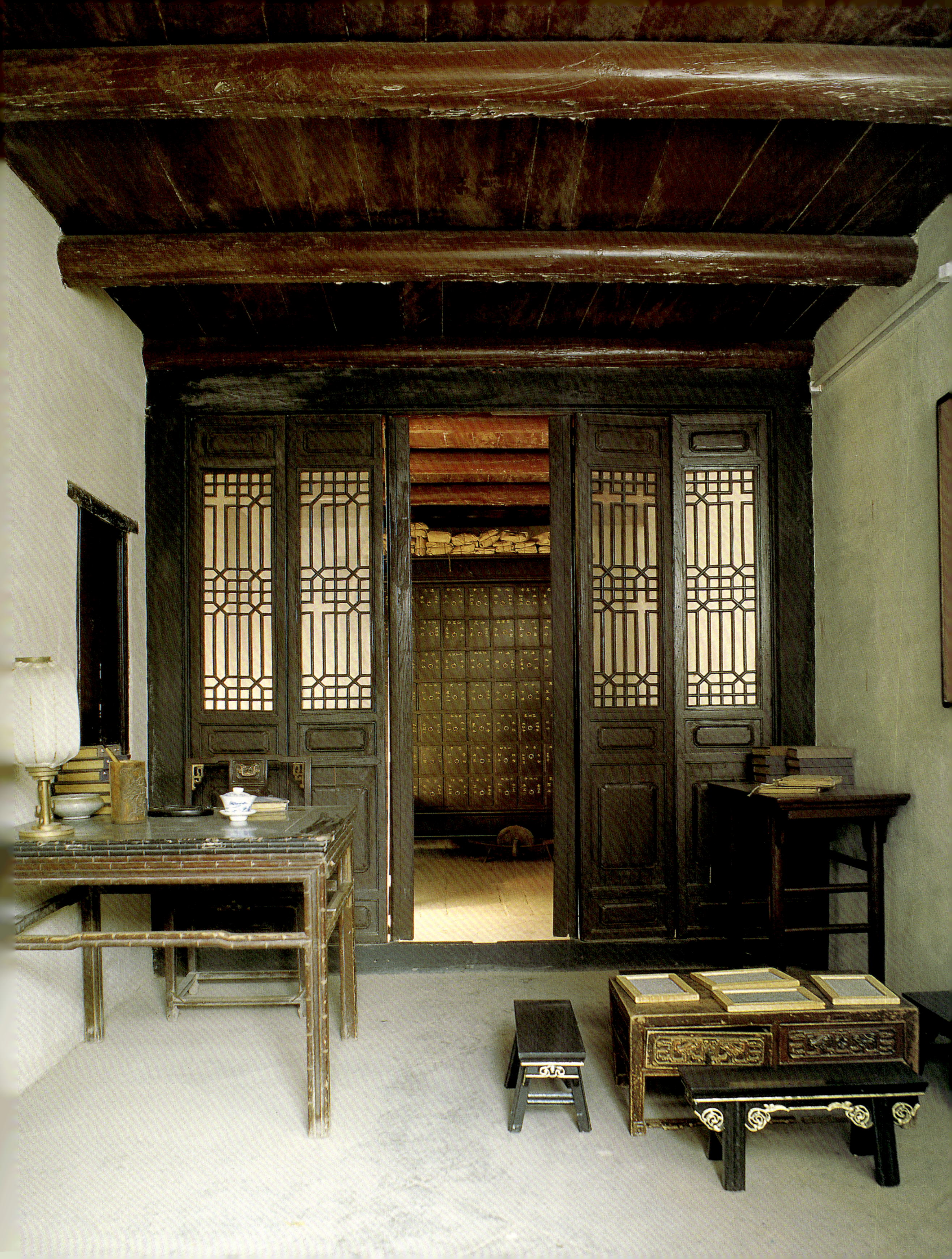

Houses as Social Templates

The structure and layout of Chinese houses reveal some common and consistent "design" principles, including attention to siting, enclosure, open–closed spaces, and hierarchical delineations. The interior layout of the house and its ornamentation serve important social dimensions for the family living within the walls. Hierarchies of generation, age, and gender are usually most clearly reflected in how interior space is divided and how it is used. After all, it is in the home, rather than in any religious or other secular structure, that Chinese life-cycle rituals—birth, maturation, marriage, and death—are carried out, sometimes in great halls but more often in open spaces temporarily converted to meet necessary ritual needs.

Viewing Chinese houses as instruments of socialization, as inculcating "texts" guiding proper family behavior, may appear as fanciful and poetic, but traditional Chinese houses indeed were "templates" in which enclosure, height, depth, proportion, gates, ritual spaces, bedrooms, beds, and kitchens, among other spaces and characteristics, mediated behavior and helped mold the actions of family members. Ritual and ethics-shaping messages, purposefully incorporated into copious ornamentation—discussed below—are as much a part of a house plan as the spaces in which they were found. As a "space of decorum" and a "space of culture," to use Francesca Bray's fitting phrases, a dwelling, a home provides

Left:
Built in 1617 by his descendants, this grand Ancestral Hall, called Baolun Ge, commemorates Luo Dongshu, a renowned scholar in the family who lived several centuries earlier. Chengkan village, Shexian, Anhui.

Below:
As portrayed in this late Qing-dynasty print, men and women have different, yet complementary, realms within the home. Women, in the lower register, tend to children as well as being engaged in the production of cloth, including reeling, spinning, and weaving. Two upper-class men across the courtyard are visiting with each other, perhaps talking about business affairs or reciting poetry.

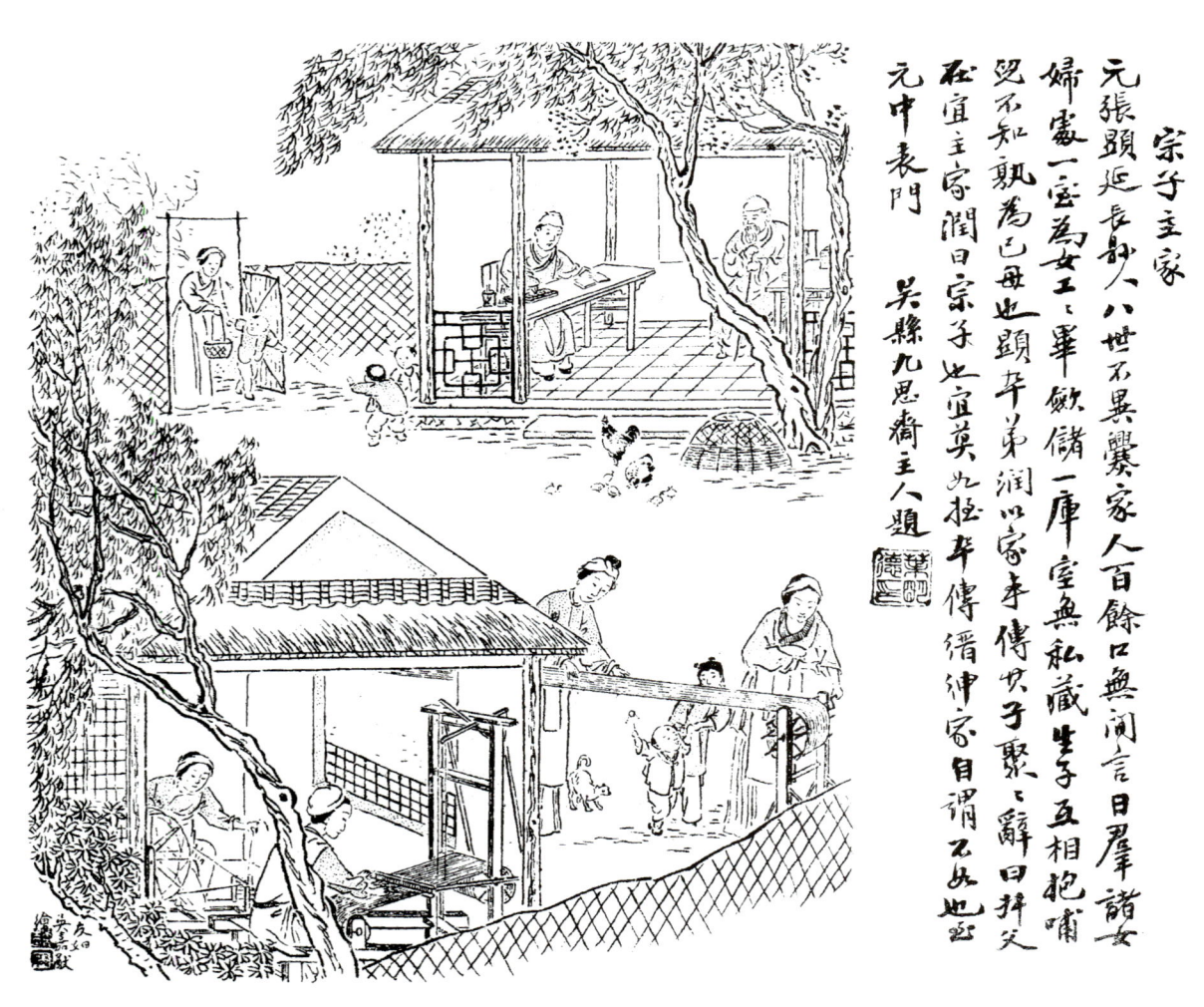

an additional means for socializing family members by applying rules of propriety and giving shape to their values (1997, 60–2; 2005).

It is, of course, no easier to describe a "typical" Chinese family than it is to describe a "typical" house. Small, simple three *jian* (bay) rectangular houses reflect the poverty of village life and have probably always been the most common house form in China, while ramified structures housing extended families are by comparison somewhat rare, although still quite numerous. The existence of large structures with multiple courtyards and structures attests to the genuine realization of the Chinese ideal of "five generations under one roof," a notion sometimes declared calligraphically if not yet actually realized. In practice, such a patrilineal family was within the same set of outer walls, but not necessarily under the same roof, and occupying different walled courtyards, usually under the authority of the senior generation male.

Complicated residential complexes more often than not mirror in their expansion, alteration, and decline the fortunes of the family itself. Within a traditional Chinese family, sons marry and bring their brides home while daughters marry out to the homes of other families, within which they are absorbed. As life-cycle events like marriage and death occur, new status relationships unfold, necessitating the movement of some family members into different rooms once occupied by others or to new rooms built to accommodate them. With family division, additional stoves might need to be set up even though families live near each other and as other spaces—threshing grounds, latrines, and wells, for example—might continue to be shared. Although the fact that so many houses never developed into anything more than a simple rectangle of three rooms with no courtyards or wings speaks more to the frustration of aspirations than to the absence of aspirations.

Three of the five relationships viewed as essential to the proper ordering of a Confucian-based society are represented within the spatial hierarchy of the home: those between father and son, husband and wife, and elder brother and younger brother. (The bonds between ruler and subject and between friends

Left:
For some, the display of four characters meaning "five generations under one roof" was a mere hope, but in the case of the Kang family such was realized at the beginning of the twentieth century. Kang family manor, Henan.

Below:
In many ways, the plan of a fully developed courtyard dwelling provides a template for guiding the behavior of family members. Status was defined by location in terms of inner/outer, front/back, upper/lower, left/right, and distance from the center.

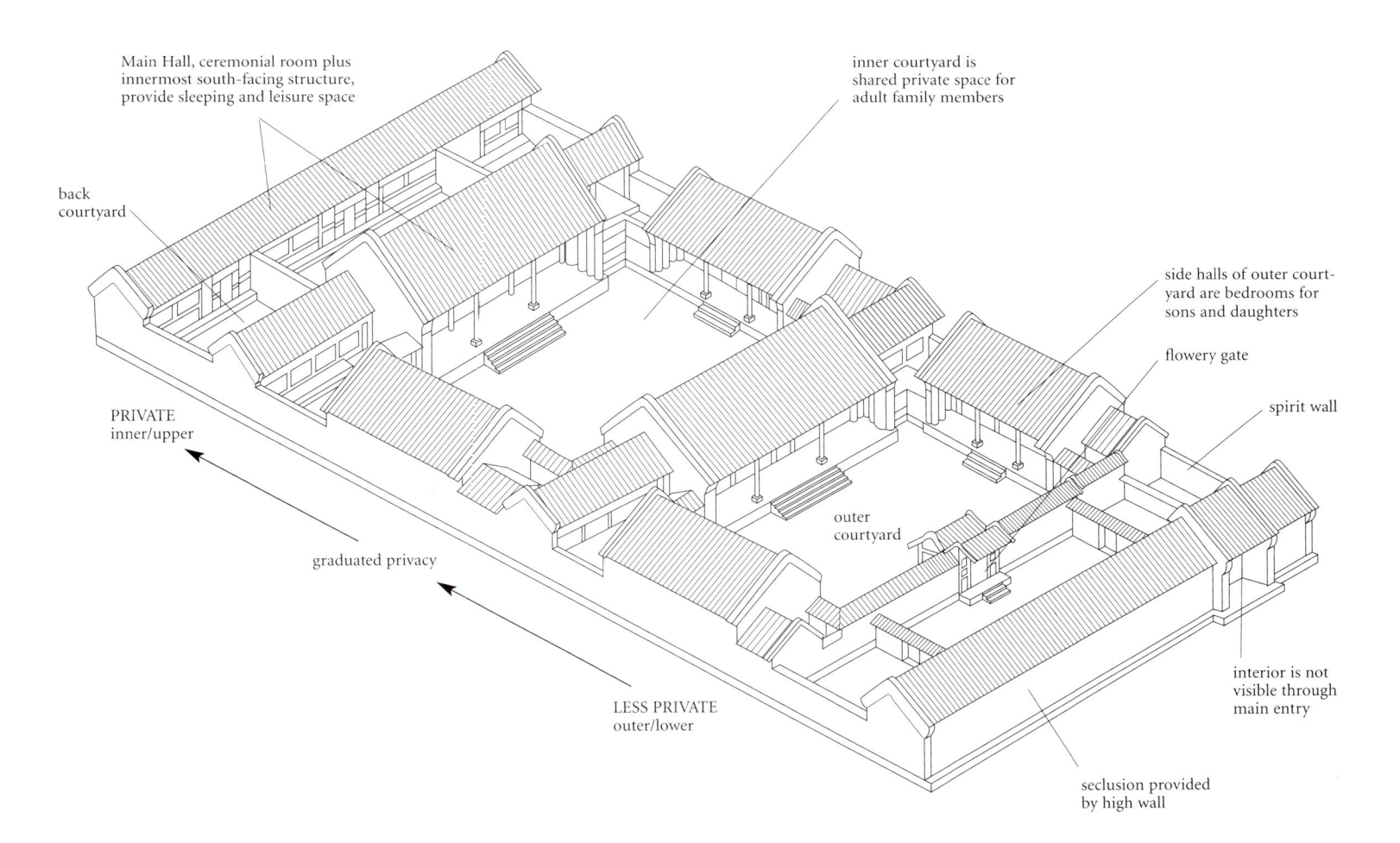

The House as Home

are the remaining two.) Except for the friend–friend relationship, each of the other four pairs is hierarchical. Each involves the maintenance of "proper" positions as well as reciprocity in the relationships.

A properly ordered home was only possible if relationships among its members were appropriate. Within a Chinese house, even a simple one, certain spatial associations—inner/outer, front/back, upper/lower, left/right, and distance from the center—are defined and well understood in terms of gates, halls, steps, and rooms, a spatial referencing system for generation, age, and gender distinctions. Some of these relationships were discussed above in reference to *siheyuan* courtyard houses in Beijing. None of these relationships, however, is rigidly demarcated or mutually exclusive. Instead, like the complementarity of *yin* and *yang*, they are relational, balanced, and even sometimes shift according to altered contexts. As will be seen in many of the larger houses discussed later in this book, the movement from public (outer) space to private (inner) space takes place through the medium of gates and halls, which themselves might be lower/upper or left/right.

In addition to mere horizontal relationships, moreover, gradations in the height of floors, steps, ridgelines, and roof slopes also underscore hierarchy and status differences that are frequently mediated along a well-delineated axis.

The full range of these spatial and familial hierarchies is seen best in a fully formed multi-courtyard house occupied by several generations. With three or more generations living together in multiple courtyards, a nested hierarchy of adjacent residential compartments emerges. In such a house, the senior generation of parents occupies the innermost, south-facing structure, which contains as well the Main Hall. Here, in the Main Hall, which goes by many names, is "housed" the ancestral altar and tablets—representing in a sense even more senior generations.

Throughout many parts of China, the bedroom with private space for parents is located "stage left," that is, on the east side of the Main Hall. Unmarried sons generally lived in the side halls, which were perpendicular to the Main Hall and facing the courtyard. Upon marriage, the eldest son would move with his new wife into the corresponding bedroom on the opposite side of the Main Hall. When the residential space is especially large and shared by many families, a separate building might be necessary to house the ancestral tablets. Enclosed dwellings are not only inward looking but are also symmetrically balanced, ritually centered, and hierarchically structured. Inner and outer are oftentimes truly relational. In a study of life in a cave dwelling in Shaanxi province, for example, the placement of the bed is considered "inner" even though it is adjacent to the entryway, serving as an intimate space for women, where she had intercourse with her husband, gave birth, trained children, and carried out her daily chores, including cooking and spinning. Deeper in the room, yet considered "outer," and visible from the doorway was the domain of the husband, a place where he received guests at the exposed table (Liu, 2000).

Top:
Here in the family's study, replete with scholarly accoutrements, a young boy's mother conscientiously attends to his use of a brush pen to practice calligraphy.

Above:
No doubt preparing part of her dowry, this young girl is engaged in embroidery, plying the needle as an expressive art in what was equivalent to the male art of painting.

Above:
Framed by tall and wide timbers, this ornamented area is just outside the Main Hall of a large home in Sichuan around 1900.

Left:
Women are enjoying each other's company while sitting on a warm brick *kang* in this late nineteenth-century photograph. With a bedroom setup similar to that shown at the top of page 77, the stove shown here is being fed and stoked in order to heat the room and the bed during winter.

The House as Home

The Main Hall

In villages in central and southern China, separate buildings are designated Ancestral Halls as a means for broad lineage relationships among common ancestors to be ritually expressed. Yet, more common even in these villages, as elsewhere in China, are spaces within the home used for the commemoration of ancestors (Ho, 2005). The nucleus of the house and a symbol of its power and continuity in a larger home is a Main Hall, whose layout follows a formal pattern based on a north–south orientation and well-defined east–west relationships.

Even in small, poorer houses, where it was not possible to have an individual room given over to ritual needs, underlying principles still could be observed in placement and orientation, even if modest in terms of layout and scale. Even in a dirt-floored dwelling, such as the boyhood home of Mao Zedong, there is a heightened formality to the room that holds ancestral tablets and religious images (see page 214).

Main halls go by different names in China, including Middle Hall or Main Hall (*zhentang*, *zhengting* or *zhengwu*), Great Hall (*dating*), Common Hall (*gongting*), and sometimes simply Hall (*tingtang* or *tingwu*). Whatever the space is called, it is symbolic of the family's unity, continuity, and even power as a corporate unit. When consulted on the proper siting

Above:
Barely hinting at the centrality of the Main Hall in times past, all of the spaces stand empty of the ancestral tablets, images, incense burners, calligraphic streamers, offerings, and other paraphernalia of ritual that once filled this space with activity and meaning. Nanchong, Sichuan.

Left:
Inserted into the wall, this black *shenkan* is a shrine that once housed ancestral tablets. Below it were tables holding both statues and objects that were the focus of rituals carried out at least twice each month by the family. Mao Zedong's boyhood home, Shaoshan, Hunan.

Above left:
Although lacking the bright red and gold ornamentation hung at the New Year, this grand doorway leading from one courtyard to another is emblazoned with three large characters meaning "Peace Means Good Fortune." Carved stone and wood serve as mediums for additional auspicious adornment. Wang family manor, Shanxi.

Above right:
Glimpsed through the leaves of a doorway, the Main Hall of Cheng Zhi Tang in Hongcun village, Anhui, is staid and formal as well as richly ornamented with calligraphy and carvings that express ethical hopes for family members.

Left:
Although stripped of the fine furniture and elegant ornamentation that once graced it, this Main Hall is still able to declare its prominence by virtue of its scale and proportions. Meixian, Guangdong.

The House as Home

View of furniture and paintings on the wall of the Main Hall of Wang Dinggui's "Hall of Inheriting Ambition," Anhui province. Some of the paintings are for sale.

The House as Home   75

of a large dwelling, a geomancer especially focuses on "fixing the beam" above the Main Hall since its proper orientation is believed critical to a family's prosperity. Domestic worship, much of it related to ancestors, was performed routinely on a daily, semimonthly, and seasonal basis in such a hall. In the Main Hall, whether grand or merely a space distinguished for that purpose in an otherwise common room, important events such as weddings and funerals took place in addition to seasonal festivities such as those at the New Year. Apart from symbolic meanings and ritual implications, many rooms of this type also served routine purposes, such as general family gatherings and the visits of important people.

Whether imposing and elaborate or uncomplicated and plain, ritual spaces also serve as the locus for didactic and expository ornamentation relating to traditional values such as filial piety, frugality, harmony, righteousness, forbearance, and diligence, among many other inculcating themes. Like the main gate of houses, these halls also are the focus of auspicious ornamentation. While conventions guided the positioning of furniture, placements that are remarkably similar from place to place in China, the furniture itself reflects a family's budget, taste, and status (Handler, 2005; Lo, 2005). Since the space itself often served a variety of purposes, furniture is considered movable and space could be flexibly redesigned to meet whatever needs arise.

Except in preserved old homes in China and with the notable exception of new houses in Fujian, Guangdong, and Taiwan, it is rather rare to encounter a Main Hall today that serves traditional ritual functions. Today, most such rooms are a family's multipurpose room, often without ancestral tablets but often with photographs of deceased parents and others, but also cluttered with a television, refrigerator, dining table, and the multifarious trappings of contemporary life. On the other hand, family altars and Main Halls remain important ritual spaces in homes in Taiwan, where they provide a venue for both the worship of ancestors and various gods.

As seen in many of the homes shown later, the obligatory pieces of furniture in a Main Hall include a high, long and narrow table, placed against the back wall, with ancestral tablets, images of gods and goddesses, as well as ritual paraphernalia, all arranged in a prescribed order. The second and sometimes third table is lower and is usually a square Baxian or "Eight Immortals" table, which also has many mundane uses that go beyond its ritual use of holding sacrificial offerings of food, incense, and lighted candles. Carried to the middle of the room, it is used also by the family for meals, by children to do their school work on, and for playing games. It is only the Baxian table, and not the high altar table, that can be carried outside as a temporary altar, and it is the Eight Immortals table, and not the hearth, that epitomizes domestic life in a Chinese home. A large painting focusing on an auspicious theme as well as at least one pair of couplets with classical quotations in harmonious juxtaposition are usually hung on the wall behind the furniture in the Main Hall.

With an inlaid marble panel, hardwood chairs of this type are placed in pairs as part of a symmetrical composition in Main Halls throughout China. Shen family residence, Luzhi, Jiangsu.

Ancestral shrines or *shenkan* are not common in Chinese homes today, even old homes, largely because of their destruction during tumultuous periods of recent Chinese history, especially the Great Proletarian Cultural Revolution between 1966 and 1976. Where they once were present, only the empty cabinet that once held them remains. Placed on the high table along the back wall or inset into the wall as a cabinet, an ancestral shrine looks much like a true-scale model of an important building because of the details of doors, lattice panels, steps, tile roof, and ornamentation. Mortise-and-tenoned joinery and pivoted hinges heighten the verisimilitude.

For families who lack a shrine made of wood, a paper print might do, showing within it not only a representative three-bay ancestral shrine but also the mansion-like structure in which it might be found, populated with representative ancestors and cluttered with auspicious imagery and calligraphy. Economic and social status traditionally guided the format and nature of visits, reportings, offerings, and sacrifices by family members at the ancestral shrine in the Main Hall. In wealthy households, the ancestral shrine was the locus of somewhat perfunctory daily attention that was augmented by more formal twice-monthly wine and tea offerings. Special foods were offered perhaps six times a year with specific ancestral rites according to the four seasons and special attention on the anniversary of the death of a parent.

In some villages, ancestral ritual occurs outside the Main Hall of a home in central as well as branch Ancestral Halls. Ancestral Halls, especially in southern China, are often imposing structures that declare the strength of a lineage and the relationships among its constituent parts. In northern China, ancestral ritual, using ancestral scrolls rather than tablets, sometimes takes place at the grave rather than in the Main Hall at home or in an Ancestral Hall.

Above:
Within an elongated arcuate cave room, the stove in the foreground was used to heat the brick *kang* bed in front of it even as sunlight also helped warm the interior as it passed through the lattice windows. Wang family manor, Shanxi.

Left:
Viewed through the lattice of a side courtyard, this side hall of a courtyard dwelling provided bedrooms for sons and daughters, with space allocated according to gender, age, and generational status. Mei Lanfang residence, Beijing.

The House as Home

Bedrooms and Beds

Bedrooms and bed in traditional China rarely served only as a place to sleep. In some areas, women's daytime household activities—chores such as food preparation, weaving, and embroidery, as well as entertaining friends—not only were carried out *in* the bedroom, they took place *on the bed*. A daughter from a rich family in late imperial times would bring to her new home a dowry, containing not only a bed carved in precious wood but also a chest replete with clothes for each season, fine textiles, and even cash, all of which were kept in her own space. Sometimes the groom's parents provided the expensive marriage bed for the new couple's bedroom as an investment of sorts in insuring grandsons in the family line.

Aside from couch-type beds, traditional Chinese beds were generally large and imposing, built on a raised platform, either with four posts and a canopy, or rather enclosed within what is commonly called an alcove bed (see pages 151, 175, 244, 245). As furniture made by carpenters, both canopy and alcove beds resemble to some degree the house itself, each functionally serving as a room within a room, an irreducible nucleus within the nested structure of a dwelling. Like the structure of a building, an enclosed bed is given shape by modular units with a timber frame structure of slender columns and beams set on a raised foundation, with infilled curtain walls and covered with a roof, as well as usually with a three-bay façade. At night, with the silk gauze or cotton curtains drawn, it became a warm, private enclosure, yet during the day when the curtains are held back by hooks and with its quilts folded along the site, the platform of the bed becomes a place to relax, work, or even visit with friends. As the most prominent element in a woman's quarters, the bed symbolized her status as wife and mother, the bearer of the family's progeny.

Built-in platform beds made of brick, called *kang* (see pages 71, 77, 115) serve these purposes throughout northern China. With a warren of flues running through them from an adjacent cooking stove, *kang* radiate substantial amounts of heat and thus are especially comfortable locations to work in winter but also preferred as being cool at other times. Usually located on a wall adjacent to windows, the southern wall being favored, *kang* provide a bright space even in summer for working, socializing, and watching children. Pillows, comforters, and low furniture multiply the convenience of *kang* as a multipurpose utilitarian space.

Bedrooms usually had windows in addition to a door, both of which, especially in central and southern China, included substantial lattice frames that provided variable levels of privacy, light, and ventilation. As winter approached, paper would be pasted on the inside of the lattice panels in order to maintain warmth yet allow diffuse sunlight to enter. Sometimes lattice panels were doubled, enhancing in the process the control of any of these variables. As can be seen in many illustrations, lattice panels enhanced not only exterior but also interior spaces even as they served as screens.

Left:
An ornate alcove bed and associated furniture and fittings of the type shown in this late Qing-dynasty drawing were brought as part of a bride's dowry to the home of her husband. A veritable room within a room, alcove beds functioned not only as a place to sleep but also as a place to pass the time during the day.

Right:
Shown here is the bedroom of the Kang family matriarch as it is said to have looked in 1901 when she celebrated her 100th birthday. The view is from her sitting room through her formal Main Hall into her bedroom with its large and elaborate canopy bed.

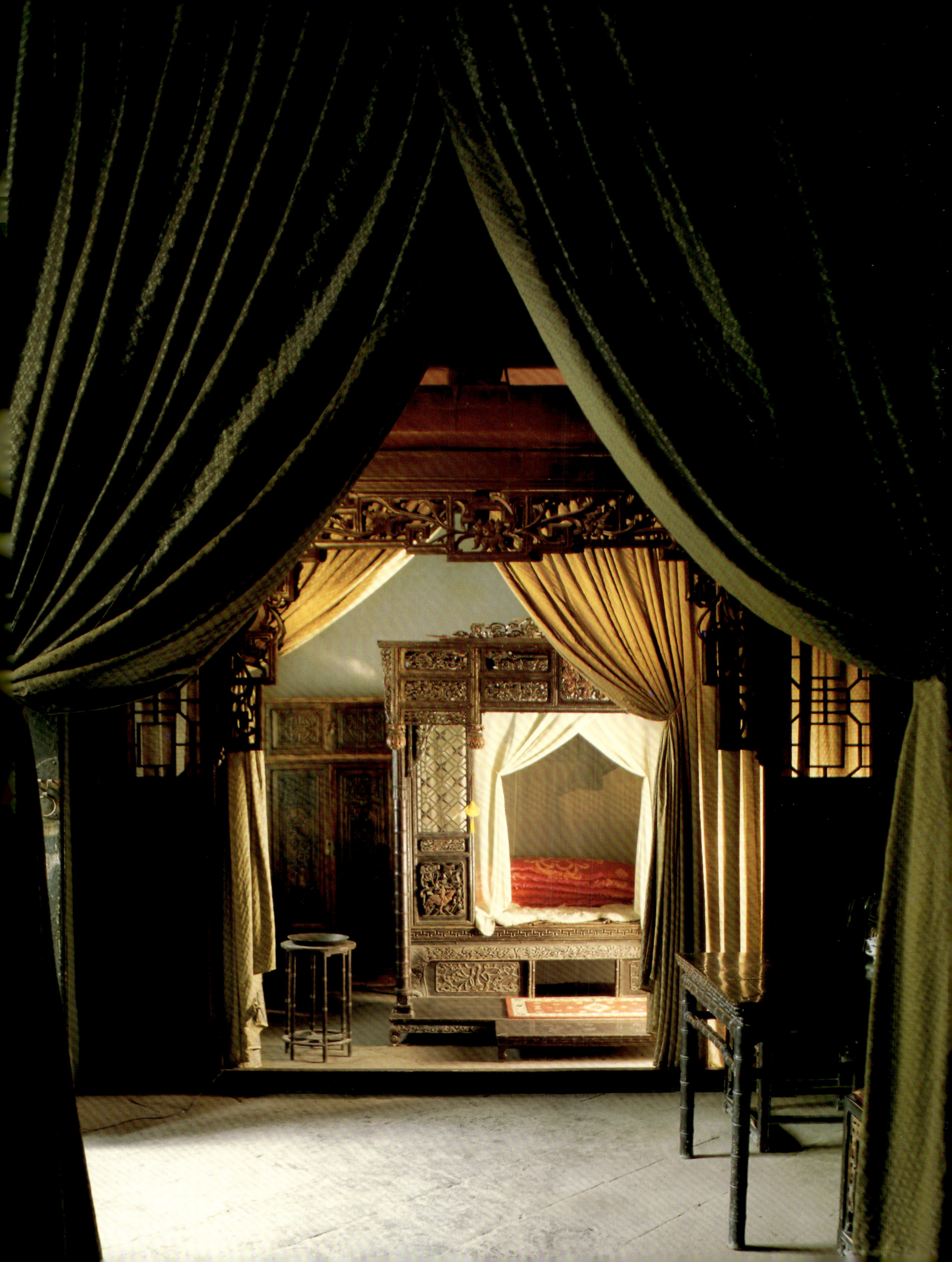

New Year's Prints and Rituals

Woodblock prints, paper cutouts, and calligraphic strips all are used by the Chinese to summon good fortune, the components of which are discussed in detail below. During the late imperial period, it is said that as many as twenty different household prints—auspicious and protective—would be replaced by a rural household during the turning of the New Year—a period that begins with offerings to the Stove God on the twenty-third or twenty-fourth day of the twelfth lunar month, continuing through New Year's eve and New Year's day, only to resurge again at the time of the Lantern Festival on the fifteenth day of the first lunar month, the first full moon of the year.

Local custom and family precedent throughout China include a veritable pantheon of "tutelary gods of the house." Chinese sources and Western observers in the late nineteenth century speak of their number being "countless" and that shops sometimes had as many as 1000 different images. Since most of the ornamental paper prints used by Chinese households to decorate their dwellings were hung as the lunar year began, they are called collectively *nianhua* or New Year's Pictures (Flath, 2004; 2005).

The subject matter of *nianhua* prints is propitious, focusing on summoning good fortune, but many also are morally instructive in that they illustrate evocative tales from history, literature, opera, and myth, portray scenes from everyday life, depict countless protective deities, and spell out moral lessons as didactic narratives. Some locally produced *nianhua* are rather crude, with colors added by hand to black ink outlines drawn with a burned willow twig. Many more are refined art skillfully produced by artisans with printmaking techniques using a relatively simple and well-developed process. Some prints would be placed only on an exterior or interior door panel, above the ancestral altar in the Main Hall, near the niche housing the Stove God, on the ceiling, or placed along the walls around a *kang* or other type of bed where moral tales could be encountered daily. Customary themes today are sometimes supplemented with contemporary imagery, for example displaying American dollars to amplify expected riches. The absence of colorful *nianhua* prints on the doors and walls of many restored old houses in China robs them of the imagery that once made each a vibrant home.

Zaojun, the so-called Stove or Kitchen God, is perhaps the most ubiquitous household deity found in Chinese houses. Rather than having any concern for the culinary arts or fire suggested by his name, Zaojun is the tutelary deity in charge of the household and the earthly representative of the Jade Emperor. As the "Overseer of Destiny/Fate of the Eastern Hall," he is said to observe and take note of both the good behavior and the misdeeds of the family, as well as reward or punish family members from a prominent position above or beside the stove. Rarely represented by a statue but almost always as a woodblock print image on a sheet of gray or red paper,

Zaojun is usually housed in a "palace," which sometimes is elaborate but more often rather crude, a sanctuary made of masonry, wood, or bamboo (see page 226). Sometimes a print of Zaojun is attached to the wall above a simple shelf or in a niche dug into the wall, with just enough room for a candle or two and a wine cup. Just prior to the lunar New Year, the paper image of Zaojun, blackened with soot from hanging for a year in the busy kitchen, is burned either at the doorway of the dwelling or in the middle of the courtyard. The rising smoke is said to carry him on a visit to the Jade Emperor of Heaven where he reports on the family members' behavior since his previous journey a year before. It is believed by many that this annual report determines whether the length of one's life will be extended or shortened, whether a person will encounter good or bad luck, success or misfortune, health or infirmity in the year to come. With a sugar paste or sweet malt taffy spread over his lips and sometimes even strong wine offered to him, Zaojun is expected to tell only good tales during his journey and then return to the family's house on New Year's eve at which time a fresh picture of Zaojun is pasted in the niche or on the wall so that he can begin anew another annual tour of surveillance, protection, and bestowal of good fortune. Ritual details vary from region to region but most share the common elements mentioned above.

At the beginning of the twenty-first century, rituals relating to various domestic gods no longer are as universal as they once were. It is still not uncommon, however, in rural and small towns in China to see images similar to those documented in past centuries but they are generally lacking in the restored homes shown later. Shops in major

Zaojun, called also the Stove or Kitchen God, is here described as the "Overseer of Destiny/Fate of the Eastern Hall." Surrounded with auspicious imagery and calligraphy, this tutelary deity notes the good behavior and misdeeds of a family throughout the year, and then reports this information to the Jade Emperor at the end of the year. At the New Year, Zaojun's image is always replaced.

cities continue to sell images as mass-produced tourist novelties and there also is a resurgence of production from traditional-style workshops that find their way into middle-class Chinese homes in urban and rural areas. Given the often-virulent criticism of folk practices, termed "feudal superstition" during the latter half of the twentieth century, it is nonetheless remarkable that uneducated as well as less educated Chinese persist in sharing deeply entrenched beliefs. Basic concerns for good fortune, long life, progeny, and other traditional desires of Chinese families remain remarkably enduring as symbols that abound within and about newly constructed homes. Whether symbolic motifs are used because of confidence in their continuing potency is, of course, unknowable. For many young people, however, the symbols appearing in old as well as new forms are opaque and obsolete, little more than ornamentation without meaning. Nonetheless, such content-rich ornamentation encountered all over the country adds layer upon layer of beauty, identity, and individualism to dwellings.

The entry of any Chinese dwelling is the focus of seasonal ornamentation. Here, in northwestern Guangdong province, the recessed doorway includes a pair of Door Gods as well as antithetical couplets and "hanging papers" or *guajian*, all of which were placed with the arrival of the lunar New Year.

The House as Home 81

The Written Word

Couplets, written on fragile red paper that will disintegrate in time, are pasted on both sides of the front gate of Chinese houses at the New Year. Unlike *nianhua* in which written words play only a supporting role to the pictorial imagery that dominates, New Year's couplets consist exclusively of two lines of Chinese characters in equal length with related but contrasting yet counter-balanced meaning. New Year's couplets are also called "antithetical couplets" (*duilian*), "spring couplets" (*chunlian*), and "door couplets" (*menlian*). A third horizontal strip with associated meaning is usually placed above the door frame. Together, these three elements look much like the Chinese character 門 for "gate." While New Year's couplets are pasted up with the coming of the New Year, their use is not limited to this annual family-centered celebration. Couplets are produced and mounted as well to commemorate weddings, funerals, birthdays, opening of shops, and even when new homes are occupied. Sometimes, minor ones are placed also at the entry of pigsties and stables where good intentions are invoked as well as on containers in which young rabbits or chicks are growing.

As can be seen in older homes of the wealthy throughout China, some of which are shown later in this book, paired inscriptions were also painted onto wooden pillars or chiseled into stone and wood columns. Large wooden horizontal presentation boards, given at celebrations, provided a further and more permanent medium for representing felicitous poetic verses.

Metaphoric imagery is usually used to communicate traditional values such as filial piety, restraint, harmony among siblings, and righteousness, notions that sometimes are expressed using abstruse language, not readily comprehended by those with limited education. Modern calligraphic additions are often more direct, as seen in the photographs at the top: "Abdundant Luck in the New Year" and "Whatever You Wish!" as well as hopeful desires for sons, grandsons, and a happy family.

In some areas, "hanging papers" or *guajian* supplement New Year's couplets and prints but are even more transitory in nature as they disintegrate from the force of wind as well as wind and light. They are also called "hanging money" or "hanging thousands," both pronounced *guaqian* but with different meanings because of a near homophonous relationship with the Chinese word for cash. Usually red in color or multicolored, they are printed with woodblocks, gilded, or cut into ornamental fretwork, and hung alone or side-by-side in sets above the doorway.

In China after 1949, the lunar New Year's celebration was transformed into the "Spring Festival," which peculiarly falls typically in the dead of winter in January or February, well before the Spring Equinox in late March. Still, it remains a colorful time of year with the posting of abundant auspicious phrases and images. Vivid and meaningful *nianhua*, *duilian*, and *guajian* transform even common dwellings into festive places of celebration in which a family expresses its hopes for happiness. The initial week of the New Year is the most important time for visiting family and friends. Celebrations conclude in the evening of the fifteenth day of the first lunar month at the Lantern Festival. Throughout this period, even the foods eaten have auspicious meaning because of homophonous associations.

Above left:
In an effort to summon good fortune, these four characters expectantly declare "Abundant Luck in the New Year." Langzhong, Sichuan.

Above right:
This entry to a reconstructed *siheyuan* along a Beijing lane includes a pair of painted couplets: "Sons and Grandsons in the Virtuous Clan Becoming Abundant," and "The Richness of Brothers in a Harmonious Family." Above the lintel, the four characters simply declare, "Whatever You Wish!"

Right:
Accompanied by ears of corn hung to dry under the eaves, red couplets and lanterns, which had been hung at the previous New Year, have become faded and frayed. Chuandixia village in rural Beijing.

Holding young rabbits, these large vats each have red strips with hopeful calligraphy applied to them: "May the Jade Rabbits Multiply" and "May the White Rabbits Multiply." Fu Yu Lou, Hongkeng village, Yongding county, Fujian.

The House as Home 83

Auspicious Emblems: Summoning Good Fortune

If one takes a measure of the proportions of the full range of symbolic ornamentation found in Chinese houses, less attention is given to warding off misfortune than is accorded the summoning of good fortune (Knapp, 1999b). Whether using words or pictures, a powerful symbolic language is employed in the pursuit of good fortune or happiness—wealth, longevity, and progeny—that together are arguably the predominant and most tenacious sentiment in Chinese life. As the Sinologist Edouard Chavannes observed at the beginning of the last century: "If the Chinese write their good wishes everywhere, it is because they believe in their efficacy. They think that the formula of benediction, like that of malediction, can be followed by effect, and that in repeating these desires for happiness ... one will multiply around oneself the chances for happiness.... It seems to me that no other people in the world has so intense a feeling regarding the intrinsic value of life" (1973, 34–5).

Chinese houses are layered with both visual and verbal messages communicating common values and aspirations, which are reinforced by similar themes embedded within the performances of ritual, ceremony, and popular entertainment. Collectively, these representative forms embody "the iconography of everyday life," to use the apt phrase of Po Sungnien and David Johnson (1992). Most auspicious emblems do not stand alone, but are incorporated in ornamented patterns dense with symbolic meaning, whether at the front gate, in the Main Hall, or in the bedroom. Even food consumed at the New Year and other times has auspicious connotations, although the specifics vary from place to place.

Using a pictorial vocabulary—punning language, wordplay, visual metaphors, as well as vignettes illustrating folktales and themes from opera performances—they are recognizable even to those who are illiterate. Pictorial puns called rebuses, in which seemingly unrelated objects are associated with a meaningful phrase, are common. The color red dominates all efforts to summon good fortune: the paper on which the emblem is printed may be red, the background color red, and the main images red, or, if there is calligraphy, the characters themselves may even be written with red ink. Auspicious objects, such as sieves and chopsticks, may appear red even though the color differs from their natural appearance. Peonies and hibiscus, while they are recognizable by their shape, may not, in fact, be red in color when included within pictures but are nonetheless seen as red, thus symbolizing good fortune, fame, and riches. A crimson rooster, indeed of any color, is a propitious *yang* creature which crows as the sun rises and then continues to ascend, and whose name *daji* is homophonous with "greatly auspicious," serves double duty as a protective amulet with a mirror around its neck. To Chinese, indeed red is a life-giving color, correlated with summer, south, and the vermilion bird that represents the element fire.

Above:
With didactic couplets, the uplifting name "Hall for Cultivating One's Mind," and auspicious ornamentation, this entry to a courtyard in the Qiao family manor is a focus of the family's hopes and aspirations. Shanxi.

Right:
A rooster, which is a propitious *yang* creature that crows as the sun rises, is usually called *gongji* but also is sometimes called *daji* or "large chicken," a term that is homophonous with "greatly auspicious." Here, with a mirror around its neck, the rooster serves double duty as a protective amulet. Nanjing county, Fujian.

Left:
Although the couplets on both sides of the altar can only be read by a well educated person, the dominating *fu* character for "good fortune" is recognized by all. Meixian, Guangdong.

Below left:
Four stylized bats, the Chinese term for which is roughly homophonous with *fu* or "good fortune," surround a large gold *fu* character. Together, they represent the "five good fortunes." Cheng Zhi Tang, Hongcun, Anhui.

Below right:
Though without its original luster, this *fu* character retains clearly the pair of wrapping goldfish with homophonous associations meaning "an abundance of gold and jade."

Bottom:
When the inverted *fu* character is read, "*fu* is inverted," it is a punning homophone for "*fu* has arrived." Wuzhen, Zhejiang.

Fu: The Quest for "Good Fortune"

The single Chinese character *fu* represents a constellation of felicitous elements that are sometimes translated as "happiness" but perhaps better rendered as "good fortune," "blessing," or "luck." Depicted in myriad forms about and around Chinese houses, *fu* is represented not only by the ideograph itself but also by pictographic objects that are homonyms of *fu*. Commonly written in black or gold ink on red paper or with red ink on white paper, often in the shape of a diamond since it is itself a configuration considered propitious, the *fu* character is pasted or carved on gates and other doors as well as at other locations, such as in the kitchen.

Sometimes at the New Year, the character is deliberately hung upside down in order to heighten its efficacy, since visitors and passers-by are expected to utter when encountering the upturned character, *fu daole*, that is, "*fu* is inverted," a punning homophone for "*fu* has arrived." The character can also be represented by a fanciful construction of other auspicious elements, such as the dragon and phoenix, rather than mere calligraphic strokes.

Bats, butterflies, and tigers often stand in for *fu* because parts of the sounds of the Chinese words naming them are homonyms or near homonyms for *fu*, varying as they do from one dialect to another. Bats especially carry auspicious meanings and appear widely as ornamentation on buildings of all types—houses, temples, palaces, among many others—but also as patterns on textiles, embroidery, paintings, and ceramics. Unlike in the West where bats are generally avoided, even seen as inauspicious, in China they are viewed as graceful and auspicious flying animals. Bats began to be featured as auspicious symbols in the seventeenth century and by the middle and late Qing dynasty had become common.

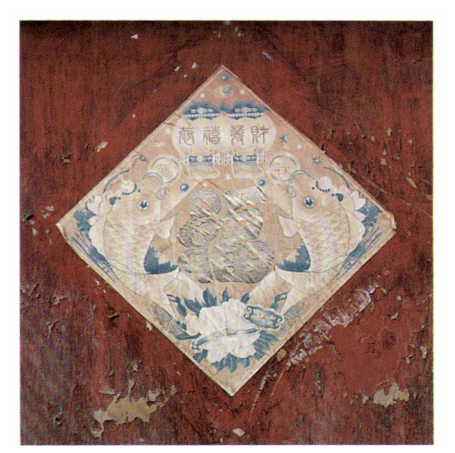

The House as Home

Because bats are often portrayed ornately and gracefully, they are often mistaken for butterflies. Moreover, the first syllable of the word for butterfly or *hudie* itself is a near homonym for *fu*, a fact that has encouraged the use of butterflies also as conventional imagery for "good fortune." Throughout southern Fujian, where local dialects pronounce "tiger" *fu*, which differs from *hu* in standard Chinese, the tiger is commonly used also as an emblem for "good fortune" as well as that of a protective beast.

Bats, butterflies, and tigers are often portrayed in pairs, doubling the effect, but more commonly in groups of five, a mythical number of significance to the Chinese. Five *fu* characters, called *wu fu*, represent the five essential components of good fortune or happiness. According to the *Shujing* (Book of History), reputedly edited by Confucius in the fifth century BCE, the five *fu* are *shou* (longevity), *fu* (wealth), *kangning* (health), *youhaude* (love of virtue), and *kaozhongming* (dying a natural death in old age). Only "longevity" and "wealth" of these "five good fortunes" are depicted in common folk ornamental motifs that summon good fortune. Perhaps this is because health, love of virtue, and dying a natural death in old age are relatively abstract notions that do not easily find symbolic representation. "Wealth" itself is a homonym for composite good fortune, also *fu*, and thus it may not be surprising that to many Chinese the mere uttering of *fu* brings riches alone to mind rather than the complete set of *fu* components. Even the crude similarity of the written forms of the different characters for both forms of *fu* confuses those who are unlettered or careless.

Written boldly on a horizontal strip of paper above a doorway, the four characters *wu fu lin men*, meaning "the five good fortunes have arrived at the door," is a comprehensive invocation regarding the full assemblage of good fortune. The same meaning is expressed using imaginative pictorial and

Above and center left:
The full and close-up views reveal auspicious ornamentation on the door panels, especially the use of stylized bats that resemble butterflies, both of which are homophonous with "good fortune" or *fu*. Beijing.

Center right:
Hanging upside down as part of door pulls, these bats too represent "good fortune." Wuzhen, Zhejiang.

Right:
With both of these carved surfaces, four ethereal bats surround a stylized and abstract medallion of the Chinese character *shou*, meaning "longevity." Together they represent the "five good fortunes": longevity, wealth, health, love of virtue, and to die a natural death in old age. Kang family manor, Henan and Qiao family manor, Shanxi.

86 The Chinese House as Living Space

calligraphic composition. Five bats, five butterflies, or five tigers—with their homonymic relationships to *fu*—are widely used as emblems for the "five good fortunes," as are four of the animals surrounding a single auspicious Chinese character such as an inverted *fu* character as well as a conventional or stylized rendering of the Chinese character for longevity. Similarly, the five petals of plum blossoms, often depicted graphically as small details on many folk arts and as architectural detailing, are associated also with the "five good fortunes." Although the five components of *wu fu* specified above can be traced to a classical text, in the minds of less literary oriented Chinese today and in the past, they frequently are simply interpreted as *fu* (good fortune), *lu* (emolument), *shou* (longevity), *xi* (joy), and *cai* (wealth). Even on the crimson exterior panels of a Main Hall of the Forbidden City in Beijing, although qualitatively stunning, auspicious emblems differ little in style or detail from those found on common houses.

Shou: The Wish for Longevity

In order to enjoy whatever good fortune might come, it is not surprising that after the character *fu*, no other auspicious character is commonly used ornamentally as *shou*, meaning "longevity," a desire for a long life, and even "immortality." Beyond the standard character and its simplified form, *shou* appears in at least a hundred variant calligraphic styles—some of which are so stylized and archaic that they are hardly recognizable. Even the layout of a housing complex, such as the courtyards and halls of the extensive Cao family mansion in Beiguang village, Taigu, Shanxi, are said to approximate the lines and spaces of the *shou* character, a powerful symbolism writ large.

Longevity and immortality are linked as well to the backwards swastika, which scholars trace to Neolithic times or to the overlapping S-curves, spirals said to represent infinity, or to the Sanskrit sign for good luck that came to China with the arrival of Buddhism. The shape was being pronounced *wan* by the seventh century. Since then, the backwards swastika has served as a common graphic representation of the actual character *wan*, meaning "ten thousand," a common counting denomination in China, meaning "that which is especially plentiful" and suitable in representing "longevity." In the case of age, it connotes eternal, or, at least long, life, and is found not only as a minor supplementary emblem filling empty spaces but also as a repeating visual element in wooden, stone, and brick ornamented patterns. Symbolic imagery is widely employed to represent the written word. Five bats, as indicated above, circling around the medallion-like character *shou* should be read as a rebus phrase "five *fu* carrying *shou* in their hands" (*wu fu peng shou*). Common emblems for longevity include the crane, pine tree, cypress, tortoise, deer, rocks, as well as the peach, chrysanthemum, hare, and monkey. Sometimes shown individually, more often they comprise composite motifs in which longevity interplays with other auspicious representations to form visual puns. White cranes, it is said, carry Daoist immortals as they ascend to heaven, while the black crane can reach the age of a thousand and is often seen holding in its beak the fungus of immortality, called *lingzhi*, an essential ingredient in longevity elixirs.

Pine and cypress, which continue to be evergreen even under extreme cold as well as living to a great age, are conspicuous symbols of longevity. This imagery is expressed in the four-character felicitous phrase, "May your longevity be like that of cranes and pines." While the pine and cypress are rather obvious symbols of longevity since they stand up well to cold, maintaining their lush color even when weather is harsh, the relatively fragile chrysanthemum might appear an unlikely sign for the same notion. The chrysanthemum nonetheless is a perennial plant with hardy roots that blooms in late autumn when other flowers have generally withered. Some say, moreover, that the homophonous relationship between the flowering chrysanthemum plant and "to stay put," both pronounced *ju*, as well as the fact that the peak bloom of the flower is said to be on the ninth day of the ninth lunar month (both *jiu*), creates a punning link with the Chinese word *jiujiu*, meaning "a long time."

The tortoise makes a natural symbol for long life, accentuated by the belief that heaven itself conferred on it a lifespan of ten thousand years. With its round, domed outer shell representing the vaulted heaven and its flat plastron suggesting a flat earth, the tortoise can be seen as a replica of the eternal cosmos. According to Daoist traditions, deer, like tortoises, are capable of living a long life and it is

Left:
Immortality is commonly expressed using the backwards swastika, shown here as part of a window lattice. As a graphic representation of the *wan* character meaning "ten thousand," its angled shape and active appearance contribute to an implicit notion of continuous ongoing movement as well as eternal, or, at least, long life. Mei Lanfang residence, Beijing.

Below:
A pair of butterflies, representing *fu* because of a homophonous association, supports representations of longevity in the form of evergreen pines, cranes, and rocks. Bainiken village, Huangze township, Shengxian county, Zhejiang.

These close-up images of the waist portion of four door panels shown on page 23 depict fruits, each of which has an auspicious meaning: pomegranates, symbols of fecundity because of the abundance of seeds that themselves are homophonous with the word for "sons"; peaches, representative of longevity, are said to be a wondrous fruit growing in the gardens of the Queen Mother of the West; citron, also called bergamot in English, a bizarre-looking citrus fruit known in Chinese as "Buddha's hand" or *foshou* because of the resemblance to an old man's fingers, represents both "good fortune" (*fu*) and "longevity" (*shou*); and, persimmons, an emblem of joy because of the brilliance of their color.

on the back of a stag deer that the "stellar god of longevity" rides. Deer, moreover, are said to be adept at finding the sacred fungus of immortality.

Individual peaches, peach wood, peach branches, peach blossoms, and the peach tree itself are all embedded with longevity symbolism, and as a result all are appropriate gifts on the birthdays of elders. Said to ripen only once in no less than a thousand years, the lush peaches of longevity are said to be a wondrous fruit that grew in the gardens of the Queen Mother of the West, Xi Wangmu. When a monkey is shown holding a peach, the imagery recalls the tale in the popular story *Xiyouji* or "Journey to the West" in which the whimsical king of the monkeys, in his quest for immortality, manages to steal and eat a peach from the Queen Mother's garden. Peach wood is believed to have powers of exorcism because of a homophonous relationship with the word "to expel."

Short of eternal life, Chinese traditionally have desired to live at least to the age of sixty, completing five cycles of the twelve-year zodiac. Playing on puns, butterflies (*die*) and cats (*mao*) are still used to suggest the homonym *die* for the age of seventy or eighty and *mao* for the age of ninety, both invocations of long life. Repeating the *shou* character a hundred times heightens the wish for longevity.

Lu: Emolument

In traditional China, the acquisition of wealth as a merchant or as a landlord was not viewed as significant as the prosperity that came from being compensated as an official—a status normally acquired by long years of study, the passing of exacting examinations, and the attainment of degrees that brought with it advantages and privileges. Since the income or emolument deriving from office is termed *lu*, deer, also *lu*, stand in for official income. Deer thus do double duty as emblems of official wealth and longevity, and it is not always clear which attribute is being represented.

The carp, a fish that must battle river currents to reach Longmen, the Dragon Gate, metaphorically emblemizes the struggle to pass examinations and achieve status and affluence. A punning relationship between *li*, the Chinese word for carp and benefit, also *li*, is accepted by many Chinese. The depiction of any fish, indeed, is a claim to prosperity because of the homonymic association between the words for fish and "abundance." Goldfish, especially, symbolize riches because the characters *jinyu* sound like "gold in abundance." Even the *yu* in "gold fish" can be transformed into costly jade, also pronounced *yu*. When shown with a lotus, pronounced *lian*, which is a homonym for "united" or "together," goldfish evoke the meaning "gold and jade joined together" (*jin yu tonghe*) or "gold and jade together fill the hall" (*jin yu mantang*).

While any fish is a claim for prosperity and abundance because of homophonous associations, the carp especially has many meanings. A single carp, shown here in the courtyard of a study, is a symbol of patience and steadfastness. Moreover, a carp represents also the struggle necessary to pass examinations since it battles currents in swimming upstream. Man family residence, Hong Kong.

88 The Chinese House as Living Space

Far left:
This carved stone ventilation port is in the shape of a bottle gourd, representing both longevity and magic. Some say it is a symbol representing Li Tieguai, one of the Eight Immortals, whose emblem is a gourd from which magical vapors are said capable of trapping evil. Meixian, Guangdong.

Left:
Monkey images serve many auspicious roles, especially as a part of various rebuses in which its pronunciation *hou* is used to represent the high rank of marquis. Wang family manor, Shanxi.

Below:
Flanked by a pair of esoteric couplets and carved into a panel are one hundred different forms of the character *shou* or "longevity." Taken together, they are viewed as an especially powerful invocation for long life. Qiao family manor, Shanxi.

The House as Home

Fu Lu Shou: Stellar Triad

Good Fortune, Longevity, and Emolument, an auspicious triad, were anthropomorphized over a long period of time into individuals whose symbolic images ornament many houses. Sometimes they were joined by a fourth figure, "Joy" or *Xi*. By the Ming dynasty, *Fu Lu Shou* together were not only elements of folk imagery among illiterate people but were also accepted by élite culture, a popularity that continues to the present. Whether arrayed as a group or shown individually, depicted in a simple paper cutout affixed to a wall, a colorful woodblock print, or more elaborately carved three-dimensionally out of wood or clay, each of them have characteristics that make them immediately recognizable. Even though Chinese popularly refer to each as a "stellar god," it is best not to think of *fu*, *lu*, or *shou* as true gods since no temples are devoted to them. Instead, their prominence suggests that they be considered as immortals or transcendental beings.

Shou Xing, the "stellar god of longevity," has a history stretching back two thousand years, longer than that of either Lu Xing, the "stellar god of emoluments," or Fu Xing, the "stellar god of good fortune." Depicted as a venerable sage with dramatic physical characteristics—long white beard and mustache, drooping earlobes, a protruding forehead with three elongated wrinkles, and a receding bald cranium—Shou Xing, also called Shoulao or "Old Shou," is identifiable to all Chinese. Accompanied by other symbols of longevity, such as pine trees, rocks, cranes, and the peach of immortality, he is sometimes shown riding a stag, carrying a staff of knotted wood, holding a bottle-gourd that is a reservoir for the elixir of immortality, and attended by a young boy as an emblem of posterity. His robe usually includes a stylized form of the character *shou* for longevity as medallions on the sleeves. The custom of giving paintings of Shou Xing and associated longevity themes as birthday gifts endures even to the present.

Neither Lu Xing, the stellar god of emoluments, or Fu Xing, the stellar god of good fortune, enjoys the kind of mythic history comparable to that of Shou Xing. Lu Xing is usually richly attired wearing a green official's brocaded robe, the color being a homonym for riches, and wearing a court official's cap with winged flaps called *guan*, itself a pun for "official." To express his identity, images of deer, also pronounced *lu* and therefore emblematic of emolument, are usually applied to the robes of Lu Xing. Lu Xing, and sometimes Fu Xing, often carries an oddly shaped object made of wood or jade known as a *ruyi*, a wish-granting scepter, that resembles the irregular shape of a *lingzhi*, the fungus of immortality.

Fu Xing, the stellar god of good fortune, usually appears as a retired scholar-official toying with some flowers or carrying a basket of flowers to suggest blessings, or a *ruyi* ("whatever you want") scepter. Wearing a "winged" hat and blue robes with the character *fu* and pictorial images of a bat or butterfly to visually verify by homonymic association who is being represented, Fu Xing embodies happiness.

Above left:
The stellar triad *fu*, *lu*, and *shou* ("good fortune, emolument, and longevity") was anthropomorphized into three portentous individuals whose symbolic images ornament many dwellings. Here they are surrounded by numerous other auspicious images including bats representing "good fortune" and young boys representing fertility. Kang family manor, Henan.

Below left:
Here, along the ridgeline of a roof, the three stellar deities representing Longevity, Emolument, and Good Fortune are deployed as auspicious ornamentation. Luzhi, Jiangsu.

Above right:
Hung on the wall, the two characters *fu* "good fortune" and *lu* "emolument" representing an official's salary, proclaim both an aspiration and an expectation. Yan Yi Lou, Chengkan village, Anhui.

Shuangxi: Doubled Happiness

Good fortune and longevity—*fu* and *shou*—are complementary wishes that taken together are known as the "doubled happiness" or *shuangxi*. This dyad, which is formed by writing together a pair of characters meaning "joy" or *xi*, is a pseudo-character not found in any dictionary but is recognized by all Chinese. Used especially at the time of a marriage, but also at other times of celebration, *shuangxi* is one of the most commonly seen "words" in and about Chinese houses. With its uncomplicated symmetry, other emblems are sometimes added to amplify its meanings. Above a marriage bed, pomegranates split open to show their many seeds become a powerful wish symbol of fertility. The intricacy and multiplicity of the strokes used to form the "doubled happiness" character are also linked to the spider's web—which itself bears a remarkable resemblance to the *bagua* or Eight Trigrams. This oblique association makes the spider, also pronounced *xi*, a creature of good omen, whose appearance portends the bestowal of good things from heaven. The portrayal of two spiders recalls the poetic verse "When joy [the spider] arrives beneath the eaves, it is always double" (*xi dao yan qian mei shi shuang*).

Two conjoined circles representing a pair of Chinese coins, pronounced *shuang qian*, also symbolize doubled happiness—the uniting of *fu* and *shou*—since they are a near homonym for *shuang quan*, meaning "both complete." The bizarre looking citrus fruit known in Chinese as "Buddha's hand" or *foshou* because of the resemblance to an old man's hand serves also as a "doubled happiness" emblem linking "good fortune" and "longevity" as a result of the similarity in pronunciation. Moreover, this aromatic and pungent fruit, also known as finger citron, is believed by some to promote the flow of *qi* and help regulate and harmonize the body's functions.

Above:
Repeated on these carved lattice panels, two conjoined circles suggesting a pair of Chinese coins symbolize "doubled happiness". Moreover, since a pair of coins is pronounced *shuang qian* and is a near homonym for *shuang quan*, they also have the meaning "both complete"—an affinity representing the uniting of *fu* and *shou*, good fortune and longevity. Ma family residence, Langzhong, Sichuan.

Left:
Made to be placed on the ceiling above the marriage bed, this intricate "doubled happiness" papercut is replete with auspicious symbolism. In addition to the *shuangxi* character at its core, the pomegranate at the top, which is shown split open to reveal its many seeds, is an invocation for sons because of homophonous associations, while the Buddha's hand fruit at the bottom expresses "good fortune and longevity." Guangdong.

Baxian: The Eight Immortals

The fabled Baxian, the Daoist Eight Immortals, who appear sailing on clouds or clustered in friendly revelry, best illustrate everlasting life, a condition that goes beyond mere longevity. They are depicted individually or as animated scenes with the full group of eight or fewer figures. Their images and personal emblems grace painted and printed hand scrolls, fans, fine porcelain, needlework, as well as ornamented structural parts of houses. Each is a folk hero, some with biographical details that indicate they were real persons, while several are certainly fictional characters. Each achieved immortality by a different route at a distinct point in his or her life and thus continues to exist without getting old. Having the best of both worlds, they are viewed as spontaneous and fun-loving in this world without the burden of worldly concerns or mortal diseases. In addition, they are said to be capable of raising the dead, curing the sick, making themselves invisible, and carrying out missions for the Jade Emperor. As a band, they represent the spectrum of Chinese life: rich and poor, scholars and soldiers, the strong and the lame, masculinity and femininity, young and old.

The Eight Immortals remain relatively constant from one part of China to another and are readily recognizable even though legends and anecdotes about them vary. Zhong Liquan, also called Han Zhongli, is the bare-bellied leader of the band with tufts of hair coiled on each side of his head and a beard that reaches nearly to his navel. His fan of feathers or his peach of immortality distinguishes him. It is said that Zhong Liquan has the ability to revive the dead, to hide the sun and moon, and he excels at calligraphy. Li Tieguai, a crippled beggar with wooly hair, an untidy beard, and protruding eyes, is viewed as understanding of others who are maimed and in physical pain. He has as his emblem a calabash gourd containing magic herbs or an elixir made from the peaches of immortality from which a bat—good fortune—is seen escaping. Lan Caihe, sometimes regarded as a female but more commonly a hermaphrodite, normally carries a basket of flowers or fruit. As a wandering minstrel, Lan Caihe is clever and said to be able to ridicule the irritations and frivolities of the world. He Xian'gu, the only woman of the eight, has a reputation for filial devotion to her mother and extraordinary feats of magic as well as an ability to resolve domestic disputes and assist in household management. Usually seen clasping a lotus stem, a long kitchen ladle, or a *ruyi* scepter, she is said to live on a diet of moonbeams and powdered mother-of-pearl and is the patron of household work. Cao Guojiu, an aristocrat, a patron of performers, and the last to join the band, is seen in elegant court dress holding a fly-whisk or a pair of castanets thought to represent the ceremonial tablets of admission to court. Zhang Guolao, a celibate recluse of great age often seen riding backwards on a white mule, is reputedly a consummate magician said to have once been a bat that turned into a man. He is not only able to raise the dead and make himself invisible, but he is said to fold up his mule like a piece of paper, put it in a bamboo wallet, and then regenerate it later with water sprayed from his mouth. His emblem is a musical instrument in the shape of a bamboo tube that is beaten with two rods. Han Xiangzi, a historical figure of the ninth century who renounced public life, is shown as a handsome and lively young man who is somewhat strong willed

Above:
The band of Baxian, the Daoist Eight Immortals, illustrates everlasting life, a condition that goes beyond mere longevity. Each has a distinct personality and an emblem recognizable by all Chinese. Here, each is signified by a papercut.

Below:
The Eight Immortals are represented in Chinese homes by a meter-square table with four trestle benches. Called *Baxian zhuo*, the "Eight Immortals table" is a material expression of the joy accompanying the sharing of food and conviviality with family and friends.

One of a set of doorways bearing Eight Immortals images, these panels depict Lu Dongbin with his sword and Lan Caihe with a basket of flowers on the left panel and the youthful He Xian'gu and Cao Guojiu in court dress on the right panel.

and rebellious. Tradition says he could entice flowers to grow and blossom at will by playing his emblem, the jade flute. He is said to represent youth and is the patron of fortune-tellers. Lu Dongbin, the most celebrated of the Baxian and said to resemble common men, especially in terms of their sexual desires and love of wine, is always seen with a double-edged sword slung from his back and a horse hair switch whisk grasped in his hand. The sword is used by Lu to sever greed, lust, and sorrow from people's lives. The Eight Immortals are represented in most Chinese homes by a meter-square table, called a Baxian table or *Baxian zhuo*, with four trestle benches to seat eight.

Whether used in the kitchen or in the Main Hall, the Baxian table is a figurative expression of the happiness accompanying the sharing of food. At the time of an engagement, a wedding, or a celebration of the birth of a son, Baxian tables are set up for the conviviality of family and friends. Folded round table tops are sometimes placed on top of Baxian tables to accommodate more than eight people.

The House as Home

Harmony at Home

Conjugal bliss and domestic harmony are a central focus of Chinese traditional life. Since Chinese believed that wives of brothers especially had the potential of disrupting harmony, much care was expended on the selection of a suitable bride for a son, fully aware that the young woman was an addition to a greater family structure. Indeed, a husband and a wife, man and woman, experienced the house and home in different ways: "A man was born, grew up and died within the same walls, and with the same male kin around him. He never had to leave his parents or his home, he knew which lineage and which landscape he belonged to from the time he began to understand the world. His house was home for life, and yet he could walk outside the family compound whenever he pleased. He lived in a kind of commune of shared patrimonial goods, in which his first loyalty was supposedly to the group. A girl grew up on borrowed time. When she married she had to leave the house of her birth, her mother and her sisters whom she loved and depended on, to move into an unknown house and a new group of women, many of whom might regard her with hostility. She would have to be self-reliant until she built up alliances and, as a mother, became an acknowledged member of her new family" (Bray, 1997: 109).

Compatibility is emblemized by the narcissus and orchid, symbolic of love, that are usually shown in pairs. Wisteria, known for their hardiness, longevity, and endlessly twining vines, are sometimes associated with pines as a symbol of the union of female and male elements. Marital bliss is depicted always as a pair—fish swimming in stylized water, flying geese, magpies entwined on a branch, or devoted Mandarin ducks. Magpies (the *xique* or "joy-bringing magpie") are birds of good omen and varied imagery that are linked to the love story of the cowherd and the spinning girl. Mandarin ducks (*yuanyang*) are an obvious symbol for conjugal happiness and fidelity since they mate for life and roost wing to wing and neck to neck. When they are depicted beside, or hold in their beaks, a lotus blossom and a lotus pod, this represents a further wish for "sons one after the other." These appear often as motifs on porcelain objects in the bedroom.

Left:
Carved in the center of this lattice panel are several emblematic elements—fish, lotus pod, peaches, and a boy—that together constitute a rebus: Good Fortune, Longevity, and Sons in Abundance. Wang family manor, Shanxi.

Below:
Although now faded, the four character red strip states "Peace throughout the Four Seasons," while the two engraved characters are a call for "happy [family] relations." Fan family residence, Pingyao, Shanxi.

This depiction of a large happy family honoring the aged parents is a stock scene understood by all Chinese. Shanxi.

A pair of lotuses, especially the lotus stem and the lotus pod shown together, symbolize marital concord and sexual union. The lotus pod, moreover, with its abundant seeds represents fertility and a happy marriage. The presence of a *ruyi* scepter, a box, and a lotus together create the rebus "may you have a harmonious marriage and may your wishes come true."

Posterity: Male Offspring
Offspring in great number, especially sons, are considered the purpose of marriage and a subject of substantial folk ornamentation. There is no need to express the gender of offspring since there is an implicit understanding that it is sons that are desired. Sons not only carry on the family name, they are necessary to perform ancestral rites. Since *zi* is the Chinese phoneme for son, child, and seed, it is not surprising that pomegranates, grapes, melons of any type, and lotus pods—all of which contain abundant seeds—are able to evoke the notion of fertility and numerous male offspring. Woodblock prints sometimes include a handsome and plump boy playing a reed pipe called a *sheng* that has the same sound as "to give birth to," together with a lotus, meaning "in succession" and an osmanthus blossom, pronounced *gui*, here standing in for the word "precious." These homonymous forms, playing on images and words, together express in a rebus the wish "May there be the birth of precious sons one after another," the carrying on of a family for "ten thousand generations."

Moral Tales: Didactic Narratives
Living together harmoniously, an ideal family is one with many sons that is blessed with good fortune (*fu*), longevity (*shou*), perhaps even supported by an emolument (*lu*), and experiencing joy (*xi*). The ideals animating a happy family, termed *quan jia fu* ("the whole family has good fortune"), are ever-present in Chinese homes as calligraphic or pictorial narratives, which are believed to have the power of exhorting expected behavior simply by expressing it, as well as offering practical advice. Didactic social themes are exhibited for the most part only in bedrooms and the Main hall, where they are found as terse maxims, evocative vignettes, or even multipart narratives, but are also abundant in and about Ancestral Halls and around gravesites. The mother's (and, not coincidentally, therefore also the wife and daughter-in-law's) bed and bedroom especially provided a primary locus for a range of didactic and expository ornamentation.

Abbreviated messages of this sort, while relatively omnipresent and encountered many times during the day, are nonetheless rather passive methods of communication that were supplemented by much more active means. All of these were periodically amplified and reinforced through storytelling and opera performance as well as in the reading of primers and other books. Opera performances, especially, offered an entertaining and dramatic mechanism for inculcating the lessons of moral tales through allusive spoken and sung dialogue. Reinforced in many ways, men and women, young and old, came to know well the various stories of filial sons, dutiful daughters-in-law, virtuous women, and brave men who, as they inhabit well-known tales, narrate moral principles and point to the means of achieving a happy life. Familiar exemplars were sometimes mortals who had achieved popularity because of some extraordinary incident in their lives or, in other cases, legendary personages who had been given human personalities. The Stellar Triad—*Fu*, *Lu*, and *Shou*—and the Eight Immortals are among this last group.

Nothing is more fundamental to family happiness than the birth of sons. Such births set in train a lengthy socialization process expected to lead to a high level of filial devotion towards the son's parents. Taken together, filial commitment towards parents, respectful offerings for ancestors, itself an act of filial gratitude, and continuing attention to the needs of perpetuating the family line by way of sons have always been seen as the foundation for family solidarity and good fortune. The *Xiaojing* or "The Classic of Filial Piety" states this succinctly: "The service which a filial son does to his parents is as follows: In his general conduct to them, he manifests the utmost reverence. In his nourishing of them, his endeavor is to give them the utmost pleasure. When they are ill,

The House as Home 95

Replete with visual puns and auspicious imagery involving cherubic boys as well as goldfish and lotuses, this colorful woodblock print has the theme "May Gold and Jade Fill the Hall" because of homophonous associations. Weifang, Shandong.

One of the twenty-four depictions of filial piety, this image portrays a tale called *Letting Mosquitoes Drink His Blood*, a story of eight-year-old Wu Meng, who showed his filiality to his poor parents who had no mosquito netting. Wu Meng, with a bare back, let countless mosquitoes nourish themselves with his own blood in order to save his parents from being bitten by them while they slept.

he feels the greatest anxiety. In mourning for them, he exhibits every demonstration of grief. In sacrificing to them, he displays the utmost solemnity. When a son is complete in these five things (he may be pronounced) able to serve his parents.... The rules of propriety are simply (the development of) the principle of reverence. Therefore the reverence paid to a father makes sons pleased. The reverence paid to an elder brother makes younger brothers pleased. The reverence paid to a ruler makes subjects pleased. The reverence paid to the One man makes thousands and myriads of men pleased. The reverence is paid to a few, and the pleasure extends to many. This is what is meant by an 'All-embracing Rule of Conduct.'"

By the Song period, young boys memorized the *Xiaojing* as they did other classical texts. In time, folk artists and literati artists and craftsmen in many media incorporated filial virtues as the subject of their work. The famous eleventh-century silk hand scroll by Li Gonglin epitomizes how moral tales came to be presented in painting, accompanied by calligraphy, to illustrate in eighteen episodic "chapters" examples of filial piety and the rules of right conduct. In time, woodblock prints, paper cutouts, and the work of wood, brick, and stone carvers came to embrace and popularize the tales that had become a central theme in Chinese culture broadly.

Even before being able to read texts or comprehend ornamentation, small Chinese children recited and memorized the *Sanzi jing* or "Three Character Classic," a distillation of the essentials of Confucian thought written in the thirteenth century. In brief couplets of three characters each, in less than 1200 characters, the *Sanzi jing* serves as an abbreviated, introductory catechism that underscores the importance of education, filial piety, family and social relationships, and exemplary behavior generally. Valued by families throughout China well into the twentieth century, its use declined over the past fifty years. Recent press reports in China in 2004, however, report of a revival by nursery school teachers who say that it only takes two months for students to commit to memory as "a way to refine young minds."

Among the best-known moral tales are those found as the "Twenty-four Paragons of Filial Piety" or *Ershisi xiao*, part of a much larger number, each with a descriptive verse. Included in illustrated booklets, almanacs, and transmitted orally, these two dozen concise tales illustrate with examples the degree of duty assumed from Chinese children: enduring suffering, risking danger, performing humbling duties, yet devoting attentive care even under difficult circumstances. Eleven of the tales speak of the relationship between a son and his mother, five between a son and both of his parents, four between a son and his father, two between a son and a stepmother, and two between a daughter and a mother-in-law.

The themes of some of the didactic compositions from the "Twenty-four" show the range of filial expectations: a seventy-year-old son acting like a child so as to amuse his aged parents, a daughter-in-law breastfeeding her aged mother-in-law (see page 263), a son procuring hind's milk for his parents by masquerading as a young deer, a son allowing mosquitoes to feed on his body in order to spare his parents from their sting, a son using flesh from his own body in order to provide medicine for his sick father, a son who tastes his mother's medicine before she takes it, a son who goes a great distance for grain for his parents during a famine, among others.

In order to demonstrate devotion to her husband's parents, a young bride might prepare an embroidered valance for the wedding bed with filial themes. As young children were born, woodblock prints with rudimentary pictorial narratives might be hung for their edification. Simple silhouetted papercuts, made to be pasted on windows or walls, were able to evoke complex tales even with only a sparse representative element of a well-known story of filial devotion, but many more invoke tales that young children can be. Whatever their form, each was a mnemonic device to help children learn proper attitudes and behavior by reciting and memorizing

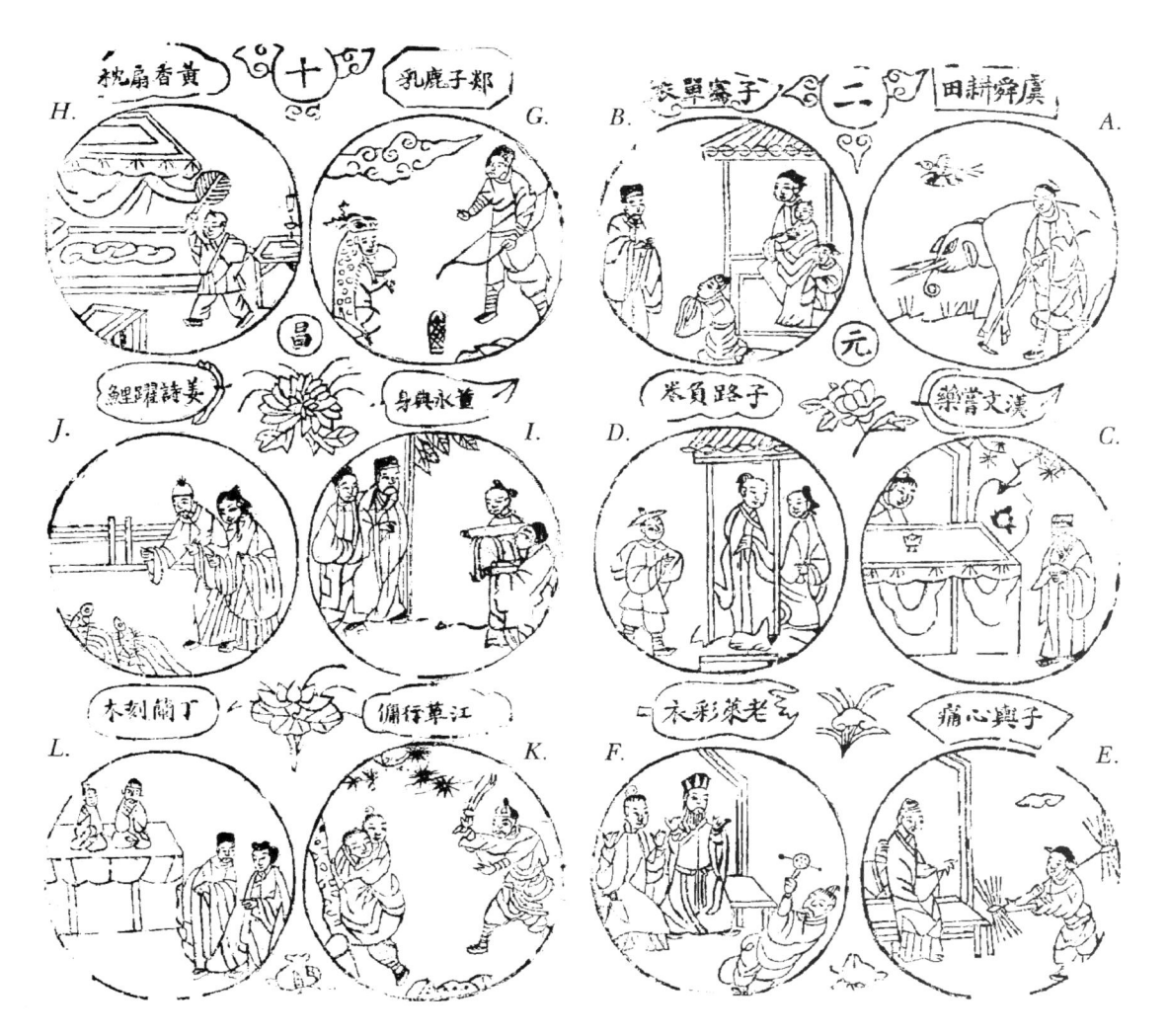

Twelve of the twenty-four paragons of filial piety are shown in this simple woodblock print. Among the tales depicted are (A) Yushun, the sage emperor who was devoted to his father and stepmother even though he was treated badly; (C) the Han emperor who tasted his mother's bitter medicine before giving it to her; (E) the absent son who hurried home when his mother bit her finger because he was able to feel her pain; (F) the son, himself old, who gamboled on the floor to amuse his aged parents so they would feel young; (G) the son who dressed himself in a deerskin and lived among the herd in order to procure deer's milk for his aged parents; (H) the son who used a fan to cool the mat and pillows of his father's bed in summer and who warmed it for him in winter by lying down in it before his father retired; and (J) the filial devotion of a husband and wife who traveled a great distance to fetch fish and water for the man's parents from their favorite river, the fish being so moved by this piety that they came to the household's doorstep of their own accord. Shanxi.

principles as well as reminders for adults of proper conduct. Sometimes booklets also included likely retributions for unfilial acts, while the availability of so-called "family instruction" handbooks offered abundant advice about how to preserve the patrimony, the family with all its resources. Tales of the rise and fall of families because of ignoring moral principles are legion just as are the anecdotes concerning the reasons for a family's inability to rise. These intertwined notions are made manifest in Chinese houses.

The *Nu xiaojing* or "Ladies' Classic of Filial Piety," focusing on virtuous women, was written and illustrated during the Tang period. It includes eighteen chapters in a didactic dialogue format with nearly similar titles to those found in the classic for men, with the addition of a distinctive chapter focusing on filial devotion to a mother-in-law. The literary text was subsequently illustrated in hand scroll form during the Song dynasty, which were suitable for didactic ornamentation within the bedrooms of dwellings.

As homes for families, Chinese houses are able to rise above the mere buildings that define them because of cosmo-magical symbolism, deeply felt beliefs and values, calendrical rituals, family hierarchies, including those of generation, gender, and age, life-cycle events, as well as myriad daily and seasonal activities. Chinese families of all kinds continue to follow calendars and precedent in applying or hanging an astonishing array of what may seem as merely ornamental items throughout and around their houses. While some of this ornamentation can be appreciated merely in terms of line, texture, and color, most such ornamentation in Chinese domestic spaces is self-consciously meaningful. Resulting from conscious action and endowed with meaning, domestic ornamentation usually has symbolic significance relating to the aspirations, fears, as well as broader cosmological beliefs of the residents and the community within which they live. In some areas of China today, it is still possible to witness manifestations of these in terms of decision-making, rituals, and actions associated with the selection of a construction site, determination of the orientation and proportions of a house, the ordering of building tasks, and choices made regarding structural and seasonal ornamentation. Some of the results are apparent and tangible while others are subtle, elusive, and even obscure. All too often, however, traditional symbols are indecipherable to young people who have only a vague consciousness of their rich meanings.

Houses usually take shape over time, sometimes growing but at others reconfigured in order to meet the changing needs of the families. Since Chinese dwellings are usually passed from one generation to another, they accumulate a history and represent the "living" and enduring patrimony of the continuing family. As the locus for reproduction, work, socialization, and leisure, the physical layout of many Chinese houses is able to reveal the complicated web of personal relationships that are not obvious by other means. As marriages occur, new members are born, and others die, a house is able to change as well.

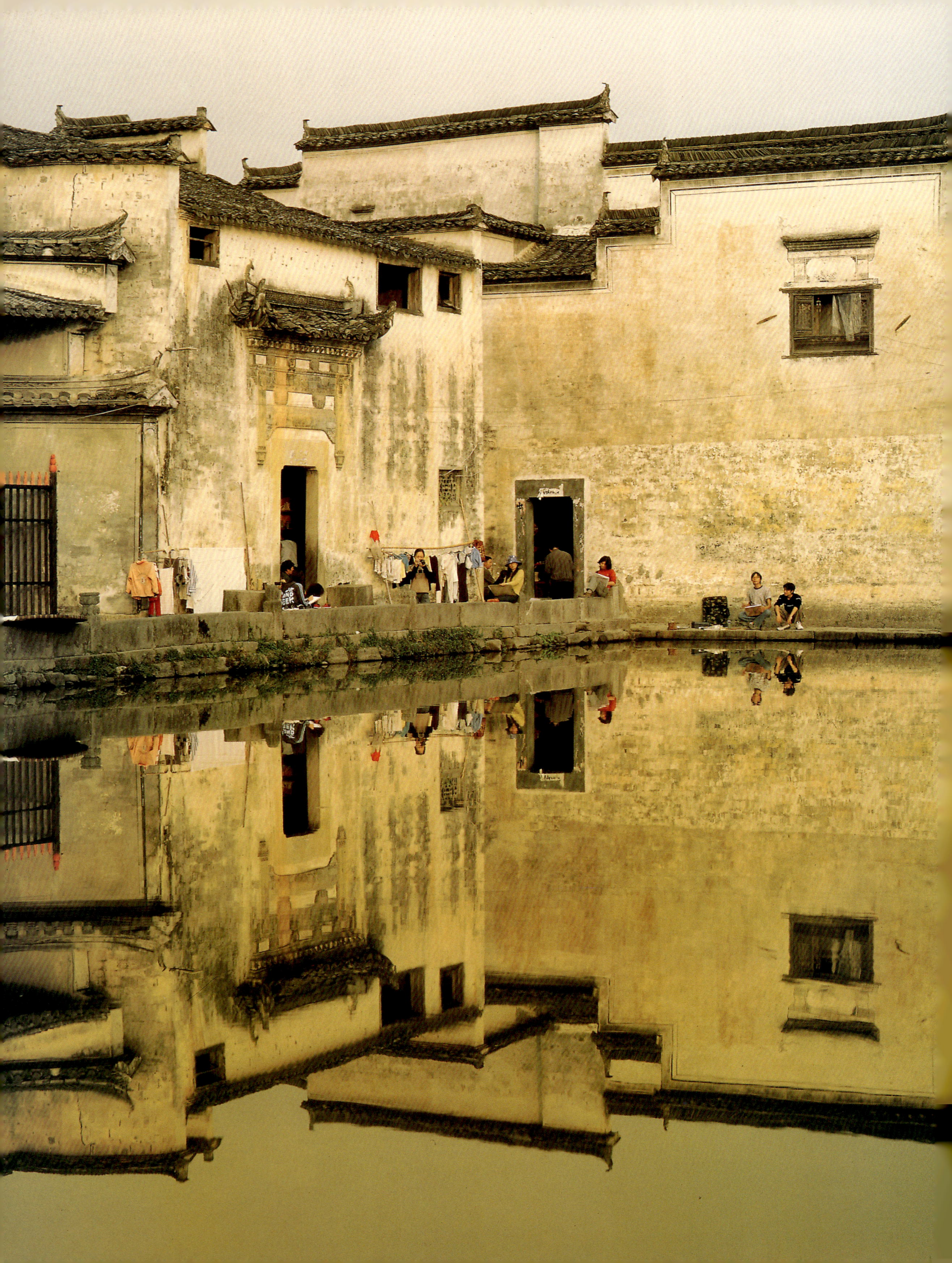

Part Three

CHINA'S FINE HERITAGE HOUSES

A BEIJING COURTYARD HOUSE
Mei Lanfang's Siheyuan, Beijing

No Chinese dwelling type is better known than the "courtyard house" or *siheyuan*, in which at least one courtyard is enclosed within four surrounding single-story buildings that face inward towards the open space. Quadrangular courtyard structures have been common architectural forms for houses, palaces, and temples in China since at least the Western Zhou period between the eleventh and tenth centuries BCE, fundamental units in the gridded urban fabric of cities in northern China.

Prototypical *siheyuan* are associated with Beijing and neighboring areas where they are found in many configurations, some quite simple but more of them rather complex in terms of layout. Among the near canonical elements of *siheyuan* are enclosure behind high gray walls with only a single off-center entry gate, which affords substantial seclusion; orientation to the cardinal directions with main structures facing south or southeast; balanced side-to-side symmetry of the dwelling complex, and a hierarchical organization of space along a clear axis. Moreover, strictly observed sumptuary regulations during the Ming and Qing dynasties in the imperial capital regulated the overall scale of *siheyuan*, including dimensions of timbers and widths of halls, as well as colors and other ornamentation, even types of furniture. As a result, the residences of ranked individuals and princes were clearly differentiated from merchants, who conceivably could have built large *siheyuan*, and of course those of common people.

Within the massive walls of the Purple Forbidden City, the cosmic center of the empire, are three parallel axes, along which are aligned the grand imperial palaces as well as the walled residences of the imperial family and their numerous retainers, including some 1500 eunuchs in the later Qing period. Along the westernmost axis in the Forbidden City's northwest quadrant, high walls enclose human-scale courtyards as the private apartments for emperors, their wives, and families. Although embellished with fine carpentry, sumptuous colors, and ornate furniture, these interconnected *siheyuan* are in plan and structure courtyard residences, which to some degree are similar to the layouts of even temples found throughout urban and rural China.

Before 1949, the Purple Forbidden City, which is still walled, was surrounded by a larger walled enclosure called the Imperial City, beyond which was another large area bounded by the actual city walls of Beijing. Walls within walls within walls created a nested structure of ceremonial, residential, and commercial spaces—somewhat like cells—of enormous cosmological and practical significance. With streets and lanes running east to west being crossed by those running north to south, much of Beijing was laid out like a chessboard beginning in the Yuan dynasty when the city was called Dadu. Well-defined neighborhoods developed along the veins of the city. These veins in Beijing are called *hutong*, narrow lanes and alleys that are said to be "like ox hair" in that their number is beyond being able to be calculated (see page 24). Here, in these *hutong* neighborhoods, princes, court officials, scholars, merchants, craftsmen, and others built densely packed single-storied *siheyuan* of many sizes, some with only a single courtyard while others had several or many linked together.

Below:
Perspective view of Mei Lanfang's residence in Beijing. At its simplest, a *siheyuan* is quadrangular in plan and surrounded by a wall with only a single entry gate.

Right:
Both the roof overhang and the brackets under the eaves of the Main Hall are colorfully ornamented with auspicious motifs.

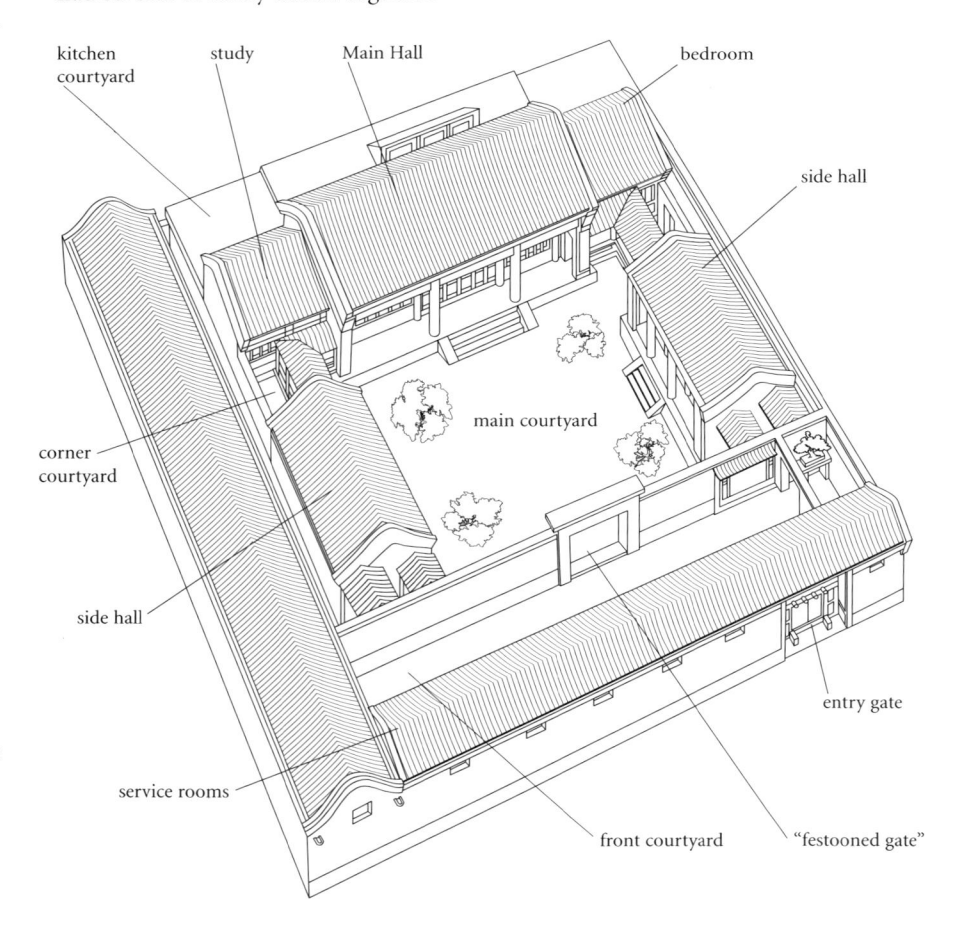

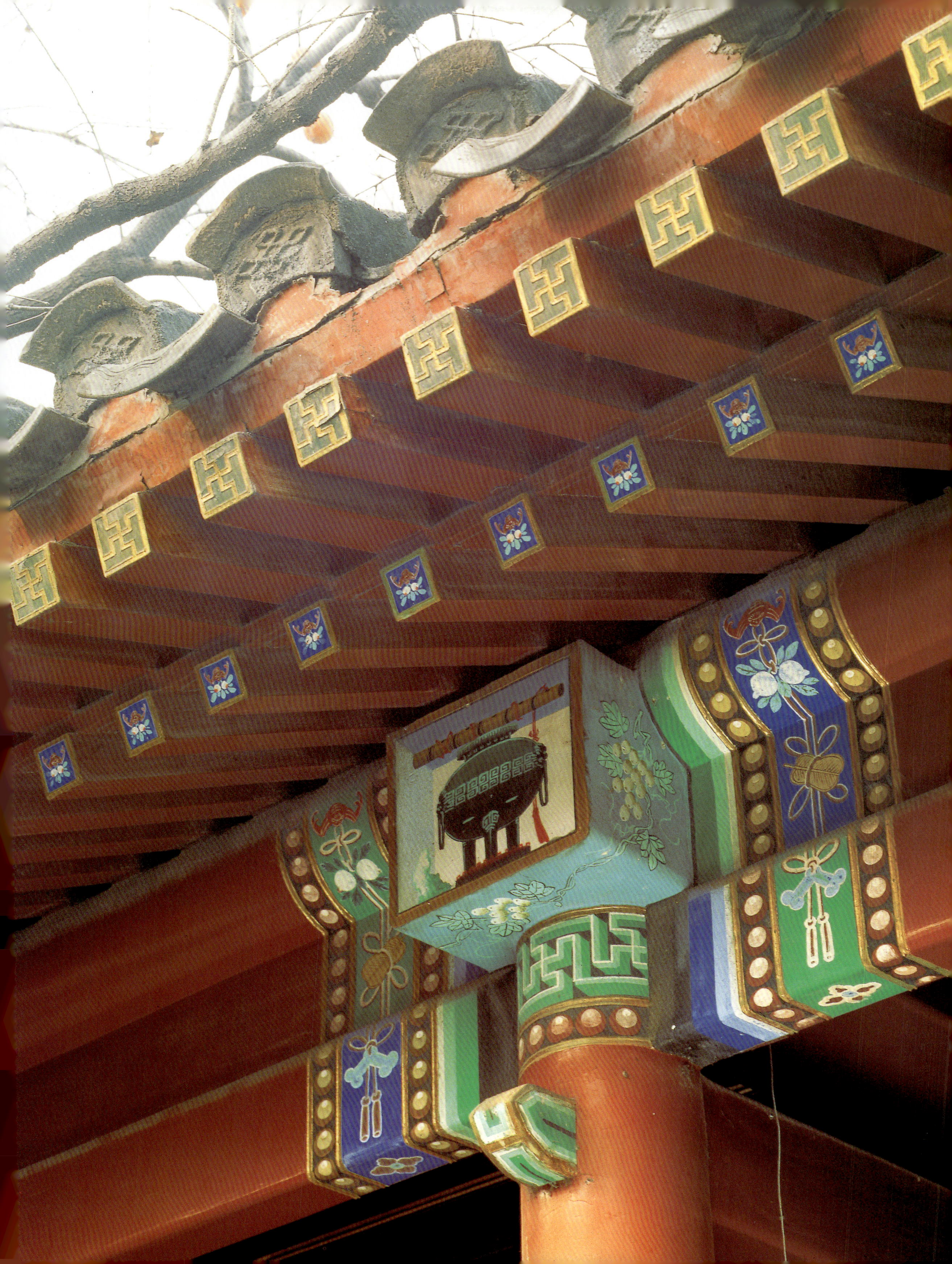

Some *siheyuan* were sprawling manors while others were crowded with several families. Princess Der Ling, First Lady in Waiting to the Empress Dowager Ci Xi who married an American in 1907 and became Mrs Thaddeus C. White, wrote, "The houses in Peking are built in a very rambling fashion, covering a large amount of ground, and our former house was no exception to the rule. It had sixteen small houses, one story high, containing about 175 rooms, arranged in quadrangles facing the courtyard, which went to make up the whole; and so placed, that without having to actually go out of doors, you could go from one to the other by verandas built along the front and enclosed in glass. My reader will wonder what possible use we could make of all of these rooms; but what with our large family, numerous secretaries, Chinese writers, messengers, servants, mafoos (coachmen), and chair coolies, it was not a difficult task to use them.

"The gardens surrounding the houses were arranged in the Chinese way, with small lakes, stocked with gold fish, and in which the beautiful lotus flower grew; crossed by bridges; large weeping willows along the banks; and many different varieties of flowers in prettily arranged flower beds, running along winding paths, which wound in and out between the lakes."

Manors of this type are essentially now extinct, having been carved up to meet the requirements of many families or torn down to accommodate modern needs. Just to the north of the Imperial City walls and adjacent to Qian Hai Lake, however, is a fine extant example. Known as Prince Gong's manor, and called in Chinese "Gong Wang Fu," the expansive dwelling complex reveals the seemingly complicated relationships of late Qing imperial times. Prince Gong, the brother of the eighth emperor Xianfeng who reigned from 1851 to 1861, moved into this imperial residence in 1852, occupying spaces that were built probably a century before. Prince Gong was also the sixth son of Guangxu, the ninth emperor of the Qing dynasty who reigned from 1875 to 1908 and the father of China's last emperor, Pu Yi. An extensive and splendid residence with three major building complexes, his manor is known especially for its garden buildings and gardens, including a labyrinth of rockeries, a teahouse, and performance spaces. Some claim that the celebrated author Cao Xueqin gained inspiration while living in Prince Gong's mansion as he wrote *Hongloumeng*, known in English as *A Dream of Red Mansions*.

Early in the Qing dynasty, there were eight major prince's manors or mansions, a number that was increased to twelve by the end of the dynasty. Except for Prince Gong's mansion, none of the others remains reasonably intact, all now having lost the grace that once characterized them and indeed even much of their original form. Over time, both in the early twentieth century and especially after 1949, government offices, hospitals, schools, arts organizations, factories, and various enterprises came to occupy them, in the process transforming once sumptuous residences into utilitarian spaces. The Ministry of Interior, for example, occupies the site of Prince Li's mansion south of Xi'anmen and Prince Rui's mansion in the Nanchizi area, built in the early Qing dynasty, has been the location for different schools over many years. Prince Yu's mansion in the Dongdan area was transformed for use by the Rockefeller Foundation's Peking Union Medical College in 1917, and is now the location for Beijing Hospital.

Mei Lanfang's Siheyuan

Located along Huguosi *hutong*, a quiet lane in the Shichahai neighborhood in the Western District of Beijing, is a gray brick *siheyuan* today known as the former residence of Mei Lanfang (1894–1961), the celebrated actor of Jingju opera, sometimes called Beijing or Peking opera. Mei Lanfang lived in the courtyard house only during the last decade of his life from 1951 to 1961. During the latter part of the nineteenth century, the courtyard was but one part of a much larger mansion of an imperial prince of the Qing dynasty, one nonetheless that was much smaller and less grand than those of other Qing nobility.

Mei Lanfang began to study Chinese opera at the age of eight, gaining an early national reputation. His tours to Japan in 1919 and 1924, the US in 1930, and the USSR in 1932 and 1935 brought his talents playing female roles before international audiences. Soon after 1949, Zhou Enlai urged Mei Lanfang to

Below:
Set upon a prominent stone base and surmounted by an imposing superstructure, the marble basin is said to have been obtained from an imperial palace. On its right is the patterned screen wall.

102 China's Fine Heritage Houses

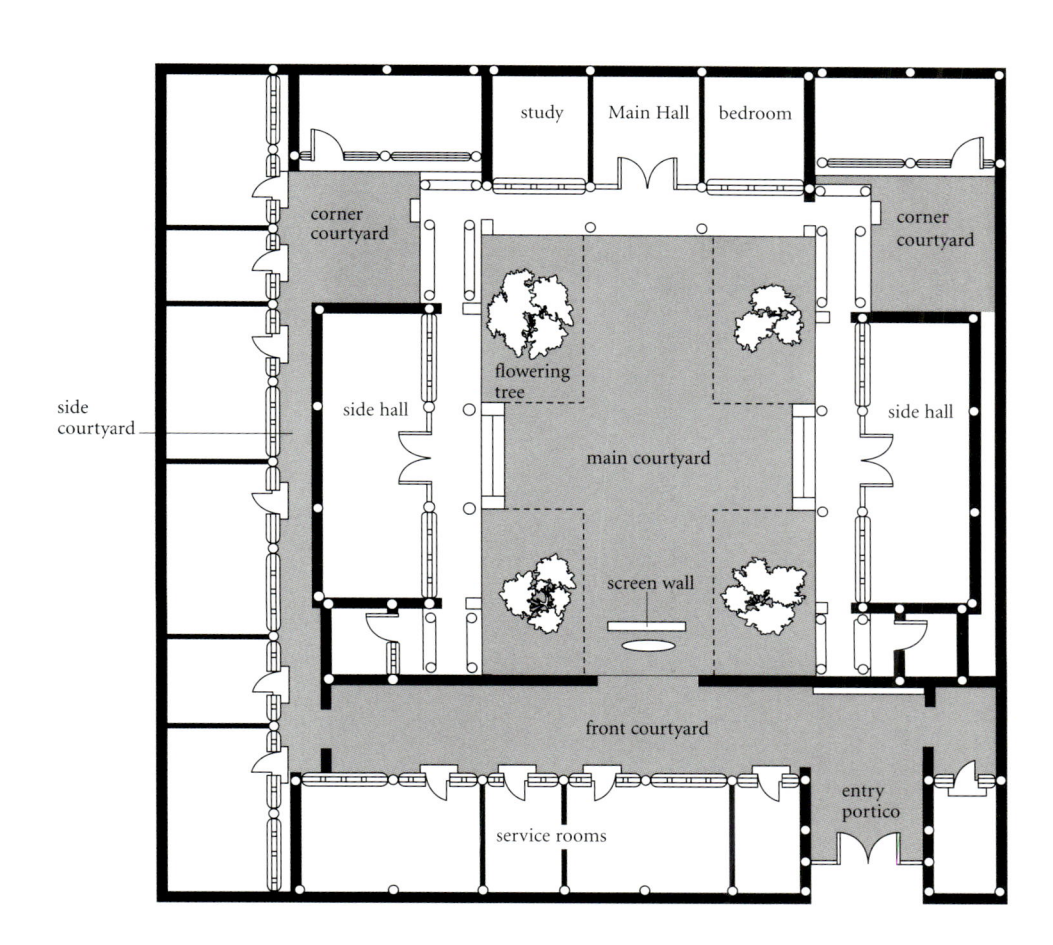

Left:
The symmetrical and hierarchical organization of a *siheyuan* is clearly shown in plan view, although in this case the outer row of rooms on the west side alters its symmetry.

Below:
Facing south on the northern side of the courtyard and usually only three bays in width, the Main Hall or *zhengfang* of most *siheyuan* is a low single-story building. Dominant in this courtyard is a pair of persimmon trees. In summer, tables and chairs from adjacent rooms would be moved into the courtyard so that family members and guests could enjoy sunny days and quiet evenings.

A Beijing Courtyard House

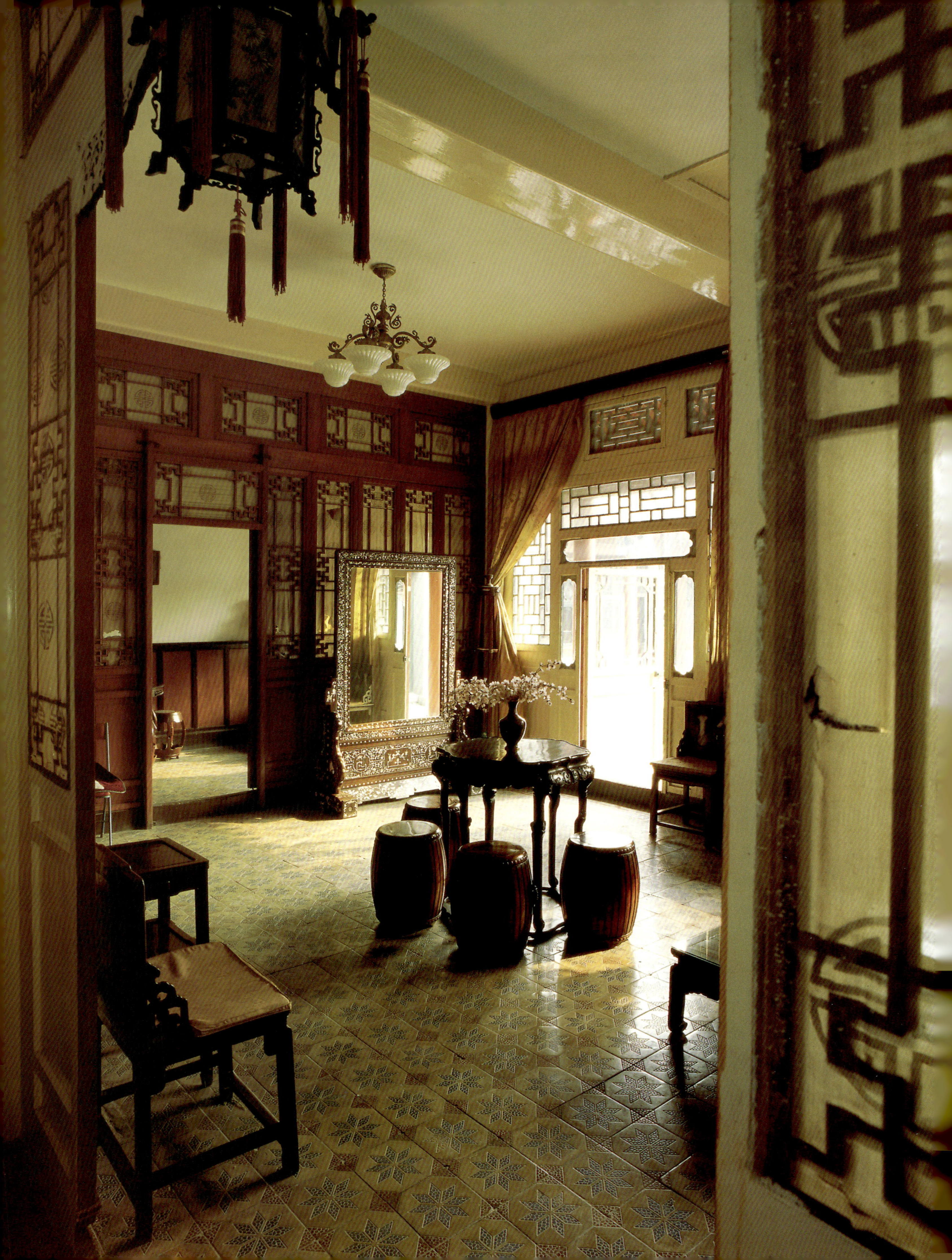

return to Beijing and serve as president of the Institute of Chinese Opera, even promising that Mei and his family could return to the old *siheyuan* courtyard they had purchased in 1921 and occupied prior to selling it in 1933 during the Japanese occupation of China. Mei Lanfang, however, was reluctant to reclaim a residence he had once sold, declining the offer, even though he had described it in his autobiography as simply an "ordinary courtyard house."

He nonetheless accepted the proposal of a gated structure on Huguosi *hutong*, which was of course only a fragment of a complete dwelling, a derelict structure that had not been maintained well for many years. At the time, only the main northern structure, which faced south, and the two facing perpendicular wings stood. In time, an outer courtyard and a side courtyard with associated buildings were built to give shape to the integrated *siheyuan* quadrangular residence still seen today. With a total area of 716 square meters and about 500 square meters of floor space, the completed structure is a mid-sized *siheyuan* facing inwards rather than outwards and somewhat larger than his earlier residence. It has a rather conventional layout comprised of a series of gates, open spaces, and independent structures that create a sequence of graduated privacy, of increasing intimacy as one moves from "outside" to "inside."

Along the southeast portion of the outer wall, the single entryway, with its pair of large leaves painted red, provides a rather plain threshold into a vestibule marked by a light gray brick spirit wall with bamboo planted in front of it. Turning left leads through another gate into a "public" zone, comprising a narrow rectangular open area that was used for the workaday activities of servants, a place for visitors to wait while they were announced, and a storage area for bicycles, briquettes for cooking, among many of the items used in a busy household. A pair of large deciduous parasol trees, with lobate leaves and racemes of tan-yellow flowers, spread their branches over the narrow courtyard. On the south side of the courtyard is a north-facing building called a *daozuo*, or "rear facing" structure, and on its right a wall with a splendid gate, called a *chuihuamen* or "festooned gate," which mediates between the outer peripheral courtyard and the inner central courtyard. In addition to offering security for the interior precincts, this magnificent gate is also a focal point of interior and exterior ornamentation. A "festooned gate," unlike the main entry gate along the lane outside, is usually highly decorated, with piled wooden structures and abundant ornamental design, but that of the Mei quadrangle is more serene. A visitor reaching this gate must climb several steps before entering the main courtyard, the view of which is blocked by a patterned screen wall or *yingbi*, set upon a prominent stone base and surmounted by an imposing superstructure. A marble basin, said to have been obtained from an imperial palace, was added as a decorative feature during Mei's occupancy of the residence but is not a common feature.

The large central courtyard as well as the rectangular one at the entry and another slender one flanking a row of guest rooms on the west side of the residence represent more than 40 percent of the total ground area of this *siheyuan*. From within the interior courtyard, which is paved with square bricks and serves as the center of family life, the sky appears to reach to distant horizons unobstructed either by the dwelling itself or by neighboring buildings, all of which are low as well. As with other *siheyuan* in Beijing, trees and potted shrubs soften the architecture of the courtyard. Careful thought was given to plantings in order to insure pleasure during all seasons, not only in terms of vegetation but also bearing edible fruit and having auspicious connotations. Dominant in this courtyard is a pair of persimmon trees, producing a yellowish fruit somewhat plum-like with a flat appearance that is rather harsh and astringent until it has been exposed to frost and becomes palatable and nutritious. Matching these is a pair of flowering trees, an apple tree and a crab apple tree, planted, it is said, because the sound of all the tree names uttered together in Chinese—*shishi ping'an*—represent the homophonic invocation "always safe." Persimmon and apple trees, moreover, live long, provide shade, and welcome birds. Pomegranates and jujube date trees, especially, because of their abundant seeds and rich symbolism are also favored as trees in *siheyuan*. On the other hand, evergreen pines and cypress trees as well as poplars are not common in Beijing quadrangles because they are believed most appropriate for gravesites. Tables and chairs from adjacent rooms are usually moved into the courtyard for family members and their guests to enjoy sunny days and quiet evenings. In the partially

Opposite:
The central room of a *zhengfang* traditionally was the location for the ancestral hall and the center for family ceremonies and celebrations. Here, in Mei Lanfang's home, this central space was used as a drawing room, an intimate space to entertain close friends.

Below:
Lacquered lattice door panels, fitted with glass and silk curtains, separate the drawing room from a family sitting room.

On the west side of the drawing room is a large bright study, which is illuminated through the south-facing wall of windows.

enclosed areas at the corner where the main building and side buildings nearly come together, flowering wisteria climb the wooden arbors that link them.

The Main Hall or *zhengfang*, as with other classical *siheyuan*, is a low single-story building on the northern side of the courtyard and faces south, following the siting axiom *zuobei chaonan*, meaning "sitting north and facing south." In this inner sanctum is the location for the Ancestral Hall and center for ceremonies as well as the residence for the household's senior generation. Mei Lanfang used the central room as a drawing room, an intimate space to entertain close friends. On its east side is another family space, a parlor, which then leads to a bedroom. On the west side is a large bright study.

Perpendicular to the main structure is a pair of flanking buildings, one facing east and the other west with rigid bilateral symmetry, which served together as living space for married sons and their families. Beyond the western building and entered from both the first and second courtyards, is a rather uncommon feature, a long structure with numerous guest and storage rooms built into it.

An important element of Beijing *siheyuan* is the set of narrow covered verandas that serve as all-weather passageways around the courtyards. Because the surrounding individual buildings are structurally separate, each side of the quadrangle is entered and exited through a door facing the focal courtyard. Since no doorways interconnect any of the adjacent buildings that comprise the courtyard complex, movement between buildings is most direct across the courtyard during fine weather. The encircling narrow verandah under the eaves offers some limited protection during times of inclement weather, whether rain or snow, and the broad overhanging eaves and stout red-lacquered columns help to buffer the blustery winds and trap the sun's heat during the course of a cold winter's day.

As a celebrated performing artist, Mei Lanfang entertained numerous luminaries during his residence in this *siheyuan*. Fitted with a mixture of Chinese and Western furniture and fixtures, the house blended elements of the past with modern elements.

After Mei Lanfang died in 1961, his sons continued to live in the house even as his wife moved to a smaller residence. Soon after the beginning of the Cultural Revolution in 1966, however, Red Guards in Beijing regularly pasted posters on the exterior walls and gate criticizing Mei Lanfang's bourgeois life. These actions led even his adult children to abandon the *siheyuan*, which then remained shuttered until October 1986 when the residence was opened as a museum. Subsequent visitation was light but has increased especially since the centenary of Mei Lanfang's birth in 1994. Domestic and foreign visitors are not only interested in catching glimpses of what life might have been like in quiet *siheyuan* along the narrow alleys that once defined Beijing but also are curious about the life of one of China's most prominent twentieth-century performing artists.

Mei Lanfang quotation:

> "Small as the stage is, a few steps will bring you far beyond heaven."

Siheyuan: Threats and Revitalization

During difficult times over the centuries, many families came to share courtyard spaces that once were elegant, reducing in the process their charm and quietude. Lao She, the playwright and author of humorous, satiric stories, wrote in his 1936 classic novel *Camel Xiangzi* about an industrious rickshaw puller and his life in the *hutong* and *siheyuan* throughout decaying Beijing. Concerning one courtyard and those who occupied it, he wrote: "There were seven or eight families living in their tenement courtyard, most of them crowded, seven to eight, old and young, into one room. Among them were rickshaw pullers, peddlers, policemen and servants. Each went about his or her job with never a moment to spare. Even the children went off with small baskets to fetch rice gruel in the morning and to scrounge for cinders in the afternoon. Only the very youngest remained in the courtyard, tussling and playing, their little bottoms frozen bright red in their split pants. Ashes, dust and slops were all tipped into the yard, which no one bothered to sweep. The middle of it was a sheet of ice which the older children used as a skating rink when they came back from scrounging cinders, shouting loudly as they slipped and slid about. The worst off were the old folk and women. Hungry and threadbare, the old people lay on icy cold brick-beds, waiting anxiously for the pittance the able-bodied ones earned to buy them a bowl of gruel."

Even as prosperity returned after 1949, it became increasingly common for courtyard houses in Beijing to be shared by many unrelated families rather than continuing as private dwellings for extended families. While conditions rarely were as hard as described by Lao She, the city's socialist bureaucratic housing allocation system gradually led to larger numbers of Beijing families living together in courtyard dwellings where they divided up once-commodious spaces into their own residential areas. As a result, the escalating use of limited space by larger numbers of people as well as inattention to repair brought with it general dilapidation that continued well into the early 1980s. Throughout the city, the infilling of courtyards with "temporary" kitchens, bedrooms, and storage sheds over time obliterated what had been the essential core of any *siheyuan*, the courtyard itself.

Over the past quarter century, high-rise apartment buildings have created new living opportunities for city residents and reduced pressures on old single-story dwellings. However, as the city is modernized and developed, new challenges have emerged regarding the conservation and preservation of the architectural soul of China's most impressive historical imperial capital. The razing of old *hutong* neighborhoods accelerated in the late 1990s, reaching alarming proportions after 2000 as demolition reached new heights. After two decades of sweeping destruction of *hutong* neighborhoods, less than a thousand *siheyuan* have been designated for preservation and saved from summary destruction. Even well-preserved courtyards that seem safe because of being listed for preservation have been summarily demolished, to the dismay of residents and preservationists.

Some old *siheyuan* have been salvaged, with all current residents relocated to new apartments, in order to meet the needs of wealthy and often well-connected individuals who wish to live in the city

Mei Lanfang, husband and father, is here shown attired in the stage dress of a young woman, the only roles he played in Beijing opera.

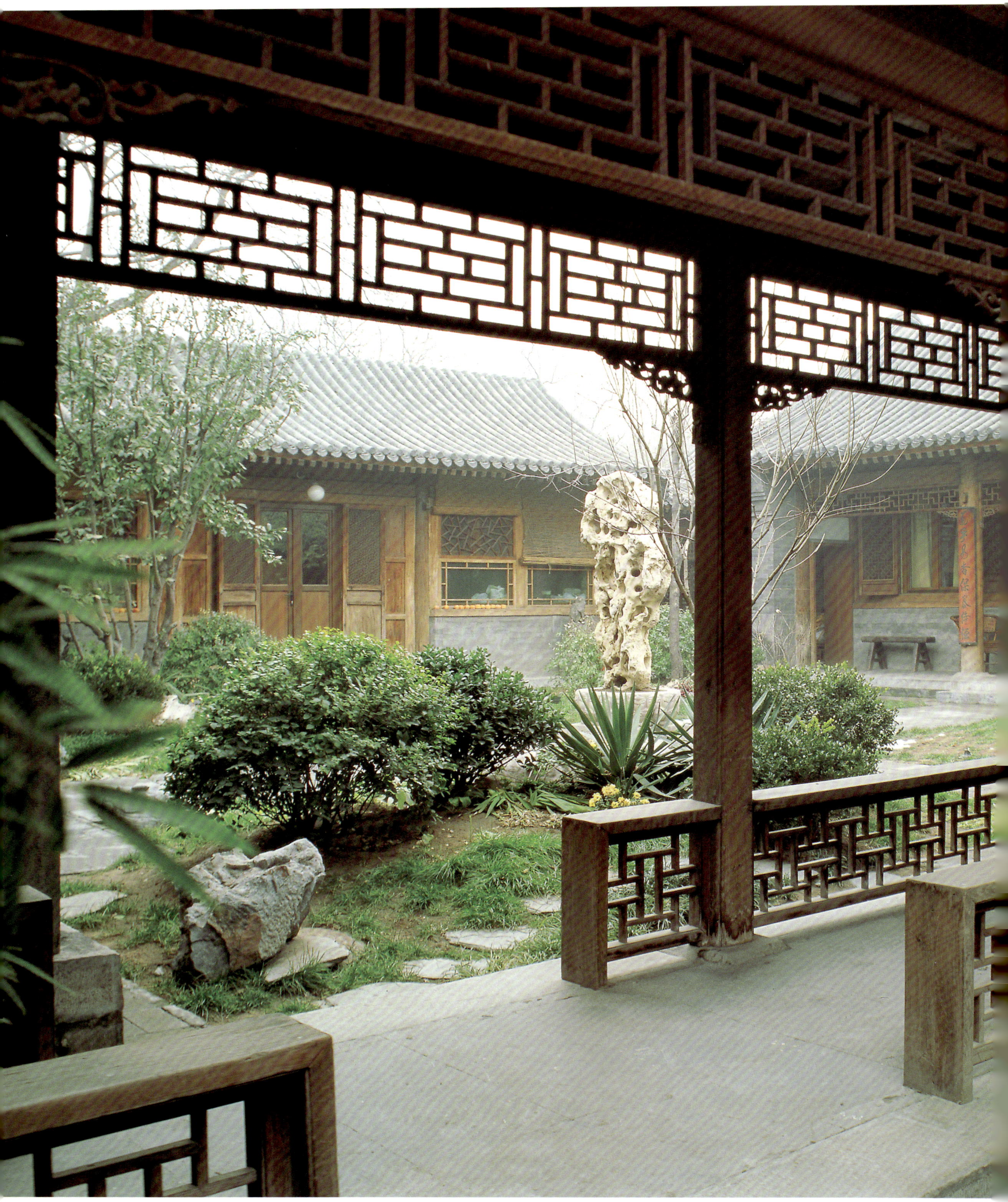

center in a style that is an improvement over past luxury. As a result, a luxury market has emerged in the districts around the old Imperial City, leading to gentrification and the fraying of the architectural fabric of old neighborhoods as rehabilitated *siheyuan* have been transformed into private estates, sometimes simply investment properties, with all of the conveniences of modern life, including automobile garages, air conditioning, modern kitchens and baths, security systems, and satellite antennas. In some cases, development companies, whose real estate arms build new villa-type courtyard residences that are multistoried, have demolished extensive areas in the city. A good example is Nanchizi, an area just outside the crimson walls of the Forbidden City, where a new term was invented—*sihelou*, meaning multistoried courtyard structures—to cloak the real estate venture with some of the historical resonance of the old word *siheyuan*. Touting the fact that two-story *sihelou* "follow" traditional old-style courtyard designs with their gray walls and open spaces, developers have produced designs similar to garden-style residences seen elsewhere in the world, embellished with traces of their Chinese patrimony in the form of mock-tile roofs (made of cement) and moon gates. Indeed, traditional *siheyuan* courtyard houses and *hutong* neighborhoods in Beijing have undergone a radical evolution as socialist economic and social policies have themselves undergone revolutionary change.

Other *siheyuan* that otherwise would have been demolished because of rising real estate values have been saved because they once were the residences of prominent persons or were occupied by party and government officials. In many of these courtyard houses, writers, academics, artists, political figures,

Opposite:
Viewed from a corner garden, replete with odd rocks, is a side building in a restored *siheyuan*.

Left:
The components of this restored *siheyuan* were moved from another area of Beijing while some of the decorative elements came from elsewhere. The intricately carved door panel showing four dragons was brought from neighboring Shanxi province.

易安居

and others lived much or part of their lives, enjoying the ambience of traditional courtyard life. Although some of these structures today ostensibly serve as museums, visitors can experience reasonably authentic Beijing *siheyuan* if they visit them even if one has little knowledge of the famous person who once lived there. Among the most interesting are those of twentieth century writers. Lao She acquired his Beijing courtyard home in 1949 when he returned from the United States and lived there until he died thirteen years later. One can only wonder if he ever considered what it would have been like to share it with seven or eight families. Lu Xun, the father of modern Chinese literature, lived in his single courtyard home beginning in 1923 but only for a little more than two years. Elsewhere in China, there are many former homes of Lu Xun, but none of them is a traditional courtyard house. Guo Moruo, a poet and dramatist born in Sichuan, lived in a Beijing *siheyuan*, which once was an annex of Prince Gong's mansion, from 1963 until his death in 1978. An oddity of his residence is the presence of an extensive grassy courtyard planted with gingko and pine trees. Other lesser known historical figures whose residences are worth visiting include the eighteenth-century Qing-dynasty scholar Ji Yun's Yuewei Cottage and the late Qing reformer Tan Sitong's home that once was a guildhall.

Large numbers of similar old *siheyuan* residences throughout the city were allocated to important governmental functionaries after 1949. One, with a rich history, is now open. Along the tranquil Back Lakes area is Prince Chun's extensive garden and house in which China's last emperor Pu Yi was born. A home was created in this space for Madame Soong Qingling, the widow of Sun Yatsen, who occupied the gardens and a newly constructed "mansion" between 1963 and 1981. However, most of the old *siheyuan* today remain hidden behind high gray brick walls, their presence only known to aging neighbors.

Opposite:
Framed with decorative lattice and illuminated at night, this small side yard in a renovated Beijing *siheyuan* provides a space for exhibiting odd-shaped rockery. The three characters translate as "Abode of Tranquility."

Above:
This small gate into a modest *siheyuan* reveals some of the damage done during the Cultural Revolution, including the lingering two characters *ge* and *ming*, together meaning "revolution," that were painted above the door at least a quarter century ago.

Far left:
At the entryway of a Beijing *siheyuan*, a pair of lions sometimes stands sentry.

Left:
Whether the dwelling behind this old gate has been restored or remains dilapidated remains a mystery.

NORTHERN MOUNTAIN HOUSES
Chuandixia Village, Mentougou, Beijing

Much of the region around Beijing is broad and flat, a product of deposition from the Huang He or Yellow River. Here, too, quadrangular *siheyuan* dwellings are generally level in their layout. To the north and west of the capital, however, are rugged mountains that provide not only the irregular landscape across which the traces of the Great Wall are draped but also the uneven building sites for tiny settlements. One such village is Chuandixia, a mountain village some 90 kilometers to the west of Beijing, in a vast, sparsely populated district called Mentougou in Zhaitang township. Migrants surnamed Han, from Shanxi province to the west, first settled Chuandixia during the Ming dynasty, in the early years of the fifteenth century, as they traveled through the difficult Taihang Mountains. Originally called "Under the Stove Village," the complicated initial character for the village's name 爨, with thirty-one brush strokes, was formally changed in 1958 to the simpler three-stroke character 川 to mean "Under the Stream Village"—both pronounced *Chuan*.

Seemingly isolated and remote, this tiny village, about two days' journey from Beijing by foot or a day by horse, in time came to serve as an essential way station along an old post road that connected the imperial capital with Taiyuan in Shanxi province. The imperial system of postal couriers carried official documents between the far-flung outposts of the empire and the capital via a series of stations situated along the roads and paths that threaded their way through the mountain passes. Elsewhere in the country, the canal and river network served a similar function, but it was in the difficult mountainous areas that reliable rest stops were most critical. While villagers in Chuandixia were able to eke out a living tilling miniscule patches of sloping ground, supplemented by game killed in the wild, a significant proportion of their livelihood came from the food, rest, and water provided to weary couriers who passed by on foot or on the back of horses or donkeys.

Because winters are bitterly cold in the mountains, the early settlers chose a building site for the

Left:
This contemporary drawing by Liu Chong reveals how the dwellings in Chuandixia village are arrayed across the steep slope, enabling villagers to take advantage of the winter sun and summer breezes as well as protect them from the cold winds that blow from the north.

Right:
Draped across south-facing hill slopes, Chuandixia village is comprised of several sections at different elevations.

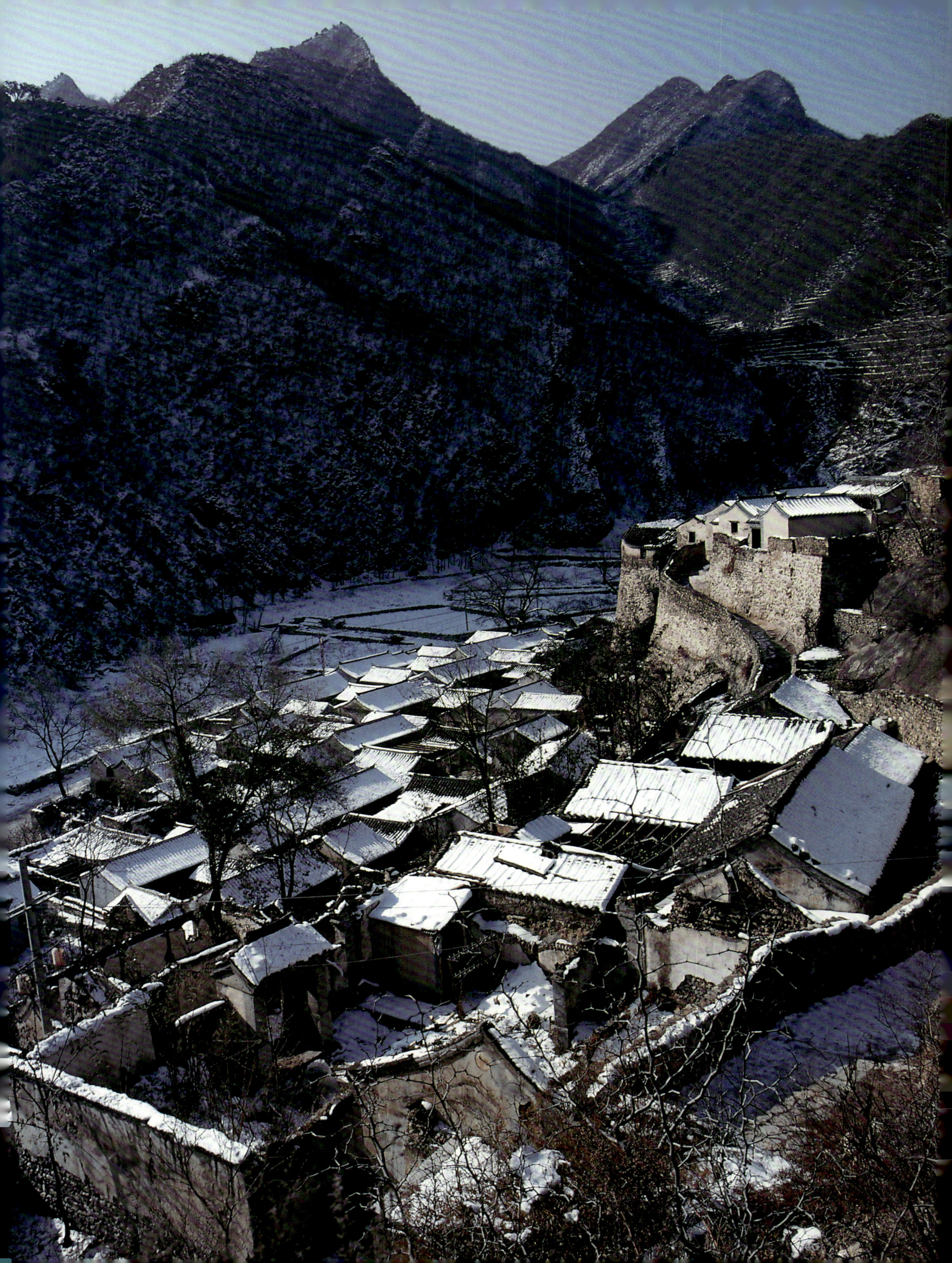

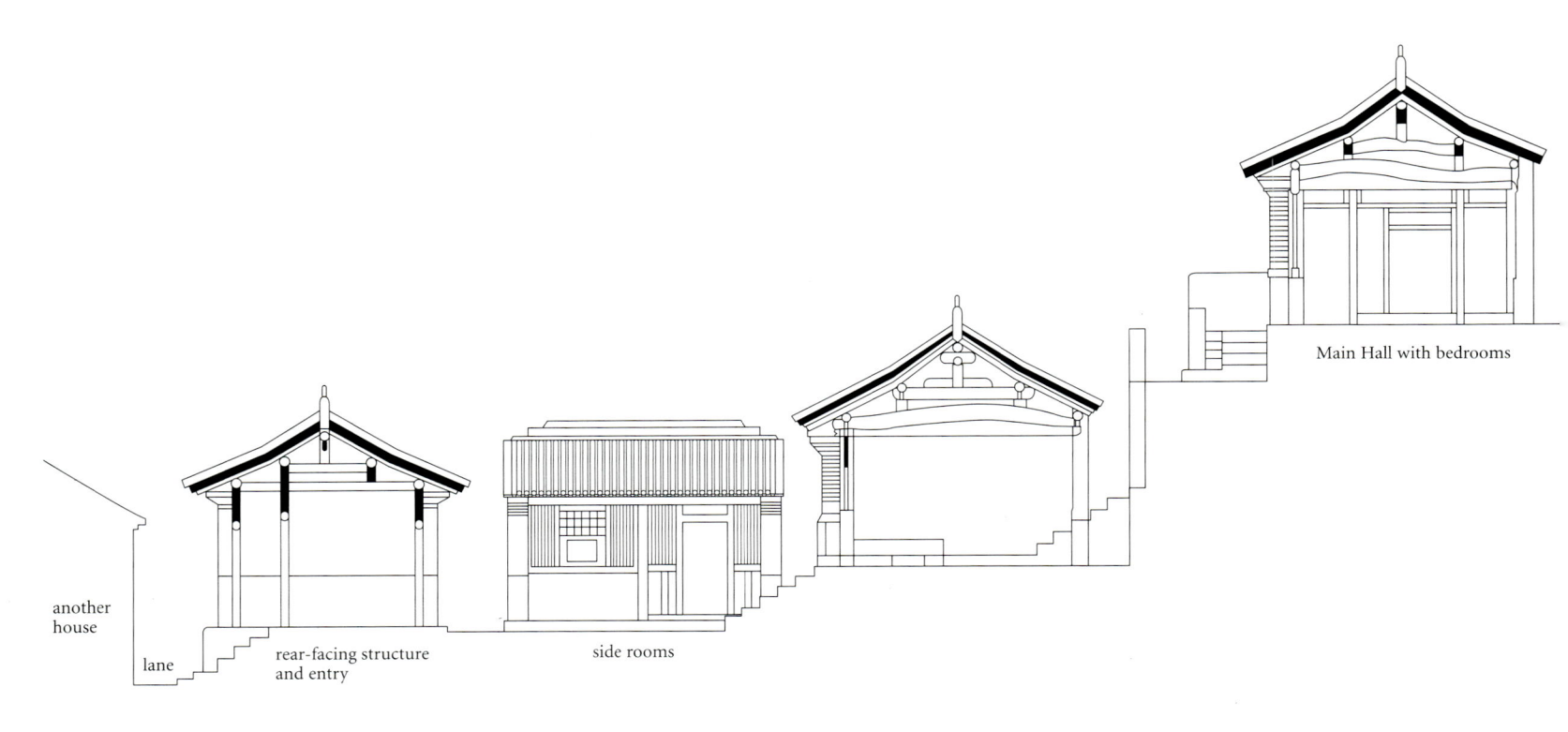

another house | lane | rear-facing structure and entry | side rooms | | Main Hall with bedrooms

Top:
The topography enforces the building of interrelated parts of a single *siheyuan* on different levels. Connected by steps, the most important building is in back and is higher than the other related structures.

Left:
Painted on the wall at the entrance to the village, the complicated thirty-one brush-strokes' character for *chuan*, meaning "stove," represents a shorthand form for the name of Chuandixia village. This character was formally changed in 1958 to a simpler three-stroke character meaning "stream."

Above:
Supported by a substantial stone foundation that rises some five meters above the steps below, this small house is connected to others by stone steps and pathways.

114 China's Fine Heritage Houses

village about 650 meters above sea level on the steep south-facing slopes. Here, the mountain to the rear provides a screen against the intense winds blowing from the Mongolian steppes, yet opens each of the houses on its south-facing slopes to the warmth of the sun. Rubble stones, abundant on the hillsides as well as sorted by water in the ravines cut by mountain streams, were the principal building materials for foundations, walls, paths, and steps. Timber for beams, purlins, windows, and doors, necessary components to complete the construction of their houses, was available nearby but only in limited dimensions and quantities. As a result, settlers were able to build only relatively compact dwellings to meet the requirements of limited building sites, available materials, and their own modest needs. While the earliest dwellings were probably constructed along the road, experience most likely showed that sites higher on the slope had the advantage of longer periods of sunlight, especially in winter. In time, an upper cluster of houses, linked to those below by stone steps and pathways, developed, which had to be buttressed from below by a 20-meter-high stonewall. The layout of stonewalls and paths also helped stabilize the slope in order to mitigate the consequences brought on by heavy summer rains. Residents claim that the village was "designed" for the convenience of people, cats, and dogs, each of which has its own narrow stone-lined pathways that allow them to move with ease from one level to another.

Practical requirements of upslope building sites lent themselves to layouts in which each *siheyuan* was stepped into the hill slope, with back structures being higher than lower structures. Entry from a lane was usually first into a lower front level of the dwelling and an adjacent courtyard, with a series of steps then leading to a higher-level back structure and courtyard. Houses in the lower village generally are more level than those higher on the hill slope. Guang Liang Yuan, "The Luminous Courtyard," the largest residential complex in Chuandixia, has three sets of stepped buildings with five meters of elevation separating the lower from the upper portion. Now undergoing restoration, it is surrounded by many other smaller U-shaped and quadrangular-shaped residences in various states of decay.

Even in the smallest courtyard structures, the conventional components of a *siheyuan* are apparent: a symmetrical plan, a clear hierarchical axis, enclosing walls, entry in the southeast portion of the outer wall, a spirit wall facing the gate, a rear-facing hall, a pair of side halls, and a south-facing main structure. Space in the main building is typically divided into three *jian* or bays although side halls often only have two bays.

In most small houses in north China, *kang*, heated brick beds, are connected to a cooking stove to capture the heat and carry it through the heat-dissipating bed. In several of the larger dwellings in Chuandixia, where bedrooms are often some distance from the kitchen, each *kang* has a firebox along its side, where burning charcoal, coal, and wood are placed to provide a comfortable space to pass bitter winter days. *Kang* of this type differ little in structure from those connected with the kitchen since both channel heated gases through flues or ducts embedded in the walls of the brick beds, where the heat is absorbed and then radiated to warm the surface above. *Kang* are fitted tightly into a space confined by thick outer walls that provide a kind of insulation to conserve heat. In those bedrooms with a south-facing wall, the lattice windows lead some additional warmth into the room even on winter days.

Left:
A *kang* or brick bed is usually built just inside the south-facing windows so that those sitting on it in winter benefit from the warmth of the sun's rays. Additionally, each *kang* is a radiating surface in that heat from the firebox passes through it on its way to the chimney, in effect then warming the whole room.

Below:
These drawings show the firebox, interconnected flues, and ventilating chimney, all given shape to the *kang* by the practical use of bricks.

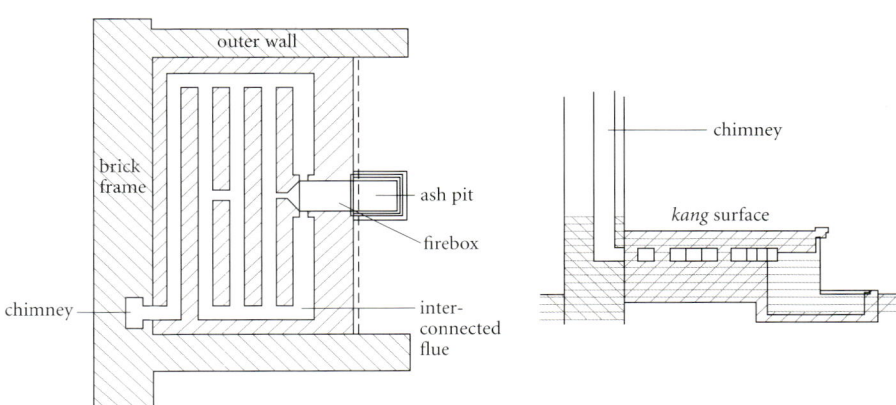

While the upper buildings in this interconnected *siheyuan* still await restoration, the inverted U-shaped structures below remain in good shape.

As can be seen in the many collapsing structures throughout Chuandixia, heavy column-and-beam wooden structural systems typical of north China lift the roof. Lattice window and door panels are simple in pattern and most still show the frayed evidence of the paper sheets that were once glued to them in order to block cold air. Houses still occupied disclose the colorful ornamentation and practicality of living in a country house: corn cobs hung to dry under the eaves, red paper couplets and Door Gods pasted to outer doors, newspapers and magazines glued to patch walls. While abandoned dwellings lack these elements, it is still possible to see evidence of political slogans written during the Cultural Revolution in the late 1960s, viewed today by visitors as curiosities from another era.

By the early 1990s, Chuandixia was a shell of its former self. It is said that there were about thirty households in the village in the eighteenth century that grew, according to some reports, to more than seventy households over the next century. At the end of the 1990s, researchers counted seventy-four courtyard houses in one form or another even though only eighteen households with forty people continued to reside in the village. Over time, no doubt houses were abandoned as their structures deteriorated and new ones were built nearby using easily available building materials, and thus it is not possible to establish clearly what the maximum population of Chuandixia ever was. Old residents recall that Japanese troops in 1942 burned a third of the residences in the village, perhaps actually representing only those that were occupied. Many of these scorched structures were subsequently left in a derelict state and remain so today.

It is said that attention was first brought to the village through the efforts of two painters, Wu Guangzhong in 1986 and Peng Shiqiang in 1992, who both were enthralled by the unity of the physical and cultural landscapes. In 1996, a television film used the village as a backdrop for scenes related to the 1900 journey of the Empress Dowager Ci Xi, who probably passed through the valley on her way to Xi'an via Shanxi province. At the same time, an entrepreneur named Han Mengliang, a descendant of those who settled in Chuandixia, began to think of ways of transforming a poor mountain village into a site supported by tourists. Via interviews in the Beijing press, invitations to television cameramen to visit, and a short typescript about the village, he single-handedly promoted the village. In 1998, the village was declared an "Historic Heritage Protection Zone" by district authorities, a status that was ratified in 2001 by Beijing's municipal authorities, with a full-scale preservation plan developed. Accessible today by a two-lane highway in less than three hours, the natural landscape of Mentougou attracts Beijingers as a place to escape the confines of the city. Most come to fish, hike, ice skate, and swim, either in the wild or at sites developed to meet the needs of weekend visitors, but some have discovered the traces of old China that litter the valleys. Although Chuandixia no longer is a quiet village punctuated with the visits of imperial couriers, it still retains the physical elements of a mountain settlement of earlier times. Work will no doubt continue to refurbish the ruins of centuries of decline but little can be done to restore a sense of the difficult, yet perhaps even satisfying, life of times past.

Above:
With tattered paper on its lattice windows, this side hall shows evidence of relatively recent use, even as now it stands unused.

Left:
Fading New Year couplets and still-bright Door Gods adorn the entry of this small courtyard dwelling.

118 China's Fine Heritage Houses

Left:
The oblong entryway of an old *siheyuan* reveals the abundant use of fired brick, thick wooden columns, and carved ornamentation.

Right:
Looking through the entryway of a partially restored *siheyuan*, with glimpses of Cultural Revolution graffiti on opposing walls and an old carved brick spirit wall inside.

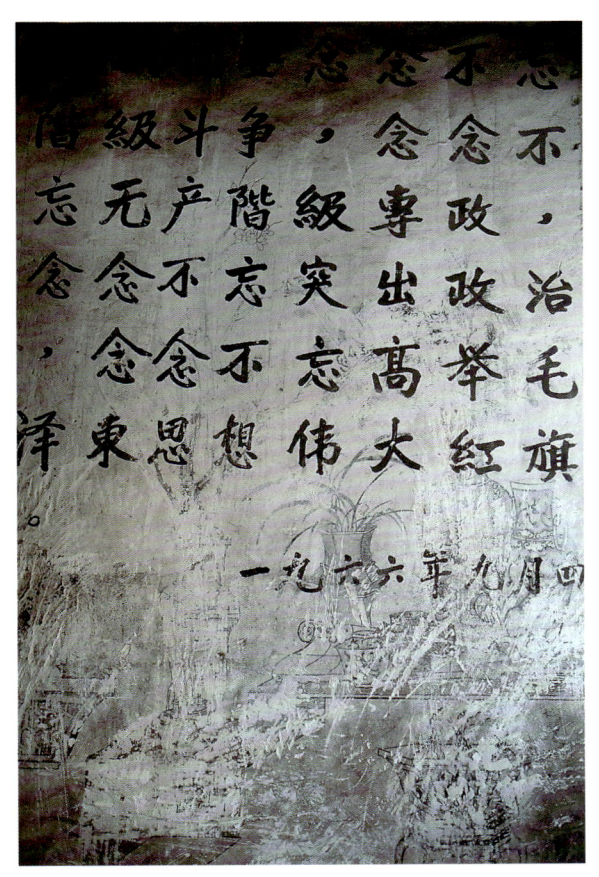

Far left:
Written in 1966 during the Cultural Revolution, these phrases call for "keeping in mind the dictatorship of the Proletariat, stressing politics, and holding high the thoughts of Mao Zedong …."

Left:
Oblique view into the entryway of an occupied *siheyuan*, showing walls papered with newspapers, corn hung to dry, and lanterns to be lit at night.

Northern Mountain Houses 119

JIANGNAN CANAL HOUSES
Homes in Yangzi Delta Watertowns, Jiangnan

The Jiangnan or "South of the Yangzi River" region is crisscrossed with countless canals and dotted with small canal-side villages and towns in addition to some of China's richest cities. To geographers, this area, which includes placid Lake Tai and extends from Nanjing eastward to Shanghai, is remarkable for its hydrography rather than its topography, its low-lying terrain, and its traditional life centering on the omnipresent water environment. At least since Sui dynasty times when the Grand Canal was built, the name "Jiangnan" rarely is used without the addition of the adjective "prosperous." As the land of abundance, "the countryside of fish and rice," and the home of China's silk industry, the water-laced Jiangnan region has long been known for its robust commercialized market-oriented economy linking villages, towns, and cities. In once-quiet cities like Hangzhou, Suzhou, Wuxi, and Yangzhou, as well as in countless settlements beyond the metropolitan centers, as both wealth and population increased a refined literati culture came to thrive and give these cities a distinctive character.

Residences with associated gardens epitomize the finest forms of domestic architecture in Jiangnan. Private literati or scholar gardens, sometimes simply called classical Chinese gardens, especially, were designed for those who expected simplicity, elegance, and poetic meaning in their daily lives. Such gardens, of course, were an integral part of a scholar's house, to the degree that the Chinese notion of a home is explicitly included in the term *yuanzhai* or "garden-house." Although some "garden-houses" are sprawling complexes that blend varieties of buildings, rockery, water, and vegetation, most resort to nature in miniature in order to array aesthetically pleasing aspects of these complementary elements into relatively small spaces. None of China's magnificent literati garden-houses is portrayed in the sections that follow. Instead, attention is brought to a small yet graceful residence of a Ming-dynasty calligrapher, painter, poet, and dramatist in Shaoxing, Zhejiang, and a canal-side residence of a merchant in Luzhi, Jiangsu, that once must have been alive with the comings and goings of family and commercial activities.

Once there were hundreds of villages and towns tied to the Jiangnan canal network, but now only a handful still echo in layout and lifestyle the waterborne settlements of the past. In a rush to modernize and industrialize in recent decades, far too many traditional settlements were hastily sacrificed when their past forms and identity were erased with the building of new houses and factories, the filling in of canals and marshes, as well as the construction of roads. Attention to the conservation of Jiangnan watertowns, however, did begin in the 1980s under the inspired attention of Ruan Yisan of the Department of Architecture of Tongji University in Shanghai, and has led to a handful of remarkable preservation successes. In the process, some watertown settlements and buildings within them, which had been seen by some as dilapidated and dysfunctional, have undergone restorative transformations and become significant heritage sites for domestic tourists. Planning principles, well thought out before either finances or tourists climbed to the levels experienced in recent years, focused on locating new construction outside the historic districts, making repairs to old buildings, improving water quality, and burying electrical and telephone lines. In order to maintain the rhythms of daily life and for villages and towns not to become merely sets of structures to be consumed by tourists, heritage issues and livelihood issues were confronted in comprehensive ways.

It is still possible, even as the twenty-first century begins, to experience authentic expressions of China's past because of the distinctive, irregular layout of each watertown and the tightly packed and often odd structures along their irregular stone-paved lanes. On and adjacent to canals and ponds as well as along the lanes, traditional activities can still be seen. Waterside pavilions, quaint teahouses, temples, memorial arches, high stone bridges, most at human scale, contribute to a generally slower pace of life welcomed by visitors and residents alike.

Among the most noteworthy of extant watertowns are Wuzhen, Nanxun, and Xitang in Zhejiang province as well as Luzhi, Zhouzhuang, and Tongli in Jiangsu province, which have been put forward as a group for designation as a UNESCO World Heritage Site. Although, sadly, many others have been developed beyond recognition as a watertown, others are in various states of preservation, especially Dongpu, Keqiao, and Anchang near Shaoxing in eastern Zhejiang, and Jinxi, Shaxi, Mudu, and Guangfu

Right:
While still important in the life of local residents, canals in many towns such as Luzhi, Jiangsu, shown here, serve as routes to carry tourists as they explore local culture.

Below right:
Throughout the water-laced Jiangnan regions, while differing in details, narrow canals, arched bridges, small boats, as well as water-side residences and shops provide convenient places for living and trading.

| docking | canal boat traffic | docking, trading | foot traffic | trading | residence or storage |

Jiangnan Canal Houses

Left:
Map depicting the hydrography of the Jiangnan region and showing the most prominent canal towns.

Below:
At the junction of two canals, a teahouse in Luzhi, Jiangsu, provides a pleasant sanctuary for locals and visitors.

near Suzhou in southern Jiangsu. Most are within a couple hours of Shanghai, China's mega city, and thus have already felt the impact of swelling visitation. Chinese tourists dominate tourism in China, enticed to off-the-beaten-track locations by websites, news reports, word of mouth, and increased affluence.

Luzhi, Jiangsu

Luzhi, like many Jiangnan watertowns and villages, greets the morning bathed in semi-transparent mist. Especially from late spring into early summer, the so-called *meiyu* or "plum rains" bring consecutive days of lachrymal drizzle at a time when plums ripen and rice is ready to be transplanted. With very little sunshine, sultry temperatures, and high relative humidity, the homophonous association of *meiyu* with "mold rains" becomes quite apparent to residents as shoes, bedding, and other stored items, even rice, in poorly ventilated areas easily grow moldy. Much attention during this period is focused on trying to prevent mold growth by moving items from the dark into the light, yet everyone recognizes ultimately the need for drying and airing such items in the intense sunshine that will inexorably follow the lingering "plum rains" by mid-July.

Until recently, it was easiest to reach Luzhi by small boat rather than car or bus, being sculled along narrow canals, the arteries of country life, through a relatively low landscape of paddy fields separated from each other by slightly elevated embankments. Virtually all of the original woodlands and marshes were extinguished as peasants replaced them with irrigated fields and perennial bushes and trees with important economic value, such as mulberry, tea, masson pine, and fruits. Chinese straightforwardly refer to these areas as *shuixiang* or "water country." In the past, these agricultural products also always were moved by boat to small canal-side settlements, like Luzhi, where they could be processed, stored, and marketed. Stone pathways and countless stone and wood bridges facilitate foot traffic.

With an area of only a single square kilometer, Luzhi is said to have once had seventy-two bridges, although only forty remain, a fact that places a convenient bridge every hundred or so paces. Hefeng Bridge, an arch-shaped structure said to be the oldest, was built of granite during the Song dynasty, but most bridges date from the Qing dynasty. Just beyond Xinglong Bridge in the eastern part of town is the Wansheng "Extremely Prosperous" Rice Company, an expansive courtyard complex built in 1910 as the center of business for a pair of entrepreneurs who had a network of a hundred warehouses for storing and milling rice in the region around Luzhi.

Below:
With lattice windows thrown open in early morning, this second-floor teahouse in Luzhi, Jiangsu, has been readied for visits by residents and tourists.

The two best-preserved houses in Luzhi are those of the Xiao and Shen families. Located on a lane in the northern part of Luzhi, what is now called the Xiao residence was actually built by a man named Yang in 1889. Sold early in the twentieth century to Xiao Bingli, who was a partner in an electric bulb manufacturing venture, the house today stands as a museum celebrating the 1960s Hong Kong movie superstar Siao Fong Fong, also called Josephine Siao, Xiao Fangfang, and Hsiao Fang Fang. Although the legendary screen actress never lived in the house, having been born in Shanghai in 1947 and moved to Hong Kong as a young child, she is the granddaughter of the Luzhi Xiao family. As a well-known Hong Kong television personality, philanthropist, and mature film actress, her fame brings countless visitors to the Luzhi Xiao residence to see the exhibits spread throughout the nearly 1000-square-meter residence, a good example of a late Qing-dynasty *nouveau riche*. The much larger nineteenth-century Shen residence, the home of an educator and merchant, is discussed in the next section.

Zhouzhuang, Jiangsu

With a history of some 900 years, Zhouzhuang watertown occupies a slightly elevated level expanse in a township that has some 24 percent of its area

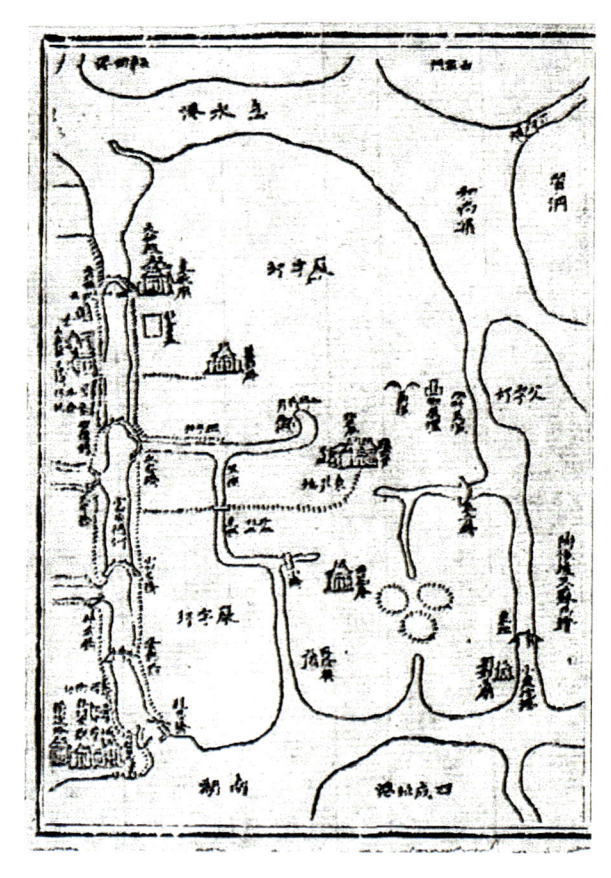

Above:
Outdoor stages for the performance of local opera are common in towns and villages throughout southern China, such as this one in Zhouzhuang, Jiangsu.

Left:
Set in a landscape dominated by water, Zhouzhuang town is shown in this nineteenth-century map as being made up of a series of islands connected by strategically located bridges.

Right:
Stone bridges throughout the Jiangnan water region rise high above the canals beneath, providing steps for pedestrians and those carrying goods. Shops and teahouses cluster around both ends of the Fu'an Bridge in Zhouzhuang.

124   China's Fine Heritage Houses

Jiangnan Canal Houses 125

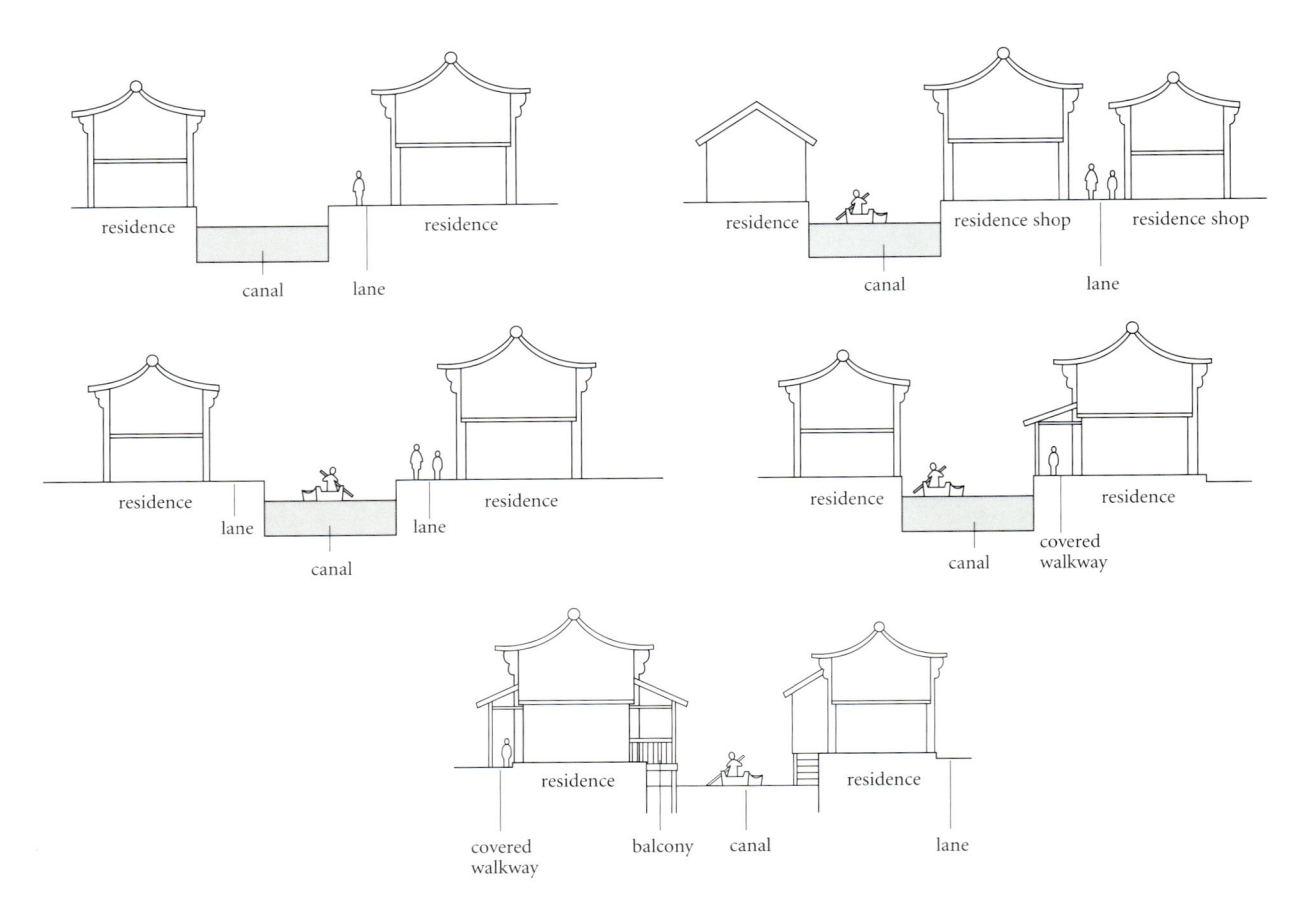

residence / canal / lane / residence	residence / canal / residence shop / lane / residence shop
residence / lane / canal / lane / residence	residence / canal / residence / covered walkway
	residence / covered walkway / balcony / canal / lane / residence

Left:
Throughout the Jiangnan region, lanes, canals, and buildings are aligned in a variety of patterns.

Below:
Here, early in the morning, well before activity disperses them throughout the town, small boats are moored in such numbers that they clog the canal.

covered by water. Its somewhat isolated physical location amidst the "water country" helped preserve it as a relative oasis within the corridor zone between Shanghai and Suzhou, which underwent extraordinary development from the late 1980s onward. In 1986, Zhouzhuang was cited as a "last frontier" settlement worthy of preservation. Even as some remarked about its backwardness, decay, and sleepy nature, others began to plan for its conservation.

Records trace the origins of the village back to a landlord named Zhou Di, who established a settlement here in 1086 during the Northern Song dynasty. However, it was in the several centuries after 1127, after the Southern Song dynasty had moved to Hangzhou in adjacent Zhejiang province, that Zhouzhuang grew and flourished. By the seventeenth century, the population of Zhouzhuang had grown to 3000, peaking perhaps at 4000 in 1953. However, by 1986 it had declined to only 1838. Over the past fifty years or so, the steady decline in the population and the effective abandonment of old buildings once alive with residents forestalled the destruction of many old structures.

Concentrated within a half square kilometer of Zhouzhuang are some 60 percent of the watertown's Ming- and Qing-dynasty structures, arrayed along a mesh of waterways that are the backbone of the old town. The principal canals are somewhat irregular in alignment yet together at the core of Zhouzhuang approximate the Chinese character 井 meaning "well." Complementing these are narrow lanes and alleyways that largely parallel the canals, with a multiplicity of juxtapositions. Canals divide the town into islets that are connected by nineteen bridges, each of which serves to link and is a hub of activity.

Tourism in Zhouzhuang began in the early 1990s, well before that of other watertowns. By then, some of the egregious damage of recent decades had been ameliorated. One spacious old residence with seventy rooms called Yu Yan Tang or "Hall of Jade Swallow," initially built for the Xu family in the fifteenth century during the Ming dynasty before being sold to the Zhang family during the early Qing dynasty, was finally emptied of the seventeen families who had come to occupy it after 1949. The Shen Benren residence, built in 1742 and covering an area of some 2000 square meters, including seven courtyards and approximately 100 rooms in its plan, was used as a machine-making factory up until the late 1980s. Today, it has pride of place as a restored structure representing the glory of Zhouzhuang in the past.

Wuzhen, Zhejiang

Situated along the Grand Canal in northeastern Zhejiang, Wuzhen is threaded with narrow canals, which are crossed by numerous old stone bridges. Only open to visitors since 2001, Wuzhen is one of a handful of beautiful canal-side towns that straddle the watery border between Zhejiang and Jiangsu provinces. Unlike some of the better known watertowns, little of Wuzhen has been restored, yet many old buildings remain in a noteworthy state of preservation. Life in Wuzhen is much as it was in the past, with remarkably few buildings specifically serving tourists. Walking along any of the narrow lanes, one can easily glimpse the rhythms of daily life: people carting fresh water, cooking meals, tending to young children, and playing mahjong. Local workshops continue to make wine and homespun cotton, in addition to items made of wood, silk, and metal.

Among the best-known bridges in China is the Bazi Bridge, which is said to have been built in 1256 during the Song dynasty. With its gentle approaches and a principal span that clears 4.5 meters, the bridge fits compactly into a tight residential area. The bridge is one of some 400 found in Shaoxing, Zhejiang, called by some "China's Venice."

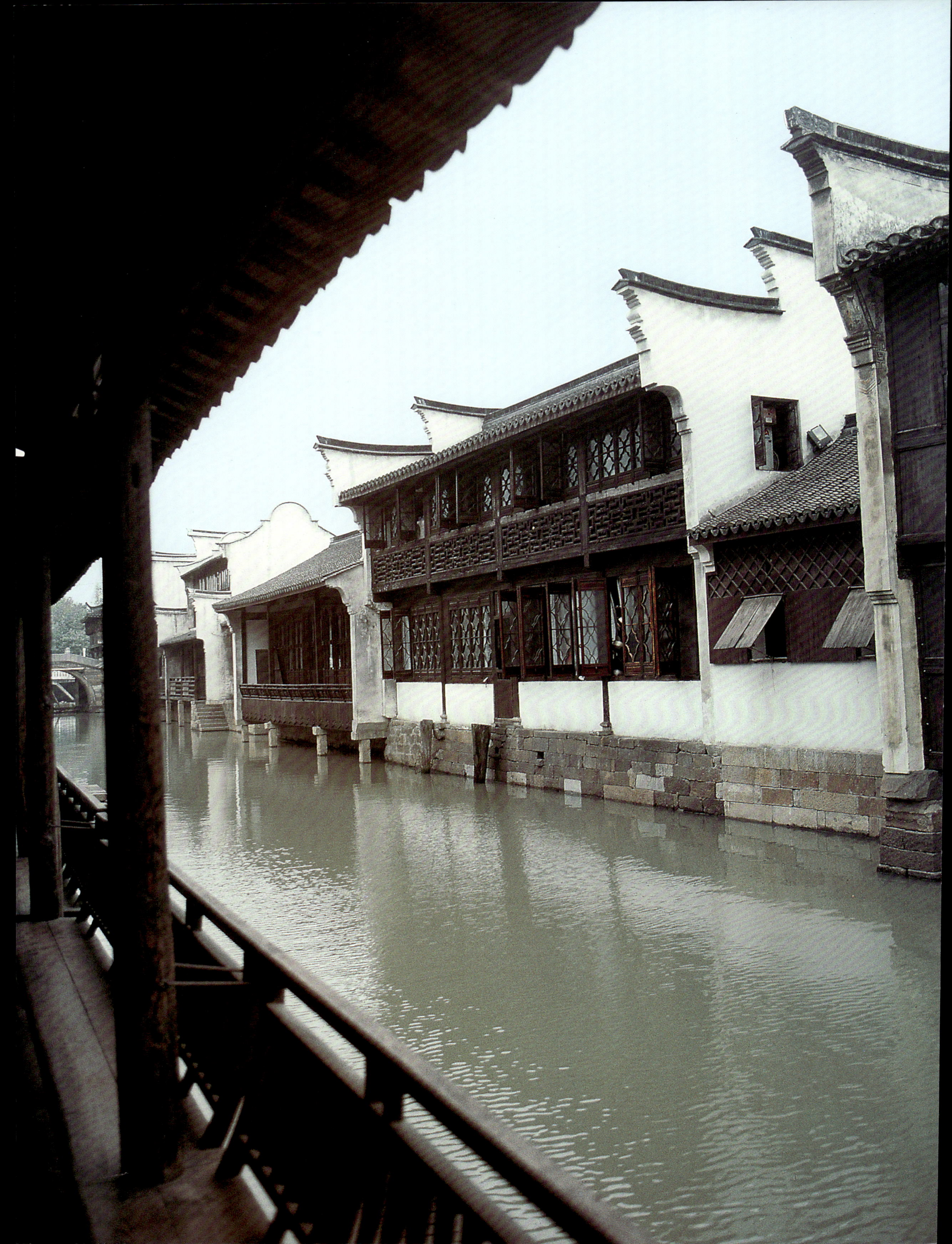

Left:
Viewed from a covered arcade along a canal in Wuzhen, Zhejiang, the backsides of shops and residences on the other side enjoy canal-side views. Some even have steps that allow access to the water. "Horses' head" stepped gables with gray tiles atop them rise above the whitewashed walls of houses throughout the town.

Above:
Two-story wooden buildings, usually with a shop on the ground floor and living space above, line narrow lanes in many canal towns, such as Wuzhen, Zhejiang. While the lower floor can be shuttered with wooden planks, the upper story remains airy because of its large lattice windows.

Right:
Carved bracket used to support the slightly overhanging upper floor.

Far right:
Decorative ornamentation of a wooden door and window panel.

Lu Xun (1881–1936), one of China's outstanding modern writers, spent the first third of his life in a canal-side residence in Shaoxing, Zhejiang. With large brick flooring, white walls, moon-shaped openings, and lattice windows, spaces are quite bright and cool during the day.

Many houses have their fronts along a lane and their backs against the water, thus function as shops or workshops and residences. With striking brick walls painted white and capped with stepped gables, which create intermittent firewalls, the structures themselves are usually constructed of wood, two stories tall, with a higher ground floor and a shallower loft. Ornamentation is rarely ostentatious, generally nothing more than carved wood brackets and supports. The patina of unpainted aged wood complements well the other natural surfaces of cut gray granite foundations, dark roof tiles, and mottled whitewashed stepped gable walls. Many of the shop-dwelling structures are raised on piers over the adjacent canal and have steps leading down to a stone landing where a boat can be tied or laundry washed.

The historic area of Wuzhen, 1.3 square kilometers in size, is entered through a recently restored soaring *pailou* or ceremonial archway leading to a high stage for Chinese opera performances. In this area, a number of structures have already been restored to their late nineteenth-century condition,

The writer Lu Xun, who was born in Shaoxing, studied the classics in a private school, depicted here, called the Sanwei shuwu (Three Tastes Studio, the three "tastes" being history, poetry, and philosophy).

including the birthplace of the writer Mao Dun, a Xiuzhen Daoist temple, a pawnshop, and a traditional pharmacy. Adjacent portions designated as part of the historic area are being developed with an emphasis on improving infrastructure, including placing water pipes and electric wires underground, repairing old walkways, removing newer structures, and assisting long-time residents to move to new housing. One prominently restored area is called "workshop area" with shops producing and selling rice wine, dried red tobacco, cotton dyeing, cotton shoes, as well as rattan, bamboo, and wood products.

Shaoxing, Zhejiang

Located just to the south of Hangzhou Bay within a "water country" similar to that north of the bay, Shaoxing has a longer and more glorious history than most Jiangnan watertowns. Some 2000 years ago, Shaoxing, which was then known as Guiji, was the capital of the Yue kingdom during the Spring and Autumn period, and it is said that Yu the Great, a legendary emperor, learned to control floods in the environs of Shaoxing some 5000 years even before that time. Yu the Great's mausoleum located nearby remains a special place of veneration. Shaoxing today is a modern city of nearly 350,000 people surrounded by economic development zones. Even if most of the traces of its earlier existence as a watertown are long gone, the city still retains sites of historic significance, including scores of homes of illustrious residents such as Xu Wei, Ming-dynasty calligrapher, painter, poet, and dramatist, and Lu Xun, progressive twentieth-century author. None of the watertowns near Shaoxing, such as Anchang, Dongpu, and Keqiao, has received the kind of attention or investment in preservation seen in other Jiangnan watertowns to the north and thus all have had their historical cores impinged upon by modern industrial development. Still, each has a number of slow-moving canals with busy boat traffic and vestiges of traditional commerce mixed with that which is modern. Coopers, stone carvers, quilt makers, bamboo craftsmen, and metal smiths occupy many workshops-cum-residences along the canals.

In each watertown, the daily life of the inhabitants continues even as the modern world intrudes. On the main streets, new cars and buses increase even as pedestrians and bicycles continue to dominate the back alleys. Along the granite-paved lanes lined with one- and two-story wooden shophouses, men, women, and children do as they have always done: shop for fresh produce, chat with neighbors, cart water, cook meals, clean out buckets, and tend flower pots. Numerous artisans work in many old workshops, producing as they have traditionally done objects made of copper, wood, cotton, silk, and paper. In order to protect an area of somewhat dilapidated traditional canal-side housing and shops, the Cangqiao lane area was rehabilitated in 2001 in an effort to improve the quality of life for residents while preserving aspects of Shaoxing's architectural heritage. Each of the old watertowns has a nearby "new town" with multistoried apartment blocks, schools, factories, and shopping centers, judged by most residents as more comfortable and convenient than the tightly packed old town.

AN EDUCATOR'S RESIDENCE
Shen Family Home, Luzhi, Jiangsu Province

One small town in the canal area of the Jiangnan region that has escaped destruction is Luzhi in southern Jiangsu province, just a short distance from the ethereal Lake Tai and only 15 kilometers east of Suzhou. Luzhi, with its relatively intact grid system, canals, bridges, and waterfront buildings of many types, remains among the least known and most attractive of Jiangnan's watertowns.

Although most of the dwellings in Luzhi are very small, often being simply a combination of shop and home in a single structure, there are a few larger nineteenth-century dwellings of note. Particularly significant is the Shen residence, which was built in 1870. Today, the focus of the Shen family is on the educator Shen Bohan, who was born in the house in 1883 and lived there at least until 1929, rather than on the commercial wealth that was at the foundation of his family's wealth. Shen Bohan's grandfather, a wealthy merchant and philanthropist in the Chinese classics, established a traditional academy in Luzhi in 1889 to educate Luzhi's youth, including his own grandson who was left in his care after the death of the boy's parents. In 1904, Shen Bohan at the age of twenty-one, like other young Chinese who were in awe of Japan's modernization and emerging power, left to study in the Department of Education at Waseda University. On his return in 1906, he transformed the traditional academy into a modern-style primary school, now called Puli Primary School, with a curriculum that included new subjects like arithmetic, history and geography, literature, and physical culture. Shen served twice as principal of the school until retiring in 1929 because of ill health. He died in Suzhou in 1953 at the age of seventy and is still remembered by townspeople for his educational innovations.

The Shen residence seen today is actually but one part of a much larger canal-side triplex structure that encompassed commercial elements, including a shop and extensive storage areas. Of the more than 3400-square-meter footprint of the larger interconnected building complex, only some 800 square meters found along the western axis are accessible today, virtually all of it comprising the sumptuous house itself. Like many Chinese homes, this one "sits north and faces south," that is, all the main halls open towards the south. Across from the front entry and perpendicular to the canal is a large spirit wall made of gray bricks, with two carved characters enigmatically proclaiming "Rippling Rhymes," an allusion lost in history. The corner position of the spirit wall and the adjacent shop are just above angled steps that lead down to the canal and provide a recessed area for neighbors to chat and peddlers to set down their wares without impeding the flow of pedestrians along the canal bank.

As a late Qing-dynasty structure, the residence is, as many might suggest, overly ornamented, some might even say gaudy, spread across a series of courtyards, large and small, as well as adjacent parallel halls of various dimensions. Just inside the front gate is an entry portico, followed by a very small skywell that leads ahead to what once was a small room to store ceremonial flags and a corridor room between the west and central parts of the complex. Now it is presented as a small library. Turning left one enters

Left:
Opposite the entry to the Shen residence is a spirit wall that was enlarged with a pair of ornamented "extending arms." The two carved characters engraved in low relief on the wall enigmatically proclaim "Rippling Rhymes," an allusion lost in history.

Right:
Viewed from the opposite canal bank, the back of the spirit wall is perpendicular both to the water and to the lane that passes before the residences and shops. Stone steps lead down to the canal, providing access to passing boats selling goods but also serving as a place to do laundry.

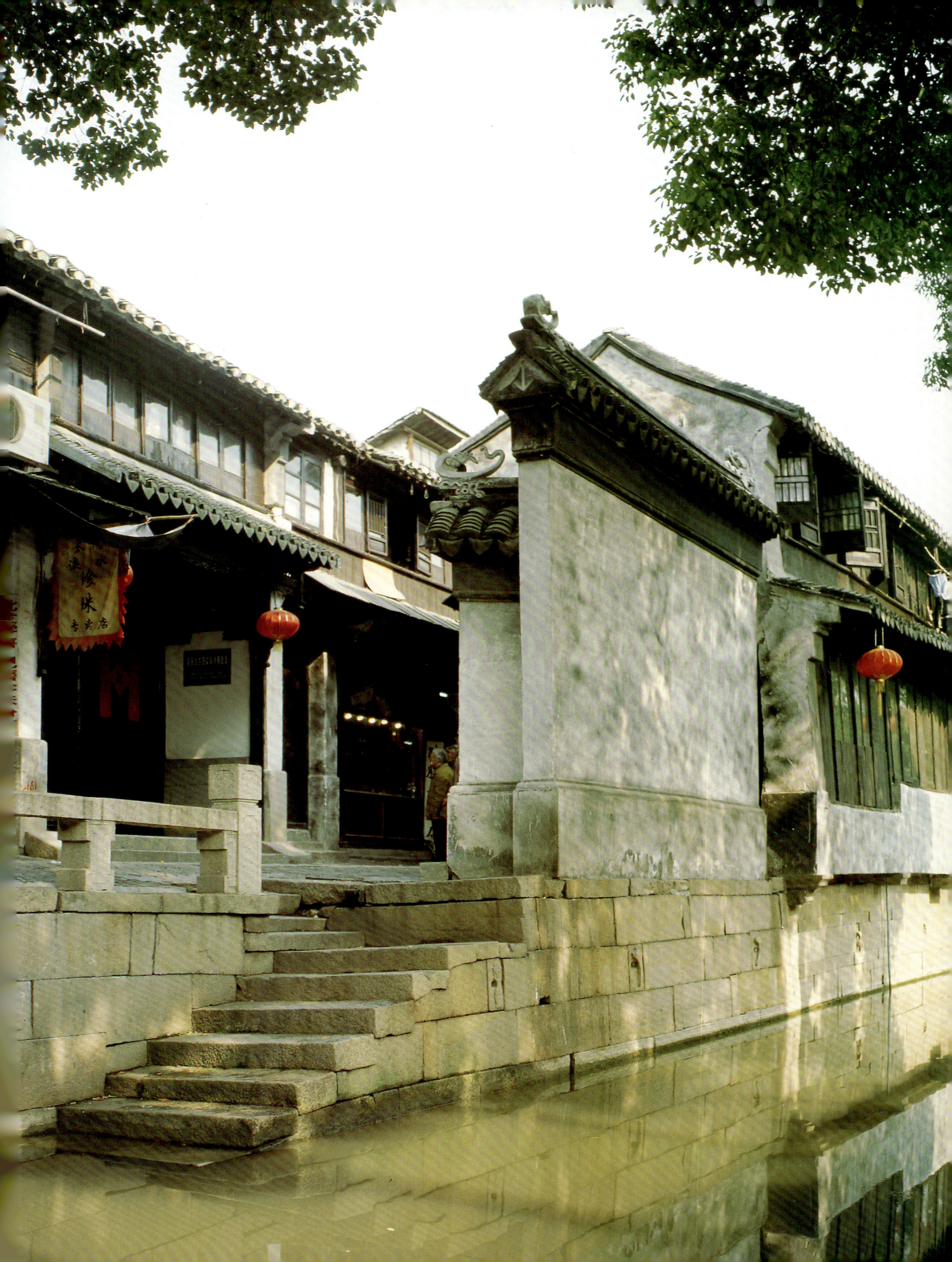
珍珠
专卖店

a narrow, rectangular courtyard fronting the first hall, once used as the family's *xi bian ting* or "western ordinary hall," now bereft of any of its furniture and used today as an exhibition hall of traditional clothing styles of the region.

As is the case with hierarchically organized courtyard houses, the next location north is another larger courtyard, which is then followed by the Main Hall, called Le Shan Tang or "Hall of Benevolence," a formal room with a full range of requisite furniture, paintings, and calligraphic couplets, and festooned with red lanterns and replete with auspicious imagery. Nearly 10 meters in height with exposed rafters and gray roof tiles, the hall is graced on all sides with profuse woodwork, including massive columns, paneling, lattice, and shallow woodcarvings.

A formal multipurpose hall of this type was the symbolic nucleus of a traditional family, representing at once its unity and its continuity from generation to generation. Important family events and ceremonies such as marriages and funerals would be commemorated as well as anniversaries and birthdays celebrated. The large courtyard and hall in front could be transformed into a banquet hall with movable round tables for relatives and guests. Convention governed the structured placement of the hardwood furniture, including rectangular and square tables as well as

Below:
The Shen residence and its adjacent commercial structures were built on the north side of an east–west flowing canal. The residence itself only occupies 800 square meters of the 3400-square-meter building complex.

Right:
Nearly 10 meters in height with exposed rafters and gray roof tiles, Le Shan Tang or "Hall of Benevolence" is the principal formal room of the Shen residence. The woodwork, including massive columns, paneling, and lattice, as well as paintings, calligraphic couplets, and red lanterns are all richly ornamented, many with auspicious imagery.

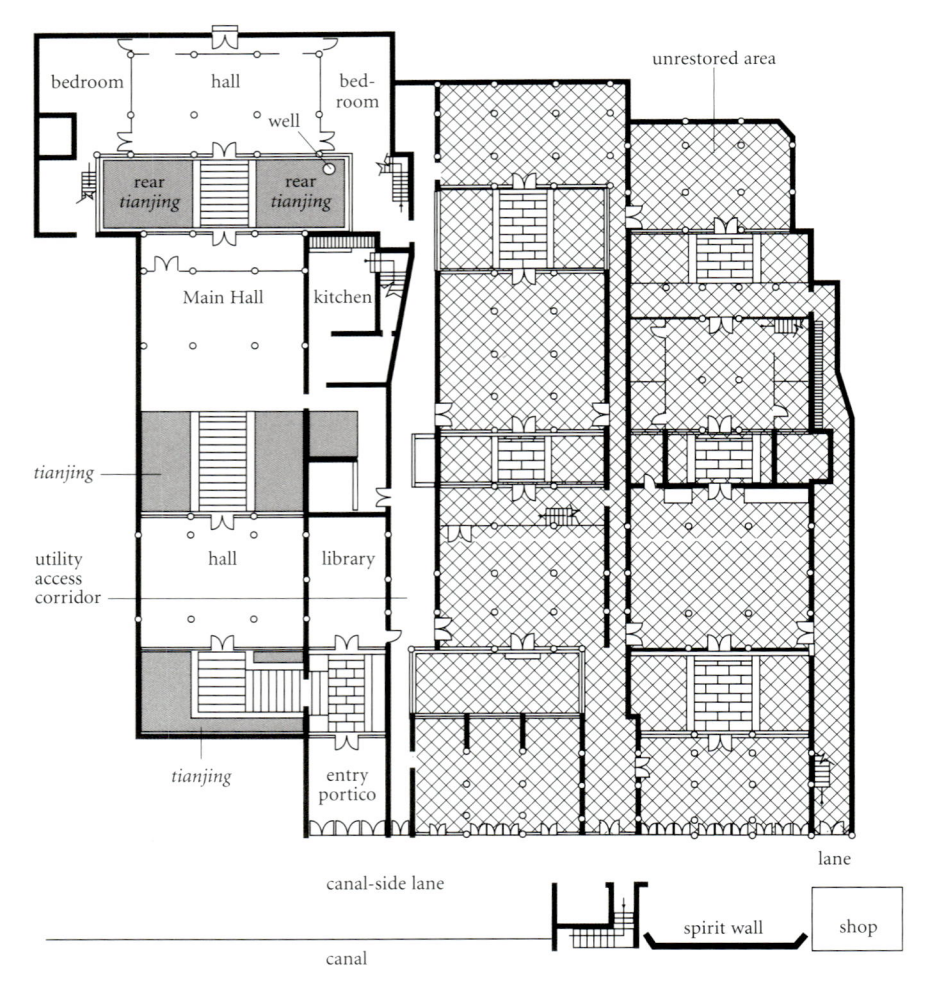

134 China's Fine Heritage Houses

An Educator's Residence 135

screens and curios. While furniture is aligned along the wall, most of it is symmetrically placed with the focus of the room concentrated in the central bay between four columns. The display of pairs of vertical couplets, horizontal presentation boards, paintings, and porcelain was expected to represent the family's status and impress visitors. To some degree, the furniture and ornamentation of the hall declared not only the household's wealth but also expressed its aesthetic sense as well as the fashions of the times.

Originally adjacent to Le Shan Hall was the Shen family's large library-cum-studio, a prominent space for a literary family of their renown. Indeed, after the Main Hall, such a library would have been considered an essential component of an educated household's residence, a kind of sanctuary from mundane matters. Peculiarly and unfortunately, a large country kitchen today occupies the space. With an impressive brick stove as well as furniture and utilitarian objects once commonly used by cooks as they prepared food, visitors can glimpse here the scale necessary to feed a large family but lose any sense of the bookish interests of several generations of Shens. It is likely that a utilitarian space for cooking originally would have been located towards the rear of one of the adjacent structures rather than here adjacent to the main ceremonial hall, but these areas today are not accessible because of incomplete restoration.

On both sides of the altar table are slender openings leading to the rear courtyard, intimate spaces for family members generally, but especially women and children. This rectangular rear courtyard is framed on three sides by a U-shaped two-story structure, seven bays wide, once used for family bedrooms with adjacent space for several servants. Below and above, on all four sides, intricately carved doors and window panels surround the courtyard. When thrown open, interior and exterior spaces become united, creating an expanded area for family interactions.

Above:
A small skywell, which is flanked by high white walls that are pierced by gates and windows, forms part of the entry portico for the residence.

Right:
Behind the Main Hall is a rectangular rear courtyard ringed by two-story structures, a series of intimate spaces for family members generally, but especially women and children.

Above:
Viewed from the northeast corner of the Main Hall are large swinging lattice door panels that can be adjusted to let in whatever air and light are deemed necessary. Furniture is arranged in formal, quite symmetrical patterns.

Left:
As light changes throughout the day, patterns of different shapes appear on the white walls of the Main Hall.

The steep wooden stairs on both ends of the courtyard lead to restricted family areas, now shown as five bedrooms with various types of furniture. Second-floor rooms, while not easy to access by the elderly, usually were cooler, better ventilated and lighted, and larger than bedrooms on the main floor. "Bedrooms" were not merely used at night. With minimal rearranging of cushions and low furniture, beds could be easily converted to sitting areas, a place to relax and talk with family and friends or care for children. Large, bulky canopy beds, couch beds, and storage cabinets could be moved up the narrow stairs because of the modular nature of the furniture that allowed it to be disassembled and reassembled easily.

From above, women and children could glimpse the activity of the men below without themselves being seen. Looking south they could glimpse the white walls and piled gray roof tiles of the "horses' head" walls that rise above the gables of the Le Shan Hall, which contrast with the blue sky and clouds surrounding them. In addition to supplying visual appeal in the tightly packed settlements, "horses' head" walls served a utilitarian function as formidable firewalls that protected tightly packed dwellings from possible conflagration as well as making it difficult for thieves to move across the rooftops from one residence to another.

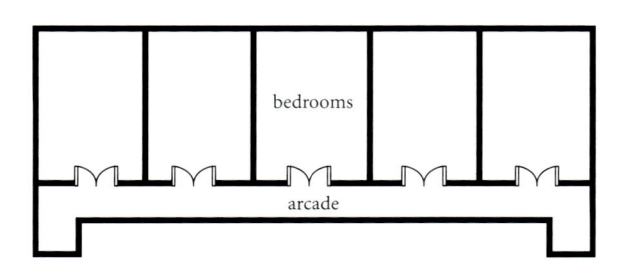

Above:
In a room that was once the family's large library, today there is a large country kitchen. With an impressive and richly decorated brick stove, visitors glimpse the scale necessary to feed a large family but lose any sense of the bookish interests of several generations of the family.

Left:
Used for storage, woven baskets of many types are common in Chinese kitchens.

Below:
On the second floor of the back building, shown in this plan, are five rooms used as bedrooms.

Above:
Dominating this bedroom on the second floor is a heavily ornamented canopy bed, with a red wedding valance, gauze curtains, and cotton comforters, as well as other utilitarian objects such as a washstand, bathing bucket, and chamber pot.

Left:
This platform or couch bed, called a *ta*, provides space for sleeping as well as sitting. With carved arms and three circular slices of marble at back whose shading is meant to mimic mountains and clouds, the bed itself is transformed into an object of art.

An Educator's Residence

A SCHOLAR'S STUDY
Xu Wei's Green Vine Studio, Shaoxing, Zhejiang Province

Tucked into a narrow lane in Shaoxing, an historic canal town on the northern coastal plain in Zhejiang province, is the unpretentious and simply elegant residence-studio of Xu Wei (1521–93), the celebrated, versatile, and eccentric Ming-dynasty literary polymath. Xu himself claimed "calligraphy is my best, followed by poetry, prose, and last painting," even as contemporary scholars in China and abroad still debate this ordering of his talents. As Xu Wei's home and study, the small structure is known today as Qing Teng Shu Wu or "Green Vine Studio" because of one of its natural elements, an old gnarled creeping vine capped with a head of green leaves.

As a calligrapher, Xu's "wild running form" of cursive script is considered rash, unrestrained, and impulsive with much of it not easily readable because of the continuous lines of black ink he drew with his brush. Xu Wei was well known as a playwright while alive. In recent years, increasing attention has been paid to his work, partially because of his play *Mulan*, based on an earlier poem, that told the tale of a woman who disguised herself as a man in order to take her father's place in the army. With computer-enhanced animation, Disney studios in 1998 released the story of *Mulan* as a coming-of-age story in which bravery and intelligence brought honor to her family. Xu Wei would have understood Disney's promotional claim, "The flower that blooms in adversity is the most rare and beautiful of all." His literary fame as poet and dramatist was established well before his expressive style of painting gained attention. Xu Wei's paintings incorporate broad strokes and splashes of ink on paper rather than silk, a style that subsequently influenced others in their expressive renderings of flowers, birds, and plants. Using imagery characteristic of the Jiangnan region in his poetry and painting, Xu's reputation as an artist during his life was rather local but spread widely in the centuries after his death.

Xu's life and work have been compared to that of the post-impressionist Van Gogh. Indeed, his reputation as a man of the arts is complemented by his reputation as a madman with a difficult and tumultuous life. His mother was a concubine who died at the age of fourteen, after which his father's second wife raised him. Much of his life thereafter was filled with torment and suffering. Married at twenty-one, his young wife died just five years later and then within another five years, he retreated to a monastery for less than a year, where he turned his energies to poetry, plays, and essays, all the while preparing to take the provincial-level civil service examinations. Altogether he failed the examinations eight times. He is said to have attempted suicide several times by ingenious but not particularly effective methods: driving a long nail through his ear, hitting his head with a mallet, and smashing his testicles. After killing his third wife, surnamed Zhang, because of his paranoia concerning an alleged affair she had, he was jailed for seven years. He was released at the age of fifty-three when the Wanli emperor ascended the throne and pardoned some criminals. For the last two decades of his life, he was mentally unstable yet was able to develop a unique style of expressive painting. During this period, he enjoyed little financial success and died in poverty at the age of seventy-two. It was only after his death that his talents were fully appreciated.

Xu's dwelling-studio in Shaoxing was a retreat from the world. It includes a comparatively large yet uncomplicated courtyard garden, and a transverse brick building at the back that serves many functions. The courtyard, crossed by a winding stone pebble path, includes within it rather sparse elements: several stone benches, an old stone well, and a variety of leafy vegetation, including a majestic grove of

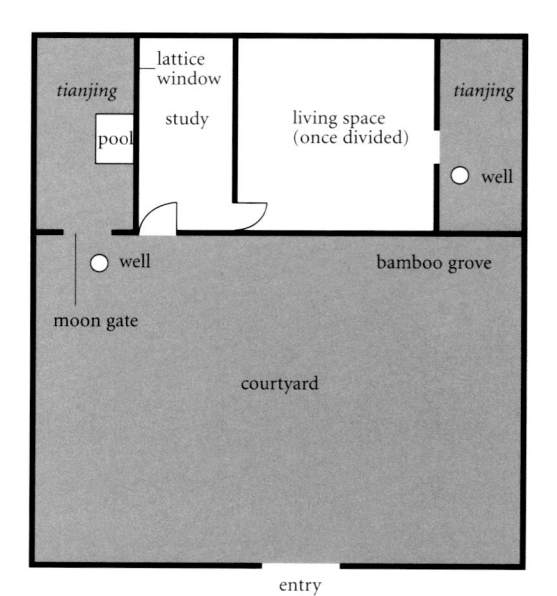

Below:
With a courtyard that encompasses more than half of the area behind the walls, the remaining space is occupied by two skywells embracing the structure itself.

Right:
Looking through the moon gate across the pebbled pavement, one sees first the simple lattice windows of the studio, the stone balustrades around a square pond, which is said to never dry up or overflow, and the green vine along the back wall that gives the residence its name.

天溪永源

spreading bamboo. Behind the bamboo on the wall are three Chinese characters meaning either "At Ease Crag" or "Unrestrained Crag," an ambiguity that may have been intended by the eccentric Xu Wei.

The building itself is divided into two rooms, a small study and a larger room, which together are flanked by a pair of tightly confined skywell-like courtyards on each end. The most important of these small courtyards, viewed and entered through a gaping moon gate from the large courtyard, is enclosed on two sides by white walls and on the fourth by simple lacquered wooden lattice panels. Strikingly unadorned, this open space incorporates three elements: an ancient tree, a pool of water that is said never to dry up or overflow, which itself is framed by a low stone balustrade, as well as signature vegetation in the form of the green vine rising along the back wall from an elevated rocky base.

Adjacent to this natural outdoor composition is a doorway leading directly into Xu Wei's stone-floored study. The study is dominated by a sturdy chair facing a long hardwood work table, on top of which are placed the "Four Treasures of the Scholar's Studio" (*wen fang si bao*): a writing brush, ink stick, ink slab, and paper, together the necessary instruments for calligraphic writing. While working at his desk and looking through the lattice window panels in front of him, Xu Wei could gain inspiration by glimpsing at or focusing on any of the natural elements situated in the skywell composition: the vine, rockery, water, and changing shadows on the walls.

Little is known of how the large room adjacent to his study was used, but it is likely that it once was divided into space for sleeping and living. Today, the room serves as an exhibition hall to display Xu Wei's paintings and writings. Beyond this room is a utilitarian space with a well and reflective walls that was probably once used for the preparation of food as well as for washing and drying clothes.

In many respects, Xu Wei's simple residence-studio is a place of solace, a contemplative retreat for a troubled recluse. Derivative perhaps of Daoist influences, it juxtaposes essential elements of water, earth, rocks, bamboo, and a green vine, all composed in ways he could observe them for inspiration. His literati paraphernalia comprise objects necessary for his intellectual pursuits—long table, chair, and bookcase, each well-proportioned and minimally ornamented—as well as the indispensable "four treasures of the studio." Xu Wei's refined taste is expressed clearly in the essentially minimalist form of his Green Vine Studio, whether in terms of the building's simple structure and ground plan, or its modest gardens, elegant furniture, and direct ornamentation.

Xu Wei's poetry:

> Half of my life so downhearted, already I'm an old man,
> Standing alone in my study, the evening wind moans;
> Bright pearls from beneath my brush can't be sold anywhere,
> So I fling them here, cast them there, amidst the wild vines.

Looking across the courtyard from the walled entry along the lane, the eye is drawn by the slightly winding pathway to the shapes of the moon gate and odd configuration of the doorway into the study. The stone lip of an old well, visible just outside the moon gate, contrasts with the scholar rocks and bamboo grove on the other side of the courtyard.

A Scholar's Study 143

Above:
Both the relatively unadorned and tranquil simplicity of the studio as well as its connections with nature outside are apparent. Sitting or standing at the desk in front of the lattice, Xu Wei gained inspiration from the rocks, vines, and water beyond while watching the changing shadows as they played across the surfaces of the skywell.

Right:
Beyond the interior living space is a second, more utilitarian skywell. Here, using another well, clothes could be washed and then hung to dry, or food preparation, even cooking in summer, could be done.

Left:
On top of the desk are the "Four Treasures of the Scholar's Studio" (*wen fang si bao*): a writing brush, a slender ink stick, a carved ink slab, and paper, together the necessary instruments for calligraphic writing.

A Scholar's Study 145

A MILLIONAIRE'S HOME
Kang Family Manor, Henan Province

Today, it is difficult to appreciate the fact that northern Henan province was once a center of gravity for imperial China, that Luoyang and Kaifeng were important dynastic capitals, and that agriculture and trade brought riches to many families in what the Chinese call Zhongyuan, the fertile Central Plains. Straddling the now rather desolate Yellow River or Huang He, this region once thrived because of a trade network linked to the river system as well as to an old system of roads. Subsequently, the shifting of imperial capitals to the south at Hangzhou and Nanjing and then during the Yuan, Ming, and Qing dynasties to the north at today's Beijing, as well as out-migration of population, brought about the region's relative eclipse as wealth and power moved elsewhere. Today, the region is best known for its railroads, factories, and cotton production, as well as a scattering of prehistoric sites, the Buddhist sculpture at the Longmen Grottoes, Han- and Song-dynasty imperial tombs, and some of the country's oldest Buddhist and Daoist temples that draw visitors to the region. Few are aware that here are vestiges of life lived in the past by some of China's great families in their great estates.

Midway between Luoyang and Kaifeng and to the south of the Yellow River in Gongxian, today called Gongyi, is Kangbaiwan *zhuangyuan*, the Kang family manor. From the late Ming dynasty into the early part of the twentieth century, the Kang family triumphed over the well-known Chinese proverb, "Wealth does not last for more than three generations" (*fu buguo sandai*), by maintaining relative unity for about twelve generations over a period of about 400 years. With little formal division of their family organization or dissipation of family wealth, their productive agriculture and trading empire allowed them to build up a complex estate centered on Gongxian. At its peak, the relatively self-sufficient estate included not only a walled compound for the immediate family and nearby residences for other kin as well as retainers, but also ancestral worship facilities, workshop areas, inns for travelers, stables for riding, pack, and work animals, livestock pens, a brick and tile-making kiln, a military camp, and a granary and stores complex. While only the traces of most of the ancillary structures exist, what does remain of their vast domain is China's largest walled complex of

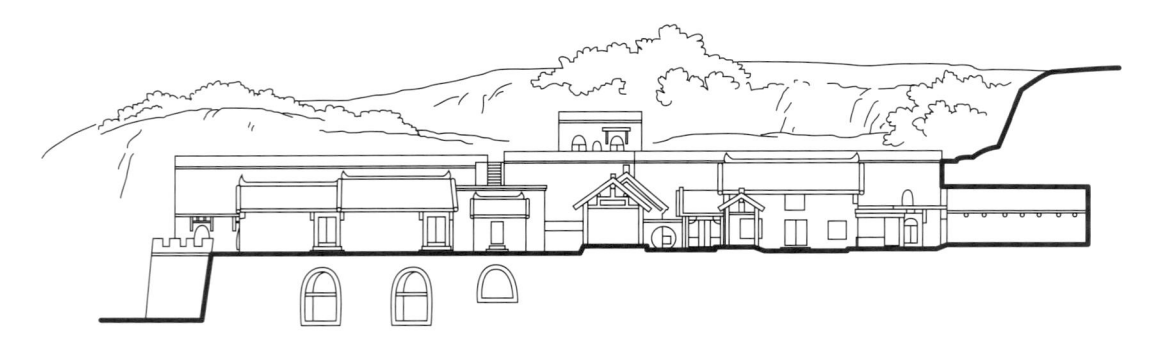

This pair of section views of the Kang family manor highlights the way in which the residential complex has been sculpted into a terrace along a loessial cliff. In addition to interconnected buildings arranged around courtyards, caves were dug into the cliff face to provide important spaces for family activities.

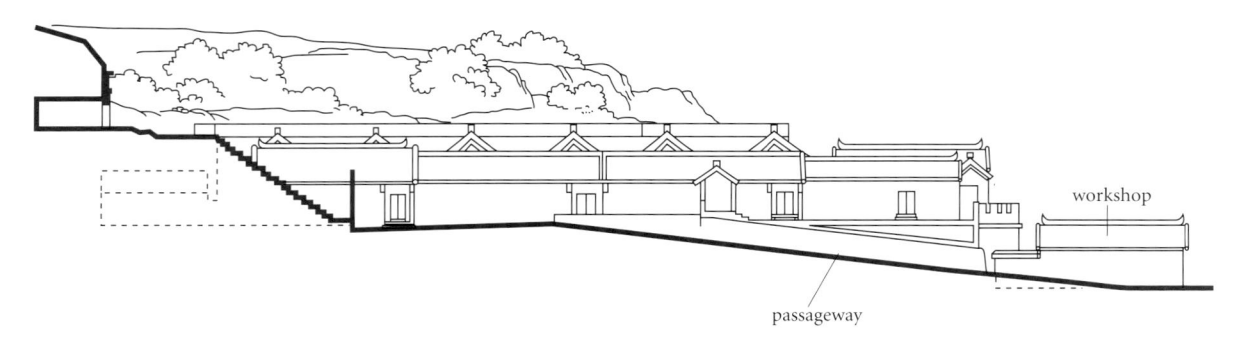

new courtyard | inner courtyard | central courtyard | old courtyard

ancestral halls

inn area | flower garden

livestock pen

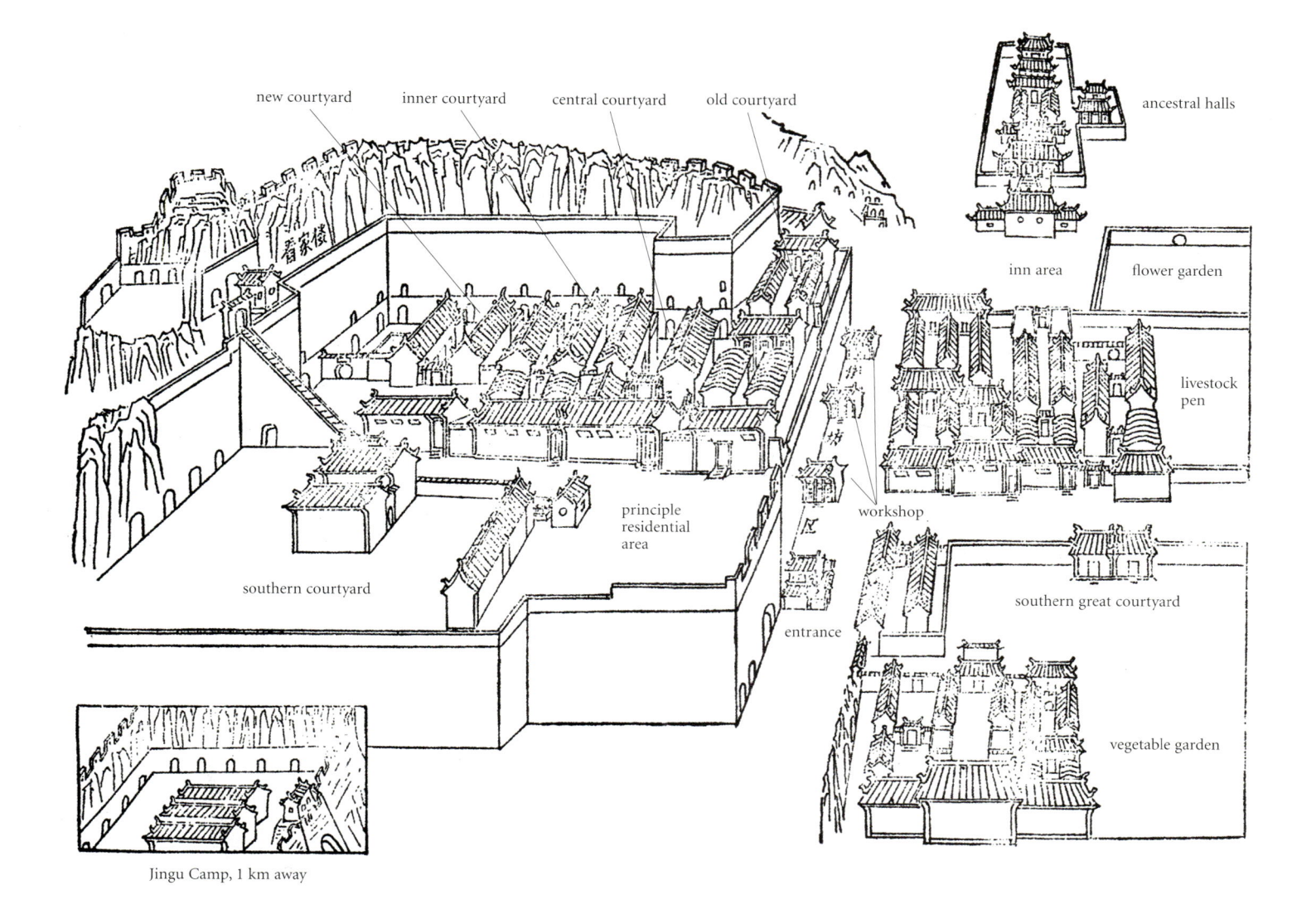

principle residential area | workshop

southern courtyard

entrance

southern great courtyard

vegetable garden

Jingu Camp, 1 km away

Above:
This nineteenth-century drawing not only illustrates a perspective view of the residential portion of the Kang family manor but also shows other parts of the self-sufficient estate, including workshops, inns, stables, livestock pens, a granary, kilns, and a military camp.

Left:
Looking towards the east from high on a nearby ridge, the parallel roofs of adjacent courtyards as well as the sculpted face of the earthen cliff are shown clearly.

A Millionaire's Home 147

Right:
At the top of the inclined passageway leading up into the manor is a carved brick spirit wall featuring the three stellar gods of Good Fortune, Emolument, and Longevity. A detailed view is shown on page 90.

Below:
The outer courtyard of the easternmost residential unit includes a heavily ornamented transitional building structure with a pair of facing side buildings.

148   China's Fine Heritage Houses

cliffside subterranean dwellings called *yaodong*, simulated subterranean structures called *guyao*, and above-ground buildings, all composed around a series of interlinked courtyards. The Kang manor dominates Kangdian village, a community of farmers, many of whom still live in subterranean dwellings, traditional cave dwellings, in the numerous gullies associated with the heavily dissected plateau behind it. It is said that the Empress Dowager Ci Xi visited here on her way back to Beijing from Xian in 1901 after the conclusion of the Boxer Uprising, and it was she, according to legend, who hailed the Kang family as *baiwan*, meaning "millionaires," leading to the place itself being called Kangbaiwan—"Millionaire Kang's."

Spread along the slopes of several loessial terraces above the Yiluo River, the Kang manor complex was begun during the late Ming period, but it was not until 1821 that the 12–15 meter-high crenellated protecting wall was built around an area that came to encompass their grand residential complex. Most construction spanned the period 1828–1909, during the waning century of the Qing dynasty, until it covered some 64,300 square meters. In order to create a sufficiently large, elevated, and level building site 83 meters from north to south and 73 meters wide, much earth was removed from the slopes and used to fill in lower elevations that were banked with massive stone and brickwork. The L-shaped cutting into the loessial soil created flat walls into which *yaodong* were dug into the ridge, supplemented by *guyao*, arcuate cave-like structures, and above-ground buildings, all fashioned around traditional, but narrow, courtyards. A 23.7-meter-long underground arched passageway, lined with bricks and secured with a strong gate, leads from below up a slope into the residential compound. At the top of this ramp is a magnificent baked brick spirit wall with carved images of the three immortals or stellar gods, representing Good Fortune (*fu*), Emolument (*lu*), and Longevity (*shou*), as well as other auspicious imagery.

The main residential area includes five distinct courtyards, aligned parallel to each other with separate gates leading into each courtyard, while smaller gates lead to connecting passageways that pierce the shared party walls between the courtyards. The easternmost, largest, and longest courtyard is called the "old courtyard." Rigidly symmetrical and with a length of nearly 55 meters and width of 14.5 meters, the courtyard sequence includes a main gate, an open courtyard, and an entry structure that leads to a pair of heavily ornamented side buildings and the main structure in the rear. The surviving matriarch of the family occupied this main structure at the beginning of the twentieth century, when the Empress Dowager

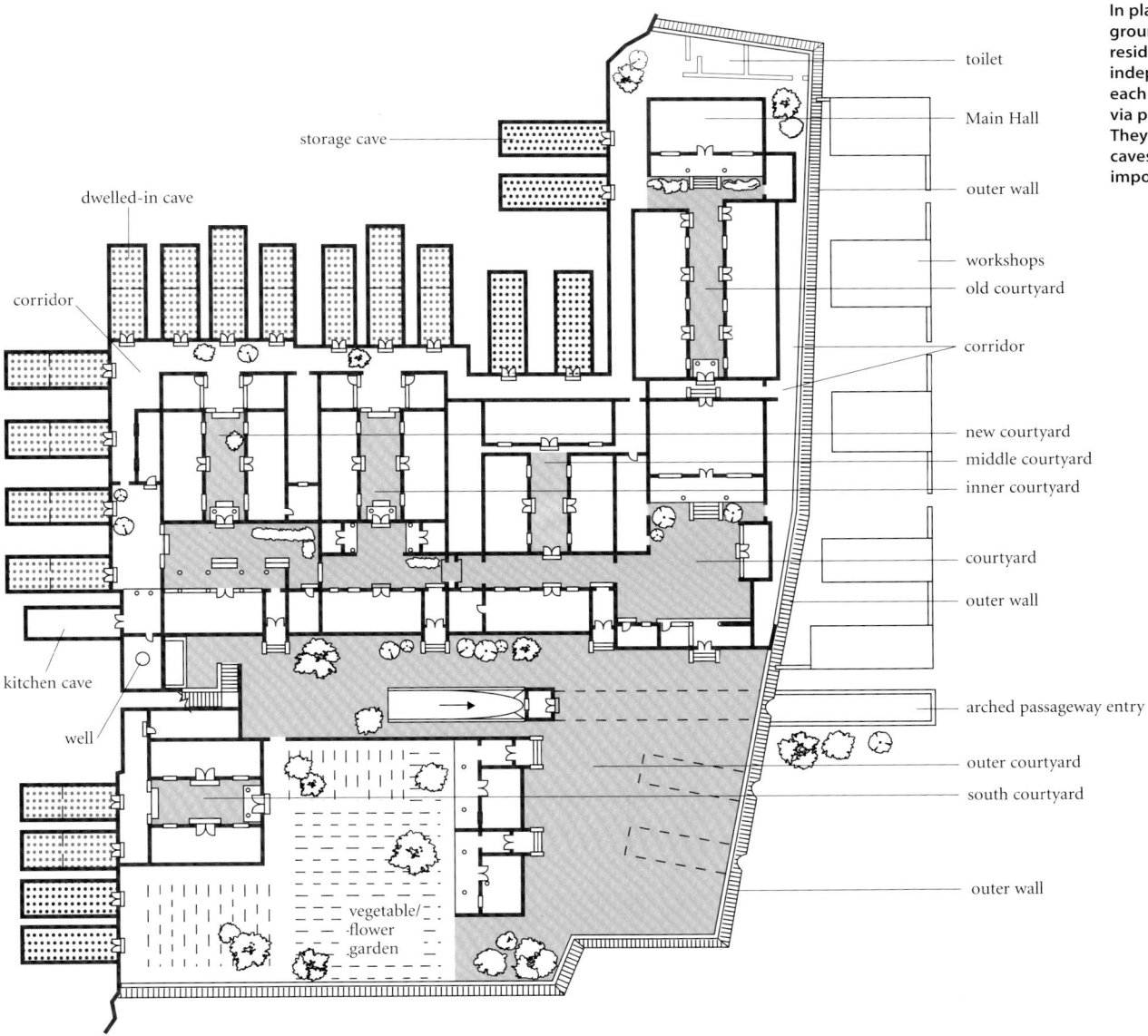

In plan view, the five above-ground multi-courtyard residences are shown as independent entities, with each connected to the others via passageways and gates. They also incorporate deep caves dug into the hillside as important residential spaces.

Left:
Carved on the frame of a bedstead are images of the three Stellar Gods.

Right:
Opposite the matriarch's bedroom and framed by heavy drapes is a sitting room in which to entertain guests.

Above:
Shown here is the bedroom of the Kang family matriarch as it is said to have looked in 1901 when she celebrated her 100th birthday. The view is from her sitting room through her formal Main Hall into her bedroom with its large and elaborate canopy bed.

Right:
This polychrome woodblock print depicts "The Three Living Gods of Wealth," including Kang Baiwan, the lord of the Kang family, who achieved the status of folk god and was said to be worshipped by villagers throughout north China.

visited in 1901. Her longevity, having already celebrated her 100th birthday, and the fact that Kang family members of four other generations still occupied the complex, brought pride to the family in that they had attained the ideal of "five generations living under one roof." Her apartment in the innermost structure included three rooms: a central hall, a sitting room on the east, and a bedroom on the west.

The four other courtyards are less grand than the first one, with each nonetheless having some distinctive feature, and all including underground cave structures as component parts. All of the buildings are made of gray brick with the type of flush gables common on palace architecture in Beijing. Steps, corridors, and gates of many types served as markers of interaction, at once linking as well as separating spatial activities from courtyard to courtyard.

One courtyard has facing side structures set up to show the different spheres of males and females, with martial arts and learning emphasized for boys while domestic talents, like weaving, embroidery, and sewing the focus for girls. In a rear cave is a shrine for "Three Living Gods of Wealth," including Kang Baiwan, folk gods said to be worshipped by villagers throughout north China. The entry to the middle courtyard has a strikingly gnarled tree as

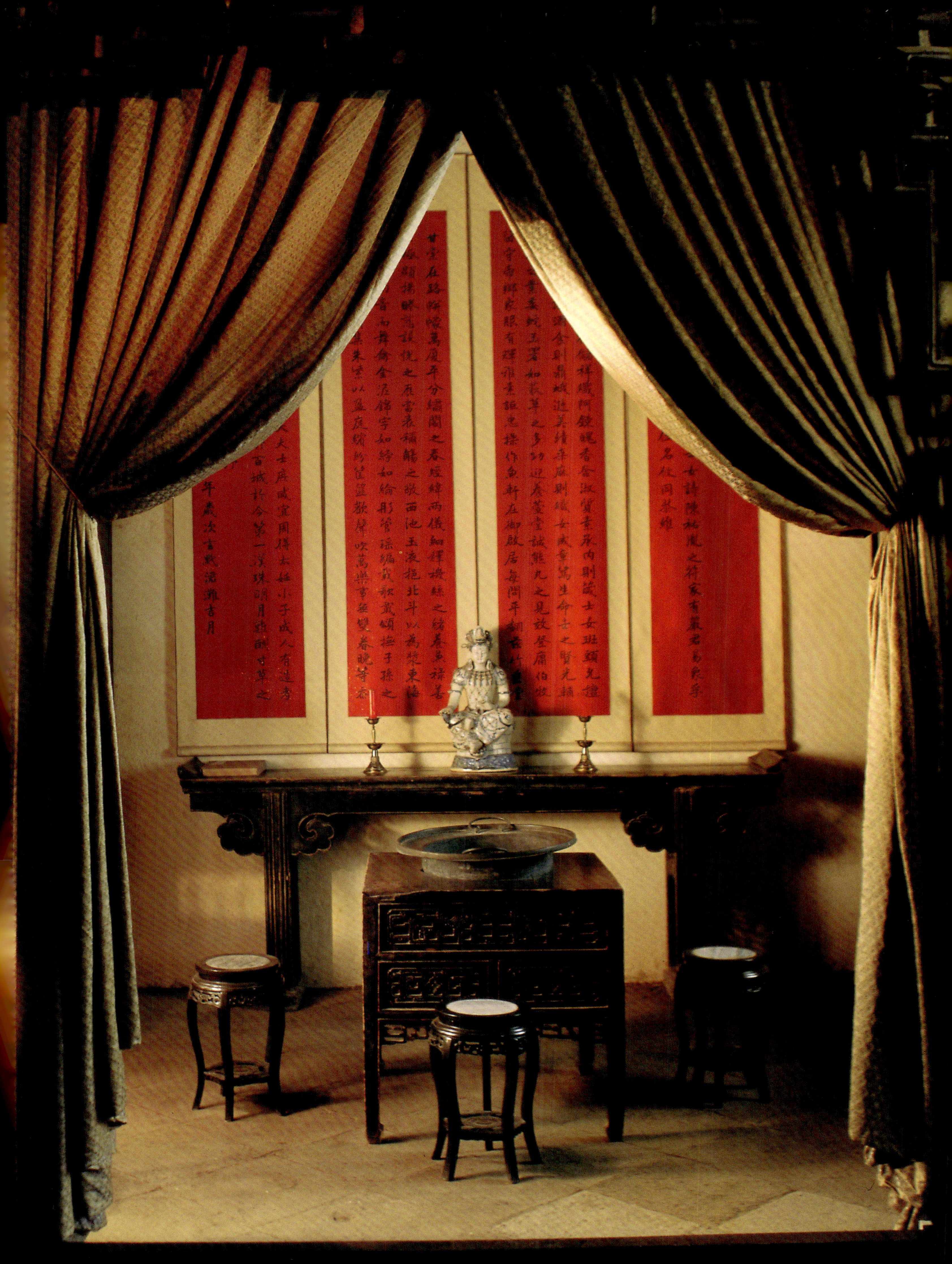

Above:
In the apartment of a young woman of the Kang family, the highly stylized Main Hall is decorated in the style of the late Qing dynasty.

Right:
In one room of the apartment of a young man of the Kang family, books are piled on bookcases and items needed for calligraphy—ink stone, ink stick, brushes, and paper—arrayed on a desk.

152   China's Fine Heritage Houses

well as a horizontal board proclaiming "Capable of Prudence in Following the Way." In the rear corner is a cave divided into two parts, the front section serving as a school for young children and the rear as a pharmacy. Both were the responsibility of the family tutor, who used the *Sanzi jing*, the "Three-Character Classic," as a principal text for rote learning and inculcating children with moral tales. Children sat around the low table to recite from texts and memory as well as to practice calligraphy. Two lines in the *Sanzi jing* express clearly the expectation that teachers were to be strict: "To teach without severity is a fault in the teacher."

By the early years of the second decade of the twentieth century, just as China itself devolved into warlordism, the Kang family's finances declined dramatically even as their power also weakened. In time, a reputation as exploiting landlords, rather than enterprising entrepreneurs, came to characterize them. After 1949, during Land Reform, all of their land was confiscated and distributed to peasants, and some 3000 objects owned by the family were seized and locked in warehouses. In 1968, during the height of the Cultural Revolution, three "evil landlords"—Liu Wencai from near Chengdu in Sichuan, Mou Erhei from near Yantai in Shandong, and Kang Yingkui in Gongxian, Henan—became the focus of a political campaign highlighting their oppression of the masses. An unintended consequence was that each of their large estates came to be preserved as sites for mass education about the evils of landlords, rather than being destroyed like so many other fine residences. Throughout the 1990s, efforts were made to restore the complex, and in 2001 the Kang family manor was granted national protection as an historic site. The fact that old family furniture could be taken from where it had been safely stored and the residential complex had suffered only minimal destruction meant that restoration has been relatively quick and straightforward.

Below:

This richly decorated bedroom used by a young girl includes an elaborate alcove bed, a dressing table, storage cabinets, small decorative objects, and a washstand. Pride of place is given to a frame holding the daughter's embroidery. It was on frames of this sort that a young girl would ply the needle as she prepared embroidered pillowcases, clothing, wall and bed hangings, and slippers, among many other articles that became part of her dowry.

A Millionaire's Home 153

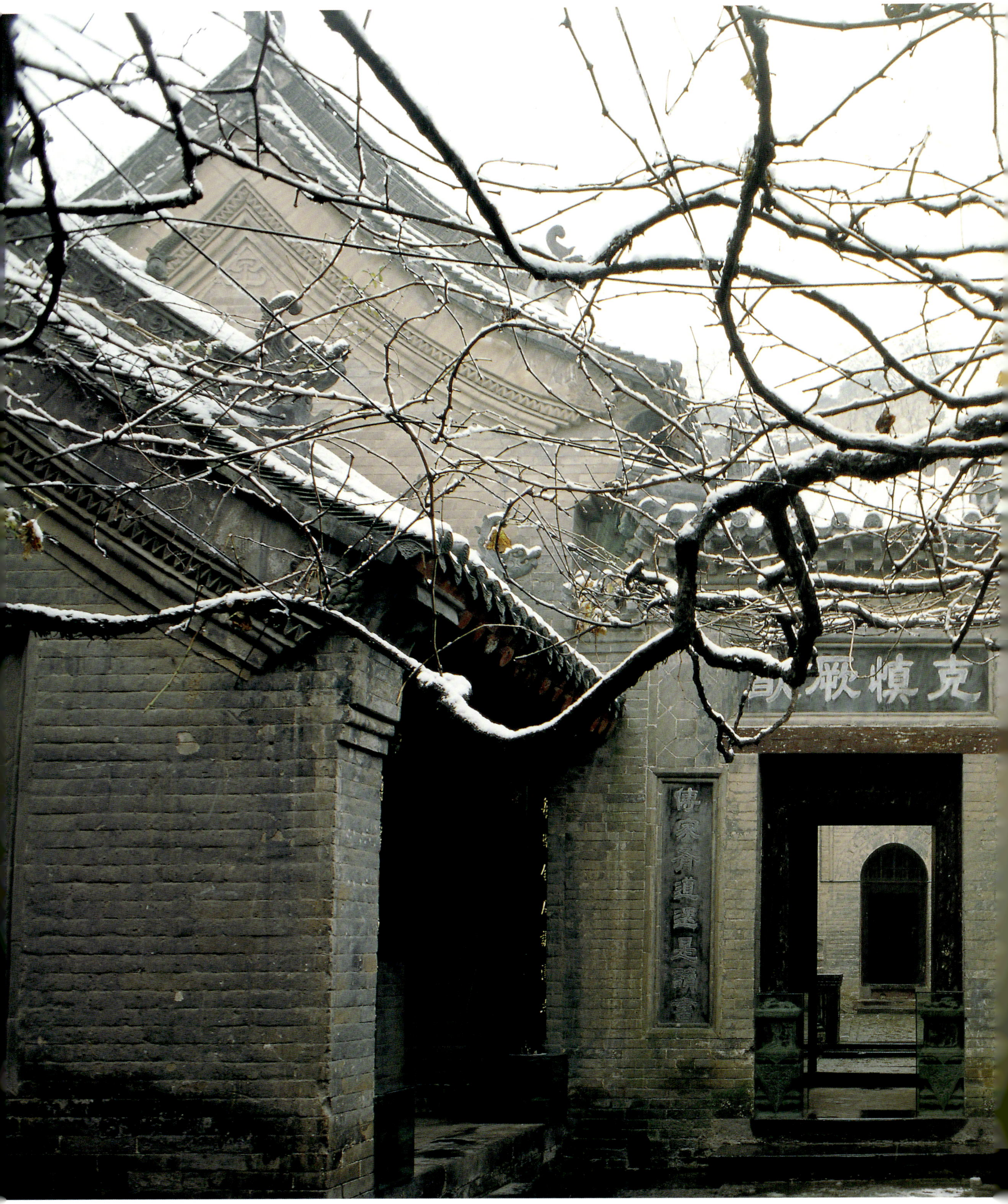

Above:
Made of gray bricks, the flush gables found on each building are similar to those commonly seen on palace architecture in Beijing.

Left:
Framed by a conspicuously gnarled tree, the entry to the middle courtyard has above it a horizontal board declaring "Capable of Prudence in Following the Way."

A Millionaire's Home 155

A THREE-STORY MING DYNASTY HOUSE
Wang Ganchen's "Swallow's Wing Hall," Chengkan, Anhui Province

Tucked within the abundant hills and soaring mountains of southern Anhui province are hundreds of old villages, some of which now boast of possessing China's oldest dwellings, an architectural heritage that has remained relatively unknown until recent times. For example, Chengkan village in Shexian county traces a settlement history that reaches to the Tang dynasty (618–906) and lays claim to being a veritable museum of old dwellings. Indeed, Chengkan is a treasury of rather simple, yet sometimes stunning, architecture with more than 200 structures—houses, ancestral halls, memorial arches, pavilions, and bridges—from the Qing period (1644–1911), as well as about twenty from the Ming dynasty (1368–1644), and at least one from the Yuan period (1279–1368).

Over time, Chengkan came to be known as the village with "three streets and ninety-nine lanes," a tight checkerboard settlement with its back and sides embraced by overlapping ranges of sinuous mountains and its front facing east towards the meandering Zhongchuan Stream. This topographic configuration shelters the village from cold winter winds blowing from the northwest and facilitates good drainage, while providing an orderly arrangement that lays open individual dwellings to prevailing winds and the penetrating warmth of winter sun. Villagers acknowledge the superior site and auspicious village location as fully in accord with optimal *fengshui* elements in which "nine dragons play with the pearl." Like other villages, the layout of Chengkan developed organically over time with unique and complex features relating to local circumstances.

Seemingly a remote and isolated village in an idyllic spot, Chengkan's wealth arose nonetheless from its connections via a prolific system of mountain fed tributaries to the historically significant Xin'an River, which itself then provided access to the Song-dynasty capital of Hangzhou and then on to other of China's great metropolitan centers in the Jiangnan region comprising the lower portions of the Yangzi River. Long-distance trade, first in timber, tea, lacquer, and especially salt, then later including the "four treasures of the scholar's studio"—paper, writing brushes, ink sticks, and ink slabs used by calligraphers—came to represent significant commercial

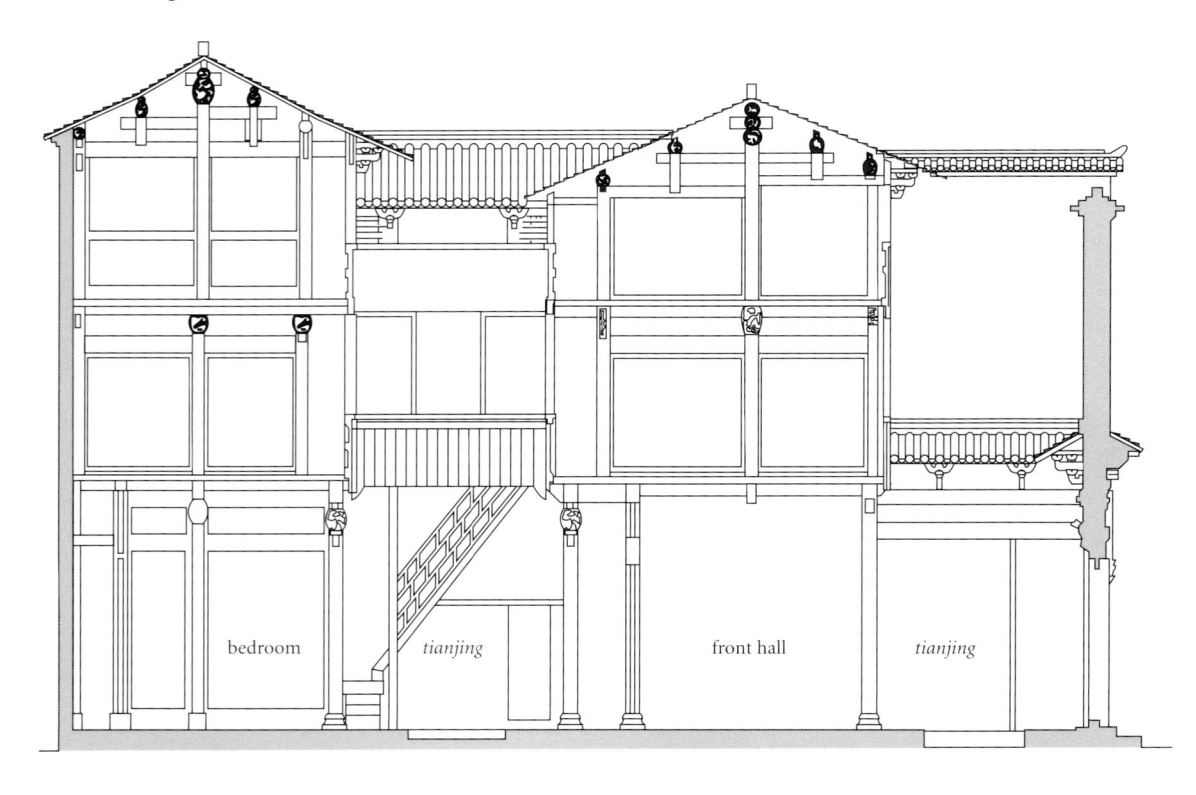

This section view exposes the columns needed to support the three-story structure as well as suggests the commodious scale of a relatively compact dwelling.

bedroom　　*tianjing*　　front hall　　*tianjing*

Above:
View across the fields of the southern portion of Chengkan village, 1872.

Far left:
Tucked within a narrow stone-slab lane and surrounded by high brick walls, the imposing doorway into Yan Yi Tang is almost hidden.

Left:
It is not clear whether this rear doorway was an original part of the house or a later addition.

A Three-Story Ming Dynasty House 157

Above:
The façades of Wu Fang Ting, a linked grouping of three sixteenth-century three-story residences that are currently undergoing restoration. Painting by Robert Powell.

Left:
Among the buildings in Chengkan village is the magnificent Baolun Ge, an ancestral hall built between 1517 and 1611 for the Luo clan.

158 China's Fine Heritage Houses

resources for a distinctive and much-heralded group called Huizhou merchants. As *keshang* or "traveling merchants," they amassed profits from trade and pawnshops, sometimes even purchasing official titles that made it possible to improve their social status as merely rich merchants by becoming gentry-literati. Huizhou merchants lived among the literati in the wealthy cities of the fertile lower Yangzi valley, where they came to appreciate fine homes, collecting art, and generally refined aspects of culture.

As sojourners in the world outside their mountain redoubts, especially during the Ming dynasty, Huizhou merchants then brought cosmopolitan values and patterns back to their tranquil rural villages where they established what is now regarded as Huizhou culture, a refined regional variant of Chinese culture. The philanthropy of wealthy merchants led to the creation of countless schools attended by promising youth in villages and towns. In time, Huizhou came to be among the regions with the greatest numbers of successful candidates passing the rigorous civil service examinations, the veneration of which is noted in villages even today. While facilities such as schools, bridges, roads, and shrines benefited from the largesse of Huizhou merchants, it was the building of their own residences that epitomizes the enriched life for the families they left behind and their own retirement sanctuaries later in old age.

Among the dwellings in Chengkan village that exemplify Huizhou culture is Yan Yi Tang or "Swallow's Wing Hall," a compact three-story residence built during the middle period of the Ming dynasty. While most of the old houses in Chengkan are associated with the influential Luo lineage, Yan Yi Tang is said to have been the residence of Wang Ganchen, about whom there is little information. When compared with garden-residences in the lower Yangzi region or the sprawling manor complexes of northern China, Huizhou dwellings like Yan Yi Tang are small in terms of the land area they occupy but still large in total floor area. Built compactly of brick, these seemingly condensed structures are often only three bays wide. Yet, because most of the residences are multistoried, with some reaching three stories, they are nonetheless commodious. Throughout Huizhou, the high brick perimeter walls are coated with white plaster and capped with contrasting gables called "horses' head" walls, which sometimes are stepped at different elevations and serve as firewalls. It is common to attribute the multistoried compact form to the limitations set by rugged terrain, but it is important to recall that Huizhou was relatively underpopulated in the past even as attention was always paid to reducing the amount of arable land

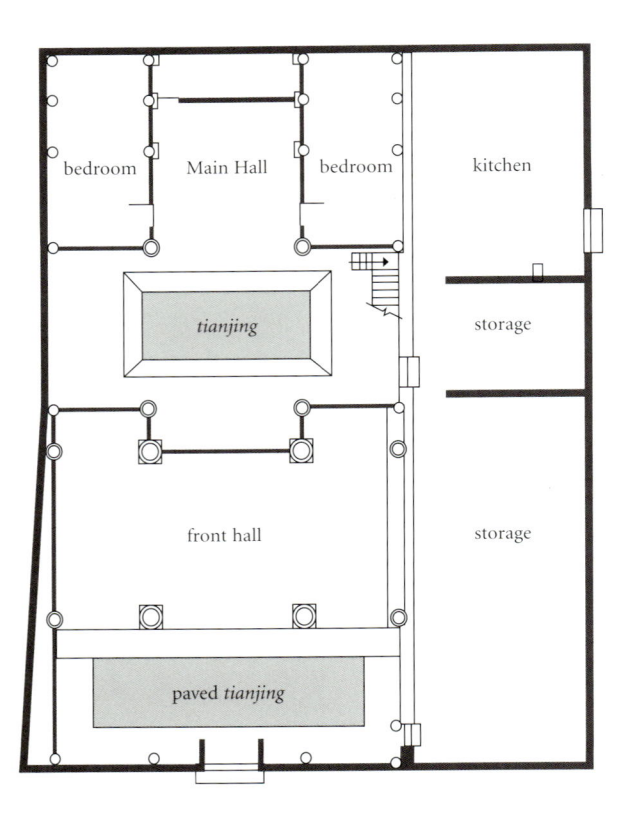

This plan view shows Yan Yi Tang to be three bays in width with a sequence involving a skywell (*tianjing*), Main Hall, skywell, and living quarters. An adjacent independent structure contained a kitchen and storage space.

used for building. The high walls and compact shape no doubt reflect as well a need and preference for security and privacy of the family members—women, children, and the elderly—who were left alone by their sojourning husbands and elder brothers.

Bounded on two sides by very narrow stone lanes, the white walls confining Yan Yi Tang soar dramatically above village pedestrians. Its main entry faces east into a tightly constricted lane to the degree that it is not possible to appreciate fully the intricacy of the brick carvings constituting the *menzhao*, the projecting "canopy" that defines it. The heavy leaves of the entrance itself are made of 4.5-centimeter-thick stone encased with metal sheets secured with protruding metal studs. On the upper floors of the south and west walls, a similar form is used with baked brick instead of stone to create sliding panels for several window portals on the south wall.

The overall floor plan of the house, covering a compact ground area of only 312 square meters, is at once dense and open with numerous confined rooms and interconnected open spaces. An interesting component of what appears at first glance to be a regular shape is that the house is, in fact, not rigidly rectangular. With a depth of 23.3 meters, the width of the front is 14.3 meters and the rear 13.7 meters, a deviation from square along the south wall that was probably completed to meet an unknown requirement related to improving *fengshui*.

The dwelling plan is punctuated with a pair of skywells or *tianjing*, relatively narrow rectangular voids that open the interior at all three levels to light, air, and rain. For the most part, verticality rather than horizontality is emphasized with *tianjing*. From the front doorway and across a slender verandah, that

Right:
View of the Main Hall through the heavy leaves of the entry door panels. The panels are sheathed with thick stone encased within metal sheets which are secured with protruding metal studs.

Far left:
From the Main Hall looking towards the entry, the space is brightened by light brought in through the rectangular skywell just inside the door.

Left:
Viewed from below and looking up to the sky above, it can be seen clearly that the inner skywell is broader in the living area on the first floor and then narrows as it moves upward. On the left is the door to a bedroom, adjacent to which are the steep stairs to the floors above. To the right is the narrow passageway to the front hall. With lattice windows along the upstairs corridor thrown open, the second floor is the airiest portion of the dwelling.

风递塘杨柳沁塘
雨轻梨叶花院音

玉树交联阆苑香
蟠桃已结瑶池露

Left:
Looking up from a position just inside the main entry, the atrium-like skywell leads light and air into the upper two stories of the central structure.

Below:
In each corner of the rear skywell is a small, rather dark bedroom enclosed with wooden panels and carved lattice windows. The stone and wooden stairs lead to the upper floors.

is barely noticeable, a visitor encounters the first *tianjing*, which then leads to a nearly nine-meter-wide central portion of the front hall. Here, in the front hall is a formal assemblage of tables, chairs, paintings, and calligraphy. Looking up from the skywell, the eye is drawn to full-length walls of lattice windows used to regulate the ambient air entering the rooms above. Adjacent to the three-story residence is a single-story utility structure with entrances into the residence, in addition to an external side entrance to a side lane.

Behind and to the side of the altar table in the front hall are doors leading to the back *tianjing*, which abuts a constrained Main Hall set between a pair of flanking narrow bedrooms, with adjacent steep stairs to the upper floors. Since the rear *tianjing* is broader than the one in front, it has the feel of an actual courtyard, an activity area where children played and women worked. Although today each of the *tianjing* is bare and empty of the daily and ritual life that once animated the spaces, it is likely that both were the locations for potted plants and vats holding water, perhaps even pools of fish. Large vats of water provided a means not only to collect and store rainfall for domestic use, but served as a reservoir in case of fire. The two back bedrooms, although narrow, are raised above the adjacent *tianjing* and hall and each is taller than the upstairs bedrooms. Older family members who might have had difficulty navigating the steep stairwells probably occupied the two first-floor bedrooms while younger women and children slept upstairs. The lattice windows that frame the two ground-floor bedrooms are the most elaborate ones in the residence. Each bedroom was crowded with an enclosed bed, chest, table, chair, and washstand. Looking up through the second

Along the corridor gallery that surrounds the second story, lattice window panels, less ornate than those on the first floor, can be adjusted to catch the breeze that enters through the opening above.

Far left:
Detail of a stone-encased window opening through the outer wall of an upstairs room.

Left:
Since the window opens towards the south, at least a narrow shaft of light comes into the room during most of the day.

tianjing, it is apparent that the opening to the sky was designed to be significantly smaller than the base of the *tianjing*, which made it possible to use the open space even during heavy downpours.

The second and third stories provided space for bedrooms and storage, with an open "hall" in the center of the back portion. Facing the same direction as the two halls downstairs and also in a central position, this open room functioned as a convenient place for women in the family to worship various deities.

Upstairs rooms on the second and third floors are both ringed by a wooden plank gallery flanked all around with swinging lattice window panels, the ones on the second floor being taller than those on the third floor. The lattice panels upstairs in Yan Yi Tang, unlike those on the ground floor, lack decorative features and are essentially formed of right-angle-crossing wooden strips. Although moving chests, dried grain, and other items up the narrow stairways was difficult, it was necessary to use upstairs for storage, not only because space on the ground was at a premium but upstairs was drier and more secure. Storage rooms contained heavy chests, wardrobes, and built-in cabinets.

From the third level, the intersecting layers of clay roof tiles outside are obvious. Each of the four roof slopes surrounding the *tianjing* leads water into the skywell where it falls to the ground, in the process affirming the local *fengshui* maxim *si shui gui tang* or "the four waters return to the hall." Like a tall container of water without holes, the house then expresses metaphorically that wealth will accumulate in the residence and not be dissipated by flowing outward.

The interior of Yan Yi Tang is flush with structural and ornamental wood, timber of many types being among the raw materials most in abundance in the surrounding hills. Unlike the wooden members found in later Qing-dynasty dwellings, as in Cheng Zhi Tang in Hongcun, those of Ming dwellings are relatively plain, that is, they have far fewer elaborate carvings. All of the interior rooms and the roof itself rely on a trabeated wooden framework structure to give them shape. As is common with Chinese architecture of many types, interior wooden structural elements are for the most part not concealed. Indeed, placing horizontal members and supporting brackets at locations in which they are apparent brings deliberate attention to the multiplicity of wooden structural parts of the framework supporting the floors and roof above. Moreover, non-structural carpentry,

Said to have been built during the Yuan dynasty (1279–1368), this dwelling continues to be used as a barn. The outline of an earlier entrance is still apparent on the wall.

Right:
Detail of a metal door hasp.

Far right:
At the juncture of two sloping angles of the roof, the ornamented tiles lead water into the skywell below.

Below left:
The bolt that secures the door leading to the kitchen, an area that is no longer accessible.

Below right:
Pairs of brass or iron door pulls, sometimes serving also as door knockers, are commonly attached to the leaves of an entryway. This doorway also includes a hasp and lockset. Exterior locks were not common in the past since security was provided by having someone always at home.

Bottom:
Access to the Yuan structure is now through a doorway on the opposite side of that shown in the adjacent view.

which resembles that of furniture making, has embellished the interior of Yan Yi Tang with cantilevered balconies framed by simple wooden panels on the lower register and tall mullioned lattice swivel "windows" above.

In addition to a bounty of restored dwellings and numerous dilapidated houses waiting to be renovated, Chengkan village contains several outstanding ancestral halls, pavilions, and bridges. Baolun Ge ("Pavilion of Precious Encomiums") and Changchun She ("Studio of Everlasting Spring") are Chengkan's architectural gems, extraordinary in scale and ornamentation as well as being faithfully restored. Baolun Ge is a mega-structure nine bays wide built between 1517 and 1611, just some six meters narrower than the throne hall in Beijing's Forbidden City. It venerates Luo Dongshu who lived during the Yuan dynasty in the fourteenth century, celebrating the numerous encomiums or formal expressions of praise offered him by emperors over the centuries. Changchun She, built as a ceremonial hall to worship the Earth God, has a foundation that is dated to the Song dynasty (960–1279), with much of the interior dating to the sixteenth century.

The houses and ancestral halls found in Chengkan, just as with Yan Yi Tang, represent a Huizhou heritage in which high levels of affluence, craftsmanship, and literacy enriched each other. It is in Chengkan that the noted New York Asian art dealer and collector Robert H. Ellsworth, who first visited the village in 1991 after it suffered from flood, began to contribute so much personally and with friends through the Hong Kong-based China Heritage Arts Foundation (CHAF) to improve preservation of old structures. Among the projects restored to a high international standard by CHAF are Baolun Ge and Changchun She. Wu Fang Ting, a linked grouping of three sixteenth-century three-story residences, is now undergoing restoration. Sadly, the reputed Yuan-dynasty dwelling is still being used as a barn, as it has for decades. Moreover, even here in a village where there is a long history of care of old structures and substantial investment in preservation efforts, the number of truly old dwellings from the Ming dynasty declined from twenty-seven in 1988 to about twenty in 2000 because of collapse, fire, and, in several cases, movement to other locations.

A MERCHANT'S RESIDENCE
Wang Dinggui's "Hall of Inheriting Ambition," Anhui Province

Cheng Zhi Tang or "Hall of Inheriting Ambition," built for the salt merchant Wang Dinggui in 1855 in Hongcun village, Anhui, is among the outstanding extant examples of multistoried residences of prosperous merchants of the Qing dynasty. Like other Huizhou merchants, Wang traveled widely, living in some of China's major urban areas. His family, meanwhile, was comfortably housed in the quieter environs of a picturesque village set amidst some of China's most beautiful and serene landscapes, which are dominated by Huangshan, the legendary "Yellow Mountains." While several centuries younger than Yan Yi Tang in Chengkan village, Cheng Zhi Tang represents a fine, yet different, example of Huizhou domestic architecture in a similar village landscape.

Cheng Zhi Tang is situated along a winding slabstone surfaced lane, paralleled by a shallow narrow channel bringing fresh water into the heart of Hongcun village. High fortress-like outer walls without windows disguise the scale and magnificence of the dwelling inside, even as the entryway hints to the discerning viewer that Cheng Zhi Tang is likely to be grander than equally disguised nearby dwellings.

Beyond the side gateway along the lane, which faces an auspicious southwest direction, is a long rectangular forecourt running east to west that leads both to the impressive south-facing main entry to the house as well as a smaller side access doorway. At a dramatic scale that is meant to impress, appearing indeed to overwhelm the doorway, is a carved brick and stone *menzhao*, a projecting "canopy" or "hood," that has more of an ornamental than a utilitarian purpose since it offers only limited protection from pouring rain. Although seeming to have been constructed of wooden timbers, the *menzhao* structure is actually assembled of richly carved brick and stone to simulate wood. The doorway itself is inserted into the wall in a shape said to mimic the Chinese character *ba*, meaning "eight." It is not clear whether there is any inherent meaning to this *ba* configuration, although it is possible that its creation was related to the eight trigrams protective amulet that is often used on the front of dwellings.

Covering a ground plan of about 2100 square meters, the sumptuous building complex includes seven interconnected structures with some sixty *jian*, interior and exterior spaces defined by the placement of four columns. In addition to several grand reception and ceremonial halls, bedrooms, guest rooms, kitchen, studies, storage areas, as well as arcades and vestibules, nine open spaces called *tianjing* of various sizes—at least one of which is large enough to be considered an actual courtyard—and a large garden are folded into the walls of the dwelling.

Tianjing or "skywells" are much more than voids, open spaces that are bounded by constructed spaces. Placed within the two-story building structures at predetermined locations, each *tianjing* serves as an elongated two-story vertical shaft, usually with a shallow indented catchment area in which to collect rainwater as well as to drain any surplus water outside the dwelling. In addition to providing light, ventilation, and water to adjacent enclosed spaces, each *tianjing* also acts as an activity hub, a place for privacy or gathering when the weather permits. The proliferation of them within Cheng Zhi Tang multiplies the variety of possible uses.

Most of the ground-floor rooms within Cheng Zhi Tang served public and service functions for the family, with rear areas reserved especially for women

Left:
Paved with cut stone slabs, the narrow and twisting lanes of Hongcun village present continually changing glimpses of white walls and dark tile copings.

Right:
Just inside the small gate from the narrow village lane, a visitor first sees an expansive walled space with a fine example of an imposing entryway that leads into the Wang dwelling.

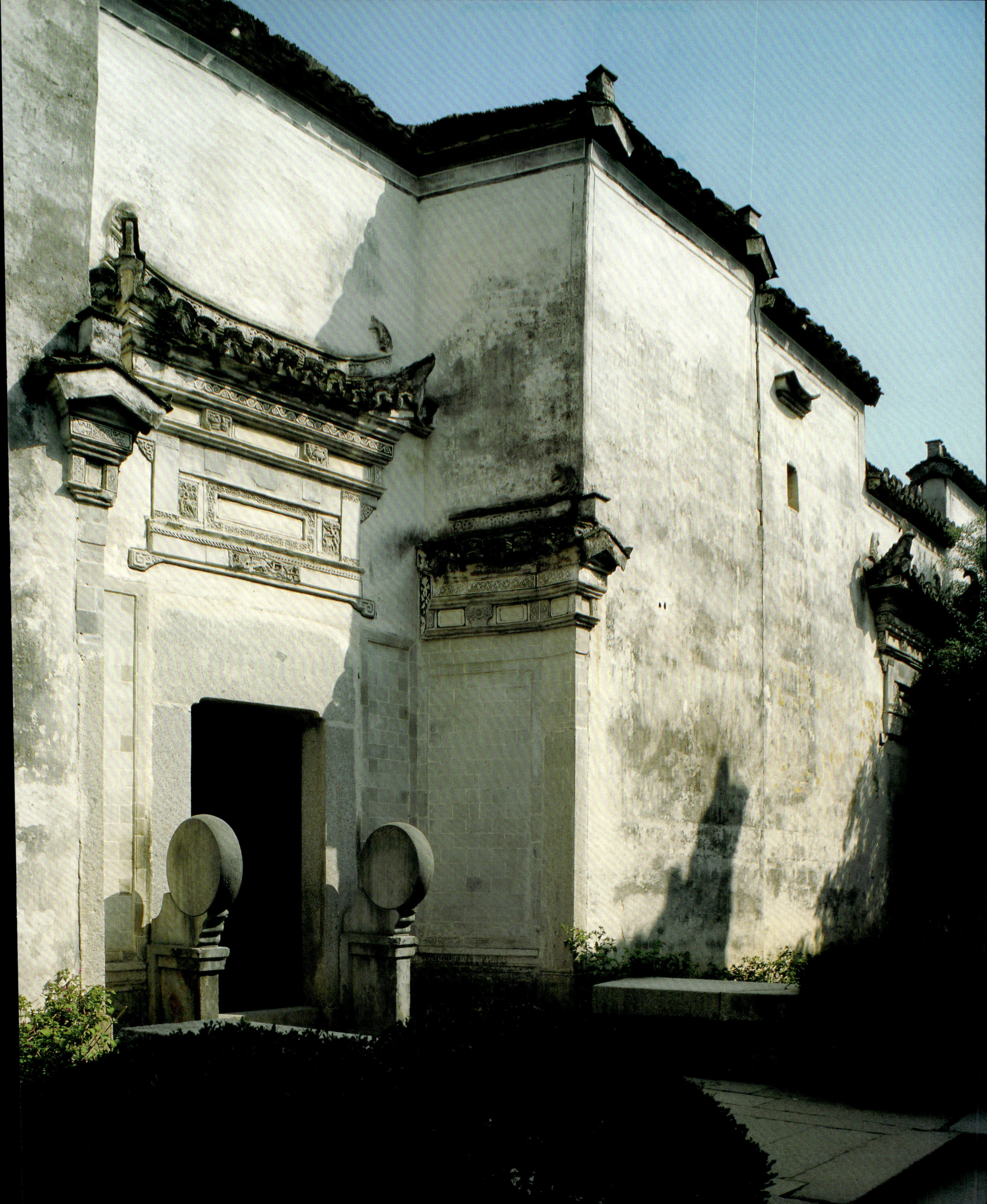

and children. Tucked into an odd-shaped corner off the first large courtyard, an area used to store sedan chairs and serve as an open corridor to other interior spaces, is an exquisite triangular "fish pond room" (*yu tang ting* or *guan yu ting*) adjacent to an exterior wall that is fed by water flowing from the outside channel of fresh water that runs constantly. Here, women and men of the family could retreat in order to find serenity and calmness amidst the activity of their large home. Overlooking the small pond is a wooden *meiren kao* or overhanging bench with a gooseneck-shaped balustrade that provides a comfortable seating area to idle away one's time.

Accessed by steep wooden stairways, the upper story served as the preferred living space in that it was better ventilated and less prone to high humidity levels than the lower level. Here, the principal bedrooms were arranged around a large common room built above the main reception hall on the ground floor. Throughout the dwelling, passageways skirt the Main Halls so that daily life could go on without infringing on formal spaces.

Like other Qing-dynasty period Huizhou-style houses, which have little exterior ornamentation, the interior of Cheng Zhi Tang is profusely ornamented with wood, stone, and brick carvings as well as couplets written on hanging scrolls, paintings, and poetic calligraphy. Especially noteworthy are the woodcarvings found on the crossbeams of the Main Hall, carved stone supports for wooden columns, as well as carved lattice windows and panels. Throughout the house are skillfully crafted partition doors and windows, which control the flow of air and light into enclosed spaces. Most are composed of three parts: an upper portion of transparent lattice, a middle crossboard, often with intricate carving with narrative subject matter, and a lower vertical panel, which is carved in low relief. When circumstances

Above:
At the heart of Hongcun, the Crescent Pond provides not only a visual delight as it mirrors the surrounding buildings but also serves as a ready source of water for the daily needs of neighbors and as a convenient emergency supply of water in the event of fire.

Below:
This section view of Cheng Zhi Tang reveals the expansive depth of the structure, none of which is apparent since the dwelling is hidden behind high walls along a narrow lane.

| outside walled courtyard | courtyard | *tianjing* | Main Hall | *tianjing* | back hall |

A Merchant's Residence

Ground Floor

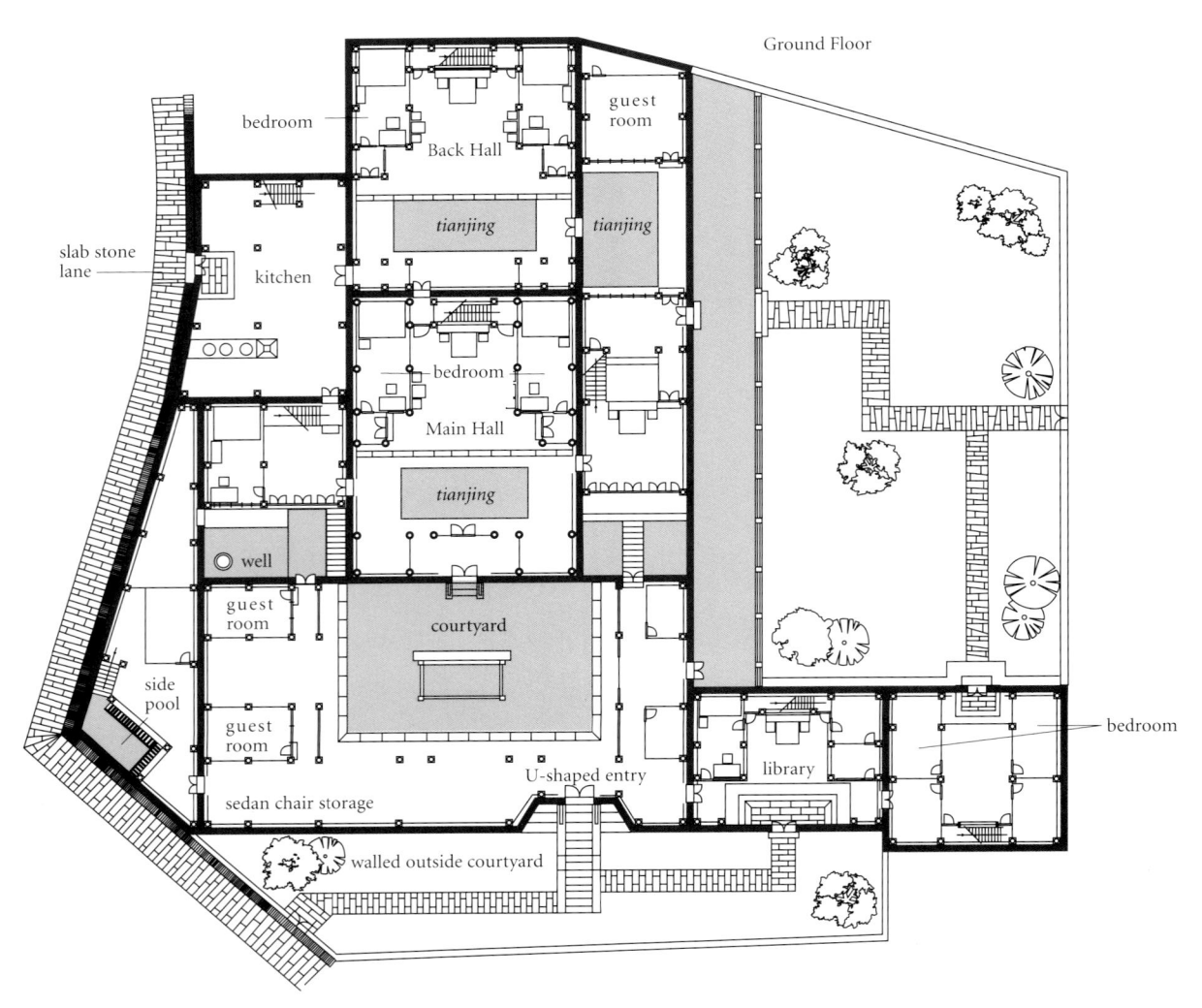

Left:
This first-floor plan shows how the shape of the dwelling was adjusted to the site, including adding a triangular-shaped open space with a pool of water. Significant attention was paid to the juxtaposition of open and enclosed spaces.

Below:
Viewed from above, this plan shows that the second-floor rooms are found only on the central and rear sections of the residence.

Upper Story

Left:
In Cheng Zhi Tang, as with other Hongcun dwellings, small skywells sometimes include a pool of water that is connected to the drainage system outside. With an opening to the sky, white walls, and wooden benches, the space provides a bright and airy area for relaxation and contemplation.

Below:
Inserted into a wall, this ornamented carved stone screen provides delight to the eyes as well as ventilation into an adjacent interior room.

Bottom:
Called a "fish pond room" or "looking at fish room," the pool is fed by water flowing from an outside channel. The wooden *meiren kao* or overhanging bench has a gooseneck-shaped balustrade that provides a comfortable seating area, a place of retreat, especially for women.

require, wooden doors can be removed in order to integrate the interior and exterior spaces.

In the rear *tianjing*, adjacent to what is called the Upper or Back Hall where ancestors were worshipped and elder members of the family lived, celebratory and didactic ornamentation is especially rich. Here, each of the stone bases supporting a wooden column has a *shou* or longevity character carved on it. If one looks up at the long wooden beams that stretch between a pair of columns, the eye catches several intricately carved festive tableaux. One called "Nine Generations Sharing the Hall Together" tells the story of Zhang Gongyi, a Tang-dynasty minister, who had been asked by Emperor Gaozong how family members from nine generations could manage to live peacefully under one roof. Zhang responded by presenting the emperor with a scroll with a hundred different forms of the Chinese character *ren*. *Ren*, meaning "forbearance," includes as well the notions of patience, tolerance, and self-control, especially in not responding to provocation. Another well-known tale is that of "Guo Ziyi Centenary Birthday Banquet," an occasion of joy and friendship. Guo,

A Merchant's Residence   171

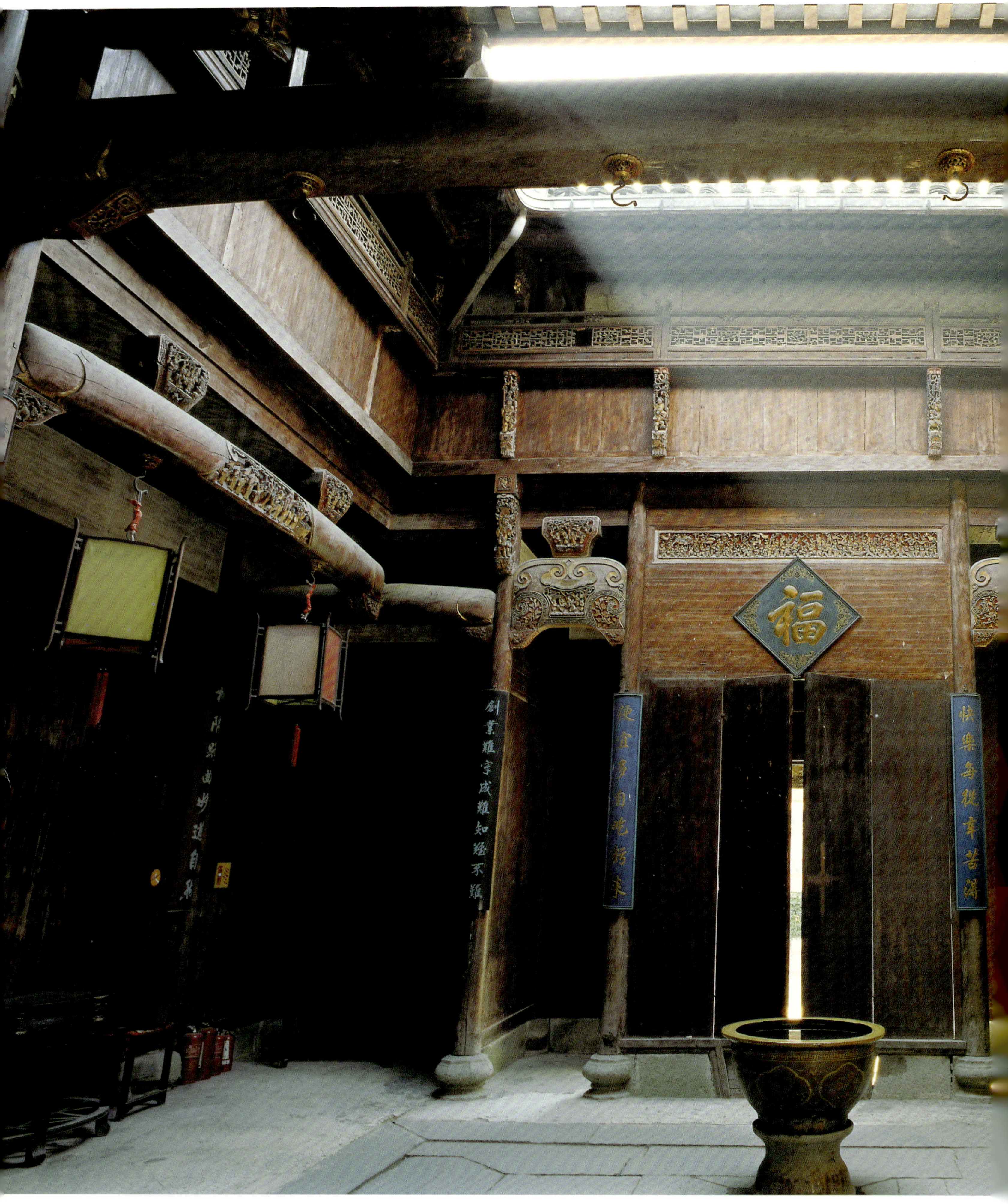

創業難守成難知難不難
福
便宜多自吃虧來
快樂每從辛苦得

Left:
The private spaces behind the Main Hall include a skywell defined by richly ornamented woodwork, including a prominent *fu* character, an auspicious invocation for "good fortune."

Below:
While serving structural purposes, woodwork like this is grand in scale and richly carved in order to heighten its ornamental power.

Bottom:
While being decorative, huge wooden bracket arms of this sort also lift timber beams.

A Merchant's Residence 173

a celebrated Tang-dynasty general, is associated with wealth and happiness. As seen earlier on page 47, this area also includes molded, ornamented roof tile ends along a high tin gutter that depict the character for "purity," offered here perhaps as an admonition for the young women living in the inner quarters.

Overlapping convex–concave gray clay tiles have been the preferred roof surfaces for Huizhou houses since the Ming dynasty when the costs of their production dropped dramatically. Here, too, as with Yan Yi Tang, the roof structures of the verandahs surrounding *tianjing*, with their richly carved eaves tiles, embody the poetic metaphor *si shui gui tang* ("the four waters return to the hall"), at once an invocation for riches to "pour" towards the family and a practical statement welcoming rainfall that will accumulate in large, easily accessible pottery cisterns populating each *tianjing*. *Tianjing* typically are paved with inlaid dressed stone, recessed slightly below the surrounding area, and connected to a drainage system that leads overflowing water outside the dwelling and into the exterior canal channel.

High brick "horses' head" walls, called *matouqiang* in Chinese, rise imposingly and rhythmically above Cheng Zhi Tang and its neighbors, complementing the expansive white walls beneath. In practical terms, these high brick "horses' head" walls surrounding the houses provide a fireproof defensive perimeter that protects the massive load-bearing timber frameworks and the valuable wooden ornamentation within, including beams, brackets, balustrades, as well as carved lattice windows and doors. The stepped silhouette of dark *matouqiang* gables, combined with the crisp whiteness of the lower walls, is a signature feature of Huizhou architecture.

Above:
Each of the two door panels leading into small bedrooms includes depictions of two of the Eight Immortals. Four of the fabled Baxian or Eight Immortals are carved on these two door panels. The matching pair of doors is shown on page 93. Here, Lu Dongbin, identified by the sword on his back, is on the left next to Lan Caihe who normally carries a basket of flowers or fruit. Cao Guojiu, in court dress, is the patron of performers, and is shown with He Xian'gu, the only woman of the eight.

Far left and left:
The lattice screen panels employed throughout the residence are intricately carved hardwoods.

174 China's Fine Heritage Houses

Left:
Since most bedrooms are relatively small in size, a canopy bed placed within them dominates the space.

Below:
In the upper stories, the balustrades of the galleries are lined with intricately carved wooden skirts.

Right:
The sunlight entering from the narrow opening above the skywell illuminates the carved ornamentation of the several layers of beams and brackets below.

A Merchant's Residence 175

THE FIVE PHOENIX MANSION
Lin Family's "Fortune in Abundance Tower," Fujian Province

Fu Yu Lou, in translation "Fortune in Abundance Tower," is an imposing architectural complex made of tamped earth and adobe bricks, with a scale and level of carpentry that elevates the building to that of a fortified mansion. The ochre-colored earthen structure was then parged with a lime-based coating to produce a white surface that contrasts with the gray roof tiles. Over time, the surface gained a mottled patina in addition to contrasting surfaces where the coating has flaked off. Chinese architects refer to this type of building as a *wufenglou* or "Five Phoenix Tower," a truly unique and imposing architectural type because of its spatial composition as well as its high buildings and sweeping rooflines. It is said that the multiple layering of the rooflines resembles a phoenix taking flight.

Built in 1882 as the residence of a fourth-grade official, Fu Yu Lou provides structural and architectural confirmation of the importance of patrilineal clan organization within a single-surname community. A handful of Lin clan members continue to occupy the building but their sparse presence pales in terms of the 27 related households and more than 200 individuals who once occupied its many rooms and courtyards. Very little is known of the circumstances leading to the construction of the structure or the history of the Lin family over the last 125 years.

Built upon a cut granite and boulder base, Fu Yu Lou is essentially square in shape, high in the back and lower in front, with a two-story structure across the front, three-story wing buildings along each side, and a dominating five-story rear structure that rises above them all. Within its wrapping walls, a series of intersecting buildings enclose courtyards of various sizes, each providing separate and relatively private spaces for individual Lin family groupings. Sitting rooms and bedrooms occupy the first three floors of the front and side structures. Two wells, one on the east side and the other on the west side, provide water for all the families living in the complex.

Entry to Fu Yu Lou is by way of an imposing gate that is angled to the northeast, like most of the structures built on the east bank of the stream in Hongkeng village, a decision that is clearly related to common *fengshui* considerations. Steps right outside the gate lead down to the stream where there is a landing where women gather early every day to do

A veritable mansion with soaring multitiered roofs, Fu Yu Lou is an imposing palace-like structure that incorporates the fundamental elements of Chinese architecture: enclosure, symmetry, axiality, and hierarchy. Early in the last century, 27 related households and more than 200 individuals occupied its many rooms and courtyards.

The Five Phoenix Mansion 177

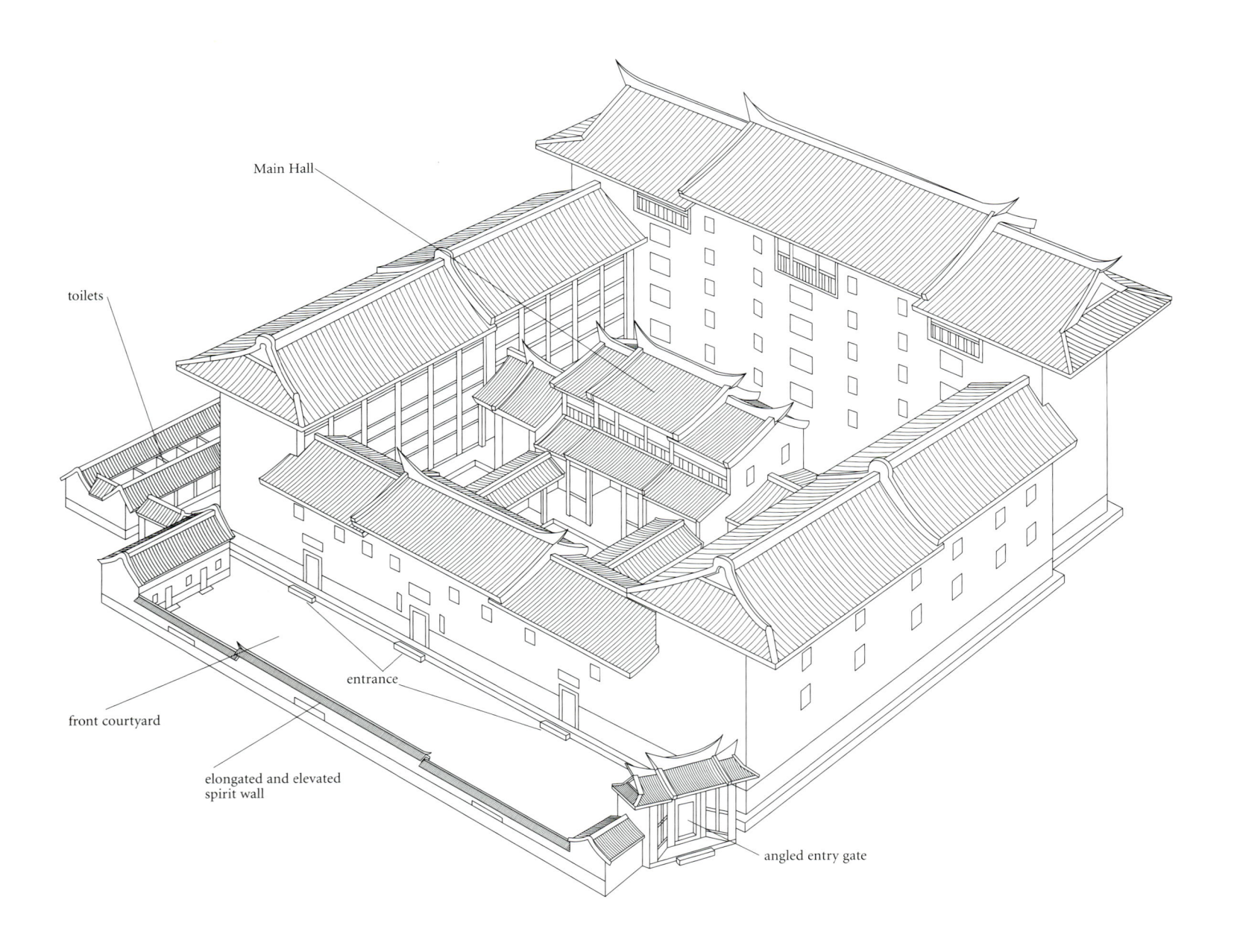

Labels on drawing: Main Hall; toilets; entrance; front courtyard; elongated and elevated spirit wall; angled entry gate

their family's laundry. The angled gate itself opens to an elongated courtyard used to dry grain, vegetables, and herbs according to the season, and to dry clothing throughout the year.

Similar to grand imperial palaces, there are three large entrances; the principal one in the center provides access to ceremonial spaces while the other two lead into common living spaces. The central entry includes a horizontal panel above it with the characters *Fu Yu Lou* as well as a set of auspicious couplets alongside. On the door panels, paper images of a pair of Door Gods are replaced annually at the New Year. Just beyond the broad entry portico is a spirit wall that blocks the view of the inside. Beyond it is a rectangular *tianjing* with flanking open spaces that abut the Main Hall, a shared ceremonial space at the ceremonial center of the complex. It was here in these interconnected open and partially closed spaces that round banquet tables would be set during *hongbai shi* ("red and white affairs")—weddings and funerals—when even far-flung family members would return to affirm clan solidarity. Elaborate and expensive wooden lattice panels surround these spaces.

Above:
This bird's-eye drawing highlights the height of the five-story rear building, the prominence of the interior hall, as well as the gated forecourt.

Left:
As with other large residences of this type, the entryway is emblazoned with a name, in this case *Fu Yu Lou* or "Fortune in Abundance Tower." A pair of permanent couplets is aligned on the wall alongside the door, while less permanent printed paper images of Door Gods are affixed to each leaf of the doorway.

178 China's Fine Heritage Houses

Behind the hall are stairs leading up to storage spaces, and then another large *tianjing* and Back Hall, which is located in the imposing five-story rear building. This structure provides shared space for the corporate Lin clan and includes rooms used for ceremonial purposes. Three sets of steep stairs connect to the upper four floors. On the second floor is an imposing room with an altar dedicated to various deities with views out over the rooftop of the Main Hall and beyond to the facing hills. Fired brick party walls, which separate the rooms, are needed to stabilize the five-story rear structure. Upper stories are currently used for activities that range from raising rabbits on the third floor to the storage of coffins on the uppermost fifth floor.

As in many areas of China, older family members purchased a lacquered wooden coffin while they were still alive, assuring in the process that they would have a suitable place for their body after death. The Lin family coffins include symbolic calligraphy employing the characters *fu* for "good fortune" and *shou* for "longevity." As an elderly family member faced death and it was considered "unlucky" to die in bed, the dying person was usually moved to the Main Hall and placed on a flat bed of boards supported by a pair of sawhorses. Having a coffin nearby facilitated the next phase involving dressing the corpse and en-coffining, which took place as soon after death as possible in preparation for rituals and the condolence visits of family and friends. After the death of a family member, white strips of paper would be placed on the exterior doors to announce the death. Since it was necessary to select an appropriate "lucky" day for burial and even a "lucky" gravesite, a coffin might be kept either in the Main Hall or moved back upstairs for storage for months or even years. It is not uncommon in old Chinese dwellings to encounter dusty coffins, both empty and with corpses within them, though it is not clear to what degree such practices continue.

Above:
The stone outer gate of Fu Yu Lou, which is angled to the northeast according to *feng-shui* considerations, is highly ornamented. Near where the women are working, steps lead down to the stream where there is a landing for women to gather early to do their family's laundry.

Left:
Inside the outer gate is an elongated courtyard, which ends at this utility building. The stone-faced courtyard is always an area of intense activity. Depending on the season, grain, vegetables, herbs, or, in this case, ripe persimmons, are dried here in order to preserve them for later use.

The Five Phoenix Mansion

Right:
The first-floor plan of Fu Yu Lou reveals a symmetrical organization of space, some shared but others delineated for equitable division among family members. Two wells and six fairly large skywells are placed among other common spaces used for ceremonial activities.

Below:
This is a view across the central skywell that is located just inside the entry portico, which is on the right. Between the entry portico and the elongated skywell is a screen wall composed of large lattice doors on pivots, which are shown here open. The steps at left lead into the Main Hall.

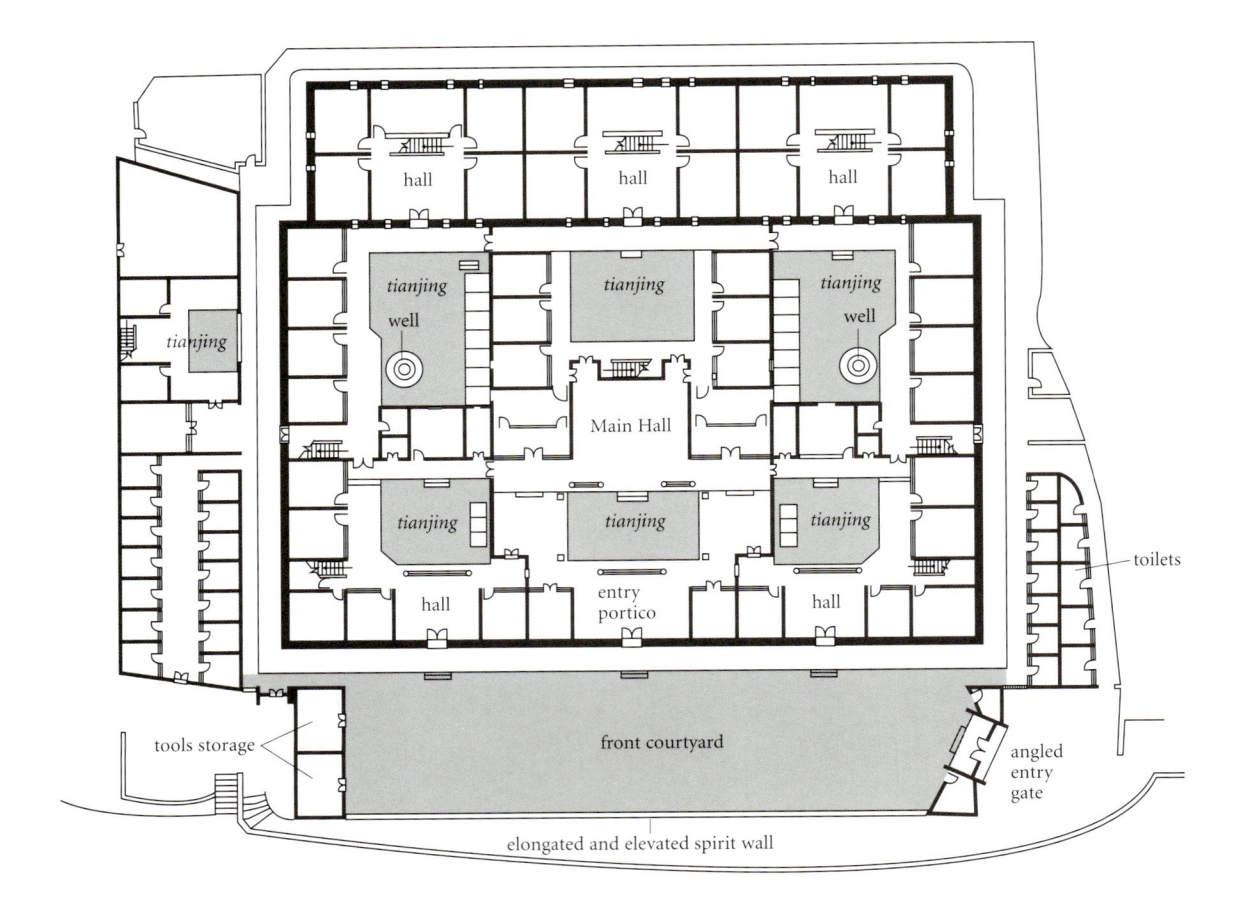

180 China's Fine Heritage Houses

This view of a side hall reveals the high ceilings and abundant use of carved wooden and stone components.

Five phoenix-style dwellings include complex associations related both to the phoenix and the number five. By juxtaposing rhetorical images and linking them to physical structures, builders and residents are able to recall classical imagery that expresses Confucian behavioral ideals. The phoenix or *feng* is viewed as an auspicious creature and appeared on the roofs of buildings built during the Han dynasty to symbolize virtuous local scholars who were filial, loyal, and served the emperor. Analogical reasoning also associates the image of five phoenixes with the stability of the five directions and the harmonization of the five colors. The body parts of each phoenix further symbolize the five virtues of a ruler: the head, virtue itself; the back, benevolence; the bosom, trust; the feet, correctness, and the tail, martial valor. Some have speculated that southern China's five phoenix-style buildings evoke a palace-type building style that once must have been built in the fabled Zhongyuan or Central Plains in Henan province of northern China but is no longer seen there. Although a large number and variety of ceramic models of buildings have been excavated from tomb sites in this region, which have enriched our knowledge of multistoried structures from ancient times, it still remains puzzling why the antecedents of *wufenglou*-type structures remain so elusive. Equally mysterious is how *wufenglou* came to be built in remote areas of southwestern Fujian, where they can still be seen today.

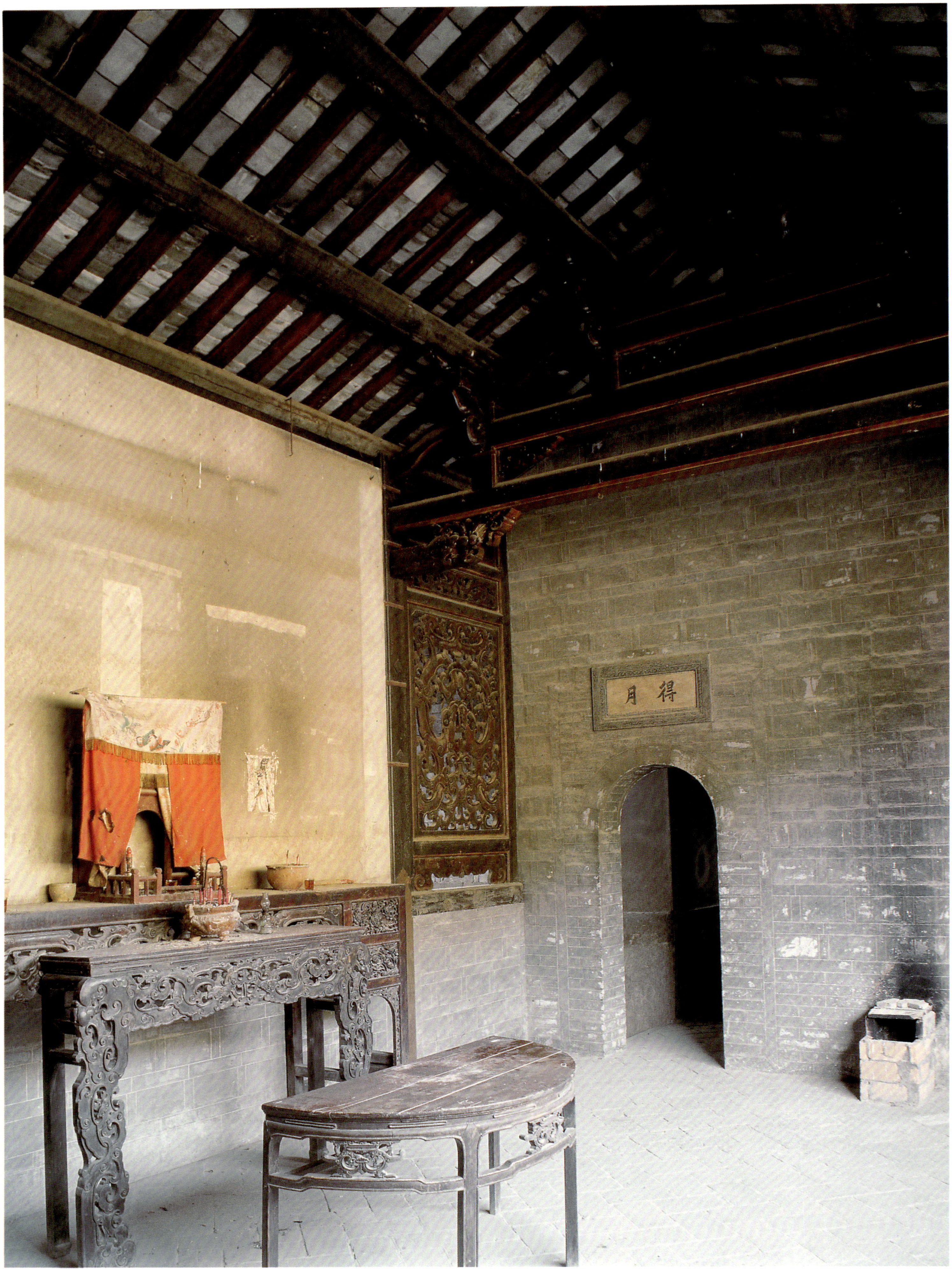
得月

Left:
On the second floor of the rear building is an altar room for worshipping deities. While some ornately carved furniture suggests the prominence of this space in times past, today the room is underfurnished and is only occasionally used.

Right:
Perspective view towards the two-story structure holding the Main Hall. Built of brick with sweeping "swallow's tail" rooflines, the building expresses the wealth of the family.

Far left:
Ornamented treatment along the rooflines and the partition walls between buildings.

Left:
As in many old Chinese dwellings, spaces are used to store coffins, which were purchased by elderly family members in order to insure a suitable burial. Here, in Fu Yu Lou, the coffins are kept above the altar room on the top floor of the rear building.

The Five Phoenix Mansion

ROUND FORTRESS RAMPARTS IN FUJIAN
"Inspiring Success Tower" and "Like a Sheng Tower," Fujian Province

Some of China's most unique structures, the so-called *tulou*, rammed earthen structures that resemble fortresses, are common in southwestern Fujian with variant forms seen in adjacent areas of Jiangxi and Guangdong provinces. Found in once remote mountainous areas characterized by narrow, sinuous valleys, *tulou* were virtually unknown and unrecorded until the last half of the twentieth century. Today, many of the villages in which they dominate are increasingly accessible and visited by growing numbers of intrepid travelers wishing to get off the beaten track. It is certain that there are even more secluded villages of *tulou* yet to be discovered and heralded in the deeper hills. In many villages, it is possible to see *tulou* in various shapes, including square, pentagonal, octagonal, rhomboid, oblong, and round, with a few built more than 500 years ago and some even just decades ago. Finding an effective translation for the Chinese word *lou*, which is part of the name of each of these buildings, is difficult. "Storied Building," the normal translation, does not do the structures justice. The term "Tower" is used here. While towers usually are taller than their diameter, architecturally the term can be used when a structure is of great size even if the height–width proportions differ from general usage.

While the term *tulou* means "earthen dwelling" and many authors write as if such structures have always been constructed of fresh earth, as indeed is the common building practice in many areas of China, most large-scale *tulou* seen today were built of a composite material known as *sanhetu*, a mixture of fine sand, lime, and soil in different ratios, rather than simply earth. Some *tulou* actually were constructed completely of cut granite or had substantial walls of fired brick. Thus, to call them "earthen dwellings" in English or even *tulou* in Chinese is clearly erroneous and insufficient. Massive round structures known as *yuanlou*, common in southwestern Fujian, are the best-known Hakka fortresses but there are many different shapes, including some with concentric circles within them. No less significant are the imposing and impregnable *weizi* of southern Jiangxi and the often magnificent *wufenglou* ("five phoenix mansions") of eastern Guangdong and southwestern Fujian. Unlike castles in Europe and Japan, Hakka fortresses in China are rarely located at high and commanding positions.

Historical and geographical reasons relating to the time of migration and relationship with neighbors help explain the distribution of different shapes of *tulou*. In the oldest settled Hakka areas, five phoenix and horseshoe shapes were common, probably because early settlers were not seriously threatened. Here, early Hakka arrivals built rather open dwellings in a style that evoked the manor dwellings of officials, the so-called *daifu zhai*, in areas of northern China from which the Hakka migrated. Imposing round or square bastions were generally built along the borders of Hakka-dominated areas and where Hakka lived among others, yet not all of them were built in response to the potential of strife. Turmoil certainly was often a factor, such as during the early third of last century when many substantial walled enclaves were built all over rural China in response to widespread banditry and general lawlessness, but there were other considerations as well.

Fully a third of all *tulou* still standing in Nanjing county in the 1990s were built before 1900, but it is a startling fact that some 427, nearly two-thirds, were built after 1900. Over the past ninety years, almost as many large round ones (192) have been built as square ones (235). This relatively recent building history suggests that reasons other than defense played roles in their construction, even given the periodic turmoil of modern times. The accelerated building of structures using traditional materials and forms after the founding of the People's Republic of China, especially, was a response to population pressures and economic conditions rather than turmoil. In the 1960s, more round structures were built than square ones, but in recent decades square and rectangular shapes have dominated while the number of related households living together has decreased as more families establish single family houses in Fujian's villages.

Zhen Cheng Lou
Hongkeng village in Yongding county, known as being at the core of a region awash with these distinctive architectural forms, was relatively inaccessible even as recently as 1990, when it was only reachable at the end of a long and rugged dirt path on foot, by bicycle, or in a three-wheeled gas-powered cart. Today, a good road with regular bus service brings backpackers and buses with international tourists.

Arranged like landed UFOs, these five enormous rammed earthen ramparts are clustered together along a steep hill slope in Tianluokeng village, Shuyang township, Nanjing county, Fujian.

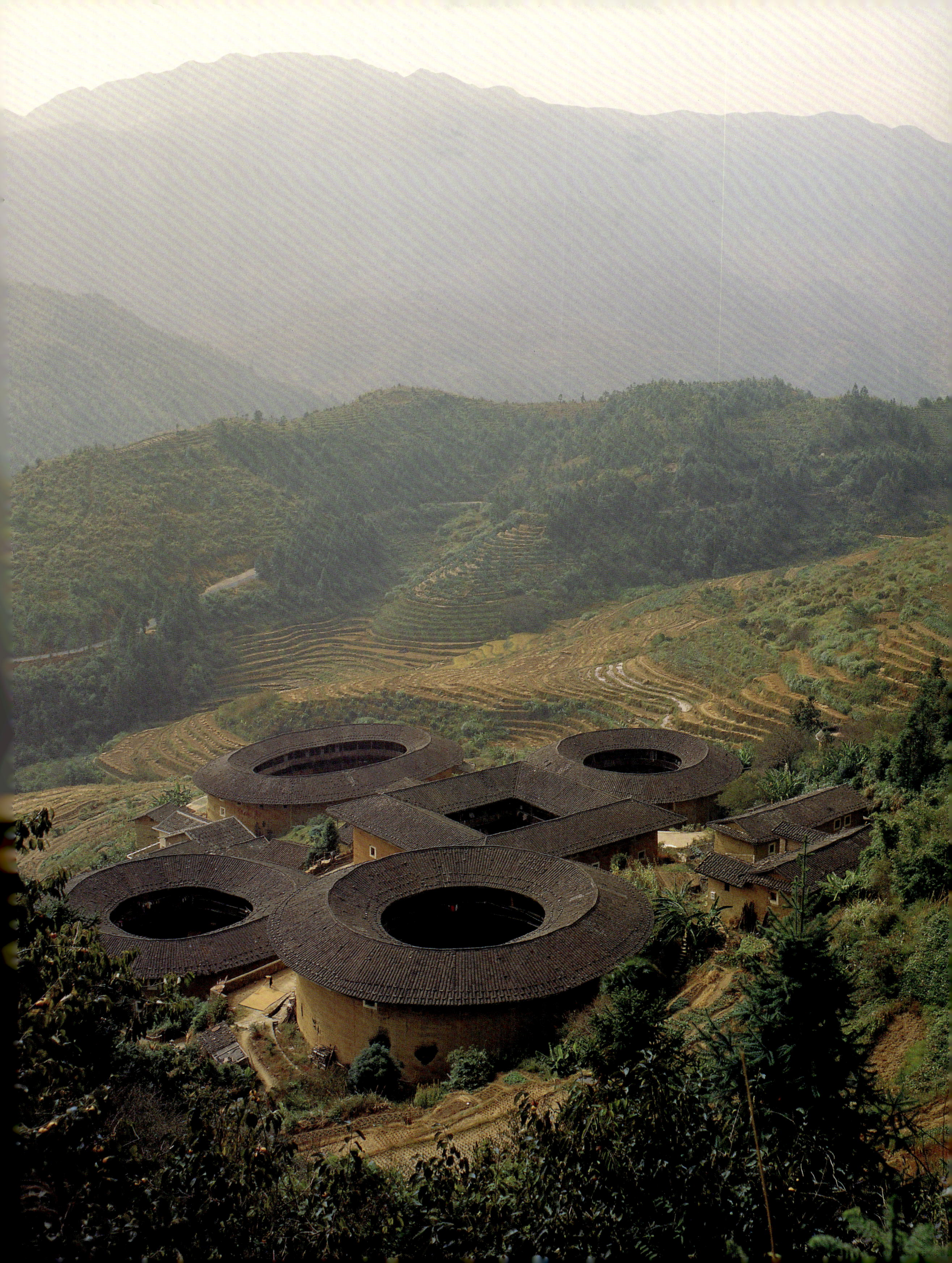

Constructed of tamped earth nearly a meter thick at the base and each with a single reinforced entry, structures of the type found in Gaobei village, Guzhu township, Yongding county, Fujian, are quite impregnable.

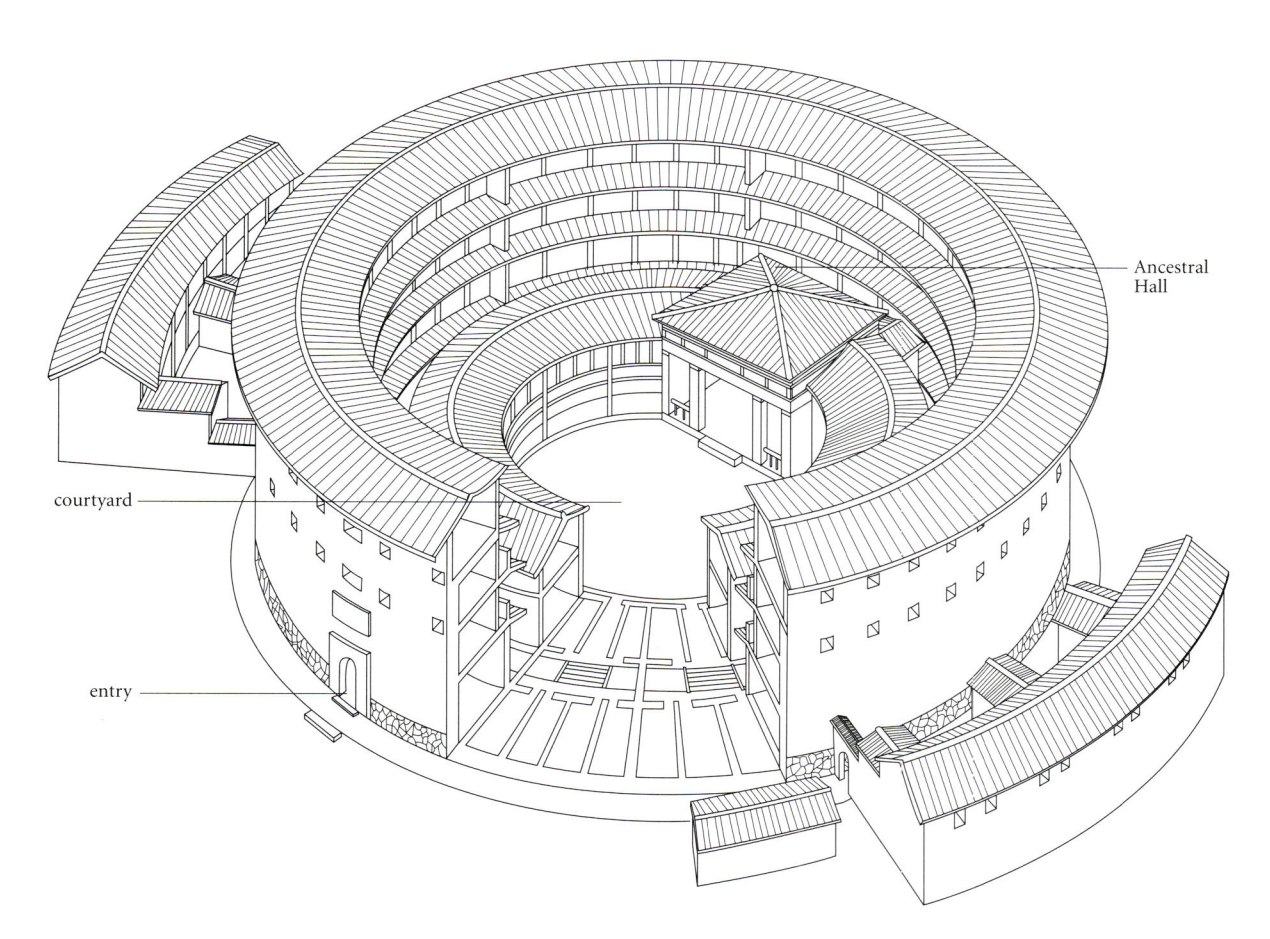

Left:
This perspective drawing captures the essential elements of Zhen Cheng Lou: a four-story round outer structure with a two-story inner ring connected to an Ancestral Hall; a large main entry and two smaller side entries; windows only on the upper two floors; and three outlying utility structures.

Below:
Both photographs reveal the texture and massive character of the walls of tamped earth structures in southwestern Fujian. Only in recent decades with increasing levels of security have residents taken to excavating window openings in the lower portions of the walls.

Zhen Cheng Lou or "Inspiring Success Tower," one of a hundred *tulou* of various sizes in Hongkeng village, is a four-story circular fortified structure with windows only on two levels of the upper wall (see pages 18–19). Built in 1912 by Lin Xunzhi during an unsettled period as the Qing imperial dynasty ended and the Republic of China was coming into existence, the windows are embrasured—their side frames are angled within the thick wall so that the opening inside is wider than that outside—for increased security and to make surveillance from inside easier.

The path leading to Zhen Cheng Lou, as it does now, once did not lead directly to the gateway but instead approached at an angle from the side before turning sharply on to an elevated platform surrounding the structure. This zigzagging shows attentiveness to *fengshui* considerations relating to appropriate siting but also probably had defensive significance as well. Today, the area in front of the structure is much more open than it was even a decade ago, cleared in order to facilitate the needs of tourist photographers. The single entry gate into the structure is oriented slightly to the southeast and has the three characters "Zhen Cheng Lou" emblazoned above it. As with other fortresses, the massive stone entry portal leads into a gate hall, an entry portico or *menwu*, an area that is normally occupied throughout the day by women, children, and old men. Here they "guard" passage into their complex as they perform work like husking rice and preparing food to be cooked (or today selling postcards). Covered with a sheet of iron, the thick wooden doors are further secured when closed with a huge beam set horizontally into sockets.

Round Fortress Ramparts in Fujian

While in many similar structures, an open circular courtyard is found beyond the *menwu*, Zhen Cheng Lou has a secondary ring of structures surrounding a central courtyard. The division of space within the outer walls of Zhen Cheng Lou is apportioned equally with most rooms of similar size so that there are individual entries into each "apartment." Closer examination reveals a carefully crafted auspicious design that, while not unique, is significant. Zhen Cheng Lou was artfully planned to express the Eight Trigrams or *bagua*, a cryptic divinatory text believed to have great symbolic power in Chinese culture and that is used in properly siting a dwelling. There are several *tulou* that are actually octagonal in shape with eight straight walls that intersect, but Zhen Cheng Lou is round on the outside while its interior living space is divided into eight clearly differentiated units to invoke the Eight Trigrams. Each of these eight units is separated from another by a tamped earth wall and then subdivided into three or six "bays" or *jian*, the common Chinese building unit, that are fronted by four linear courtyards that face the animal sheds. Several wells within the courtyard supply the residents with water.

Above:
Swept by the asymmetrical arc-shaped shadow of the late autumn sun, the interior core of Zhen Cheng Lou reveals its striking three-bay Ancestral Hall with an inner circular core of utilitarian spaces covered by a tile roof.

Left:
Brick walls placed perpendicular to the outer round walls help to buttress the structure. Within the building, wood dominates as the building material. Wooden floor joists are sunk into each of the tamped earthen walls of the upper three stories, while a wooden framework of interlocking mortise-and-tenoned pieces gives shape to rooms and verandahs.

188   China's Fine Heritage Houses

While the outer walls that ring Zhen Cheng Lou are of an earthen composition, the structural space within is all built of wood. Wooden floor joists for each of the upper three stories are secured deep into the tamped earth walls, and a wooden framework of interlocked pieces is assembled to support much of the weight of a heavy tile roof. Thin baked bricks are placed on top of the floorboards of the arcade around each level as a fire prevention measure. The two-story inner ring connects with a tall three-bayed Ancestral Hall with a four-sloped hipped roof, which itself is the focus for auspicious ornamentation. At the center is a nearly circular open courtyard, large enough for family ceremonies. This core area is connected to the outer structure by four roofed corridors that pass around four square skywells, two of which have wells.

A pair of symmetrical arc-shaped two-story structures lies adjacent to Zhen Cheng Lou, a combination that is rarely seen. Local lore refers to the pair as being symbolic of high position since they appear like the flaps of a traditional hat worn by officials during imperial times. One served as the location of a school for children of the Lin family, while extra space was used for storage and bedrooms for visitors.

Ru Sheng Lou

Among the smallest round earthen dwellings is one built more than a hundred years ago by a branch Lin family somewhat upstream in Hongkeng village. With an external diameter of 17.4 meters and an internal diameter across the circular courtyard of only 5.2 meters, its compact shape and size have given rise to the name Ru Sheng Lou or "Like a Sheng Tower," since its form is said to evoke the Chinese canister-like volumetric dry measure for grain, called a *sheng*.

The single arch-shaped entryway is oriented somewhat towards the northwest, differing significantly from others in the village. Directly opposite the entry is the Ancestral Hall, which occupies a single central bay and juts out slightly into the round courtyard. Paved with stones harvested from the nearby stream, the courtyard is the center for daily activities because of the presence of a well and the sunlight that enters during the day. A pair of stairs leads to the two upper stories, which are framed in unpainted wood.

A fair question is, why round shapes when most Chinese structures are square or rectangular? In some areas, there was a clear transformative progression with square fortresses being supplanted by round

This view between the two rings of structures reveals the abundant use of fired bricks for interior walls and partitions, which are then capped by fired clay roof tiles. Individual families have four-story "apartments" consisting of a series of rooms arranged vertically.

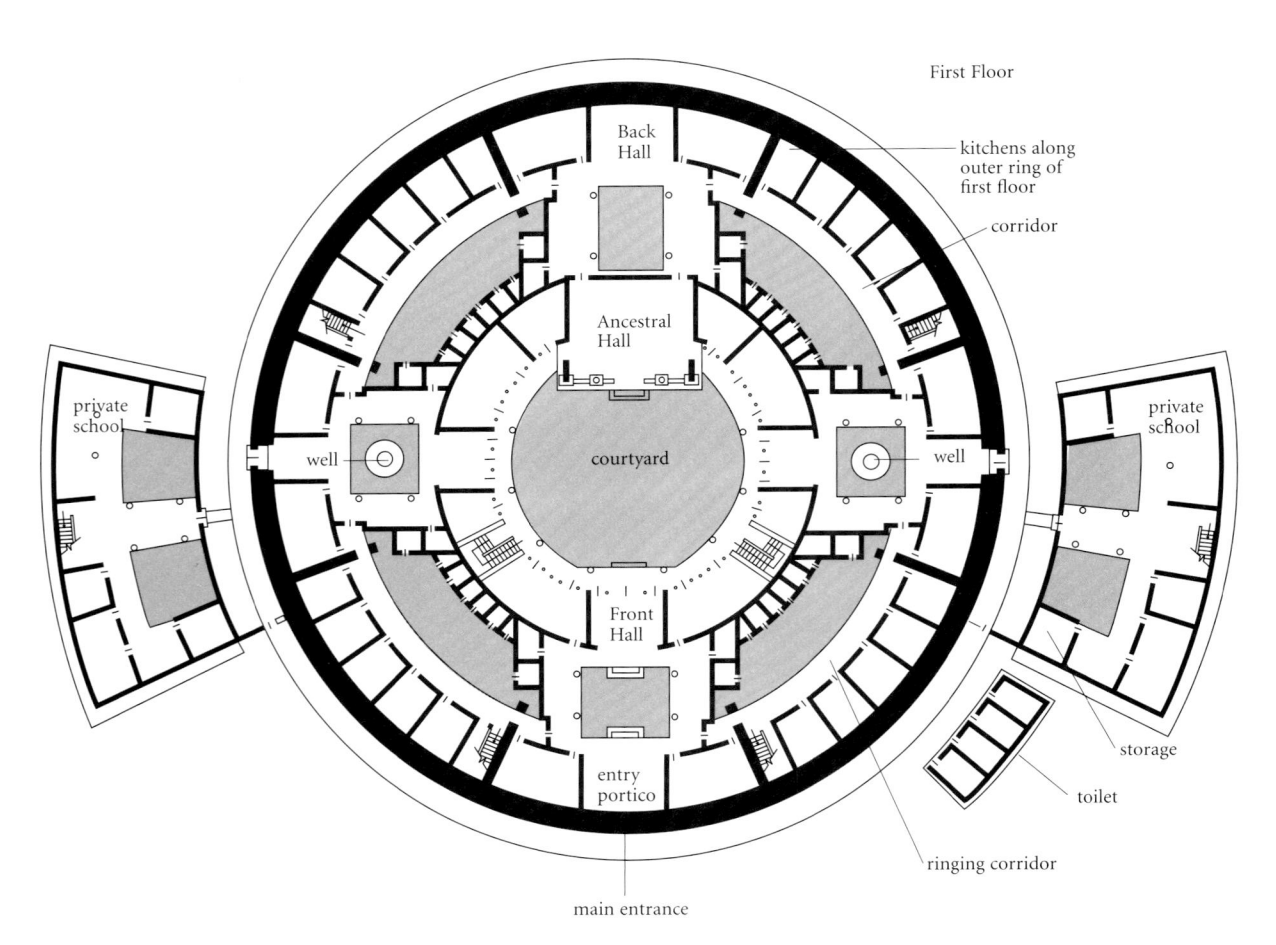

First Floor

Labels (first floor plan):
- Back Hall
- kitchens along outer ring of first floor
- corridor
- private school
- well
- Ancestral Hall
- courtyard
- well
- private school
- Front Hall
- storage
- toilet
- entry portico
- ringing corridor
- main entrance

Left:
This plan of the first floor shows the division of the interior space into eight segments, a separation that has cosmological meanings associated with the Eight Trigrams. Much of the layout is symmetrical, including a pair of wells and side entries, corresponding skywells positioned throughout the building, stairways, and two wing structures. Only the toilet is not duplicated on both sides. A hierarchy of spaces is apparent from the entry straight through to the Back Hall.

Below:
This plan shows rooms on the second floor of both the outer and inner rings. Roofed passageways allow individuals to move freely across and around the structure even in the most inclement weather.

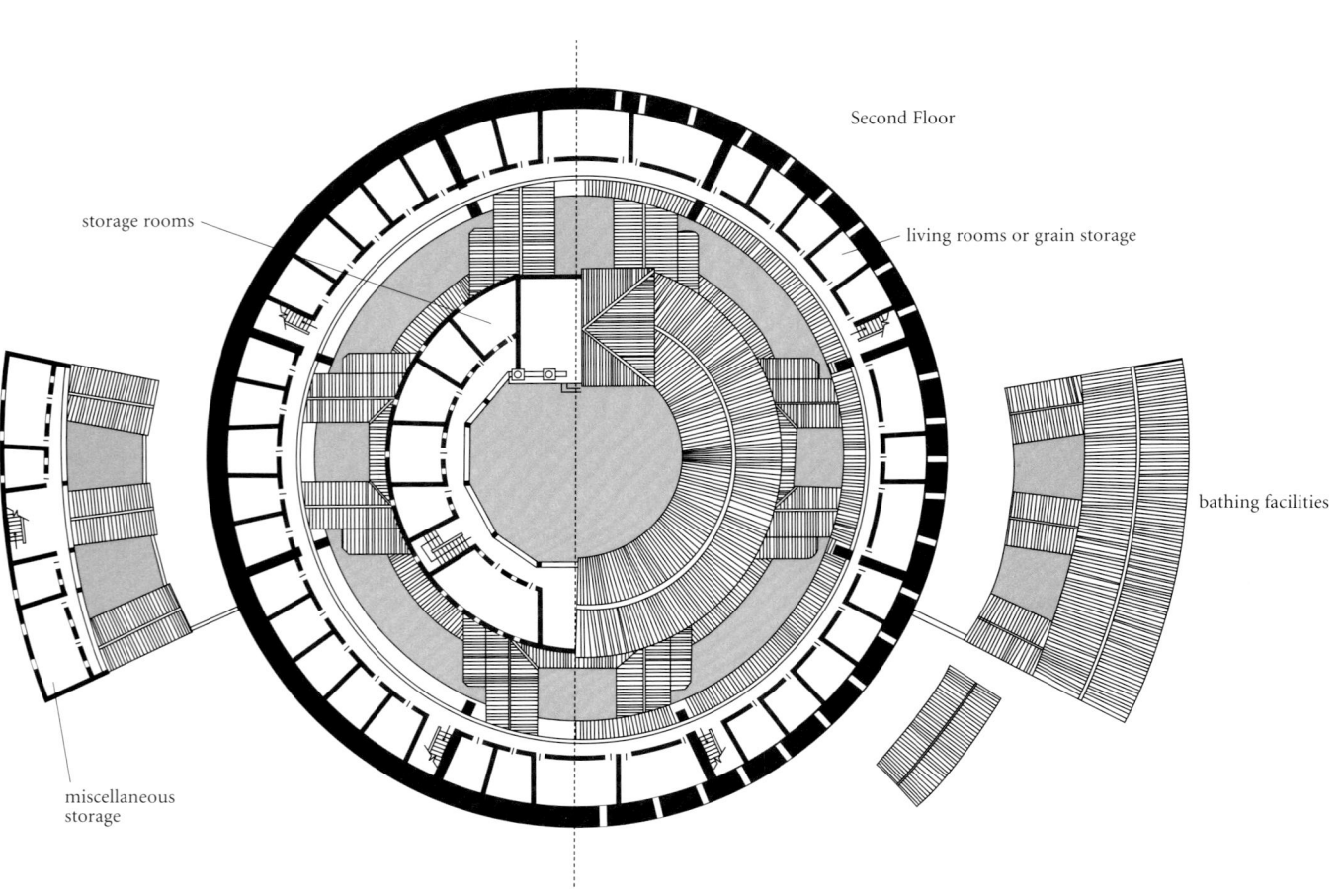

Second Floor

Labels (second floor plan):
- storage rooms
- living rooms or grain storage
- bathing facilities
- miscellaneous storage

190 China's Fine Heritage Houses

ones. Once builders experimented with curvature, it took little time for circular structures to emerge from curved framing systems. For one thing, a circular wall is able to wrap approximately 1.273 more interior space than a square wall of the same length, according to Chinese calculations. Thus, constructing circular exterior walls as compared to straight ones saves scarce building materials. Within a circular structure, moreover, the wooden members used to frame interior living quarters can be standardized in dimension, thus reducing the level of carpentry skills needed to complete the project. The modularization of components with a circular roof eliminates the difficult joinery necessary to link the intersecting planes atop a square structure. Some observers also suggest that round shapes are more resistant than other shapes to earthquake damage and are able to deflect the strong winds of seasonal typhoons. In terms of social structure, residential space can be divided more equitably than is the case with a square shape. Doing so provides egalitarian division of assets and a spatial affirmation of an aspect of Hakka life that differs from the hierarchical associations so often seen in Chinese architecture. Using these criteria, the benefits are clear with larger structures even though little is gained by building a small round building in comparison to a small square one.

Above:
More than a hundred years old, Ru Sheng Lou is among the smallest round structures. It has an external diameter of more than 17 meters from outside to inside with little more than a five-meter-wide interior courtyard. This view is from the Ancestral Hall towards the only doorway. At ground level, the space is divided into twelve rooms, an Ancestral Hall, and an entry portico.

Left:
This view of the exterior of Ru Sheng Lou is from inside the gate of Fu Yu Lou, discussed earlier, which is immediately across the stream that passes through the village.

HAKKA ENCIRCLING DRAGONS
De Xing Tang and Ning'an Lu Weilongwu, Guangdong Province

Between the fourth and nineteenth centuries, five great waves of migration brought northerners from the Central Plains of the Yellow River valley southward, first to the Gan River valley in southern Jiangxi province and then successively into the rugged contiguous mountainous portions of a small triangle framed by southwestern Fujian, northern Guangdong, and southern Jiangxi. In spite of centuries of residence in these areas, this population is still referred to as Hakka, Kejia in Modern Standard Chinese, an ambivalent term that translates simply as "Guest Families" and has been used since at least the Song dynasty. The name was applied by local Chinese settlers to the newcomers and, somewhat curiously, was subsequently adopted by the in-migrants themselves as a name. Through their migrations and eventual settlement among other Chinese, Hakka have maintained a separateness and identity as a distinct Han Chinese sub-ethnic group. Some forty million people today identify themselves as Hakka, viewing Meizhou in northeastern Guangdong province as their adopted homeland where at least sixteen counties are considered "pure" Hakka areas.

Wherever Hakka pioneers settled, they created dwellings of impressive size, strength, and structural complexity that offered protection against communal

Below:
De Xing Tang. *Weilongwu* are usually built at the break-in slope along a gently inclined hillside. The curved rear portion is elevated and matched to a lower front area that is defined by a half moon-shaped pond. Together they have geomantic properties.

One of the two secondary entrances at the front of the dwelling. While the center entrance traditionally was used rarely and generally only for ceremonial purposes, the pair of secondary entrances met the needs of day-to-day movements in and out of the large structure.

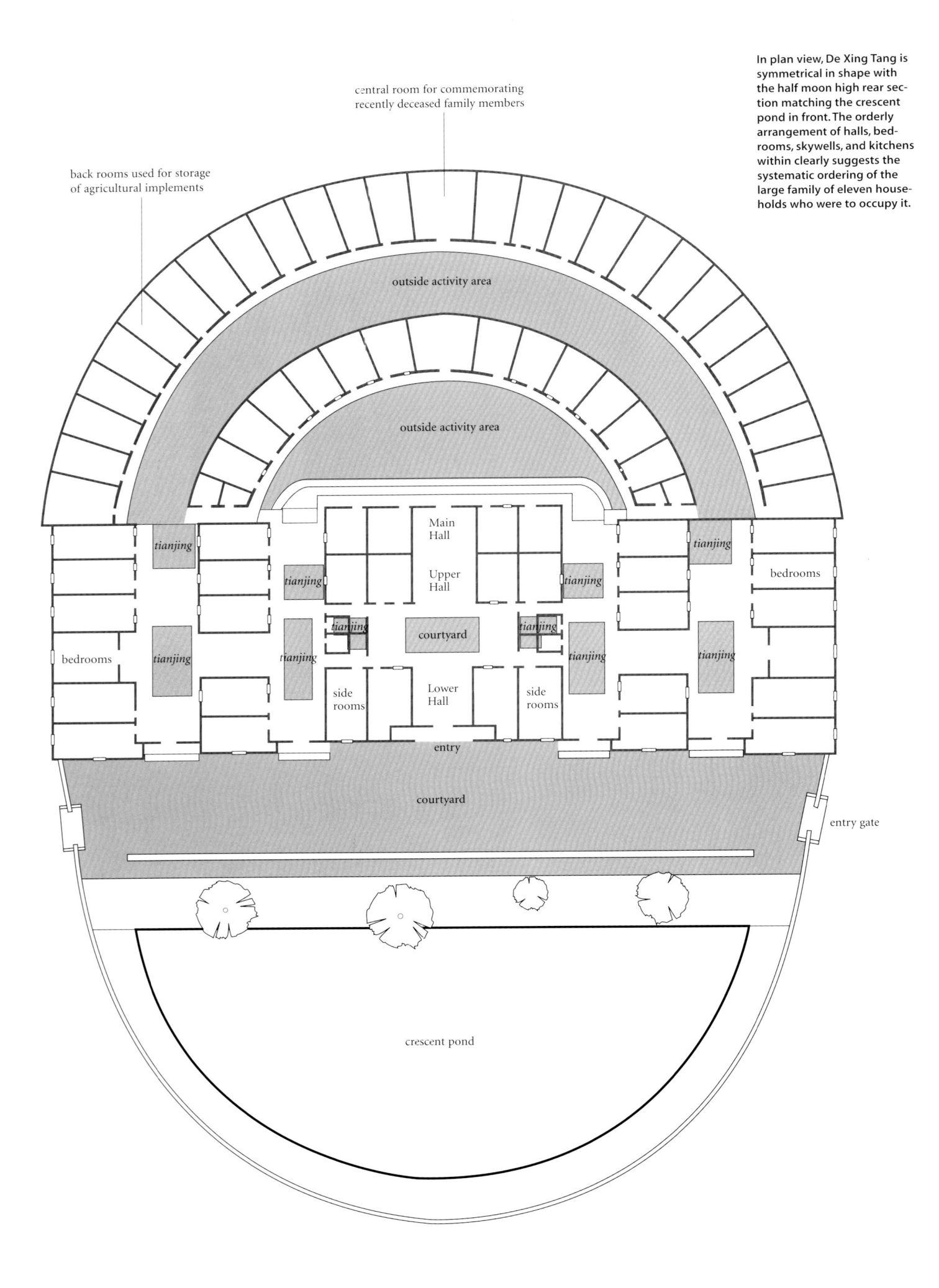

back rooms used for storage of agricultural implements

central room for commemorating recently deceased family members

In plan view, De Xing Tang is symmetrical in shape with the half moon high rear section matching the crescent pond in front. The orderly arrangement of halls, bedrooms, skywells, and kitchens within clearly suggests the systematic ordering of the large family of eleven households who were to occupy it.

outside activity area

outside activity area

bedrooms

tianjing

tianjing

tianjing

Main Hall

Upper Hall

tianjing

tianjing

bedrooms

tianjing

tianjing

courtyard

tianjing

tianjing

side rooms

Lower Hall

side rooms

entry

courtyard

entry gate

crescent pond

194　China's Fine Heritage Houses

Left:
The rear portion rises on both sides, appearing horseshoe-like in shape, with storage and bedrooms aligned along its outer wall.

Below:
This view is from the central Main Hall looking across a small courtyard towards the main entry. The depression helps drain excess rainwater out of the building. Normally, large vats would also be located here in order to collect rainwater for household use.

violence as well as met the requirements of their cooperative patrilineal clan system. While the massive and imposing round fortresses and "five phoenix" towers of Fujian, discussed in earlier sections, are fine examples of Hakka dwellings, equally distinctive are the lesser-known *weilongwu* of northeastern Guangdong. Here, where Hakka dominated and had less need for impregnable fortresses, they built a distinctive dwelling style that echoed the manor dwellings of officials, a variant of the so-called *daifu zhai* once common in northern China a millennium ago, but curiously no longer evident there.

Termed *weilong* ("encircling ridge" or "encircling dragon"), Hakka dwellings in Meizhou are built at the break along a gently sloping hillside, with the curved rear portion elevated and matched to a lower front portion that is defined by a half moon-shaped pond, both of which have geomantic properties. With their encircling arcuate back walls, *weilongwu* appear like an enormous omega Ω, or horseshoe-shaped armchair, securely set on a sloping hillslope in order to protect residents from danger and provide them prevailing breezes and effective drainage. *Weilongwu* combine elements of the traditional *siheyuan* courtyard styles—bilateral symmetry, axiality, hierarchy, and enclosure—with distinctive features: the presence of upper, middle, and lower halls, the change in elevation from high in back to low in front, and the large pond. Combining the upper hemisphere with the lower hemisphere, some say, created a *taiji* diagram, the circular composition that includes the complementary *yin* and *yang* pairs that represent stability, interdependence, and mutuality.

De Xing Tang Weilongwu

Among the most dramatic *weilongwu* is De Xing Tang, built between 1905 and 1917 by the grandfather of the current resident Pan Zhengfeng, a businessman who had returned from Southeast Asia after having made his money. Like many other *Huaqiao*, or returning "Overseas Chinese" at the turn of the twentieth century, he invested in a residence that not only showed his wealth but also expressed his understanding of Chinese norms and his expectations for his family. De Xing Tang, meaning "to promote virtue," was designed as a co-residential complex with space for each of the families of his eleven sons, numbered serially from one to eleven as a separate branch or *fang*, with space allocated according to the sons' birth order. There is no doubt that his hope was that many generations of Pan family members would continue to live together at this idyllic location in a dwelling complex that covered a total area of 8500 square meters with 1690 square meters of enclosed buildings.

The selected building site for De Xing Tang was judged auspicious, chosen by a geomancer who paid attention not only to the configuration of the landscape but also to the *bazi* or "eight characters" related to the moment of birth of the dwelling's owner. Construction was carried out carefully so that the hillslope was not cut into since doing so would harm the dragon that resided there and bring misfortune to the family. The arching upslope part of the house appears like an open fan with ribs formed by an inner concentric arc of fifteen rooms complemented by a longer outer arc with twenty-seven rooms. Except for the larger central room in the outer arc, which was considered the "Raised Mound Hall" or "Dragon Hall," depending on which of the homophonous characters for *long ting* are employed, each of the roughly quadrangular rooms is the same size. This hub space was wider than adjacent rooms and was used for ritual purposes. Other rooms in each of the two arcs, which are identical in size, were distributed equally among the resident families. Between the two convex arcs of rooms are parallel open areas, one that is linear yet crescent-shaped while the other is nearly hemispheric. Both sweep upwards towards their middle portions and then slope downwards towards the level middle portions of the residential complex, creating odd courtyard-like open spaces because they are not level but undulate. The outer crescent-shaped open space is connected via a matched pair of corridors, alternatively open and closed, that run the length of the central building. Each juxtaposes a pair of skywells and adjacent verandah-like spaces, leading to a pair of doors at the front. These slightly recessed doors serve as the regular entrances for family members as they move in and out of their residence during the day. The central entryway, which is recessed and highly ornamented, was reserved in the past for use only during formal family occasions; today, its double-leaved door is left ajar for anyone to use at any time.

The floor plan of the core building is both symmetrical and hierarchical, comprising a pair of five-bay-wide horizontal structures flanked by two sets of perpendicularly oriented structures. The outer pairs of perpendicular structures are adjacent to the

Below:
Today, appearing only as if it had been tidied up from recent usage as a storage area, the grandeur that characterized the Main Hall for a large family is barely suggested.

Left:
The skywells and the sheltered spaces surrounding them provide comfortable places to work as the sunlight illuminates them in different ways throughout the day.

Below:
A warm corner of a skywell.

skywells, providing pleasant living space for family members. The two structures at the center of the complex are principally ritual spaces, comprising a Lower Hall just inside the entry and an Upper Hall beyond a courtyard. A pair of doors leads from the back of the Main Hall into a shallow vestibule and then on to the sweeping parabolic back areas. Today, all of these spaces are without the kinds of ornate furniture and uplifting ornamentation that must certainly have characterized them in the past. There is no doubt that in recent decades this magnificent structure must have housed a large number of families whose day-to-day activities brought substantial wear and tear, even damage, to the building. Accumulated debris has been removed and the walls and columns have been stripped of nearly a century's worth of paper and grime, yet restoration work has still to be completed.

Across the front of De Xing Tang are two spaces that complete the oval shape and that affirm its symmetry. One space is a large rectangular area that serves both as a family courtyard as well as a utilitarian space that can be used to dry, thresh, and winnow grain as well as other crops. Agricultural equipment, such as plows, harrows, and winnowers, is stored just inside the adjacent rooms, where it can be kept until needed. The main external entry for the complex leads into this courtyard and then on to the three doors into the building. Just below the rectangular courtyard is a half moon-shaped pond or *chitang*, whose location and scale were determined by the geomancer who selected the site and established proportions; it serves not only *fengshui* needs but also provides a source of water for washing clothes and for a fire emergency. Just beyond are the irrigated rice fields, whose colors change from many shades of green through shades of gold as the seasons advance. Exterior walls wrapping the complex are all without windows, so that whatever breezes and light enter the dwelling come from the front, drawn into the doorways or entering via the open skywells that punctuate the structure.

Hakka Encircling Dragons   197

Hakka dwellings throughout Fujian, Guangdong, and Jiangxi offer some of China's most distinctive shapes. While rectangular shapes are ubiquitous, there is an extraordinary number of square, round, arcuate, pentagonal, octagonal, and horseshoe forms. Given that many of these structures are multistoried or have portions that are multistoried, each is the product of refined building skills and careful planning. It is remarkable that craftsmen, even in what must have been remote mountain villages, employed modular construction principles and comprehensive systems of proportions to replicate extensive shapes relatively simply in order to build grand structures. Utilizing the *bagua* and other abstruse cosmological instruments, moreover, it was possible to schematically organize a complex ground plan pregnant with meaning yet functionally useful for family life. For the most part, the underlying meaning of odd structures like these remains elusive and open to debate.

Ning'an Lu Weilongwu

Throughout Meizhou and adjacent areas, *weilongwu* vary in scale, reflecting the needs of individual families as well as the resources needed to fulfill their requirements. Smaller *weilongwu* only have a single outer rear arched structure while larger ones have two or three, with the number of formal halls also increasing as the overall scale increases. In some places, a single *weilongwu* represents a hamlet or village while elsewhere multiple *weilongwu* comprise the settlement.

The Ning'an Lu *weilongwu* in Nankou township of Meizhou is a representative example of a modest structure of this type for a Hakka family of indeterminate size. Built on a lower hill slope, its building site does not intrude upon paddy land needed for crops. Wrapped with walls and with no fenestrations along the perimeter, as well as sturdy doors, the complex provides a secure sanctuary. Outer walls

Top:
One of the many communal-type kitchens that today serves the needs of different families who use their own gas stoves to cook.

Above:
The spaces above the entries throughout De Xing Tang all display complex patterns of painted, drawn, and carved ornamentation.

Right:
Hung at the New Year, these five auspicious streamers represent the "five good fortunes." Above them is the calligraphic phrase "financial resources will flow in."

Far right:
Paper amulets ask for the protection of Guandi, who personifies trustworthiness, strength, and loyalty. Usually hung at the New Year, protective prints of this type can also be invoked at other times of the year.

Right:
Ning'an Lu is a *weilongwu* of modest size as this perspective drawing shows, yet it clearly has the same elements of more extensive examples of *weilongwu*.

Below:
This view along one of the passageways shows the sequence of open and closed spaces leading to the rear area, which rises on an incline up the sloping hillside.

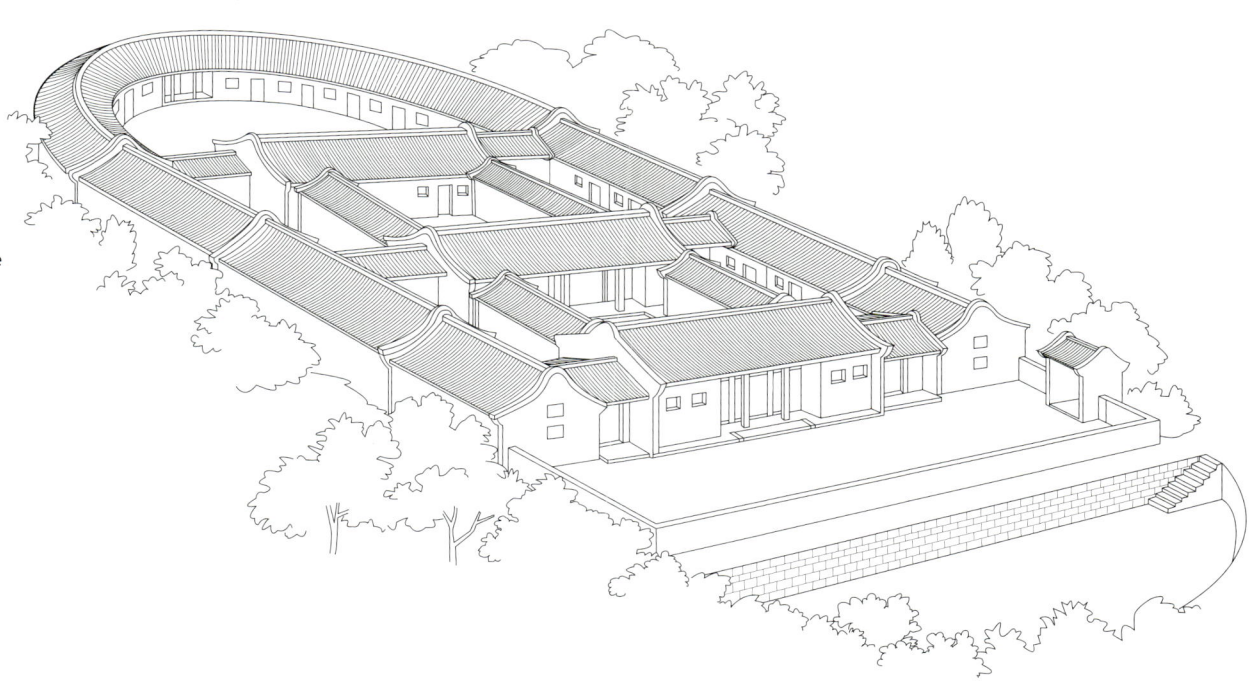

Hakka Encircling Dragons 199

are constructed of a tamped material, composed principally of earth but also sand and lime. Wooden and stone columns are used to support the roof of each internal structure, whose interior walls are all nonload-bearing. With a single arc-shaped rear profile connected to a crescent pool in front, the overall structure is symmetrical, elongated, and imposing, whether viewed from the front or the side.

While the arcuate *weilongwu* in the homeland of Hakka in Meixian, Guangdong province, and the imposing multistory circular Hakka structures in southwestern Fujian province are truly unique architectural forms, strikingly different walled dwellings and dwelling complexes are also found in the hinterland of urban Hong Kong, across the border in Shenzhen and Guangdong, and scattered throughout the Gannan region of southern Jiangxi province. Formerly situated relatively alone in areas of small populations, unlike today where the structures are crowded together, these oval, semicircular, pentagonal, octagonal, horseshoe, and even half moon-shaped structures are mixed with round, square, and arcuate shapes. In rural Hong Kong, which shares some of the linguistic and cultural characteristics of adjacent Guangdong and which historically was indeed part of Guangdong province, are found numerous walled residential compounds. Some of these were built by Hakka or their descendants.

Left above:
The richly ornamented upper gable wall at the end of a building is in a shape that represents wood, one of the elements in "five phases" cosmology. A bat representing "good fortune" appears above the circular ventilation port.

Left below:
Exterior view of the southwest corner of Ning'an Lu showing three different stone windows, each carved so that air is drawn into the dwelling.

Below:
This side elevation view clearly shows the substantial depth of the receding structure, including the portion that climbs up the slope.

Bottom:
The walls of the recessed entryway serve as a canvas for paintings as well as auspicious paper amulets, including images of Door Gods on the leaves of the doorway, with five red paper slips hanging above.

Hakka Encircling Dragons 201

A MANDARIN'S MANSION IN HONG KONG
Man Chung-luen's Residence, Hong Kong, SAR

Beyond the hyperkinetic metropolis of urban Hong Kong is the relatively slow-paced area known as the New Territories, a district that has itself undergone rapid transformation in recent decades. Fifty years ago, the New Territories was still largely rural with villages and market towns in the lowlands supporting a largely agricultural population growing rice and raising fish. By the 1970s, however, many old villages were being abandoned by those who sought work in the urban area or overseas, leaving behind only the elderly and very young. Increasingly, the vibrant social and economic fabric that had been established by the Five Great Clans—surnamed Tang, Hau, Pang, Liu, and Man—was left in tatters, with derelict houses, still-occupied walled villages, and a collection of scattered old buildings—residences, ancestral halls, temples, shrines, study halls, forts, even a single short pagoda—that only hinted at life in the past. Challenged by the quickening pace of destruction, some in Hong Kong have made valiant efforts to identify and conserve the declining examples of its built heritage as well as to foster cultural identity and pride. One of the early successes was Tai Fu Tai, located in Wing Ping Tsuen village, San Tin, Yuen Long district, which was declared a protected historical site in 1987.

The Man (pronounced Wen in standard Chinese) lineage, the last of the Five Great Clans to arrive on the south side of the Shenzhen River, first settled in what was to become the northwest corner of Hong Kong's New Territories in the fifteenth century. Here, as pioneers, they transformed an expansive shallow wetland into productive, yet still somewhat brackish, paddy fields in which a hardy variety of red rice could be grown. They named their single-lineage village San Tin or "New Fields," a name still used today, which in time developed into eight hamlet-like settlements. Most of the village hamlets included a lane or two of adjacent compact brick houses that shared party walls, and several wells where women would congregate during the day. Brick walls and gated passageways provided security for the Mans by keeping out intruders. Over time, five looming, temple-like ancestral halls and fifteen study-halls called *shufang* were constructed to meet the ceremonial needs of different segments of the Man lineage.

Unlike the common small village houses in San Tin, which reflect the difficulty of accumulating much wealth, there is one "mansion" among the residences of those belonging to the Man lineage. This single residence is Tai Fu Tai (*pinyin* Daifu Di), considered today to be an outstanding example of

Right:
Solidly built of cut stone and brick, the front walls are pierced by a main entry as well as a pair of side entrances for daily use.

Below right:
The ground-floor plan (left) reveals an expected symmetry with the three-bay core structure, which is then rendered asymmetrical by additions to both sides, one of which includes a narrow alley leading to the toilet as well as the kitchen and utility courtyard. The upper floor (right) is relatively inaccessible, providing some dry storage space as well as a place for young women to observe guests below without themselves being seen.

Far left:
Drawing showing the structural framework of Tai Fu Tai as well as details along the roofline.

Left:
The upsweeping tip and heavy ornamentation of the ridgeline are common features of fine dwellings in southeastern China.

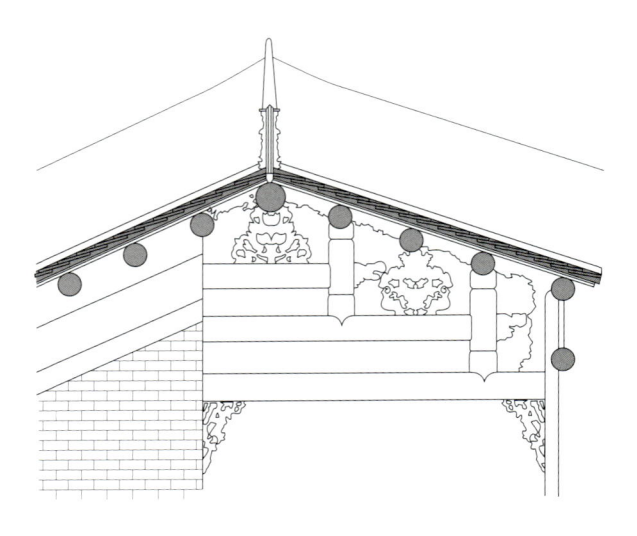

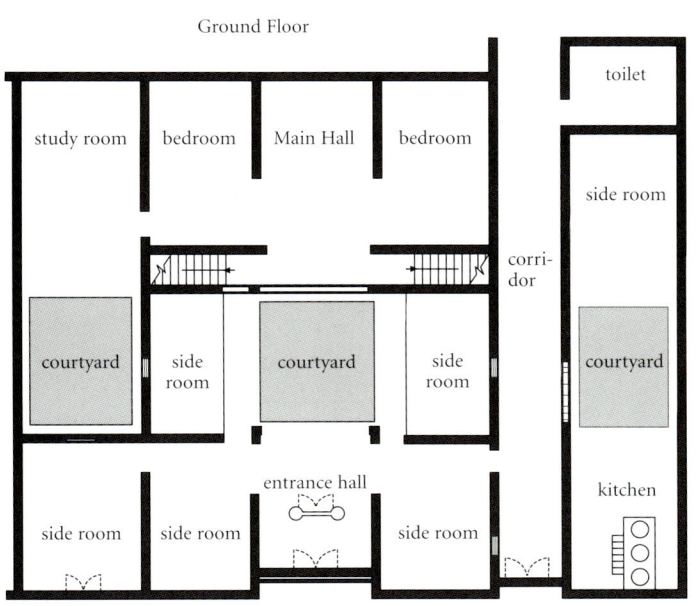

Ground Floor

| study room | bedroom | Main Hall | bedroom | | toilet |

| courtyard | side room | courtyard | side room | corridor | side room |

| | | | | | courtyard |

| side room | side room | entrance hall | side room | | kitchen |

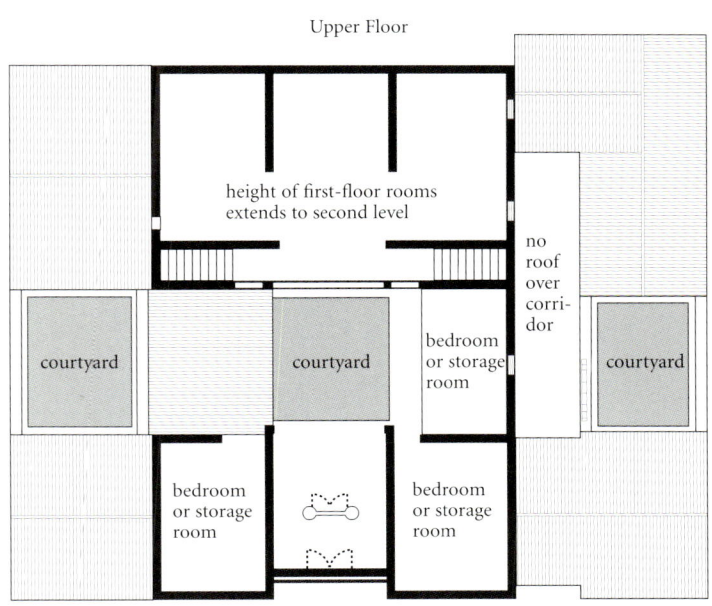

Upper Floor

courtyard		height of first-floor rooms extends to second level		courtyard		courtyard
			bedroom or storage room		no roof over corridor
	bedroom or storage room		bedroom or storage room		

A Mandarin's Mansion in Hong Kong

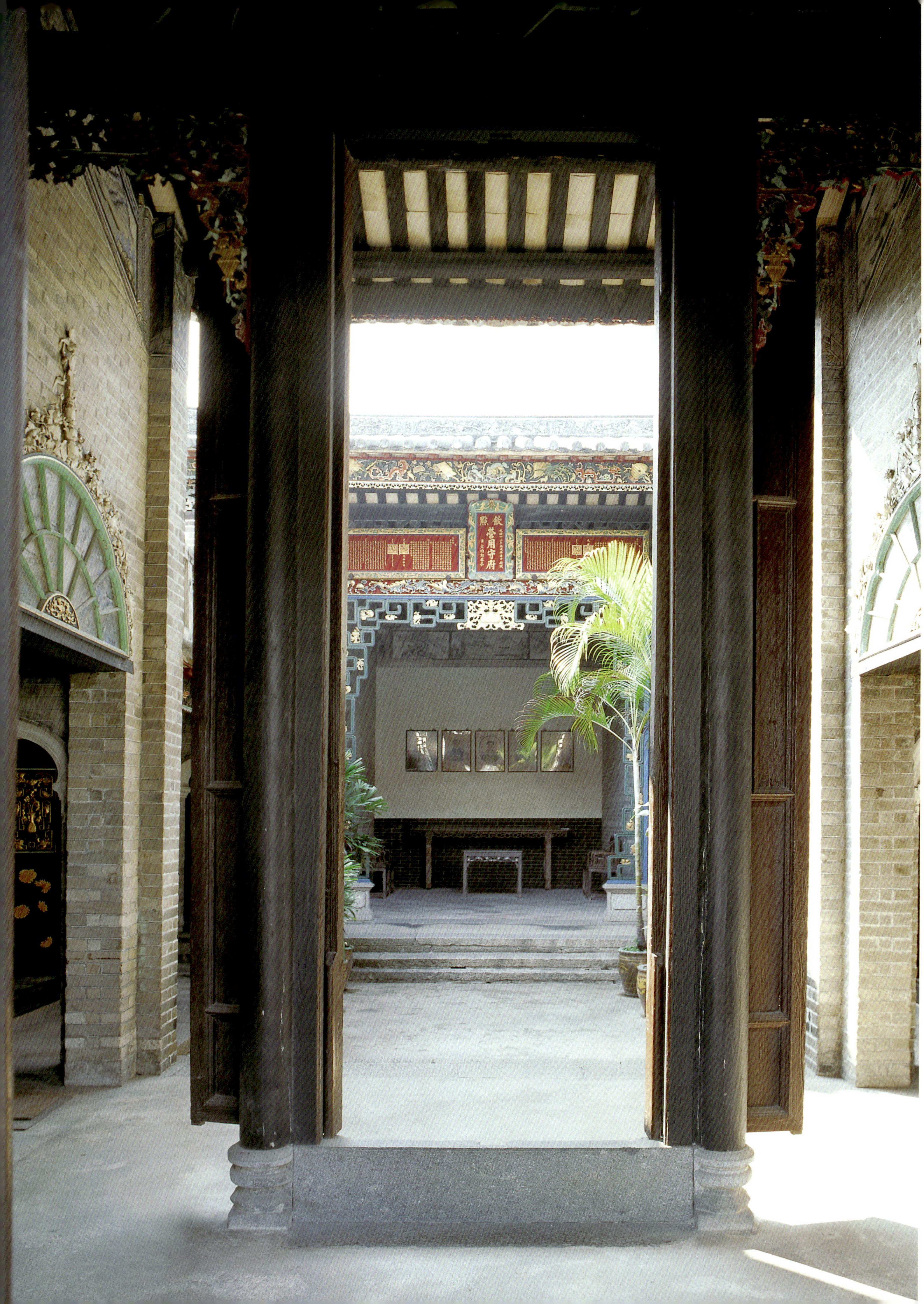
欽點
營用守府

Opposite:
From the entry, this view looks through the entrance hall containing the open screen or spirit wall and across the courtyard towards the Main Hall.

Left:
Profusely ornamented, this U-shaped wooden lattice panel graces the entrance to the Main Hall. Included at its center is a pair of hanging horizontal honorific boards and a vertical plaque given to Man Chung-luen by a Qing-dynasty official.

Below left:
Alongside both sides of the entrance hall are semi-hemispheric painted glass panes with rather rococo-like plaster moldings, which most see as having a Western flavor that hints at the emerging cosmopolitan nature of Hong Kong in the latter part of the nineteenth century. In addition to traditional woodcarvings and ceramic figures, the house ornamentation also includes idiosyncratic elements.

Below right:
Four of the Baxian or Eight Immortals are depicted in a boat in this painting high above a wall perpendicular to the Main Hall. A complementary set is on the opposite wall.

a nineteenth-century multi-courtyard scholar-gentry residence, which is both stately and simple while having elaborate ornamental elements.

Man Chung-luen, a member of the twenty-first generation of the Man clan, built the Tai Fu Tai residence in 1865. Usually the name "Tai Fu Tai" attached to a dwelling commemorates the fact that the owner had passed the triennial Imperial Civil Examination at the *jinshi* degree, the highest of three levels. Such an individual was eligible to be addressed as *Tai Fu* in Cantonese or *daifu* in standard Chinese, an honorific indicating a high official, sometimes called a Mandarin in English. Using both Chinese and Manchu characters, the two red horizontal boards suspended above the entry to the Main Hall of Tai Fu Tai declare that the Qing Emperor Guangxu himself in 1875 bestowed the Tai Fu title. In this case, however, the title was an honorary designation in recognition of Man Chung-luen's reputation as a successful merchant and philanthropist. Man thus was not a high civil official who had earned the title by passing the examinations, but instead had "purchased" the title, some say with gold he found from a cache hidden by pirates. The third character, also pronounced *Tai* in Cantonese, but *di* in standard Chinese, simply means "residence." In some other areas of China, such a house might be identified with three characters, *Jinshi Di* ("residence of a *jinshi*"), written on a similar board above the entry.

The broad façade of Tai Fu Tai reveals a three-bay center section with a pair of flanking additions that are lower and set back in a subsidiary position. The granite foundation stones and the bonding pattern of gray bricks emphasize the side-to-side symmetry of the structure, which is then accentuated by a grand central entryway and a pair of parallel doors leading into side buildings. Along the ridge of the roof and within a three-dimensional frieze below the eaves, ornamentation is similarly balanced. Like other dwellings, ancestral halls, and temples throughout neighboring Guangdong province, the three-dimensional fired pottery figures from the famous kilns in Shiwan, Foshan, as well as polychrome moldings, are used to add both color and allegorical meaning to the residence.

Tai Fu Tai differs from many Chinese houses in that the overall floor plan is not rigidly symmetrical, even as the core area is symmetrically proportioned and there is a clear axis running from the entry in front to the Main Hall in the rear. The central entryway leads first into an entrance hall or entry portico, whose view from the outside is blocked by a two-leaved screen wall. Beyond the screen wall, which may be opened, is a large courtyard with another pair of side rooms. Adjacent to the entry portico is a pair of flanking side rooms for the convenience of servants.

Ahead is the Main Hall, which looms large between flanking bedrooms. Dominating the entrance to the Main Hall is a profusely ornamented U-shaped wooden lattice panel, above which is a pair of hanging horizontal honorific boards with a vertical plaque given by a Qing-dynasty official. On the back wall are portraits of Man Chung-luen, his wife, and some other family members. Only a few pieces of family furniture made of *hongmu*, called "redwood" in Chinese but "blackwood" in English, remain in the hall, barely suggesting the sumptuous state of the hall at the end of the nineteenth century. On both sides of the Main Hall are bedrooms. A rather inaccessible upper floor provides storage space as well as a place for young women to observe guests without themselves being seen.

Immediately adjacent to the Main Hall is a quiet, elongated *huating* or "study room" with its own courtyard, which taken together provide a

Left:
A pair of arches of this type, which show Western influence, leads from the open space in front of the Main Hall into adjacent areas

Below:
While only a modest "mansion" by Hong Kong standards, Tai Fu Tai is a rare example of a nineteenth-century multi-courtyard scholar-gentry residence.

Right:
Located immediately in front of the *huating* or study room is a rectangular courtyard, which taken together because of their inspirational ornamentation, provide both a place for thought and a refuge. Above the ornamental screen wall ahead are two characters, *wan yue*, meaning "to find pleasure in the moonlight," which is suggestive of it as a place of leisure for examining the night sky.

A Mandarin's Mansion in Hong Kong

study   Main Hall   corridor   kitchen

rear   front

Above:
Transverse section, longitudinal section, front elevation, and rear elevation of Tai Fu Tai.

Right:
This moon gate leads from the main courtyard into the kitchen area.

Far right:
A view of the corner of the kitchen, including, on the left, a side of the brick stove.

place of refuge and introspection. Here, much of the ornamentation is inspirational, such as the carp swimming upstream and the elegant calligraphy on either side of the tile-filled window. The struggling carp signifies perseverance, the effort required to succeed, and a wish for success in passing examinations leading to official position and success. At the head of the enclosed courtyard is an ornamental screen wall made of patterned bricks with two characters, *wan yue*, atop it, meaning "to find pleasure in the moonlight," suggesting a place of leisure for examining the night sky.

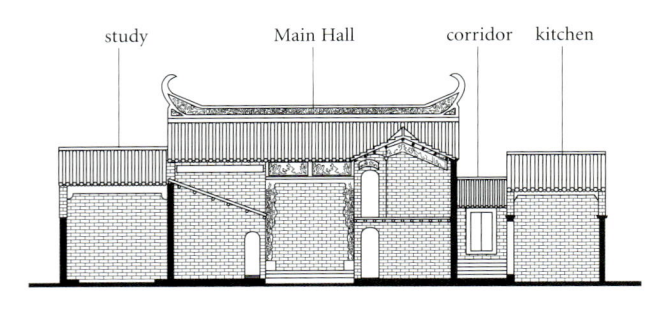

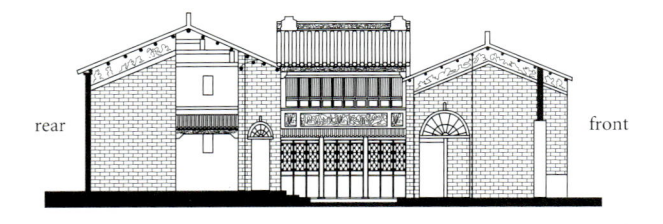

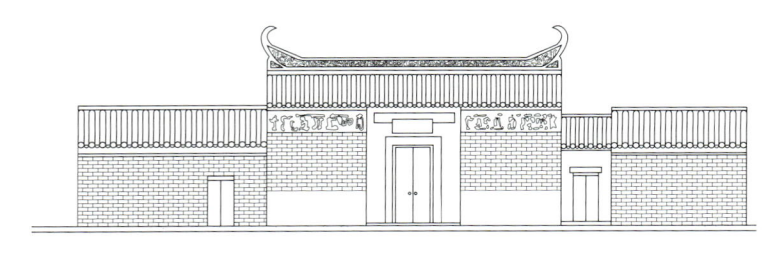

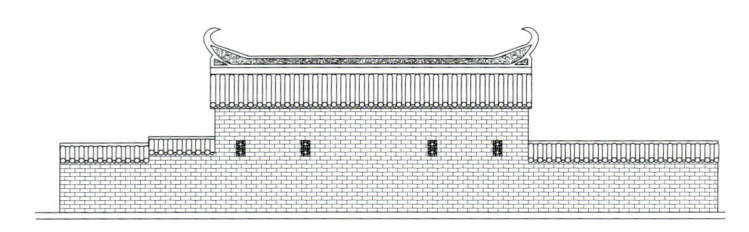

In a separate wing building, which is entered through a corridor running the full length of the building and that has its own door to the outside, is the utilitarian section of the house, including a toilet in a back corner. The elongated side building, which is accessed through a beautiful moon gate, includes a kitchen, a side chamber, as well as a courtyard that served as an outdoor work space. Like other traditional Chinese kitchens, the brick cooking area was designed so that large cooking vessels, called woks in Cantonese, could be set in place above the wood fire, as well as clay cooking pots along the side. The hollowed-out log along one wall is a press used to crush peanuts in order to extract peanut oil for cooking.

Among the most distinctive features of Tai Fu Tai is its abundant ornamentation, some of which has a Western flavor that hints at the emerging cosmopolitan nature of Hong Kong in the latter part of the nineteenth century. In addition to traditional woodcarvings and ceramic figures, somewhat idiosyncratic elements such as painted glass panes and rather rococo-like plaster moldings demonstrate

Young women could peek from this upstairs area and observe visitors or ceremonies taking place in the Main Hall below, where family portraits are hung above the altar table.

new influences from the West. Auspicious symbols, including vases, symbolizing peace, with playful lions each side and many different sorts of flowers, fruits, and leaves are seen throughout Tai Fu Tai.

When the Hong Kong Antiquities Board advised in 1978 that the residence had historical value, two families were living in the old house and it had begun to show evidence of wood rot and other structural dilapidation. After lengthy negotiations with Man Wah Cheung Tong, the corporate body representing the Man lineage, Tai Fu Tai was given full protection in 1987. Restoration took approximately a year, including the replacement of rotted timbers and broken bricks, the cleaning of wall paintings and other ornamentation, repairs to the bracket systems, and the relaying of roof tiles, which left a patina of age. Nearby is the Man Lun-fung Ancestral Hall, which was probably built at the end of the seventeenth century. Today, historical sites like Tai Fu Tai and Man Lun-fung Ancestral Hall are easily accessible by bus and taxi from central Hong Kong.

Not too far from San Tin are other villages established by settlers of the Five Great Clans. One of the better preserved villages is Pingshan, inhabited by the Tang clan since the twelfth century. Utilizing what is called the Pingshan Heritage Trail, established in 1993 under the auspices of the Antiquities Monuments Office and the first of its kind in Hong Kong, visitors can follow a well-marked one-kilometer trail that links an old temple, well, trees, study hall, shrine, and ancestral hall, as well as Sheng Cheung Wai, an old walled village that is still occupied. Because so many modern multistoried villa-style residences and parked automobiles crowd the narrow lanes, it is difficult to perceive Pingshan as a "village" and a repository of old structures. Yet, each of the sites along the heritage trail remains a part of the life of Tang family members.

A COUNTRY FARMHOUSE
Mao Zedong's Boyhood Home, Hunan Province

The boyhood home of Mao Zedong is a strikingly simple farmhouse not too different from other adobe brick structures still seen nearby in the cloud-draped hills and fertile rice-producing areas of northern and central Hunan province. When the baby Mao was born in this house in December 1893, imperial China had experienced nearly a century of humiliation and was entering an especially bleak period of political disintegration. The turmoil did not subside until the adult Mao Zedong proclaimed the establishment of the People's Republic of China in 1949. Subsequent decades brought still more catastrophes to the Chinese, some of which were stimulated by the actions of Mao himself, yet he and his birthplace have remained iconic elements in the drama of China's modern history.

Mao Zedong's great grandfather, Mao Enpu, purchased the house lot and adjacent farmland in Shaoshanchong around 1878, fifteen years before his grandson was born. The distinctive Hunan word *chong* can be translated as "hamlet," in that it describes the small parcels of flat land suitable for building lots in the hilly area. This purchase was made principally because the extended Mao family's homestead farther up a nearby valley was already overcrowded. The dwelling, initially consisting of merely a small rectangular, thatched five-room cottage that was used while the land was tamed and terraced, grew over time into a sprawling, inverted U-shaped structure comprised of eighteen interconnected rooms covering an area of about 556 square meters. This was the home of Mao Zedong's youth that is still seen today. The well-ventilated dwelling is nestled on the lower portion of a steep hillside within a glade surrounded by bamboo and Masson pine trees. Its doorway and fronting courtyard face north, looking out over terraced rice paddies that cascade down towards a pond.

Right:
The Mao farmstead is sited on a narrow patch of land at the base of a hill slope and adjacent to cascading terraced paddy fields.

Below right:
In this ethereal Cultural Revolution era poster, the birthplace of Chairman Mao is shown as a pilgrimage destination for Red Guards. Some one to three million youths journeyed to Shaoshan each year between 1966 and 1976.

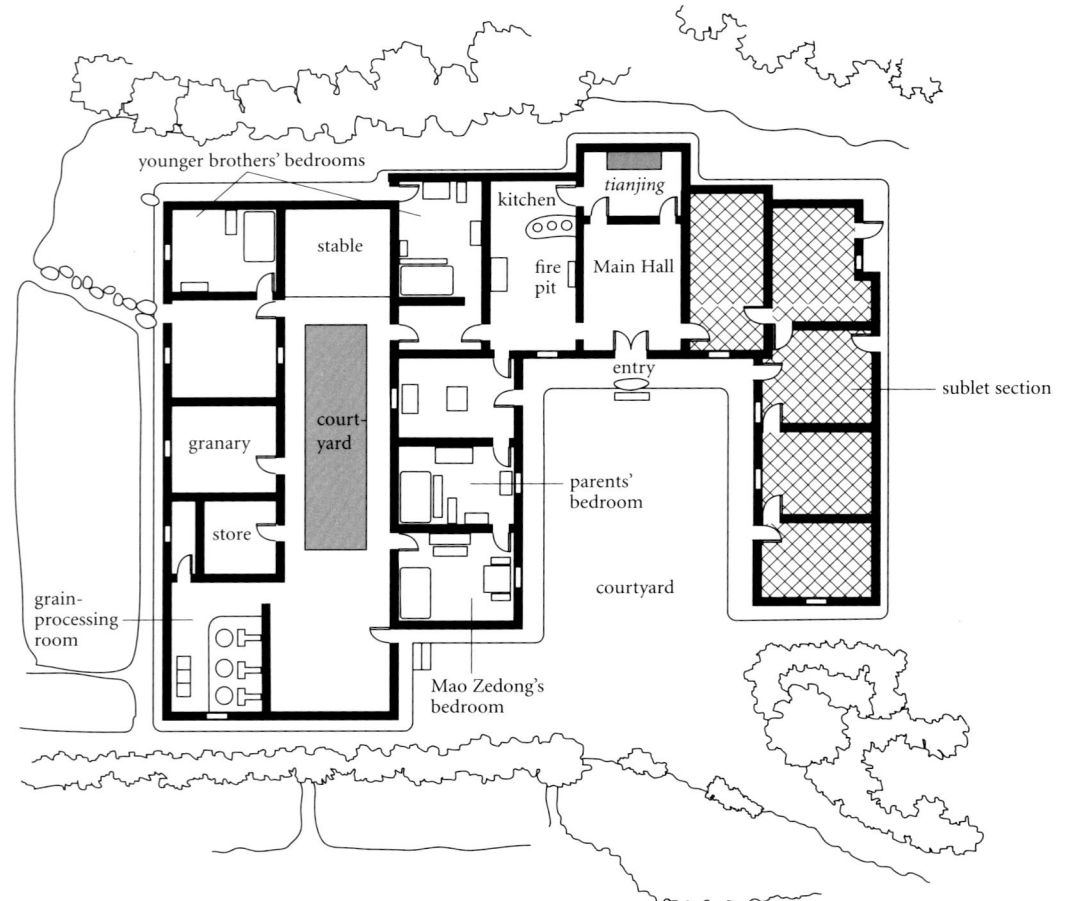

The Mao family farmhouse over time evolved into an inverted U-shaped plan with an adjacent wing that included an elongated "skywell," called a *tianjing*, which is surrounded by bedrooms and working places.

The expansion of the residence mirrored the rise of Mao's father Shunsheng from a "poor" to a "middle" to a "rich" peasant—to use terms of social analysis developed later during Mao's revolutionary life—as his small farm grew and additional income came from the buying and selling of grain. Such transformations of families and their residences were seen throughout China when fortune smiled. Typically, this involved the addition of, first, one wing, then another; the replacement of thatching with roof tiles; the setting up of an additional kitchen to service a newly married son; and the renting of surplus space to kin or neighbor. Sometimes even adobe brick walls would be replaced—one at a time—with fired bricks. Mao's mother bore seven children in this house, two daughters and five sons, but only three boys survived. Zemin, born in 1895, and Zetan, born in 1905, like their elder brother Zedong, each had his own bedroom in the expanding dwelling. Lore has it that Mao's immediate family only occupied the eastern thirteen rooms, which were capped with a tile roof in 1918, the year that his father reached the peak of his wealth. The western wing, with its thatched roof and five rooms, was sublet to a neighbor, also surnamed Mao. The two families jointly shared a single Main Hall. Today, the thatched roof section is not accessible to visitors.

It is said that young barefooted Mao began to labor in the nearby paddy fields when he was six, and, even after enrolling in the nearby village school, continued to help with farm work in the mornings and after school. Mao's early schooling included the Chinese classics. However, his stern and parsimonious father was more interested in his mastering the abacus so that he could keep the increasingly complicated household accounts.

The record of Mao's life over the next decade is replete with inconsistencies and conflicting information. It is said that in either 1907 or 1908 a marriage was arranged between the fourteen-year-old Mao and a girl of eighteen, but Mao Zedong himself did not mention such a youthful marriage. If they had been married, it is likely that the young couple would have lived together in his parents' home, probably occupying the bedroom adjacent to theirs. The young wife, it is said, died three years later at the age of twenty-one when Mao himself was still a teenager.

Mao never wrote about traditional practices, such as nuptial customs, which most likely were observed by his family. He readily acknowledged that his mother was a devout Buddhist, unlike his father who was a non-believer. It is said that Mao fled the family farm (and perhaps his wife) in 1909 to continue his education away from the influence of his father, this time in the Tongshan Upper Primary School in Xiangtan county town. After that it was on to a school in nearby Xiangxiang, the home district

Starkly clean at present, this front courtyard, embraced by buildings on three sides, was once the principal activity center for the Mao family during daylight hours.

Far left:
The substantial eaves overhang of the west wing helps shelter the adobe brick from being eroded by rain. The "hanging fish" is a representation of "abundance" because of a homophonous relationship between the words.

Left:
Protruding wooden bracket arms lift the purlins that support the overhanging eaves.

of his mother's family. Finally, he moved to Changsha, capital city of Hunan province, in 1911, to study at the First Provincial Normal School,

Mao's eyes were opened to new social and political possibilities as he encountered activist notions in radical newspapers and in the thinking of teachers and students in Changsha. Mao now felt the urgency of reading "the wordless book," the society around him, and he probably saw for the first time a map of the world. In the fall of 1918, he traveled to Beijing where he obtained a minor job in a university library working for the Marxist thinker Li Dazhao. In May 1919, he returned to Changsha, but left again, before finally returning in 1920 to teach and also to marry Yang Kaihui, usually referred to as Mao's first wife. (She was later executed by the Nationalists in 1930.) The years away from his family and village exposed Mao to the fundamental changes taking place in China, including Sun Yatsen's revolution in 1911, as well as to ideas flooding in from the West. By 1920 he considered himself a Marxist and on July 1, 1921 led the Hunan delegation to the fledgling First Congress of the Chinese Communist Party in Shanghai.

Above:
Looking down a slope towards the house of a neighbor, this view along the east wall of the outer wing shows the stone base, plastered lower wall, adobe brick above, as well as the tile roof.

Left:
Visiting his boyhood home in 1959, Mao Zedong walked with an old relative and other family members from his home, behind, to a nearby restaurant.

A Country Farmhouse 213

Mao had returned to Shaoshan in 1919 after the death of his mother, who was simply known as "Seventh Sister of the Wen family," but he did not come back just several months later when his father died. Subsequently, Mao only revisited his home village four times, always at critical junctures in China's revolution. In late 1925 and 1927, he used his old home as a base to carry out a survey of peasant associations, which was the basis for his famous "Report of an Investigation of the Peasant Movement in Hunan." This seminal document declared peasants to be China's major revolutionary force. He also returned during the Great Leap Forward in 1959 for twenty-six days, when local peasants gave him sobering news of fabricated grain output, contrary to what others were reporting. He returned one final time in 1966 during the Cultural Revolution.

The dwelling one sees today is neatly restored and preserved. In spite of its bare walls, spartan furniture, scant farm implements, scattered photographs, and terse signs, it is not difficult to imagine what life might have been like for the farm family more than a hundred years ago. The interlinked rooms are indeed commodious, but it is important to recognize that in such Chinese farm dwellings these spaces—all under a common roof—also served as barns, granaries, and places to store brush for the kitchen stove and straw for animal fodder. They also accommodated indoor pens for animals. Throughout most of the year, the sunny front courtyard was used to dry rice and vegetables as well as to socialize with family and neighbors. Only in winter, when days are short and the sun low behind the hill, is this area in shadow throughout most of the day.

The house was elevated upon a foundation of rubble stone, requiring a stone slab step to reach it from the courtyard, even extending beyond the walls so that it is possible to move from one door to another under the cover of the overhanging eaves even when it is raining. The structure was built with relatively thick walls. The large 34 by 11.5 centimeter adobe bricks were made in molds and hardened over time in the sun. Unlike wealthier houses that have columns to support the roof, the walls here are all load-bearing. Each triangular gable directly carries the roof structure, which is made up of wooden purlins and rafters and the tiles that they support.

Viewed from the front door, the high-ceilinged Main Hall is dominated by a black lacquer *shenkan*, a shrine housing ancestral tablets and statues, which is set into the wall above tables containing ritual paraphernalia. Shrines were essential pieces of ritual furniture in traditional households and can still be seen in the countryside. Looking somewhat like a "building," shrines of this type range from remarkably plain to richly detailed with carved ornamentation and mortise-and-tenon joinery. The Mao family *shenkan* is quite simple, lacking any refinement and reflecting essentially only practical functions (perhaps the one seen today is only a crude reconstruction). In this room is also found a square *Baxian zhuo* or Eight Immortals table with four trestle benches. As the center of family gatherings, tables of this type, covered with a cloth, might serve during a wedding or funeral as an offering table in front of the altar, or they could be moved to the center of the room or even into the courtyard outside where meals could be eaten or games played.

Behind the Main Hall is a transitional space under a sloping roof with an opening in the ceiling. Here rays of sunlight make food preparation for the contiguous kitchen easier. In addition to letting in light and ventilating smoke, the skywell also directs rainwater into large vats where it is stored. The area also provides space for fuel for the cooking stove: brush, grass, and charcoal collected from the hillsides. The adjacent kitchen is dominated by an imposing brick and mortar stove that sits immediately inside. Although Chinese kitchens are frequently dark and sooty, this one is commodious, with abundant work and storage space as well as places for the family to gather. There is also a fire pit. In the Hunan and Jiangxi regions, fire pits are common features in rural kitchens where, in winter, an open charcoal or coal fire could be kept burning in the recessed hearth

Opposite above:
With its soaring high ceiling, the Main Hall is clearly an important room even as the open adobe brick walls and modest furniture mark its relative modesty. Stripped of ancestral tablets, the simple *shenkan* inserted into the back wall only hints at its centrality in times past.

Opposite below:
Located behind the Main Hall is a transitional space that served as a pantry for the adjacent kitchen, a place to store firewood and to process vegetables. The opening in the roof lets in sunlight, ventilates smoke, and facilitates the collection of rainwater in a large vat.

Above:
When Liu Shaoqi, once China's President, and his wife visited Mao Zedong's birthplace in 1961, they seem to marvel at the size and utility of the old stove.

Left:
Viewed from behind and showing the three apertures used to insert fuel into the burning chamber, this large stove dominates the Mao family kitchen.

Far left:
As in other areas of south-central China, homes in Hunan often have an open hearth, a charcoal or coal fire pit, that in winter provides a warm space for the family to gather. The adjustable hanging trammel can suspend a kettle of boiling water.

Left:
This country cupboard provided a place to store bowls, plates, and chopsticks while the baskets on the wall held herbs and spices.

in order to boil water in a kettle suspended from a trammel, an adjustable iron rod with a hook. The fire pit was also a place for the family to gather when it was cold. It is said that the young Zedong even assembled young members of his extended family around the warmth of the fire pit where he spoke to them of the need for peasants to participate in revolutionary activities.

There is now no evidence of a shrine to the Kitchen God, called Zaojun or Zaowang, but it is likely there once was one. Serving as tutelary deity in charge of the household rather than having any connection with the culinary arts or fire, a Kitchen God was a ubiquitous household fixture in late imperial China and relatively common even today in the countryside. Found in imperial palaces as well as in humble huts, the enshrined image had incense and candles lighted before it daily in addition to periodic food offerings. Prior to the lunar New Year, the paper image of Zaojun, blackened with soot from a year in the kitchen, is burned. As the smoke rises, he ascends to Heaven to report to the Jade Emperor on the family members' behavior since his previous journey.

Just beyond the kitchen, past a small room with a square table and benches, is Mao's parents' bedroom. It contains the bed where his 26-year-old mother gave birth to him and his siblings. Adjacent to this is the bedroom of Mao Zedong's youth. Like all of the bedrooms, this small room is dominated by a bulky wooden canopy bed, called *babu chuang*, a veritable room within a room. Gauze curtains offered little seclusion but some respite from mosquitoes. Marital beds of this type were sometimes brought as part of a new bride's dowry, but it is not clear where this particular bed came from. On the wall nearby is a *tong* oil lamp made of bamboo. The young Mao, who was known as a voracious reader, is said to have used it to read late at night. The flame resembles a bean in shape and size, casting just enough light to read but not enough to arouse the suspicion of his strict father. He sometimes retreated for more privacy, through a trap door in the ceiling of his room, to the airy loft above, which has a window. In this bedroom, Mao is said to have gathered family and other villagers in 1925 and 1927 to talk about the peasant movement. When Mao returned home during the Great Leap Forward, thirty-two years after an earlier visit, he spotted on the wall across from the bed a photograph of his mother, himself, and his two brothers, taken in 1919. He asked where the photograph came from, declaring that it was probably the earliest picture of him, taken when he was about twenty-six. He often stated that he resembled his mother.

Just beyond Mao's bedroom is a very large rectangular courtyard surrounded by storage rooms for farm implements and produce, livestock sheds, and the bedrooms of his two younger brothers. Bathed in sunlight for parts of every day, this courtyard, with its recessed core and shaded margins, provided a work space for husking and cleaning harvested rice. In the southwest corner room sits a hand rice mill for separating the hulls. Nearby are several foot-balanced pestles and mortars used to polish rice in order to remove the glumes. Adjacent is a large room that served as the granary where a large amount of unhusked rice was stored. The bedrooms of Zedong's two brothers lie adjacent to the pigpen and stable for cattle. Rear and side exits open to a broad terrace used to dry harvested rice in preparation for its storage inside the house.

The young boy, of course, became the Great Helmsman, and the hamlet of Shaoshan and his boyhood residence played their roles in his fluctuating fortunes. After a youth spent working around the house, the young Mao left the village for education.

Introduction into social movements led rather quickly to his role in the formation of the Chinese Communist Party. When he returned in the later 1920s, he appears to have gained inspiration from the struggles of peasants, with whom he was familiar.

In 1929, the Nationalist government confiscated the house and its furnishings. Substantial deterioration and destruction had occurred by the time the house and land were returned to Mao's brother's family in 1937. After 1949, the building itself was restored and some furniture returned. In 1953, the site was put under national protection and opened to visitors. During the high tide of the Great Proletarian Culture in the decade after 1966, Shaoshan became a kind of pilgrimage destination for between one and three million people a year, especially Red Guards drawn by the mystique and the veritable cult of Mao Zedong. When Mao himself retreated to Shaoshan for ten days in June 1966 to meditate on the course of the Cultural Revolution, he stayed in a newly constructed villa near Dripping Water Cave not far from his grandfather's original farmhouse. He spoke of retiring to this bucolic village with the hope of living in a simple thatched-roof cottage.

Left and below:
Mao Zedong's small bedroom is dominated by a bulky canopy bed, a veritable room within a room. On the nearby wall is a *tong* oil lamp made of bamboo (left, shown enlarged), which cast just enough light for the young Mao Zedong to read. The small flame resembles a bean in shape and size.

A Country Farmhouse 217

Far left:
Adjacent to the elongated skywell, a room holds equipment to process farm products, including a number of foot-balanced pestles and mortars used to polish rice.

Left:
In addition to farm implements such as the winnower shown in the rear, the room also holds a hand rice mill for separating the hulls.

Below:
This elongated skywell has around it not only storage rooms, a granary, pens for pigs and cattle, but also the bedrooms of Mao Zedong's two younger brothers.

After Mao's death on September 9, 1976 until the hundredth anniversary of his birth in 1993, the number of visitors to Shaoshan dropped precipitously. When the peripatetic travel writer Paul Theroux came in the 1980s, he discovered that "the tide was out in Shaoshan; it was a town that time forgot— ghostly and echoing." Since then, however, especially as domestic tourism has become a growth industry, local pride and civic boosterism relating to Shaoshan's native son have led to the revitalization and commercialization of the village. Important historical sites, such as Mao's residence, Mao's school, and the Mao clan Ancestral Hall have been fitted into a tapestry of visitor experiences that now include a multitude of Mao family restaurants, an extensive Mao museum, a Mao library, a Mao research center, and landscaped public gardens. In addition, a comprehensive Mao Zedong theme park operates nearby, where visitors can in a single day savor *each* of the significant places throughout the country associated with the life and legend of the Chairman. Mao Zedong—revolutionary hero and common man— has become a cottage industry in his transformed village, a socialist icon commodified by capitalist entrepreneurs. The immediate environs around Mao's birthplace nonetheless remain relatively unchanged, providing a quaintly ageless glimpse of a late nineteenth-century farmstead. In a country that today is undergoing a truly "revolutionary" transformation, one can find quiet whispers of the circumstances that propelled the young Mao on his extraordinary path.

Poem written by Mao Zedong to commemorate his visit to Shaoshan in 1959:

Shaoshan Revisited, June 1959

Like a dim dream recalled, I curse the long-fled past...
My native soil two and thirty years gone by.
The red flag roused the serf, halberd in hand,
While the despot's black talons held his whip aloft.
Bitter sacrifice strengthens bold resolve
Which dares to make sun and moon shine in new skies.
Happy, I see wave upon wave of paddy and beans,
And all around heroes home-bound in the
evening mist.

Mao Tsetung Poems, Peking: Foreign Languages Press, 1976

Quotations from Mao Zedong:

"A revolution is not a dinner party, or writing an essay, or painting a picture, or doing embroidery; it cannot be so refined, so leisurely and gentle, so temperate, kind, courteous, restrained and magnanimous. A revolution is an insurrection, an act of violence by which one class overthrows another."

Report on an Investigation of the Peasant Movement in Hunan (1927)

"A man in China is usually subjected to the domination of three systems of authority [political authority, clan authority, and religious authority].... As for women, in addition to being dominated by these three systems of authority, they are also dominated by the men [the authority of the husband]. These four authorities—political, clan, religious and masculine—are the embodiment of the whole feudal-patriarchal ideology and system, and are the four thick ropes binding the Chinese people, particularly the peasants."

Report on an Investigation of the Peasant Movement in Hunan (1927)

"All men must die, but death can vary in its significance. The ancient Chinese writer Sima Qian said, 'Though death befalls all men alike, it may be weightier than Mount Tai or lighter than a feather.' To die for the people is weightier than Mount Tai, but to work for the fascists and die for the exploiters and oppressors is lighter than a feather."

Serve the People (1944)

"You can't solve a problem? Well, get down and investigate the present facts and its past history! When you have investigated the problem thoroughly, you will know how to solve it. Conclusions invariably come after investigation, and not before. Only a blockhead cudgels his brains on his own, or together with a group, to 'find a solution' or 'evolve an idea' without making any investigation. It must be stressed that this cannot possibly lead to any effective solution or any good idea."

Oppose Book Worship (1930)

"Letting a hundred flowers blossom and a hundred schools of thought contend is the policy for promoting the progress of the arts and the sciences and a flourishing socialist culture in our land. Different forms and styles in art should develop freely and different schools in science should contend freely."

On the Correct Handling of Contradictions Among the People (1957)

Regarded as the first photograph of Mao Zedong (right), this image taken in 1919 when he was twenty-six includes his mother, himself, and his two brothers. Mao sometimes declared that he resembled his mother.

A LANDLORD'S VILLAGE HOME
Liu Shaoqi's Boyhood Home, Hunan Province

When Mao Zedong proclaimed the founding of the People's Republic of China atop the rostrum facing Tiananmen Square on October 1, 1949, a fellow Hunan native named Liu Shaoqi was at his side. Liu was a pragmatic theorist and seasoned administrator whose abilities led many to see him as the steward of Mao's revolutionary legacy and Mao's presumptive successor. Tragically, Liu's fortunes instead abruptly turned as his promotion of practical economic policies eventually came into conflict with Mao's more ideological urges. Despite having served as China's Head of State from 1959 to 1967, Liu Shaoqi was labeled the "number one capitalist-roader" and "renegade, traitor, and scab" during the early stages of the Cultural Revolution. Although thrown onto the "ash heap of history" and banished to oblivion, Liu has since undergone a political resurrection that also provides a peek into his formative years.

Liu Shaoqi (originally called Liu Shaoxuan) was born in Tanzichong hamlet of Huaminglou township in Ningxiang county, just 30 kilometers across a mountain range from Mao's birthplace in Shaoshan. Unlike Mao, Liu was born into comfortable family circumstances and in his early years enjoyed a significantly more cosmopolitan life. In 1948, he married, some say for the fourth time, a new wife named Wang Guangmei, a university graduate some twenty-four years younger than he. During the nearly twenty years that he served as a high official, together they paid state visits to many countries. In Beijing, they lived in Zhongnanhai, the walled sanctuary for China's Communist rulers, but the imposing walls did not ultimately provide safe haven for either of them. In January 1967, Red Guards were able to break into their residence and post "big character posters" on the walls. They dragged them out for public criticism and humiliation in their own courtyard. Liu, it is said, offered to resign, telling Chairman Mao that he would like to return to live and work either in his home village in Hunan or in the revolutionary caves of Yanan. However, in 1968 Liu Shaoqi was stripped of power and disgraced. He became bedridden with untreated pneumonia, and died a lonely death on the floor of an unheated building in Henan province in 1969, midway between his boyhood country home in Hunan

Below:
This oblique view of the long façade of the boyhood home of Liu Shaoqi reveals that the surface of the adobe walls has been parged with a thin coat of viscous mud. It is likely that there were no windows in the early house and that those now seen were opened later.

Right:
Built around 1870, the Liu house was sited so that it is wrapped from behind by a copse of trees on a hilly slope and faces a large pond.

Below right:
Oriented so that it faces west, this expansive farm dwelling, shown here in plan view, includes two large courtyards and several smaller skywells.

ancestral shrine

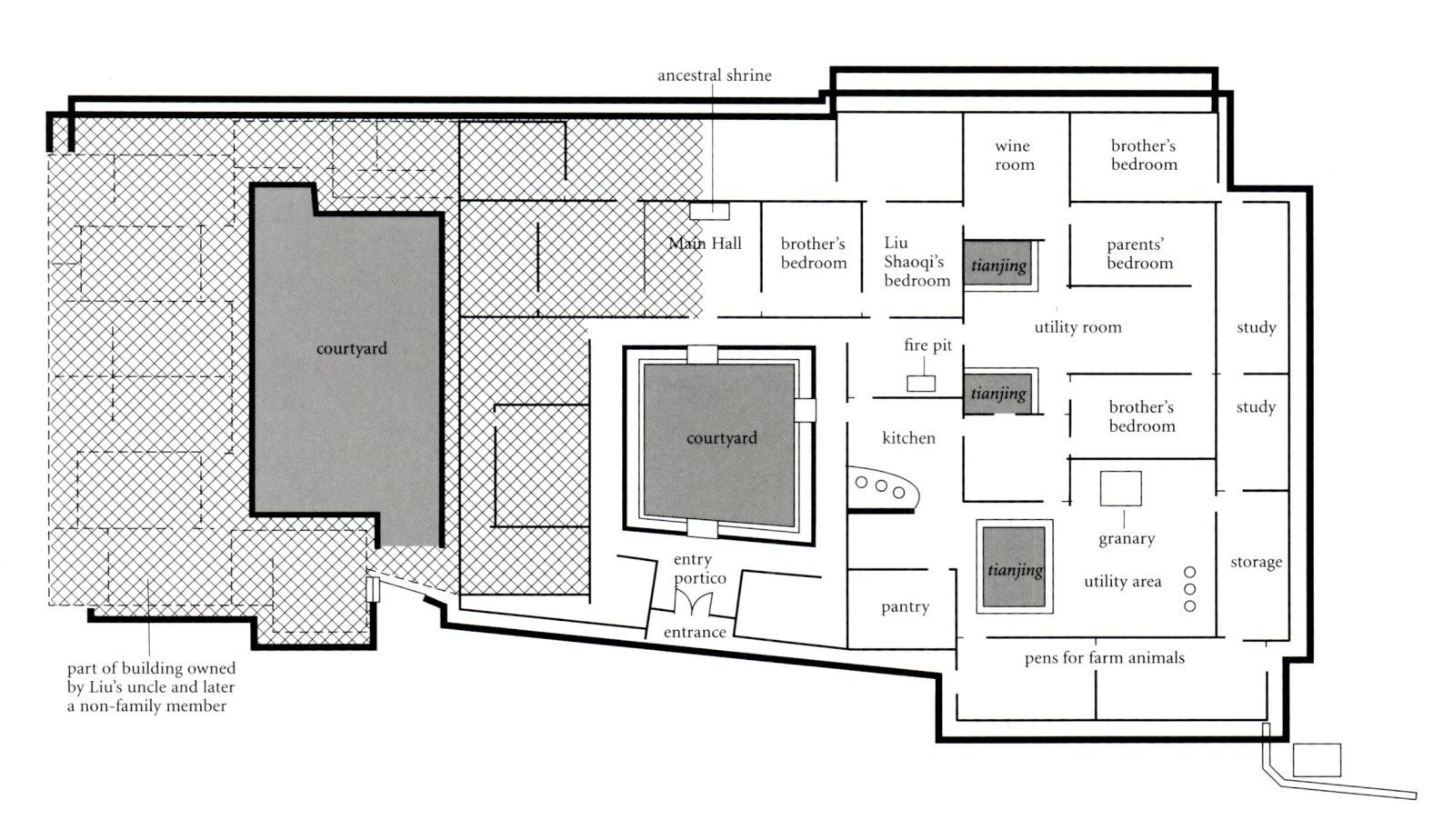

wine room | brother's bedroom

Main Hall | brother's bedroom | Liu Shaoqi's bedroom | *tianjing* | parents' bedroom

courtyard

utility room | study

fire pit | *tianjing* | brother's bedroom | study

courtyard | kitchen

entry portico

entrance | pantry | *tianjing* | granary | utility area | storage

pens for farm animals

part of building owned by Liu's uncle and later a non-family member

A Landlord's Village Home 221

and Beijing. His death was not made public until 1974, while his wife, who had accompanied him to his boyhood home in 1961, suffered confinement for ten years until her release in 1977.

Little is known of the history of the Liu family dwelling except that it was built in 1871 by Shaoqi's grandfather when Shaoqi's father was six years old, twenty-seven years before China's future "President" was born there on November 24, 1898. Once the grandfather died in 1875, the two surviving sons raised their own families in the large house. At some point the building was divided and a line drawn down the center of the Main Hall to indicate a sharing of ritual space. This created two attached, yet separate, residences joined across a courtyard.

Both brothers came to be considered rich landowners and supported large families. Liu Shousheng, Liu Shaoqi's father, died in 1910 when his son was not yet a teenager. His mother managed the large family of four sons and two daughters, living with her sons until she died in 1931. Liu Shousheng's elder brother struggled to hold onto his half of the estate but went bankrupt in 1930. He sold his interest to a neighbor surnamed Xia. Thus, a significant portion of a residence built by the prosperous grandfather—with the hope that it would house many offspring of the Liu family—had in just two generations been

Left
The rehabilitation of Liu Shaoqi from political oblivion is suggested by the fact that the characters above the door that declare "The Former Home of Comrade Liu Shaoqi" were written by Deng Xiaoping.

Below:
Barren of activity and ornamentation once characteristic of such a central room, the Main Hall is today dominated by a large empty wooden cabinet which once contained a *shenkan*, the family's ancestral tablet shrine.

222 China's Fine Heritage Houses

divided, with partial ownership passing to a non-family member, a common practice in difficult times.

Shaoqi, meanwhile, continued to live in the house with his mother and brothers, until he left in 1919 to attend middle school in Changsha, the provincial capital. He later journeyed beyond Hunan to Beijing to study either French or German, and then to Shanghai to study Russian. In 1920, he joined a socialist youth group and had the opportunity to live and study in Moscow for less than a year. It was at Moscow's Communist University of the Toilers of the East (KUTV), a special institution for budding Communists from Asia, that Liu Shaoqi came to appreciate Leninist ideology. And it was here that he joined the newly formed Chinese Communist Party. After he returned to China, he became Mao's confidant, rising rapidly, becoming first a member of the Central Committee in 1927 and then of the powerful Politburo in 1934. Often working in the underground, he honed his skills as a labor and party organizer. Even though he differed from Mao in temperament and in his approach to revolutionary change, by 1942 he was championing the study of "Mao Zedong thought" as a contribution to Marxism, whose form already had gone beyond the rudimentary stage.

Through the end of the 1950s, Liu Shaoqi remained the steady bureaucrat supporting the ideologue Mao. The euphoria of nation building, however, was soon dampened by the apocalyptic failures of Mao's Great Leap Forward and the creation of Peoples Communes. Beginning in 1958, this movement led to famine and the deaths of at least twenty million people over a three-year period. Mao contemplated "retiring" from political life and the country turned to the pragmatic Liu Shaoqi to lead the economic recovery. To many in China, intractable problems began to increasingly emerge.

Liu Shaoqi's bedroom contains a bulky wooden alcove bed, an enclosed space within an enclosed space, fitted with curtains made of a loose open-weave thin gauze fabric and with padded cotton bedding. Near it is a writing desk with an oversize armchair. The picture on the wall portrays Liu using the desk during the week in 1961 when he stayed in his boyhood room. Rare in bedrooms is an interior window that opens to an adjacent skywell, allowing light and air to enter.

Right:
Baskets are hung on a kitchen wall near the stove in order to store herbs and spices.

Far right:
Volumetric measures used to determine an amount of grain.

Below:
In the kitchen or in the bedroom, an ornamented washstand serves to hold a metal washbasin and as a place to drape a washcloth to dry.

It was at this juncture, in May 1961, that Liu Shaoqi, together with his wife, returned to his boyhood home, which he had last seen in 1919, in an effort to personally understand the failure of the commune system. Traveling for a month in Hunan, including time in Mao's home village in Shaoshan, he spent six nights in his old bedroom in the family homestead in Ningxiang. Even though the Liu residence had been designated an historic site and converted into a little-visited museum in 1958, Liu Shaoqi requested that this designation be rescinded and that local peasants be permitted to live in the old dwelling. After he became a pariah and scapegoat during the Cultural Revolution, his ancestral residence was ransacked and its contents scattered or destroyed. A neighbor took down the sign declaring the site "The Former Residence of Comrade Liu Shaoqi" and feigned destroying it by turning it upside down and using it as a tabletop. After being cleaned up, this original sign now hangs above the entrance to the Main Hall. Above the main entry is a similar sign, but this one in the calligraphy of Deng Xiaoping a powerful affirmation of Liu's rehabilitation.

While Liu Shaoqi's birthplace appears similar to that of Mao Zedong's, closer inspection reveals a definite class difference between the two. The expansive Liu residence is clearly that of a successful and rich landowner while that of the Mao family bespeaks the struggle of a small peasant to make the transition from scarcity to self-sufficiency. Located in a hamlet called Tanzichong, the Liu homestead is situated among undulating low hills also known for the production of tea and rice. Like other well-sited farmhouses, it is wrapped from behind with a copse of trees and faces a large pond. Both features far exceed the scale of those of the Mao family homestead. The house faces west, a rather uncommon direction, but the overall setting was obviously

224   China's Fine Heritage Houses

carefully chosen. The middle third of the front wall, which includes the main entry portico, was not built parallel or perpendicular to other walls of the house. A deviation of this sort can only be explained as a *fengshui* master's attempt to assure the good fortunes of the family. As with the Mao house, the Liu dwelling was built using adobe bricks. However, all the walls, inside and out, were parged with a thick coat of ochre mud plaster that required regular maintenance. This represents a qualitative improvement over common adobe brick.

When viewed from the outside, it is relatively easy to divide the residence into two parts. The right or southern half is the portion inherited by Liu Shaoqi's father, while the rest belonged to his father's elder brother who sold it. A large courtyard, entered via a substantial portico, leads directly to the Main Hall, which is dominated by a large wooden cabinet with a *shenkan*, or ancestral tablet shrine above it. The room today is barren of any of the life and ritual that must once have animated its spaces. From the Main Hall, a door leads to the bedroom of the second eldest son with another door leading into Liu Shaoqi's own bedroom.

Liu Shaoqi's bedroom is nicely situated in that it has not only three doors but also a window that opens to an adjacent *tianjing*, allowing light and air to enter. Like Mao's bed, Liu's is a hulking wooden alcove or canopy bed, an enclosed space within an enclosed space, fitted with curtains made of a loose open-weave thin gauze fabric and with padded cotton bedding. Adjacent to the bed is a substantial writing desk with an oversize armchair. The picture on the wall portrays Liu using the desk during the week in 1961 when he stayed in his boyhood room.

Outside his bedroom, around the *tianjing*, is a room for making and storing wine, a bedroom for his elder brother, his parents' bedroom, a spacious utility room, which has a second *tianjing* alongside it, and another brother's bedroom. Behind these are several "studies," some of which may have been used by tutors engaged to help educate the sons.

Completing the circuit of rooms in the southwest quadrant of the house is a very large barn-like area for unhusked grain, with adjacent milling and polishing equipment. The rice container is nearly two meters high and capable of holding a year's worth of grain. Next to this are a large pigsty, a cattle pen, and a storage room for farm implements, fuel, and foodstuffs. Adjacent to this space is a rectangular *tianjing* open to the sky, which brings abundant light, air, and water into this functionally important part of the house.

On the opposite side of the *tianjing*, separated from the main courtyard by a wall, is the kitchen, the largest room in the dwelling. The brick and mortar stove is situated just inside a window overlooking the courtyard. The three circular openings can hold various round concave pans, which with their flared sides and depth concentrate heat at the bottom and minimize the use of oil. Commonly called in English "woks," from the Cantonese pronunciation of the generic Chinese word for cauldron, bowl-shaped pans of this type are multi-use vessels that allow a cook to stir-fry, steam, braise, sauté, simmer, deep fat-fry, stew and even smoke without the need for other types of pots or pans. Stoves of this sort usually require two individuals to operate them. One cooks in front while the other squats feeding fuel into the rear of the stove. The two must work together to maintain the proper temperatures. Since there is no chimney, a rush mat is tilted between the top of the stove and the ceiling in order to direct some of the smoke towards the window and keep it from the cook's face or the food. Nearby is a pantry where jars of salted and pickled vegetables were kept and where dried herbs hung in baskets. Unlike the Mao family kitchen, which includes a fire pit, here the fire pit is in a smaller adjacent room, where the heat can be better concentrated and not dissipated by the greater space of the open kitchen, *tianjing*, storage areas, and animal pens of the Liu house.

Liu Shaoqi was posthumously rehabilitated in 1980, four years after Mao's death, reclaiming his place in the Communist pantheon as a "first generation leader." In January 1988, his former residence

Below:
Between the kitchen and a dry storage area for fuel and grain is a recessed skywell, which provides a lighted area to work as well as a place for rainwater to be collected and stored. On the far right is a hulking storage container for unhusked rice, with sufficient volume to meet family needs over the winter months.

was designated a national historic site with substantial expenditures allocated to renovate it. Over the past decade and a half, moreover, hundreds of acres of surrounding farmland have been transformed into a park-like precinct celebrating the life of Liu Shaoqi. In addition to long paths and abundant gardens, an imposing statue square, memorial hall, comprehensive museum, and even his airplane, have joined his former residence as elements representing a long life in service to China. Today, Liu Shaoqi's 1939 pamphlet *How to be a Good Communist* is hailed as a classic that synthesizes Communist ethics with Confucian virtues, and he himself is declared to be a revolutionary with "boundless rectitude, awe-inspiring righteousness."

Quotations from Liu Shaoqi:

> "There is no such thing as a perfect leader either in the past or present, in China or elsewhere. If there is one, he is only pretending—like a pig inserting scallions into its nose in an effort to look like an elephant."

> On self-cultivation: "We should not look upon ourselves as immutable, perfect and sacrosanct, as persons who need not and cannot be changed."

Top:
Whatever the size of the kitchen, a large brick stove usually dominates. In this nineteenth-century print, one woman enters as another sits to eat. Woven baskets are hung on the wall and brush for fuel is stored behind the stove. The Kitchen God's altar, with incense placed before it, sits atop the stove.

Above:
Close-up of the fire holes at the rear of the stove. Using metal tongs, fuel is inserted deep into the belly of the stove in order to maintain a constant temperature.

Left:
Adjacent to a window for ventilation, this stove also employs a screen to block the cook from being buffeted by smoke rising from the fire holes in the rear. Two persons must operate a stove, one controlling fuel in the rear and the other cooking in front.

Far left:
In an alcove just beyond the kitchen is a table with benches for eating and working.

Left:
Using a bench and a frame laced with twisted strings of straw, a worker could make some of the household's own utilitarian footgear. After "weaving" a sandal, it is necessary to beat it with a mallet on the stone floor in order to soften the straw before it can be worn.

Below:
This large storage area adjacent to the kitchen also has a doorway to the outside. Here farm implements are stored and agricultural products stacked before being processed and used.

A Landlord's Village Home   227

URBAN DWELLINGS IN NORTHERN SICHUAN
Ma and Feng Family Residences, Langzhong, Sichuan Province

Located in northeastern Sichuan province, Langzhong is heralded as one of the province's oldest and best-sited towns. Viewed from atop the undulating Mount Jinping ("Brocaded Screen Mountain"), which sits across the Jialing River to the south of Langzhong, the town appears to have been cupped by the curvature of the river. In fact, the overall site of Langzhong with its encircling mountains to the rear, a river sweeping along its sides and passing to its front, together with Mount Jinping, provides what many consider to be one of the most complete *fengshui* landscape configurations in China. The city is strictly orientated according to the cardinal directions, with its principal buildings facing south towards the river and hills beyond. Although the city has a history that reaches to the Qin dynasty in the third century BCE, it was not until the Tang dynasty in the seventh century that the current city site was chosen and a rectangular wall built to secure it. The city wall with its four gates is long gone, yet the location of the lanes and style of shops is said to evoke patterns of the Tang dynasty. What largely remains is the area that had developed outside the East Gate of the walled city, which is said to have had ninety-two streets and lanes, a compact town of approximately 1.5 square kilometers.

When viewed from atop 36-meter-tall Huaguang Tower, with its sweeping upturned roofline, the low rooftops of Langzhong in this area outside the old walls appear as an expanse of gray-tiled single-storied structures punctuated by courtyards and skywells of different sizes, which are aligned along a grid of streets and lanes. Commercial areas with shops and workshops are separate from the better residential areas, but shopkeepers live in spaces built adjacent to their workplaces. More than a thousand old structures, including residences, shops, guildhalls, temples, and an examination hall, line the lanes, with most having a projecting eaves overhang to shield the wooden fronts from heavy rain and provide some relief for pedestrians during downpours. During

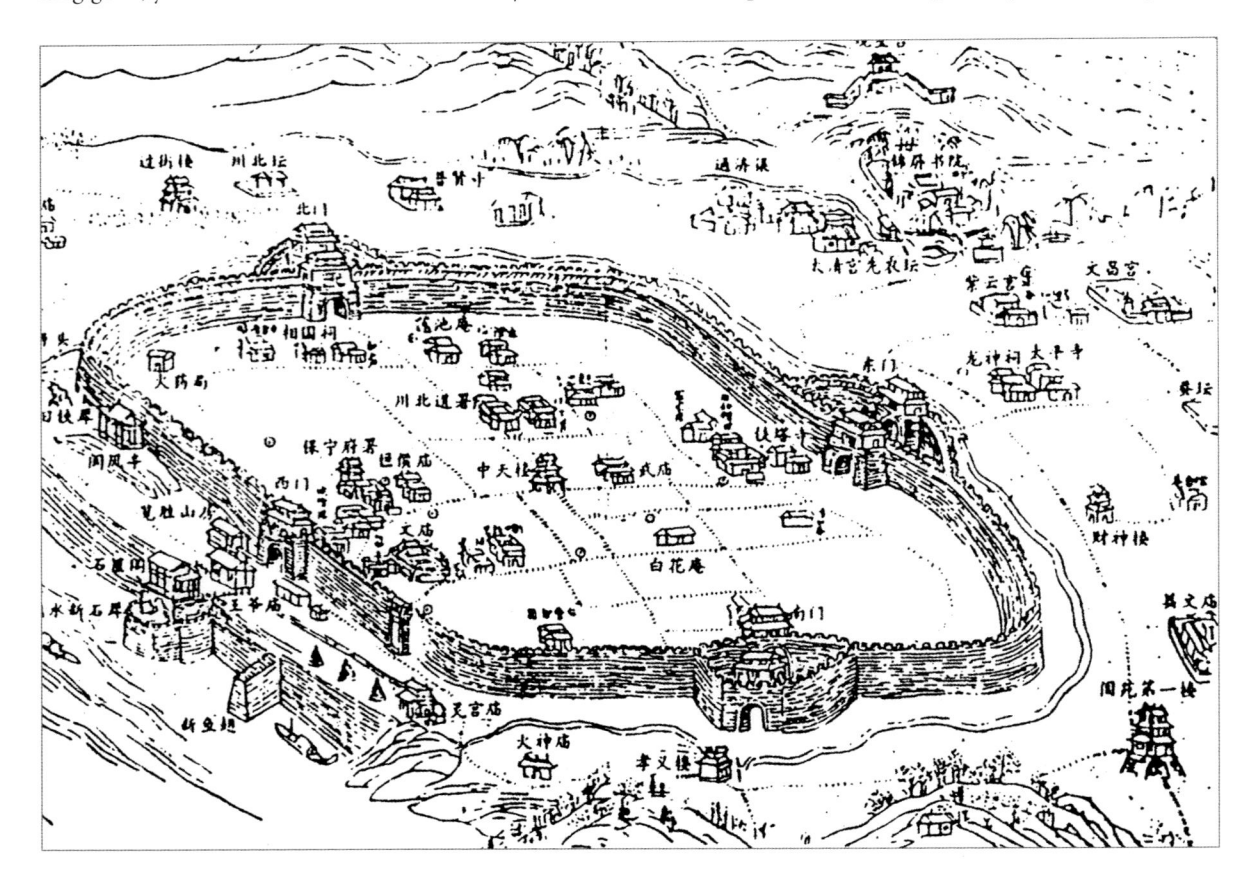

This 1871 map of Langzhong, looking north, is said to exemplify one of the best *fengshui* sites of any Chinese city. The wall surrounding the settlement is said to date to the seventh century during the Tang dynasty, but what is depicted, including prominent buildings, is a view during the nineteenth century.

Left:
Viewed from above, the low rooftops of Langzhong appear as an expanse of gray-tiled single-storied structures that are punctuated by courtyards and skywells of different sizes.

Below:
Paved with stone slabs, the streets and lanes of old Langzhong form a relatively consistent grid.

Urban Dwellings in Northern Sichuan 229

summer, bamboo poles are used to support canvas canopies to shade the lanes, and merchants bring their goods out onto the street.

Most of the old houses in Langzhong are still occupied by their owners, and visitors only come in relatively small numbers. It is easy to taste the atmosphere of times past since there are relatively few modern intrusions into the old town. Lanes are too narrow for buses or cars, so pedestrians, pedicabs, and bicycles dominate. Utility poles for electricity and a simple sewage system have made life somewhat more convenient for residents. As in many Sichuan towns and villages, teahouses and periodic fairs were traditionally intimate parts of the cultural landscape. Itinerant peddlers and craftsmen still ply the lanes in Langzhong, where they sharpen knives and scissors, collect paper, bottles, and cans, sell fruits and vegetables, give haircuts, essentially supplying most of the needs of women, especially, who spend most of their time behind the gates of their houses. One indispensable commodity in Langzhong is Baoning vinegar, which can be purchased in some twenty varieties from shops throughout the city. Full glasses of Baoning vinegar are consumed as a beverage by residents each day, since vinegar brewed from wheat bran is said to cure ailments, especially those relating to internal organs. Meals in Langzhong are usually served with two glasses, one for wine and one for the dark vinegar, sometimes called "Langzhong tea."

Several old residences are still relatively intact, with little evidence of the senseless ravages of past political campaigns or the abuse by large numbers of people living in them in modern times. Even some of the *dayuan* or "big courtyards" of old families are cared for by aged family members. Tourism has led to the conversion of some old houses into inns, but, for the most part, Langzhong has yet to attract the attention of visitors. Among the better preserved old dwellings are those of the Du family, Zhang family, Hu family, Sun family, Hua family, and Kong family, but only the Ma and Feng family residences are discussed below. Little written information is available about any of these families.

What is today called the Ma family residence is said to have been built by a migrant from the southeast coastal province of Guangdong, who came to the region in the middle of the 1600s, a time of dynastic change when people moved long distances to better their fortunes. At some point, the dwelling was sold to the Ma family, which has occupied it at least since 1895. The rectangular plan includes three parallel structures, two with double-sloped roofs and the third only with a single-sloped roof. The first structure abutting the street is four bays wide, a configuration that is relatively uncommon since most people view four as asymmetrical and unlucky in that the number four is homophonous with the word "death." One of the four bays serves as a broad and deep entry

Below:
Looking south towards the curved Jialing River, which embraces the town and its agricultural hinterland, this drawing reveals the multiplicity of named sites of Mount Jinping that constitute the rich inherited cultural landscape of Langzhong. Huaguang Tower is shown here as being outside the walled city.

Right:
As it did in centuries past, the 36-meter-tall Huaguang Tower, with its sweeping up-turned roofline, dominates the old section of Langzhong.

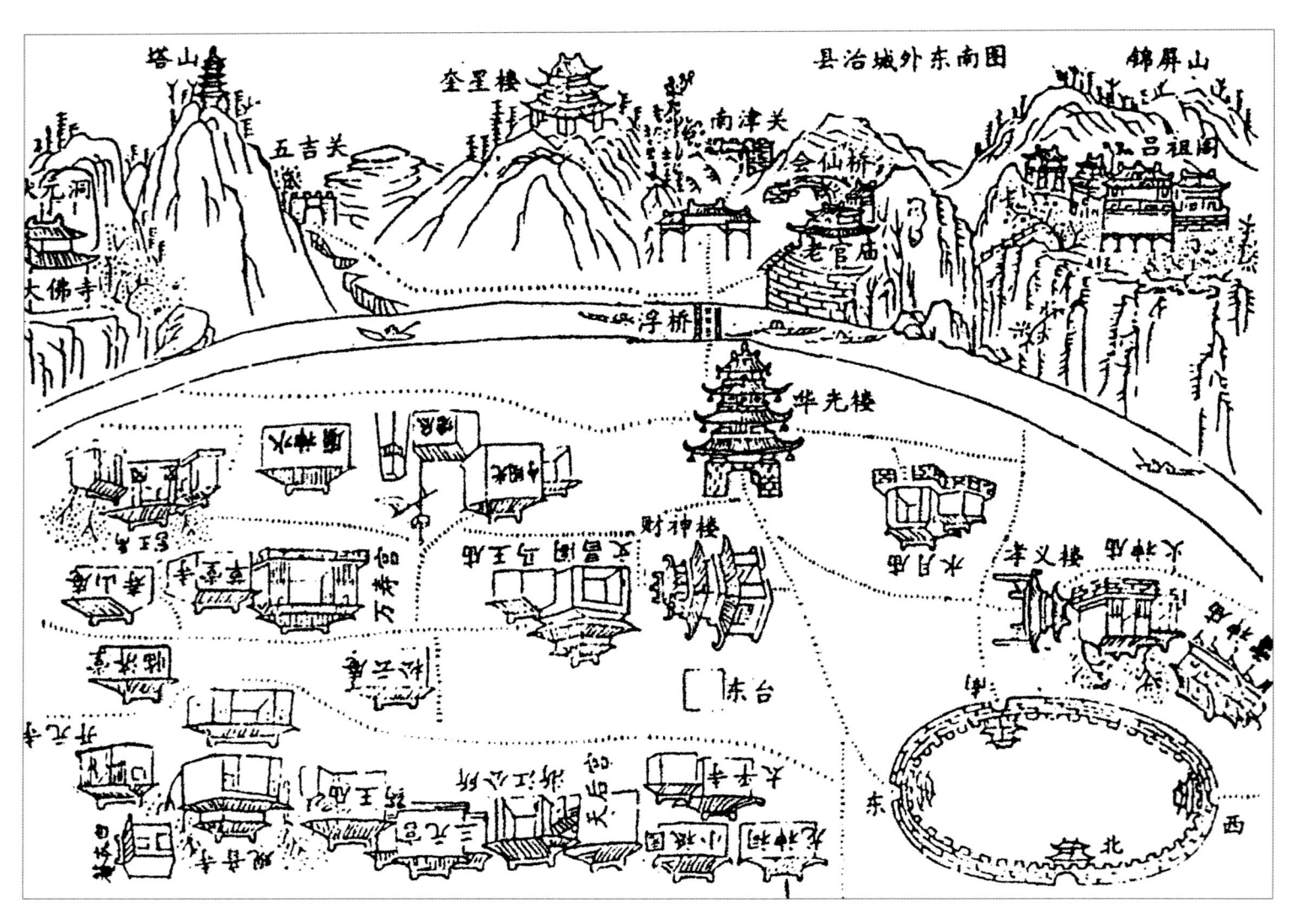

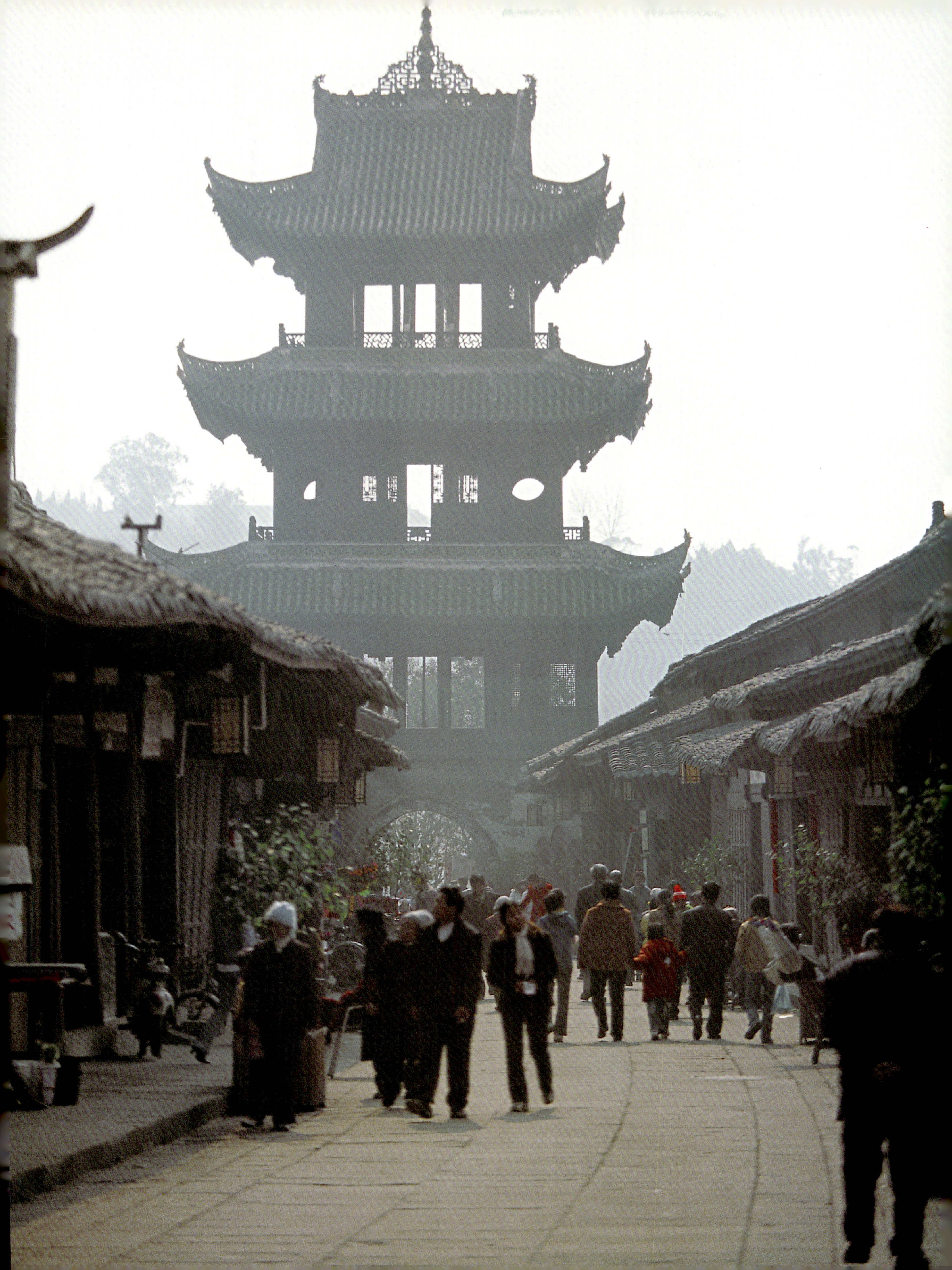

"Olde Town" Langzhong today preserves many of the traditional shops, with their removable wooden panel fronts, that once lined its lanes and streets.

portico, with six adjacent small rooms, which then opens into an outer courtyard leading directly to the large open Main Hall. The side rooms as well as those adjacent to the rear courtyard served as bedrooms. Today, all the rooms stand vacant, clearly tidied up but not yet brought to life with furniture and ornamentation. The flanking side rooms are decorated with beautiful lattice door and window panels as well as structural supports. Unlike the lattice windows in common dwellings, these were sealed with semitransparent thin leaves of mica, a crystalline mineral found in abundance in the province. In addition to the two courtyards, there are three *tianjing* that open up the interior spaces. A kitchen and toilet are located in the rear of the house. Adjacent to the rear courtyard are stairs that lead to a second-story structure, said to be a room used by the family for leisure purposes. In Sichuan, elevated rooms of this sort are called "rooms for gazing at the moon," with their importance underscored by being placed directly on the axis passing through the Main Hall. From the upstairs room in the Ma residence it is possible to see Jinping Hill in the distance. The amount of structural and ornamental wood seen throughout the house clearly indicates that someone with wealth built the house, although virtually nothing is known of the circumstances of construction. Like farmhouses throughout Sichuan, the depth of each structure is substantial, made possible by employing a pillar-and-transverse tie beam wooden framework in which the outer portions act as buttresses to stabilize the building. The Main Hall structure at the center is broader, deeper, and higher than either of the other buildings, underscoring its centrality and importance.

The Feng residence is similar but larger than the Ma residence, covering an area of about 1000 square meters with some thirty rooms. Like the Ma residence, the house was built by one family, in this case named Wang, who sold it in the late nineteenth century to an in-migrant from Gansu province named Feng. In 1935, the complex was taken over as the local headquarters for the Red Army until after 1949 when it became the office for the Baoning township government. It is likely that occupation by government officials saved the structure from the collateral damage associated especially with the Cultural Revolution. The Feng residence was opened to the public in mid-2003.

Entered directly from the street, the entry portico leads to a rectangular courtyard with flanking side buildings. As with other structures with tall lattice doors, the door panels can be removed in order to open and connect interior and exterior spaces. One must cross a threshold to enter the high Main Hall

Above:
View into the narrow courtyard of the Ma family residence showing the sloping rooflines that draw water into the house.

Far left and left:
Shown from a distance and in close-up, the well-carved lattice doors and windows of the Ma home were sealed with semi-transparent thin leaves of mica, a crystalline mineral found in abundance in the province, rather than with the thin rice paper used in many other parts of the country.

second-story leisure room | side hall | open hall

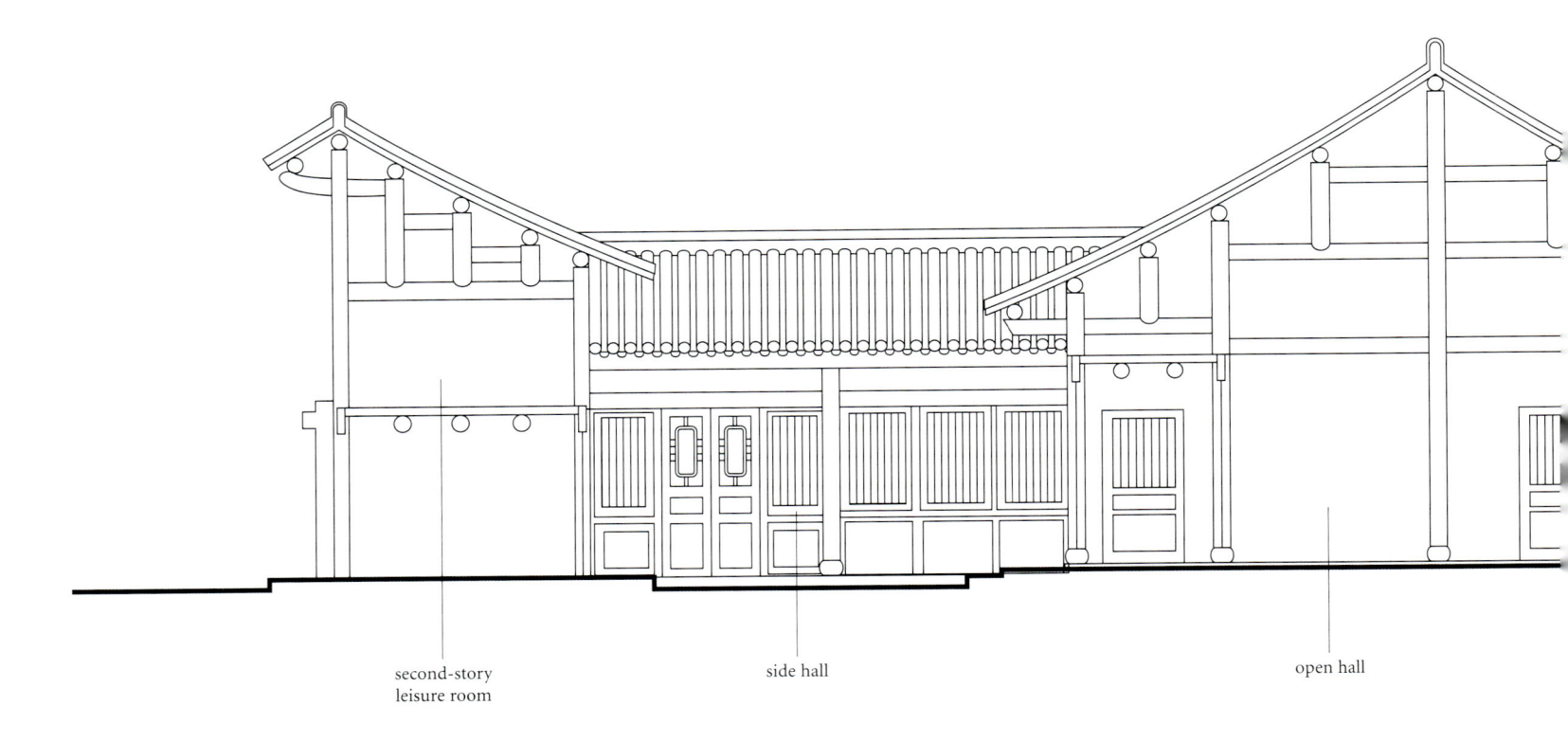

or *tangwu*, where a suite of hardwood furniture, comprising tables and chairs of various types, are placed in standard symmetrical positions relative to each other. Lattice and door panel carvings here are especially exquisite and well-preserved. Decorative motifs, whether on furniture, on door or window panels, or high under the eaves on brackets, are rarely without an auspicious meaning. Ornamented with both geometrical and didactic forms, the upper portions of doors and windows usually include perforated lattice in order to maximize ventilation, while the lower solid panels are frequently carved in bas relief patterns.

The inner or second courtyard also is stone-lined, with deep overhanging roofs protecting the wooden panels from rain-wash. Here, under the branches of several tall trees, children and women, especially, had privacy in their daily lives. The two-courtyard pattern found in most of these dwellings is said to resemble the Chinese character *duo*, meaning "many," thus is said to serve as an auspicious symbol invoking the hope for "many children."

Interest in preserving and rehabilitating the oldest parts of Langzhong began in earnest in the late

Above:
Four of the wooden panels along the façade of this side hall are removable or may be opened on a pivot while four others are stationary.

Right:
Detail of a carved lattice panel with running chrysanthemums, a symbol of long life. Under it is a pair of interlocking circles, which serve as decorative struts between the stretchers.

Far right:
Carved ornamented bracket in a pattern of spiraling vines used to support a beam.

side hall

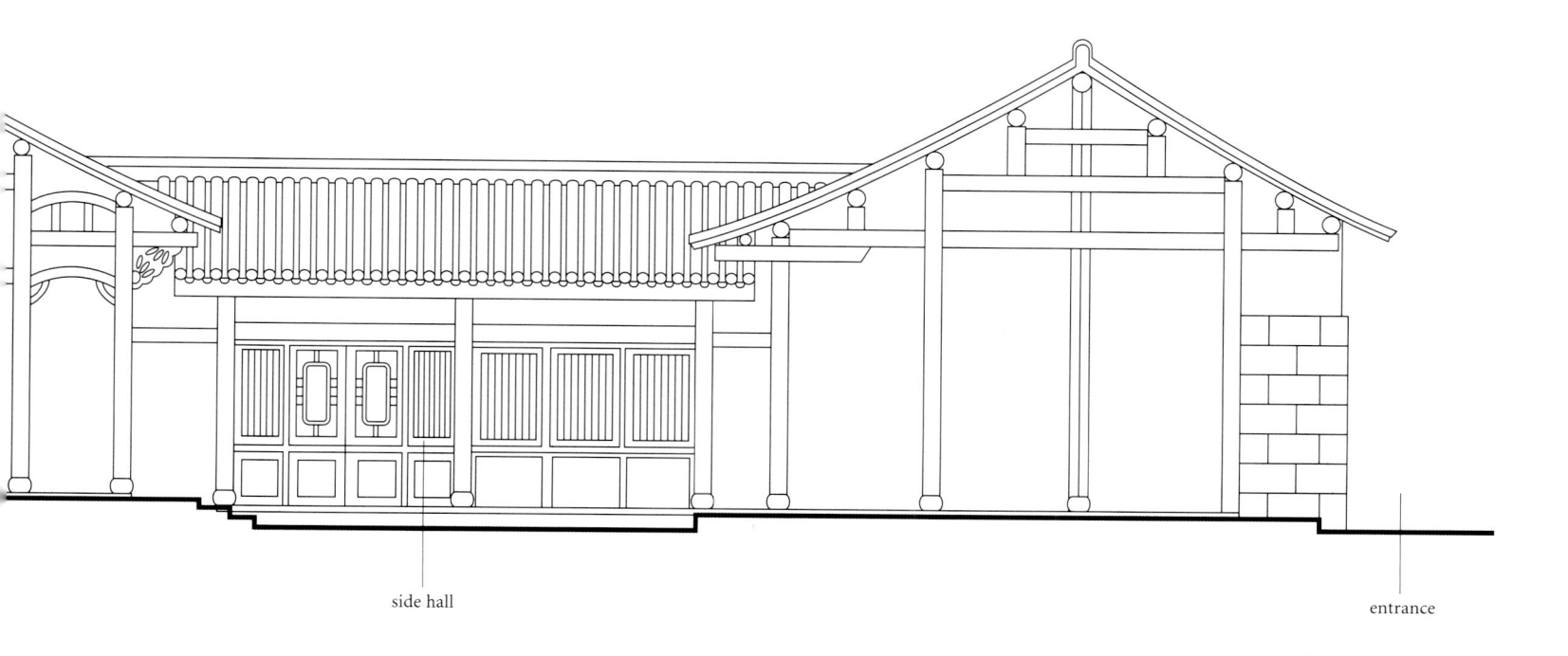

entrance

Above:
This attenuated section view of the Ma residence portrays the two courtyards and the three transverse structures that dominate its spatial organization. It also illustrates the pillars-and-transverse tie beams wooden framework employed throughout the residence.

Right:
This floor plan reveals that the Ma residence has an odd four-bay structure, two large courtyards, several small skywells, and a second story in the rear, the latter described as a "room for gazing at the moon." Indeed, it is possible to see Jinping Hill in the distance and, periodically, the moon when it is in the southern sky.

Below:
This elevation drawing portrays the asymmetrical façade as well as the textures of brick, tile, and wood.

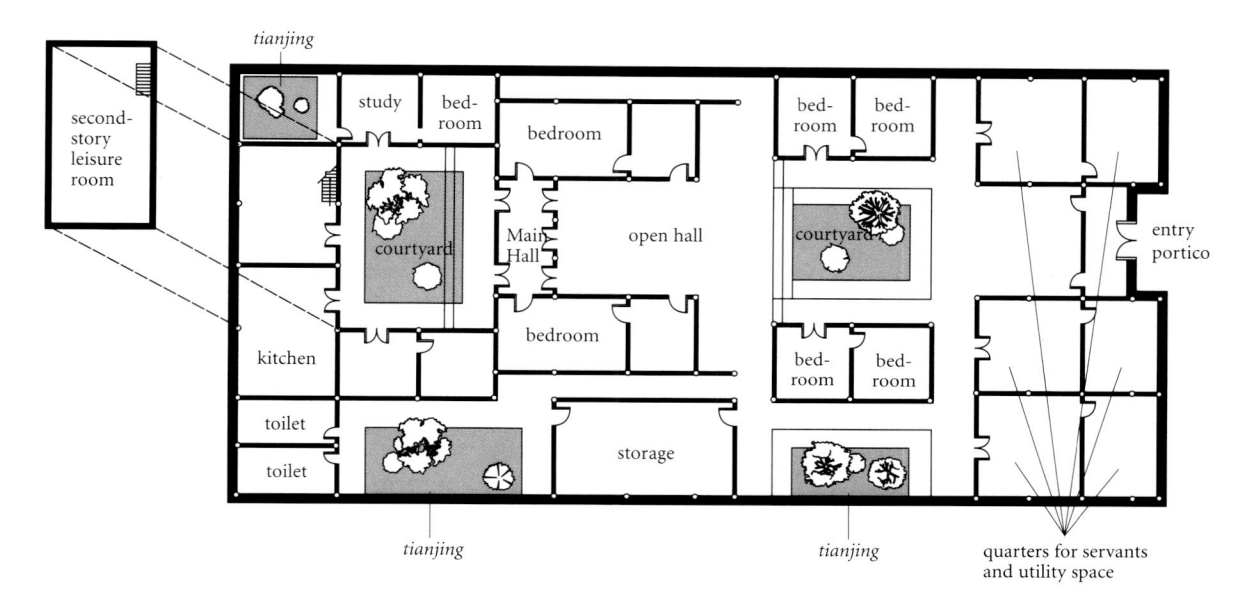

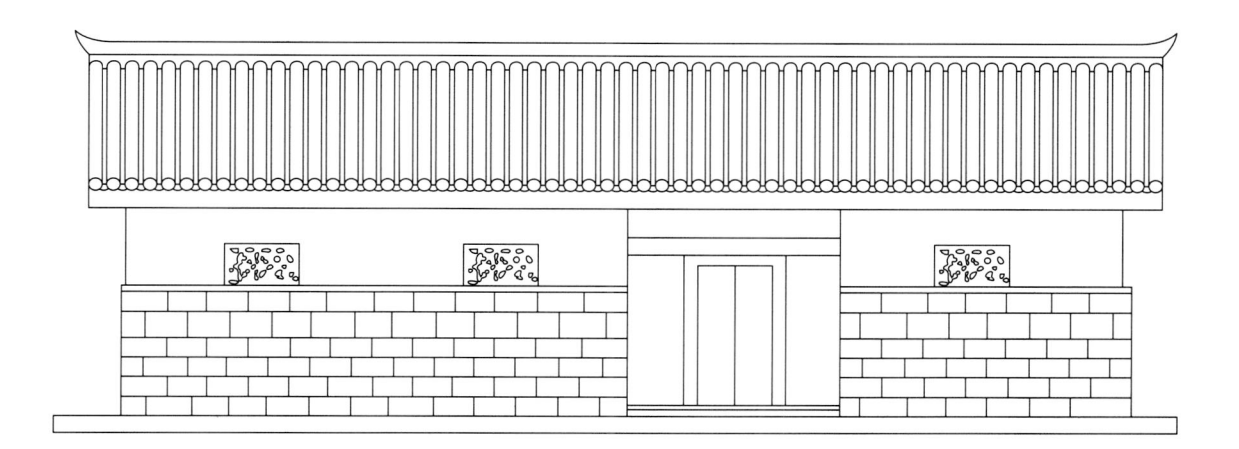

Urban Dwellings in Northern Sichuan   235

1980s. With indiscreet modern buildings increasingly overlooking the old town and impinging on its authenticity, local boosters began to call for the development of a conservation policy in order to forestall change and to begin plans for revitalizing the historic town through tourism.

More recently, voices have been raised calling for the preparation of documents to elevate Langzhong to UNESCO World Heritage Status. A decade ago, some 30,000 of Langzhong's total population of 860,000 lived along the old lanes. About 10,000 have already been resettled elsewhere in order to upgrade their living conditions and lessen wear and tear on the old structures. Intrusive utilities like telephone and electric poles have, for the most part, been placed underground, and drainage has been improved. Newer structures that had been built over the years amidst the old ones have been torn down, with their building lots infilled with new structures that match. In Langzhong, as in some other areas of the country, there is also concern for the preservation of local folk arts and crafts, which like buildings themselves, are under threat.

Left:
Yet to be filled with furniture and wall hangings, this corner of the open Main Hall in the Ma residence reveals its exceptional breadth and height, which were made possible by the use of a pillars-and-transverse tie beams wooden framework, also called the *chuandou* **framing system.**

Below:
Shaded courtyard of the Feng family residence viewed from a covered structure that is usable even during periods of heavy rain.

Right:
Opened to the public in 2003, the expansive Feng family home is hidden behind this relatively modest doorway.

秦家大院

京院蘇園韻川渝靈悟巴闕風

秦磚漢瓦魂唐宋格局明清貌

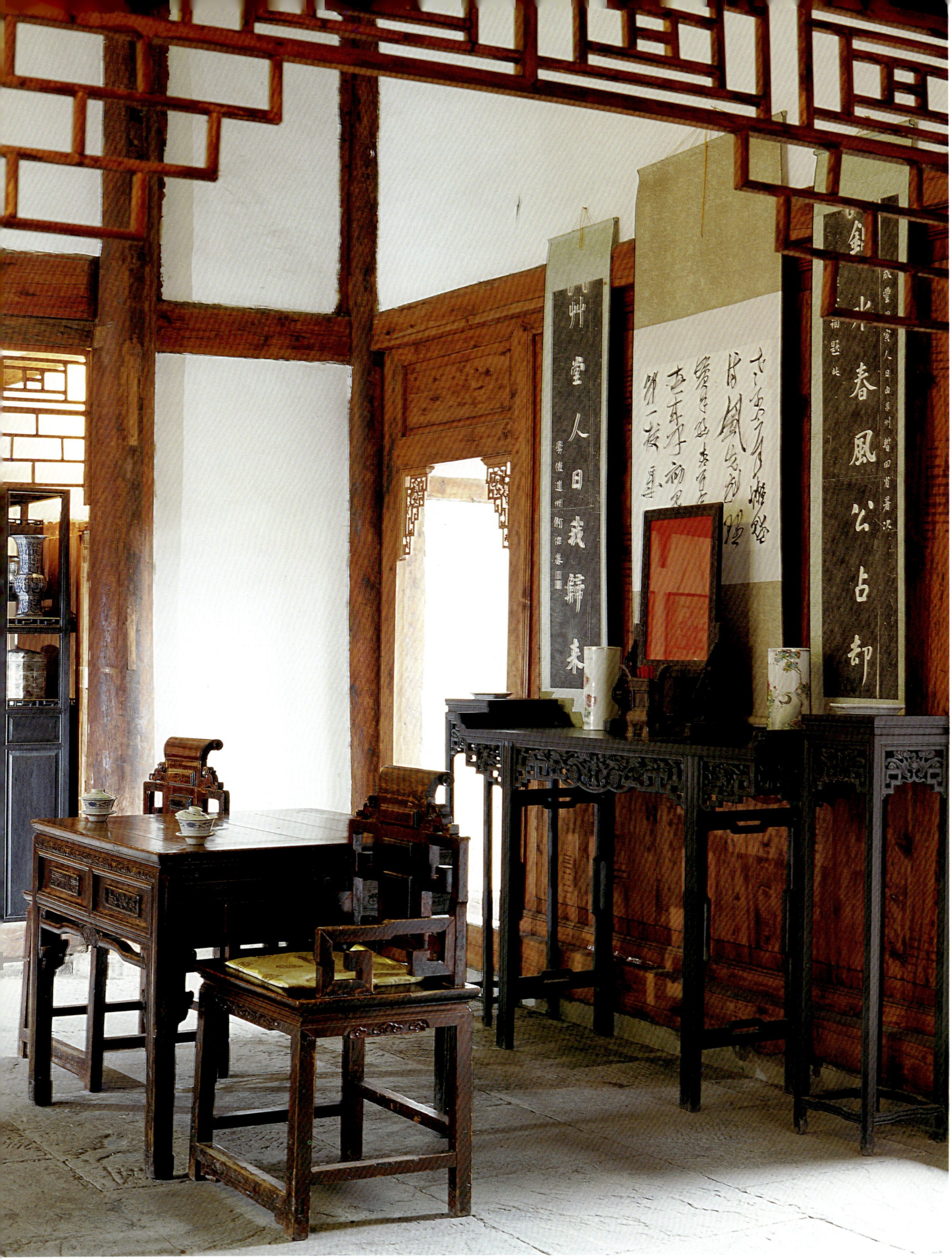

Left:
The Main Hall is furnished and decorated as it would have been early in the twentieth century when the Feng family occupied it.

Right:
When thrown open on their pivots to link interior and exterior spaces, the richly carved doors serve as an ornamental feature.

Below:
View under the projecting protective eaves that shelter the carved wooden lattice panels of the living quarters in the second courtyard of the Feng residence.

Below:
Close-up of a shallow carved panel of the door shown to the left. Five intertwined bats, which have a homophonous relationship with the word *fu* for good fortune, represent the "five good fortunes," namely, longevity, wealth, health, love of virtue, and to die a natural death in old age.

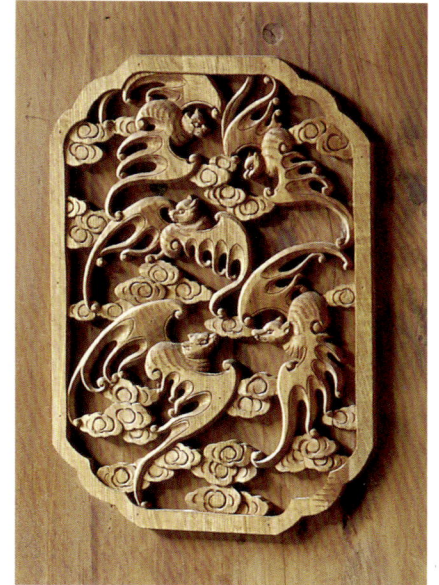

Urban Dwellings in Northern Sichuan   239

A U-SHAPED FARMHOUSE
Deng Xiaoping's Boyhood Home, Sichuan Province

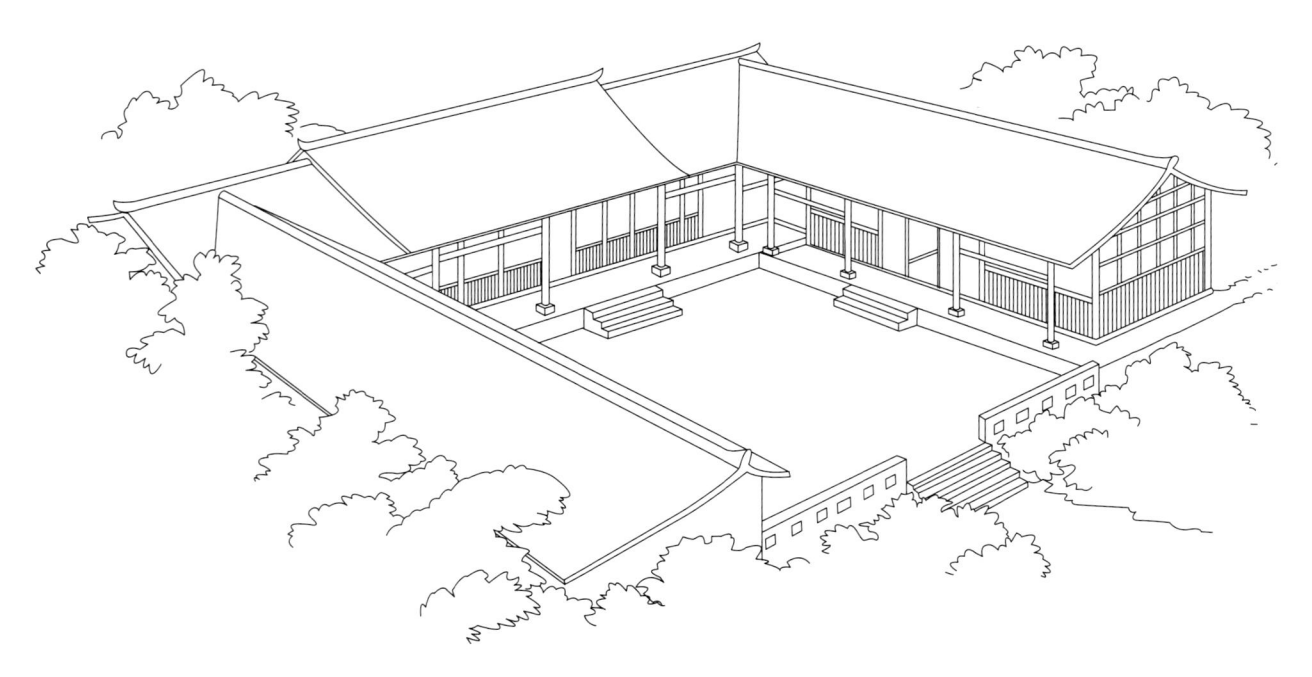

Set within a green copse of bamboo, the Deng family *yuanzi* or courtyard is an inverted U-shaped building of substantial proportions. As a relatively symmetrical *sanheyuan* or "three-enclosed courtyard," it includes a pair of perpendicular wing buildings flanking the main horizontal building.

After the death of Mao Zedong in 1976, no Chinese has loomed larger than Deng Xiaoping. The two had worked together but also against each other, intensively and intermittently, in giving shape to Communism in China over six decades. Yet, it was Deng, once a committed disciple of Mao, who, when he ultimately emerged from Mao's shadow, articulated *gaige kaifang* (reform and opening)—Socialism with Chinese Characteristics—a host of economic and social policies that then accelerated China's remarkable transformation over the past quarter century.

Born in 1904, eleven years after Mao, and living a little more than two decades after Mao's death in 1976, Deng's 92-year life essentially ranged across the full length of the twentieth century. In some ways, Deng's journey from the remote interior province of Sichuan to the world stage paralleled China's own passage from the isolation of the Middle Kingdom to a looming global presence at the beginning of the twenty-first century. His own rural family clearly embraced old ways while at the same time urging the young Deng to raise his eyes and look beyond his remote village for new opportunities.

Mao's birthplace in Hunan province became a much-visited revolutionary shrine during the Great Helmsman's lifetime, whereas Deng's childhood home in Sichuan remained essentially unvisited until recent years. Deng himself never returned to the house of his birth after leaving it as a teenager, never visited his parents' graves, and, according to his daughter, "did not allow us to do so either, on the grounds that our arrival there would disturb a lot of people as well as the local government." Yet, just as others were beginning to discover his quiet home village, Deng's daughter Maomao and his younger sister Deng Xianfu visited the Deng family homestead in October 1989, seemingly more out of curiosity than any attempt to search for family roots.

A Sichuan proverb says, "When the sun shines in winter, the dogs bark." Especially from October to March, days are often gloomy, the sky is gray, the sun is hidden, light rain falls, and temperatures are mild, with the result that vegetation remains lush. Often wreathed in clouds, northeastern Sichuan is a region of jade-green hilly landscapes, its well-tended fields a veritable mosaic of rice, vegetables, corn, fruit,

240 China's Fine Heritage Houses

mulberry, and bamboo. The region boasts a long history of intensive farming but only relative prosperity. With a year-round growing season, three crops traditionally were the norm and, as a result, hardworking farmers generally were able to eke out at least a comfortable life for their families. The young Deng was born on August 22, during summer, when the sky was clear and temperatures intensely hot.

The ancestors of Deng Xiaoping had been in Sichuan for many generations, some say for 600 or 700 years, most likely arriving as migrants from Jiangxi downriver because of turmoil. Like other lineages whose members can be traced over long periods, those who passed the civil service examinations and became "officials" usually receive the most attention from their descendants. One or two family members many generations removed from Deng Xiaoping had passed the highest *jinshi* degree and been named to the Hanlin Academy in the imperial capital during the Qing dynasty. Indeed, the name "Paifang village" proclaimed the presence of a multitiered memorial arch or *paifang* commemorating such an ancestor during the eighteenth century. The arch was smashed during the Cultural Revolution, and the name of the village itself was changed to Fanxiu xiaodui or "Anti-Revisionist Production Brigade," a label it carried until the early 1980s.

Left:
Taken in France two years after he left his Sichuan village, this studio photograph shows Deng at the age of sixteen.

Below:
Both the broad courtyard and the dwelling itself are raised above the surrounding area and are accessible by a series of stone steps.

A U-Shaped Farmhouse

Far left:
Nearly two meters in depth, the front verandah is covered by a broad overhanging roof that is supported by a tier of projecting tie beams of different lengths.

Left:
Some of the vertical supports for the projecting tie beams are carved as ornaments.

The ancient phrase *shan gao, huangdi yuan* ("the mountains are high, the Emperor is far away") describes well the Sichuan countryside at the end of the Qing dynasty. Villagers lived relatively self-sufficient lives, with both the strengths and constraints of family tradition, and were linked to the outer world only via the market town in which peasants, merchants, and others mingled on periodic market days according to cyclical dates. Complementary spheres of work, succinctly stated as "men plow, and women weave," not only made it possible for families to be essentially self-reliant but allowed the amassing of modest wealth if cash income increased.

Farming, domestic handicrafts, petty trade, and service as village leaders likely provided the Deng family the means for economic progress over time. Certainly, they never became wealthy because of land holdings, merchant trade, or high office. Increasing wealth supported improvements to the family dwelling as well as education for the children, but the circumstances relating to how the U-shaped farmhouse took shape are lost in the fog of history.

Paifang village, like other villages in Guang'an county, still has a dispersed pattern of rural settlement. Instead of villagers living together in a compact rural settlement of tightly packed dwellings, approximately a hundred households in Paifang inhabit housing clusters loosely dispersed along a stream. The stream, villagers say, helps bind separate families to membership in a single village. In Sichuan, each of these diminutive hamlets is called a *yuanzi*, often translated as a "courtyard." But each is much more than an open space surrounded by structures, since a *yuanzi* may include several actual courtyard-type dwellings. Delineated and protected by a dark green circular grove of bamboo, each dispersed *yuanzi* is rather secluded and appears to float amidst the extensive terraced paddy fields.

Only a few essential facts are known about Deng family circumstances as the twentieth century dawned. Many particulars remain conjecturable, in part because of the later political vicissitudes of Deng Xiaoping himself. His father, Deng Shaochang, was born in 1886, probably in the same hamlet in which he was to raise his own family but possibly in a smaller dwelling. When he himself was a young boy, Deng Shaochang lost his own father, who left behind a widow, who was mother to at least two children, including an elder daughter, and head of household with several additional family retainers.

While this small family of the Deng grandfather cannot account for the extensive dwelling seen today, it probably was the serial conjugal activity of Deng Shaochang, the father himself, that led to its construction. When Deng Shaochang was about thirteen, he took a young wife who, by marrying in, replaced his sister who had married out to a family in another *yuanzi*. The young wife, however, proved barren and Shaochang sought another woman, some describe as a wife from a wealthier family but others say was merely a concubine required to increase the probability of a much hoped for son. In any case, this woman, surnamed Dan, gave birth in 1901 to a daughter and then three years later a son, first called Xiansheng, then Xixian, among several other names, and then later Xiaoping, the name he carried during his adult life. Two other sons were subsequently born before Deng Shaochang brought two other women, more likely concubines than official wives, into the family courtyard where each required her

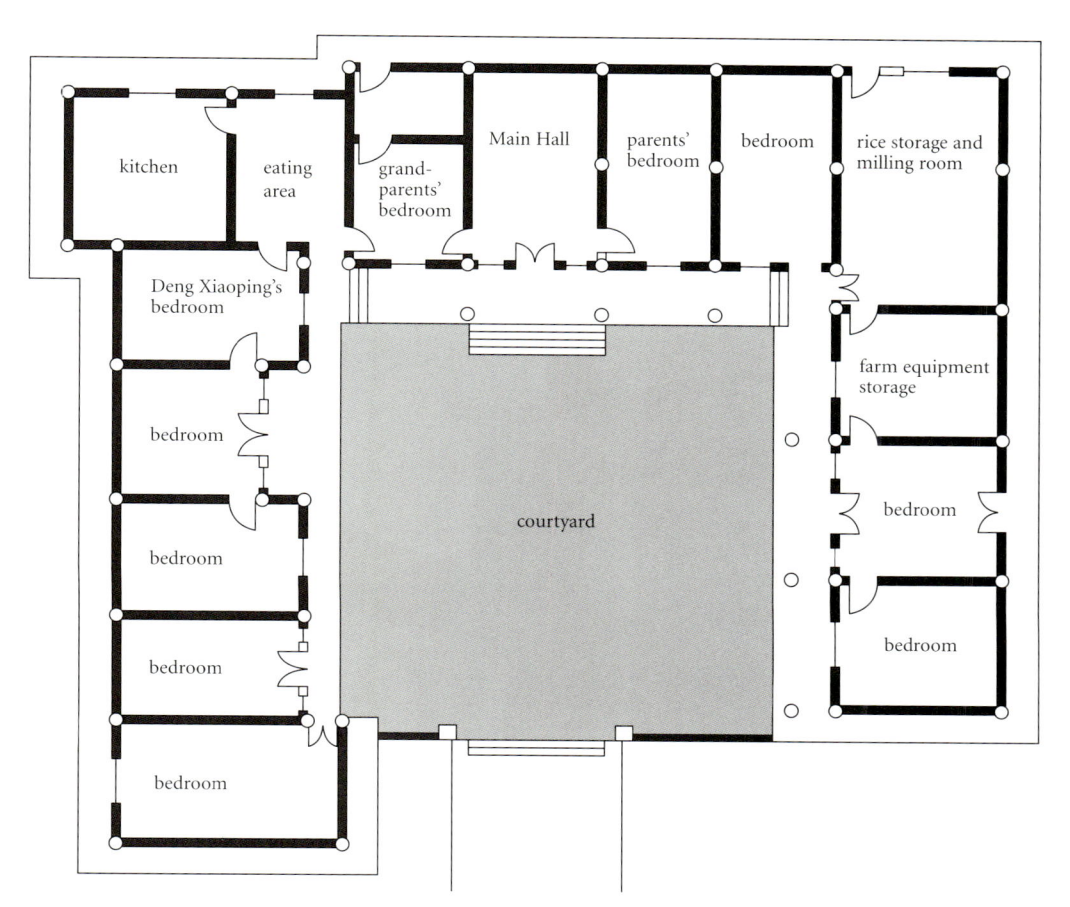

Floor plan labels:
- kitchen
- eating area
- grandparents' bedroom
- Main Hall
- parents' bedroom
- bedroom
- rice storage and milling room
- Deng Xiaoping's bedroom
- bedroom
- bedroom
- bedroom
- bedroom
- courtyard
- farm equipment storage
- bedroom
- bedroom

Left:
As this plan shows, more than half the rooms in the Deng home were bedrooms, a pictogram suggesting the complexity of multi-generational family life during late imperial times. Some other large rooms provided space for looms that were used for the production of textiles.

Below:
Today, the tidied up Main Hall of the Deng residence barely suggests the formality and activity that would have characterized it at the beginning of the twentieth century.

A U-Shaped Farmhouse

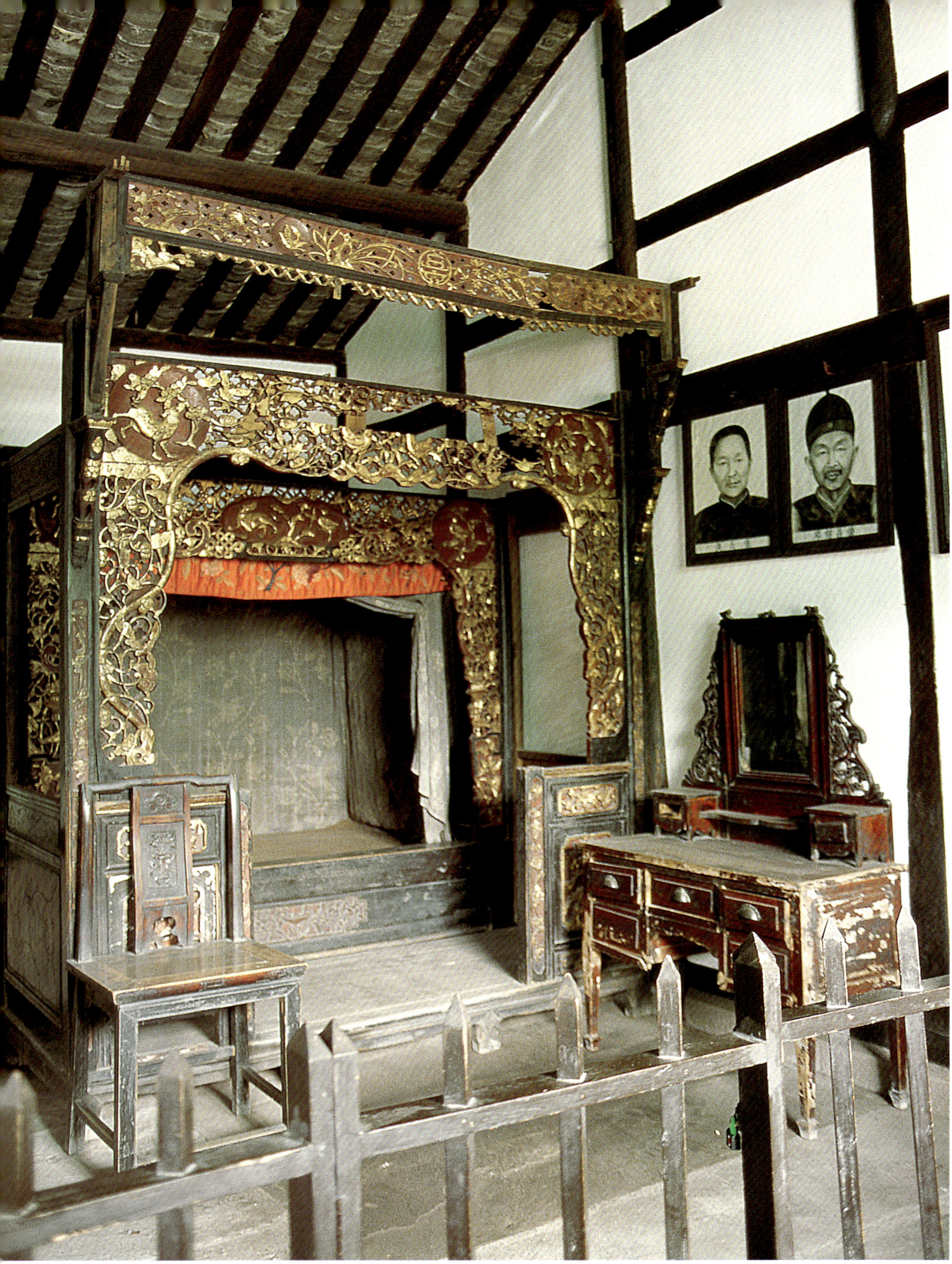

Left:
The old ostentatious furniture described as belonging to Deng Xiaoping's parents actually replaced plainer furniture seen in the house a decade earlier. It is unlikely that what is shown originally belonged to his parents.

Bottom:
In a corner of the grandparents' bedroom is an ornamented canopy bed.

Below:
Even in the late 1990s, the Deng farmstead essentially stood alone within a traditional agrarian landscape but has been transformed in recent years. In preparation for the centenary of his birth in 2004 and expectations of increasing visitation, a vast interpretative Deng Xiaoping Memorial Park has been created around the farmstead.

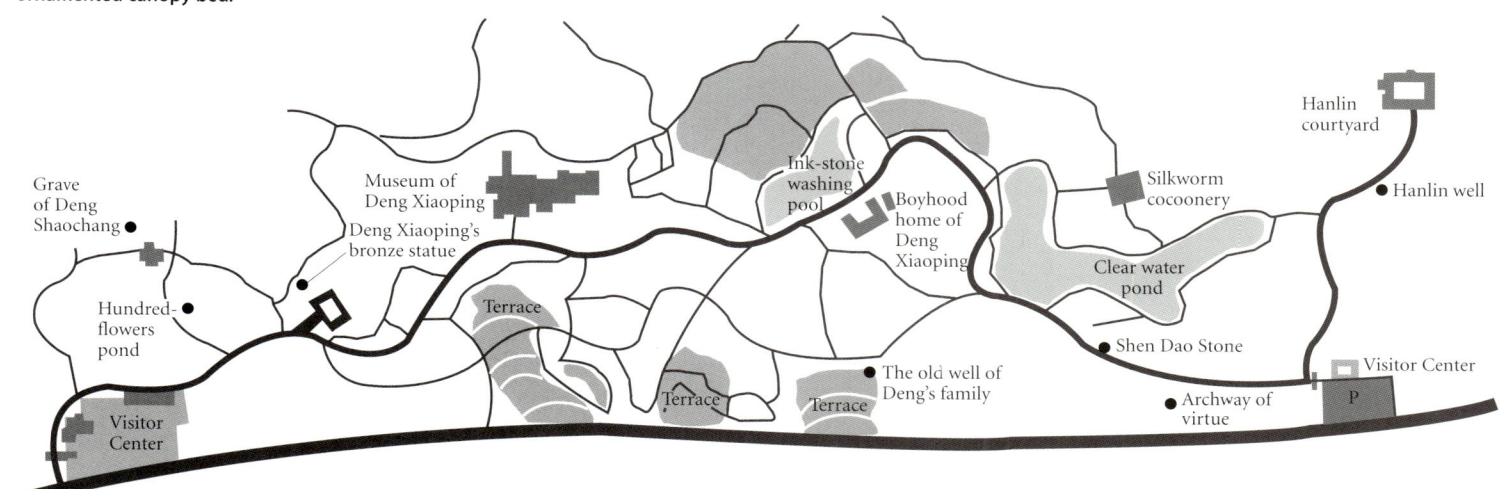

own bedroom and support. The third woman gave birth to the fourth son of Deng Shaochang. The fourth woman brought into the family as a wife, Xia Bogen, was a young widow with a daughter who then gave birth to three other daughters.

As a testament to what might appear as fluidity in Chinese family structure, Deng's own daughters considered this fourth wife as their grandmother, who after 1949 came to live with the Deng family in Beijing. During Land Reform in the early 1950s, various local peasant families, including some cousins, were given spaces in the old house to call their own, and some continued to occupy the house until the late 1980s when the dwelling was emptied out and tidied up. Today, only cousins of Deng remain as representatives of the family's origins in Paifang village. The rambling house, with its twenty rooms, is at once a pictogram representing fecundity during late imperial times while remaining strikingly mute about the memories it holds within it.

The rapid growth of Deng Xiaoping's father's "family," undoubtedly acceptable in terms of traditional norms, came to be accommodated easily in what must have been the most impressive house built in a village where most farmhouses were mere three- to five-room rectangular structures with thatched roofs. During the decade when his family expanded with "wives" and children, Deng Shaochang did little farming, depending more on hired laborers and increasingly spending time as a leader of local organizations, all of which is clear evidence of his increasing power and wealth.

Whether Deng Shaochang was "a cruel landlord, who lived the life of a parasite sucking the sweat and blood of poor peasants" or "a good man,

A U-Shaped Farmhouse 245

Characteristic of dwellings in this part of eastern Sichuan are walls composed of white infill panels set among slender pillars and multiple transverse tie beams that make up the wooden framing system called *chuandou*.

hard-working by himself and sympathetic to others" depends upon whether the evaluation was made by Red Guards in the late 1960s when Deng Xiaoping was a political pariah or in the 1980s after he had been politically "rehabilitated" and became "Paramount Leader." In any case, Deng Shaochang provided an imposing farmhouse for his changing family as wives arrived, babies were born, and children grew. A tutor was hired for the eldest son, the young Xiaoping, as he was later to call himself. The lad was enrolled in a primary school outside the village in 1910, where he studied for the next five years, before being sent off to a boarding school in Guang'an county town some 10 kilometers away. In 1918, a few days after his fourteenth birthday, he and his slightly older uncle left China for France, by way of Chongqing, Shanghai, and a thirty-nine day ocean voyage. With his father's blessing, they were participating in a work–study program that came to involve some 1500 young Chinese between 1918 and 1920.

It is said that the young Chinese sojourners hoped more to "study" but the French wanted them more to "work," yet both work and study in a foreign land proved transformative for those who participated. Effectively abandoning his boyhood home and family, Deng Xiaoping indeed embarked on a remarkable journey to the pinnacle of power in China. Remaining in France for more than five years, he worked longest as a laborer in the Schneider & Cie Iron and Steel ordnance factory in Creusot. He also worked as a fitter in the Renault factory in a Paris suburb, as a fireman on locomotives, and as a kitchen helper in restaurants. Throughout this period, he came to meet and know other young men who subsequently became well-known Chinese Communist leaders. Among them were Zhou Enlai, Jiang Zemin, Zhu De, and Chen Yi. Now more aware of China's ferment, even though a continent away, and attracted by Marxism, many of these work–study youths, including Deng, joined the fledgling branch organizations of the Chinese Communist Party while in Europe. In January 1926, he went to Moscow to study and then returned to China in early 1927. In July of that year, he met Mao Zedong in Wuhan. It was at the age of twenty-three that he changed his name to "Xiaoping."

It appears that Deng Xiaoping never seriously pondered the circumstances of his early life in Sichuan, either to acknowledge the fortunate paths set for him by his father or to contemplate what his own life might have been like if he had not left. Meanwhile, his father continued to gain status as a member of the village élite and a commander of a regional security force, living until 1936 or 1938. It is said that Deng Xiaoping sent revolutionary pamphlets home and his father sold some land to provide funds for his eldest son's revolutionary activities.

The open U-shaped courtyard dwelling of Deng Xiaoping's boyhood can be described as a *sanheyuan* or "three-enclosed courtyard," somewhat similar to others in southern China, yet it has striking Sichuan characteristics. In Sichuan, inverted U-shaped houses are called *sanhetou*, which has a similar meaning to *sanheyuan*. They are raised above the ground, their rubble stone base supporting a stone foundation that requires several sets of steps. All open areas probably were originally made of pounded earth although over time stone slabs were used to surface the courtyard, floors, and verandahs. Such improvements entailed significant expense.

A pair of wing buildings flanks the main building; space is symmetrical and generous in both extent and volume. Comprised of a horizontal building joined with a pair of perpendicular wings, space is clearly delineated in relatively large, high, deep, and airy rooms for a range of activities characteristic of a prosperous farmstead. The rooms in the main structure are all much taller than those in the wings. Buildings of this type have a wooden framing system called *chuandou*, consisting of slender pillars that are tied together with multiple transverse tie beams. The latter are similarly slender in dimension yet serve to stabilize the structural framework. Each pillar is set on a simple stone base or on the encircling stone plinth within the interior walls. The weight of the heavy tile roof is carried to the ground directly by the pillars. In order to create a broad verandah ringing the dwelling, the roof is extended via the use of substantial eaves supported by protruding horizontal tie beams. Although mortise-and-tenon joinery is seen everywhere on the outside of the house, it is most outstanding on the overhang framework that supports the eaves across the front. Nearly two meters in depth here, the weight of the roof tiles requires a tier of projecting tie beams of different lengths in order to bear the load. Even during heavy rain, the front verandahs allow the large lattice windows to be left open for ventilation against oppressive heat.

The unvarnished natural patina of wooden pillars, wainscot paneling, and lattice window frames provide a contrast to the whitewashed infilling between the columns. The complicated and costly wooden structural framework is a statement that the owner is prosperous. Each infilling between the pillars is a nonload-bearing curtain wall made of split bamboo culms woven into panels and then sealed with a mud or mud-and-lime plaster before being whitewashed and made impervious to air and moisture.

Little of the house has been interpreted except for the Main Hall, kitchen, parents' bedroom, grandparents' bedroom, Deng Xiaoping's own bedroom, and the large grain-processing area in a corner room. The original family furniture indeed was scattered over the years, replaced after 1949 by what was needed by the nearly dozen peasant families who occupied the space. By the late 1980s, several old wooden bedsteads, some square tables and benches, as well as paired side chairs and tables, accompanied by some photographs, calligraphy, and household ephemera, had been installed in the newly empty rooms. They failed, however, to give any sense of the daily life that must have once been common in the Deng *yuanzi* a century ago. In recent years, a few pieces of ostentatious furniture have replaced plainer ones seen a decade earlier. Most noticeable are the large old beds seen in early 2004 that are more likely to be of the type used by a prosperous rural family than the simpler ones in the house in the 1990s. Whether they have any connection with the Deng family is indeterminable.

There are large empty rooms that were probably once used for the household economy, especially the production of textiles. This type of handwork is said to have interested Deng's mother and, as a cottage industry, was likely a source of additional income for the family. Textile production in Sichuan meant both cotton and silk. Sericulture entailed a lengthy process involving many stages and bulky equipment such as bamboo racks, feeding trays, reels, and looms. No such equipment is evident in the farmhouse today. Raising silkworms, especially, was a labor-intensive activity since great care was required to satisfy the voracious appetite of the silkworms and to regulate the temperature, humidity, light, and noise that affect their development. Family members recall the courtyard being filled with chickens and geese, which were raised principally to guard the house because they made loud noises when strangers approached and were known to be almost as fierce as dogs.

Until the late 1990s, the farmstead essentially remained as a solitary and silent connection with Deng's remarkable life. However, with the centenary of his birth in August 2004 and expectations of increasing visitation, a vast interpretative Deng Xiaoping Memorial Park, weaving the natural setting of terraced fields and ponds with a wealth of interpretative facilities, has been created. These include an exhibition hall and theater, a reconstructed *paifang* or memorial arch, an array of memorabilia including the old family well, and even the black open-topped Red Flag limousine Deng used to review the troops parading in Beijing's Tiananmen Square.

Anchoring this park is Deng's boyhood home, which provides only vague hints of the early life of this remarkable leader. Yet, significantly, the preserved birthplace represents a type of fine dwelling once found throughout this region where houses still are "of the land and the people." In their form and structure, they reveal accommodations to climate, available building materials, and the cultural dynamics of families that live in them.

Below left:
Along the front and side verandahs, large, relatively simple lattice windows provide ventilation for the interior in an attempt to reduce the often oppressive heat and high humidity.

Below right:
The stacking of thin roof tiles along the ridgeline not only offers ornamentation but also serves to stabilize and seal a critical seam where two slopes join on the roof.

A GRAND QING MANOR AND A SIMPLE MING COURTYARD HOUSE

Qiao Family Manor and Ding Family Village, Shanxi Province

Shanxi province has some of China's grandest manors of the Qing dynasty and, by contrast, some of the simplest dwellings from the Ming dynasty. They are spread rather randomly in what appear to be desolate areas of central and southern Shanxi, but their locations point to old trade routes and optimal settlement sites whose nature is not yet fully understood. In the case of grand manor complexes, their presence hints at a level of merchant culture and wealth in the past that seems anachronistic today given the prominence of dirty industries such as coal-mining and cement-making, which plague the province with leaden skies filled with cough-producing soot. Yet, today in China, where "making money" through commerce and entrepreneurship are touted as the engines of economic development, it should not be surprising that a new focus is being put on the country's commercial history as well as on surviving residential architectural gems of wealthy families in the past.

The study of China's long-distance merchant networks is still in its infancy and there are many gaps in our understanding of the respective roles of private individuals and the imperial state in the economy's rise and fall over five centuries. Even less is known about the specific circumstances leading to the design and construction of extensive residential manors in far-flung areas. Some of the earliest merchants gained wealth in the lucrative salt trade. Later on, iron, cotton, soybeans, tea, and silk became part of the trade mix, and by the nineteenth century individuals grew rich from pawnshops and banking. During the Ming dynasty, "Shanxi Merchants," called Jin Shang using the conventional abbreviation for the province's name, amassed wealth by transporting grain to feed troops along the northern Great Wall frontier and from licenses entitling them to sell salt at monopoly prices. Long-distance trade of this sort, especially along the borders with Mongolia and

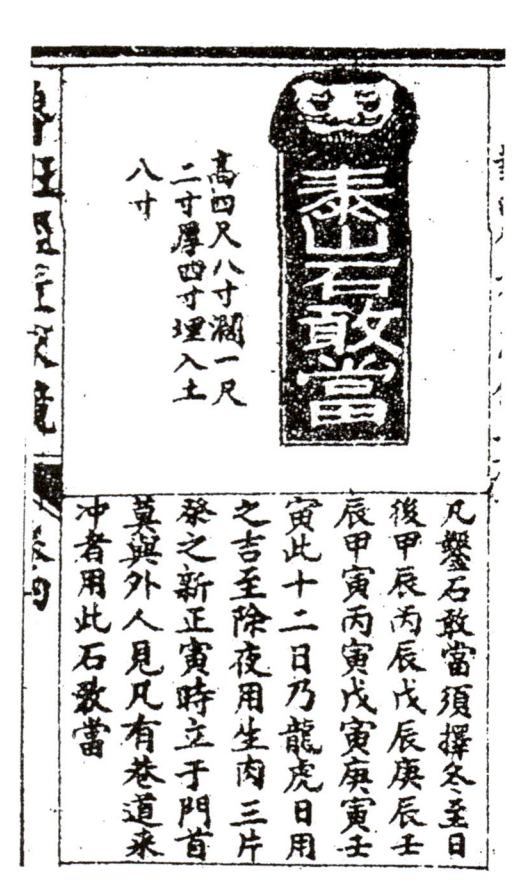

Far left:
The *Lu Ban jing* carpenter's manual spells out not only the dimensions of an efficacious *Taishan shi gandang* ("resisting stone") but also the time when it should be carved and then set in place.

Left:
With the five characters *Taishan shi gandang* and a threatening animal face chiseled into its flat face, this defensive stone is placed on a wall at a T-junction where one lane reaches another outside the Qiao family manor.

Right:
The approach to each courtyard complex in the Qiao family manor is through an imposing entryway constructed of brick, wood, and tile.

248 China's Fine Heritage Houses

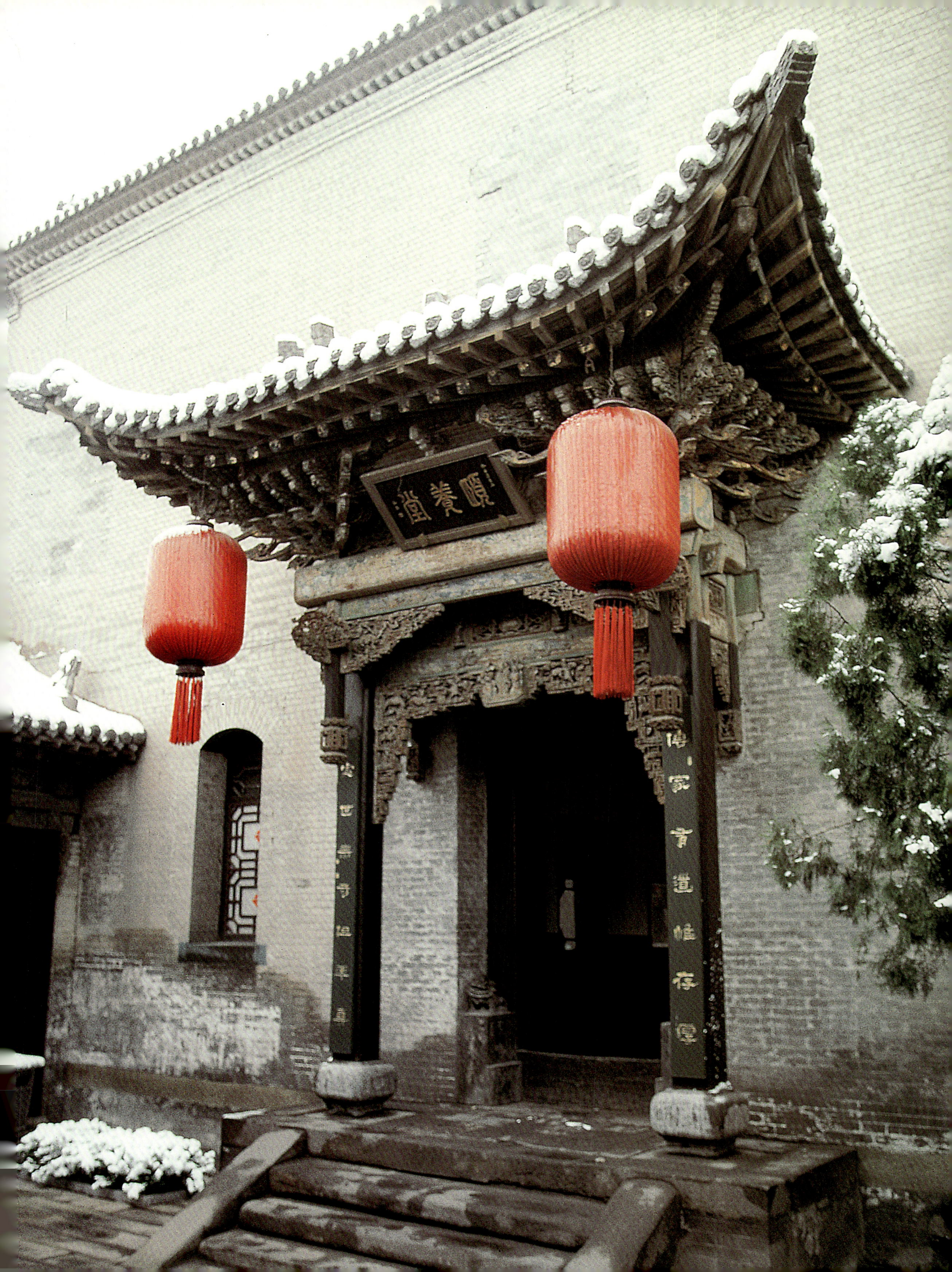

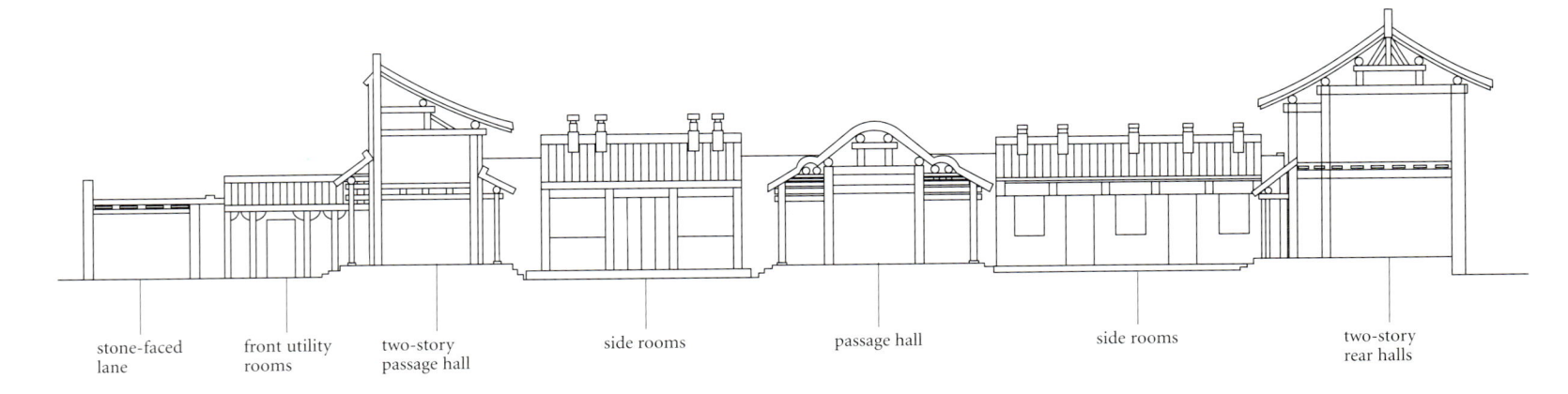

stone-faced lane | front utility rooms | two-story passage hall | side rooms | passage hall | side rooms | two-story rear halls

Russia, expanded between the sixteenth and eighteenth centuries. Just as "jumping into the sea" (*xia hai*) today suggests danger as well as opportunity for Chinese entrepreneurs who explore uncharted territory, in Shanxi during the Ming and Qing dynasties, *zou Xikou* or "going to Xikou" meant trekking beyond the Great Wall to find potentially lucrative prospects not available at home.

Most of the residential complexes of Shanxi merchants are walled and located within villages or towns in what today are considered remote locations. Few provide obvious evidence of the economic and social factors that contributed to their formation over a period of several centuries, especially during the prosperous seventeenth and eighteenth centuries but even continuing during the less flourishing nineteenth century that followed. Each is usually designated as the *dayuan* or *zhuangyuan* (manor or estate) of a single family or clan. It is said that there are seventeen such manors in Qixian county alone and perhaps as many as a thousand scattered throughout the province. Although some have deteriorated markedly over the last two centuries because of neglect, natural forces, as well as deliberate destruction, others remain remarkably intact and beautiful, providing clues to past social and economic forces that are evident in no other way. In recent years, local boosterism has brought many of these to light, but only a handful have been extensively renovated and promoted, especially the manor complexes of the Qiao family, Qu family, and He family in Qixian county, Jiang family of Yuci city, Wang family of Jingsheng village in Lingshi county, Shi family of Shijiagou village in Fenxi county, and Cao family of Beiguang village in Taigu county.

Fortified residential complexes usually are an architectural response to unsettled conditions. In China, rebellion, banditry, and the general turmoil associated with the change of dynasties usually led to the building of high walls in order to provide security. In many cases in Shanxi and other parts of northern China, village walls were rather temporary forms made of earth that survived only as long as there was a clear purpose for them. When they were no longer needed, they were razed as stability replaced strife or eventually nature would obliterate them. In cases where the wealth of affluent clans made it possible, substantial fortifications of fired brick and stone, with parapets, towers, and sometimes moats, were built around existing as well as new settlements. Once completed, walled residential complexes of this sort were generally preserved as markers of a clan's strength and power. In Shanxi, walled villages and residential complexes are often called *baozi* or *bao* ("fortresses"), toponyms that remain even in the absence of the fortifications themselves.

Above:
Section view of the Qiao family manor from south to north (left to right) showing the three main horizontal buildings, including a two-story structure in the rear, and the perpendicular structures that together form sets of courtyards.

Right:
View from the first courtyard through the passageway structure into the second courtyard, and the two-story structure that constitutes the rear or upper hall within the Qiao family manor.

Right:
This decorative door panel incorporates a pair of complementary motifs: bats, which are homophonous for "good fortune," and a stylized longevity character.

Far right:
Ornamental brass door loop in the shape of a flower vase, the sound of which is homophonous with "peace."

A Grand Qing Manor and a Simple Ming Courtyard House 251

Qiao Family Manor

Widely regarded as an outstanding example of a *bao* is Qiaojiabao, the grand fortified settlement of the Qiao family in Qixian county. Begun in 1756 by Qiao Guifa, the Qiao family manor or *Qiaojia dayuan* came eventually to occupy a total area of 8725 square meters as a result of two major expansions, one in the middle of the nineteenth century and then again at the beginning of the twentieth century just as the Qing dynasty was ending. The Qiao family thrived from trading activities centered at Xikou, today called Baotou, beyond the Great Wall, in what is now Inner Mongolia. Specializing in trade in pigments, flour, grain, soybeans, and oils as well as running several pawnshops, the Qiao clan prospered, eventually expanding their business far beyond the borders of northern China. By the end of the nineteenth century, they operated coalmines, specialized shops, and an extensive banking network. Empress Ci Xi stopped at the Qiao family manor in the summer of 1900 as she fled to Xian with the young emperor in the wake of the arrival of an international expeditionary force in Beijing at the close of the Boxer Uprising.

Changes in the national economy in the first decades of the twentieth century reduced the family's income and, according to popular beliefs, the profligacy of the fifth-generation descendants of the clan's founder led to bankruptcy of the clan. By the early 1930s, the family had divided up its assets and the manor began to fall into disrepair, finally being abandoned after the Japanese invasion in 1937. After 1949, the complex was taken over by local authorities who used it as an army barracks as well as for other governmental functions. Substantial destruction occurred during the Cultural Revolution. In 1985, the manor's fortunes, if not of the clan, turned again as the complex was designated a museum with substantial funds apportioned for its repair. The grandeur of the Qiao family's *dayuan* is apparent to viewers of Zhang Yimou's 1991 film "Raising the Red Lantern." Zhang's story is one of deceit, treachery, and sexual favors in a wealthy Chinese clan at the beginning of the twentieth century—all occurring within the confines of a grand feudal mansion. His tale, however, is not that of the Qiao family whose rise and fall is itself worthy of being told.

As the manor complex took form, gray brick outer walls were built to connect the even higher back walls of courtyards. Capped with parapets, these 10-meter-high walls without windows presented a formidable and secure enclosure for the Qiao family. Because the manor is approached via narrow village alleys and never viewed from afar across the fields, its overall scale appears even more imposing as one encounters its main gate because of the height of the adjacent brick walls. Atop some of the flat roofs, several tall towers were built to rise high above the walls so that patrolling night watchmen could survey the inside and outside of the complex from passageways and steps that circuited the complex. Just inside the front gate, an east–west running lane paved with stone leads to the Ancestral Hall at the end and the

Right:
The blank space in the northwest corner of this plan was once a large courtyard complex that was destroyed during the Cultural Revolution. Beyond it are the outlines for buildings and narrow open spaces that make up the Qiao family manor's remaining two multiple courtyard complexes on the north and the three smaller ones on the south.

Below right:
What appears today as a pleasant garden represents the filling in of vacant space left over after the destruction of the courtyard complex during the Cultural Revolution.

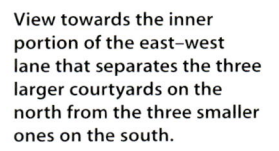

View towards the inner portion of the east–west lane that separates the three larger courtyards on the north from the three smaller ones on the south.

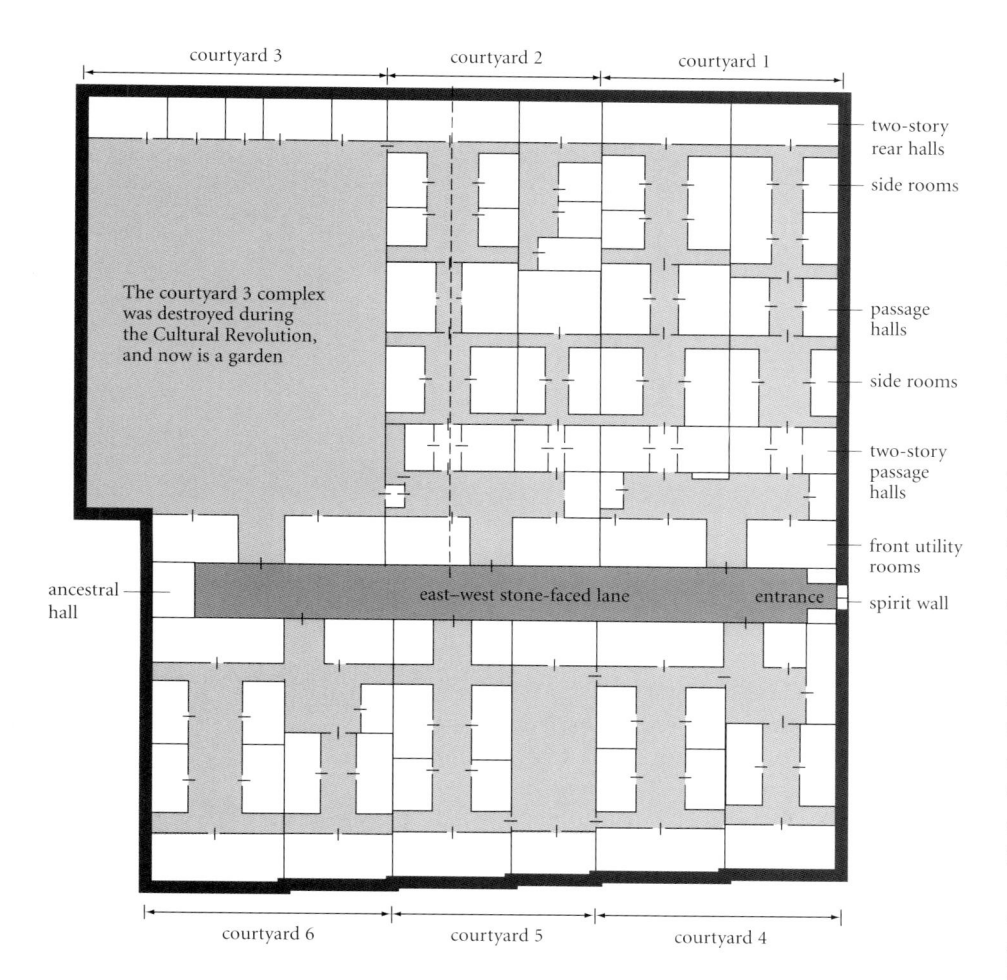

courtyards making up the manor. In order to meet the needs of a large and growing extended household, the manor complex eventually came to comprise six major courtyard compounds, three larger ones on its north side and three smaller ones on its south side. Each set of steps leading to the gate of one of the six courtyard complexes is entered from the east–west lane and each of the steps and gates is staggered so that it is not directly opposite another. Near each of these entries are stepping stones to assist riders on horseback as they mount and dismount. Some say that the layout of the courtyards, rooms, and lanes auspiciously resembles the character 喜 for "joy."

Beyond each of the entry gates to the six courtyards on the north and south sides of the lane is a complex of twenty smaller courtyards and side yards as well as 313 enclosed rooms with a total floor space of 3870 square meters. On the north side, only two of three sets of courtyards remain. Courtyard 3 in the northwest corner was completely destroyed during the Cultural Revolution and has been replaced with a garden. Of the two remaining courtyards on the north side, each has an east to west entry courtyard as well as several narrow rectangular inner courtyards that run north to south. The oldest is Courtyard 1, called *laoyuan* or "the old courtyard," which was built in the mid-eighteenth century by Qiao Guifa.

Once past an entry courtyard that runs east to west, there are two narrow inner rectangular courtyards that run north to south that are linked by a hall. Midway between these two longitudinal courtyards

A Grand Qing Manor and a Simple Ming Courtyard House   253

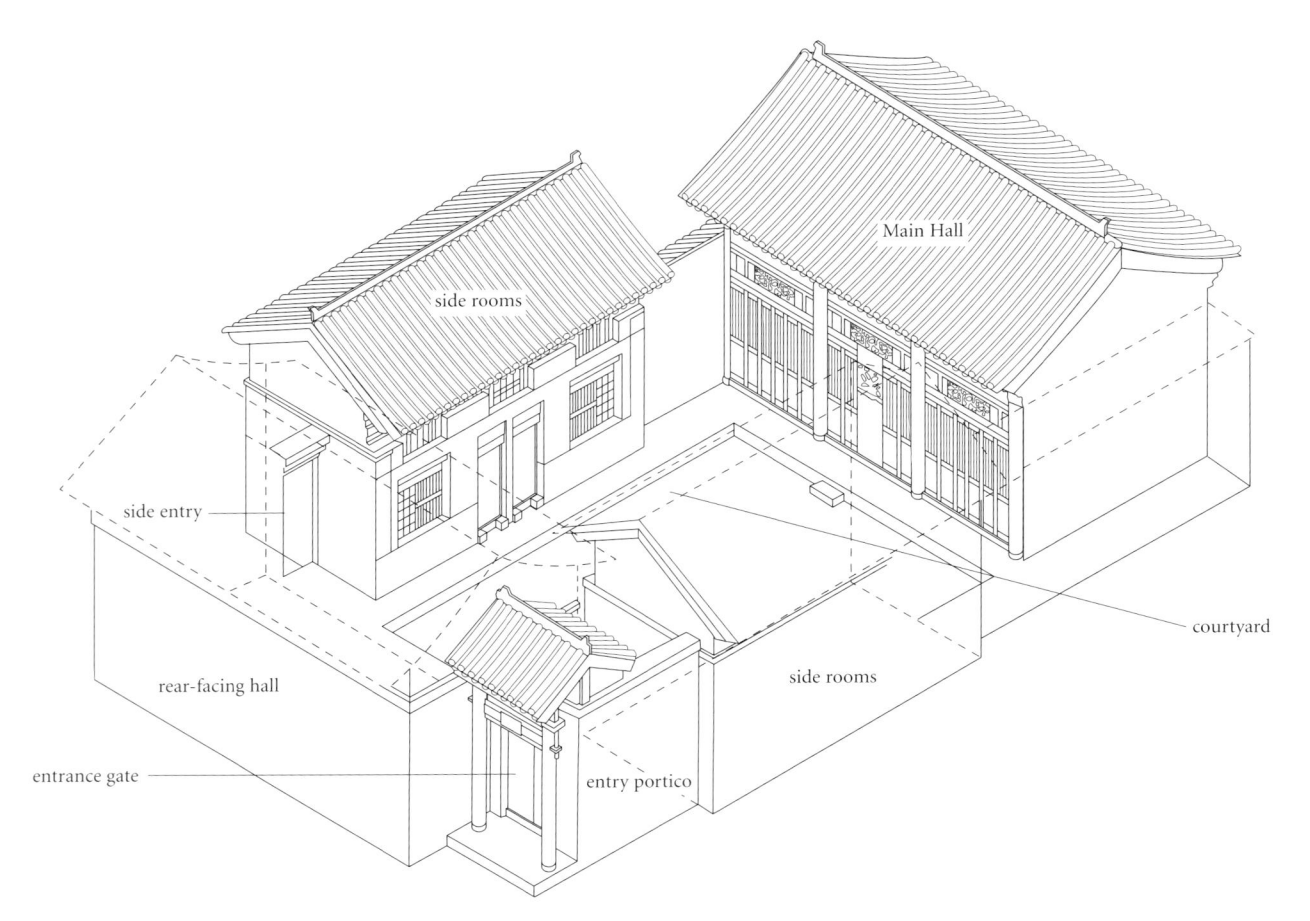

Above:
Axonometric drawing of a Ming-dynasty house in Dingcun, the Ding family village, showing a tight plan of built structures and open spaces.

Right:
The slightly irregular quadrangular plan of a Ming-dynasty dwelling includes two pairs of facing structures, with the paramount one placed to the north and facing south.

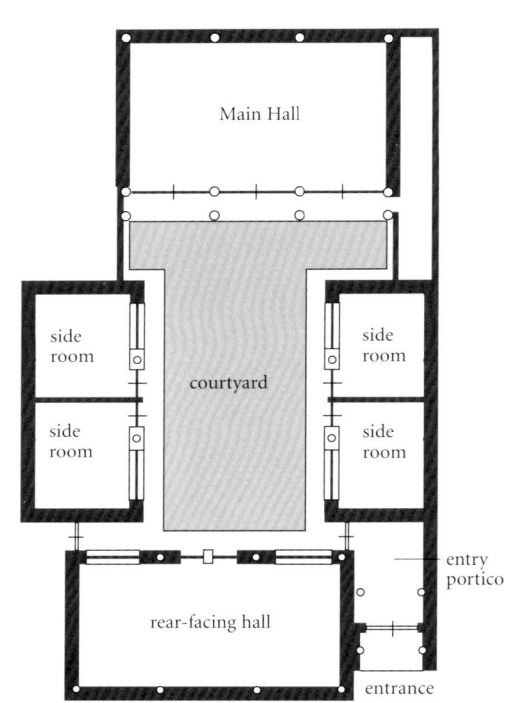

is a single-story *guoting* or "transitional hall" with a rolled roof that leads to a dramatic courtyard framed by side buildings with somewhat curved roofs. On the north side of the second courtyard and entered through an elaborate gate is a two-story *zhengfang* or main structure. Called here an "open or bright building" or *minglou*, it faces south and has a sweeping double-sloped roofline. Although five bays wide, the *minglou* has no internal partitions so that it can be used as a single room. Its second story cannot be accessed directly via an inside stairway but can only be entered from an adjacent rooftop. Unlike elsewhere in northern China, the Qiao family used its *zhengfang* exclusively for ceremonial purposes such as making offerings and welcoming guests. Five-bay-wide side buildings, called *xiangfang*, run north to south alongside the narrow inner courtyard, and contrast with three-bay-wide *xiangfang* in the outer longitudinal courtyard. Although perpendicular to the *minglou*, they are not physically joined together. Both side structures have single steeply pitched roofs at a 45-degree angle that rise higher on the outer wall in order to dampen the impact of winter winds and then lead rainwater into the courtyard. Household members used the *xiangfang* or side rooms for daily activities such as eating and sleeping. Inclined towards the interior and with a prominent eaves overhang, the lower roofline of these side halls creates a human scale for the otherwise constricted courtyards and surrounding high walls, providing at the same time a sense of openness that belies their narrow shape and diminished size. Internal passageways with open portals provide corridors around the complex for women and others who need not enter the main courtyards and gates.

The high exterior walls helped to buffer winter winds while the inclined roofs drew sunlight and rain into the narrow courtyards. The use of elevated and curtained beds instead of heated *kang* by the Qiao family is at variance with general northern practices that provided winter warmth from the radiated heat of *kang* upon which members of the family would spend much of the cold winter. Much of the Qiao family complex, however, was heated by a more expansive system that involved extravagant consumption of fuel necessary to keep whole rooms warm, clearly expressing the wealth of the household. This was accomplished by linking large stoves to chimneys via a warren of flues that ran under the brick floors and through some walls in order to supply radiant heat from many directions. As a result, more than 140 chimneys, some of which are elaborately ornamented, populate the upper walls and roofs. Except for the embellished exterior entryway that faces a wall with 100 variations of the Chinese character for longevity carved on it, brick, wood, and stone carvings were limited to inside locations that only the family could experience. Around 1921, renovations introduced Western-style ornamentation as well as modern features such as bathrooms, electricity, and etched window glass without changing the traditional character of the residential structure.

Ding Family Village

Perhaps the oldest residences in Shanxi are those in Dingcun or "Ding Village" in Xiangfen county. Of forty designated structures, ten have halls and courtyards that were built in the sixteenth and seventeenth centuries during the Ming dynasty with two complete dwellings said to date to the Wanli period (1573–1620). The earliest *siheyuan*, dated to 1593, is located in the northeast part of the village and preserves characteristics of Beijing-style residences: an entry gate on the southeastern wall, a spirit wall, a rear-facing *daocuo*, a colonnaded south-facing three-bay-wide Main Hall, a pair of flanking side rooms three bays wide, and brick *kang* beds.

The second oldest, dating from 1612, was built with two courtyards and associated structures, but today only fragments remain. Some dwellings may be older although they have undergone such modification that they do not represent Ming styles. For the most part, Ming dwellings are characterized by relatively simple *siheyuan* quadrangles that conform to the sumptuary regulations of the times.

While some of the Qing-period dwellings in Dingcun are uncomplicated, others involve receding and interconnected courtyards with substantial attention to hierarchy and the separation of outer and inner realms. Local historians attribute the survival of fine examples of Ming and Qing dwellings not only to the remoteness of Dingcun from the past centuries' tumult but also to family inheritance practices that demanded shared ownership. When two brothers divided their father's real estate, one would take an "upper" share and the other a "lower." This horizontal division worked against any one individual's desire to demolish and rebuild without the consent of the other. In 1985, six contiguous dwellings built between 1723 and 1786 were designated as the "Dingcun Folkways Museum," reputedly the first such specialized museum in China.

Below:
Looking north towards the three-bay Main Hall of a Ming-era dwelling in Dingcun village. The pair of flanking side buildings faces a narrow courtyard that is ringed by elevated stonework sheltered by a broad eaves overhang.

THE MANOR OF A BEAN CURD MAKER

Wang Family Manor, Jingsheng, Shanxi Province

Among the least-known, largest, and most interesting manors on the loessial plateau in Shanxi province is that of the Wang family, once one of the four most powerful families in Shanxi and the ancestors of Wangs who today live throughout China. The *Wangjia dayuan* or Wang Family Manor extends across a gentle loessial terrace along the slopes of Mianshan Mountain in Jingsheng village, some 12 kilometers from the small county seat of Lingshi and 150 kilometers south of the provincial capital Taiyuan.

Wang, romanized also as Wong in Cantonese, Heng in Teochew, Ong in Hokkien, and Vong in Vietnamese, contends with Li and Zhang as the most common surnames found in China. Together these three surnames are held by more than 270 million Chinese—nearly equaling the total population of the United States—with each of them representing about a third of this number. Today, the Wang surname belongs to more than 10 percent of families in north China, while it is only second in the Yangzi River region, yet does not rank even in the top five in southern China. Meaning "king" or "ruler," Wang, according to many authorities, originated as a surname in central Shanxi province during China's first unified dynasty, the Qin, in the third century BCE. As one of China's oldest family names, it thus has its roots in northern China, with a complicated dispersion history throughout the country and indeed in Chinese diasporas around the world.

There are detailed records that trace the arrival of the Wangs from Taiyuan to Jingsheng village in 1312 during the Yuan dynasty. According to legend, the family began to supplement its farming with income derived from the making and selling of bean curd, an enterprise that enriched the family over time. These humble origins are highlighted today in the descriptive exhibits in the manor, but it was business, trade, and official position that eventually

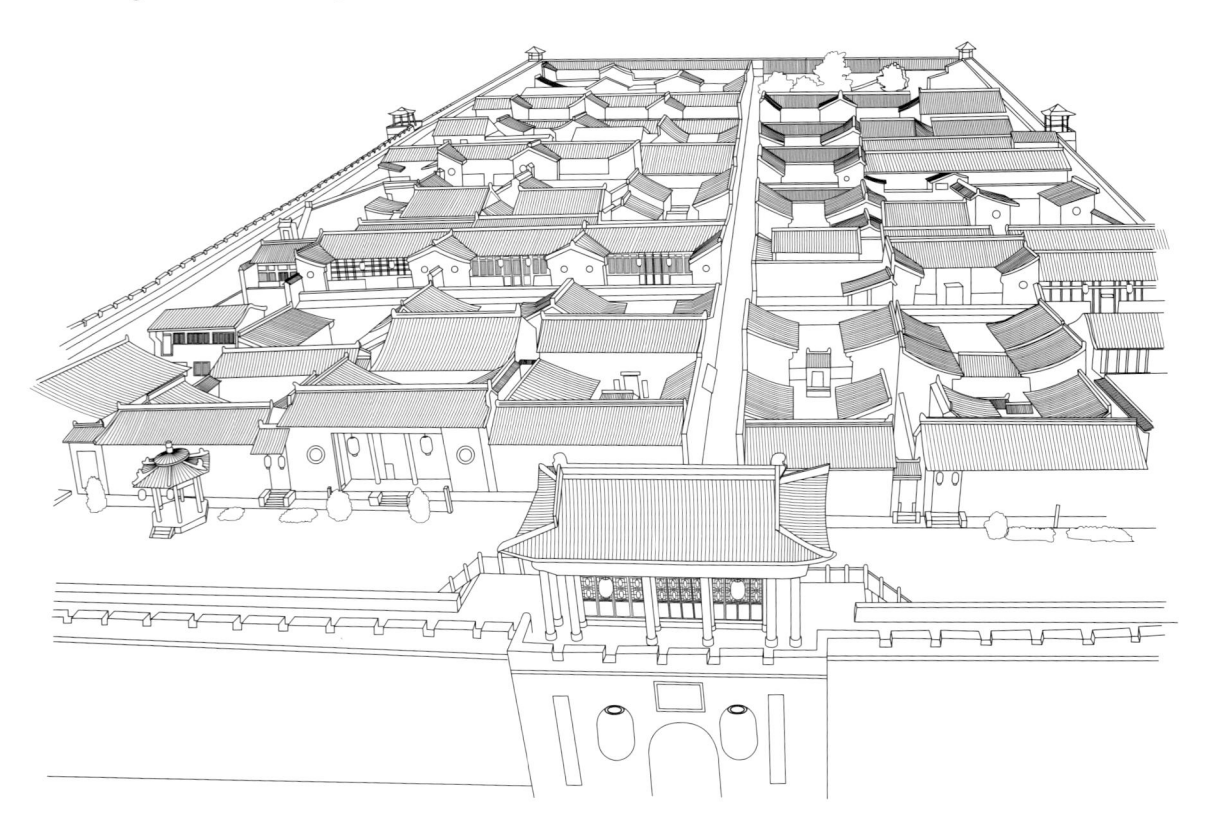

Left:
Bird's-eye view of a major portion of Hongmen Bao, the "Red Gate Fortress," revealing the impregnability of its eight-meter-high encircling brick-faced wall and the complexity of receding and interconnected courtyards.

Right:
The single south-facing gate, colored red, is the source for the name Red Gate Fortress and leads to a 3.6-meter-wide north–south lane.

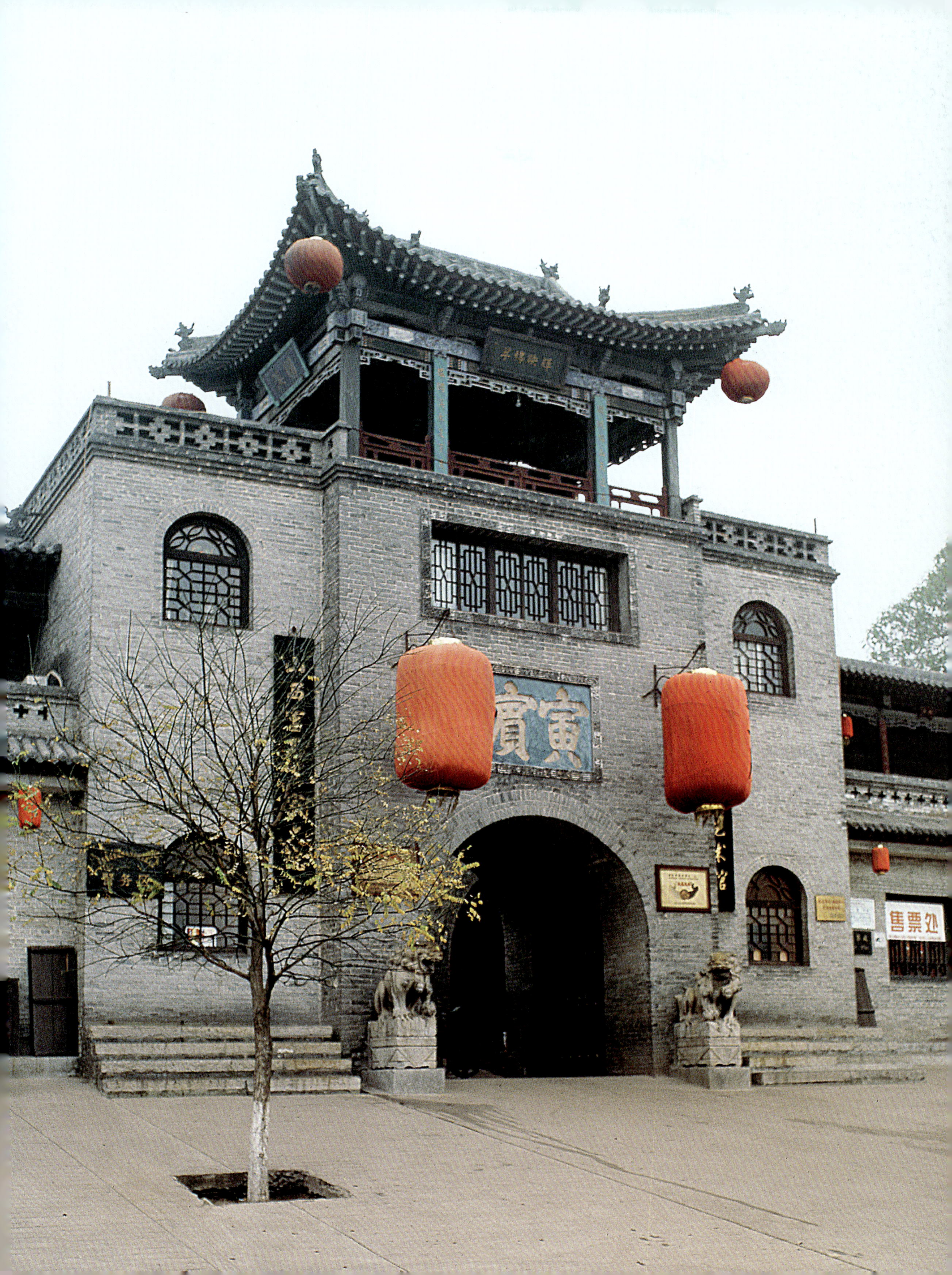
寅賓
售票处

Above:
As shown in this plan, the north–south lane is crossed by three east–west lanes in order to represent auspiciously the Chinese character for Wang, the family's surname.

Right:
One of the south-facing residential courtyards shows the cave-like main structure and abundant carvings as well as the pair of facing two-story buildings with upstairs rooms and balconies that provide private spaces for young women.

The Manor of a Bean Curd Maker

品行兼優

brought greater wealth. The eighteenth century is always highlighted as a peak in the Wang family's development, since it was during this century that resources and talents accumulated to such a degree that large residences, ancestral halls, as well as private academies were built. The family used its wealth also for public benefit by building roads, bridges, water conservancy projects, public granaries, opera stages, and temples. Moreover, the Wangs built a Confucian temple in Jingsheng village, a rarity in China's countryside, which served as an academy for educating young boys, leading many of them to success in civil examinations. Yet, as the Qing dynasty itself waned in the nineteenth century, the Wang family's fortunes in Shanxi also declined, according to family histories, for many reasons, including profligate and self-indulgent sons. Some claim that by 1949, most of those surnamed Wang had abandoned Jingsheng, their home village, leaving for Beijing, Sichuan, Taiwan, and even the United States.

In the village, it was said that among the so-called "nine gullies, eight fortresses and eighteen lanes"—cave dwellings, walled compounds, and compact village—"five gullies, six fortresses, and five lanes" belonged to the Wangs. Built first over a seventy-five year period in the seventeenth century, the full Wang family manor complex sprawls across nearly 32,000 square meters (eight acres), and is divided into two distinct eastern and western "fortress courtyards" or *baoyuan*, each with its own gate, as well as a separate Ancestral Hall complex. The east courtyards are collectively called Gaojia Ya or "High Family Ridge" and those on the west Hongmen Bao or "Red Gate Fortress." The structures and courtyards in both complexes are arranged in ascending tiers on a hillside, with courtyards of various sizes and shapes aligned along several north–south axes running up the slope. With encircling walls, courtyards within courtyards, and numerous gates, the Wang family manor fits well with the terrain, offering at once protection from external threats and security for the extended family within. Facing south, the building complex has a commanding presence as it overlooks smaller village dwellings below it, even suggesting to some that its dominance is castle-like.

Within the four walls of Gaojia Ya, built between 1796 and 1811, the courtyards are arranged in six parallel tiers that rise along the mountain slope, with a gate at each of the four cardinal points of the walls. At the core of Gaojia Ya is a set of three courtyard complexes, each with a layout having the Main Hall in front and the bedchamber to the rear, with kitchens to their east and a school and garden on the west. Each of the courtyards is divided into three building units, comprising a *zhengfang* or main structure to the rear and a pair of flanking *xiangfang* built to look like subterranean dwellings, but which actually are above-ground cave-like dwellings called *guyao*. Thirteen actual cave structures, called *yaodong*, each with four attached courtyards, are found along the rear of Gaojia Ya where they have a commanding position overlooking the entire area. It was on top of these caves and inside the wall that watchmen patrolled at night to insure safety of the Gaojia Ya residential complex below.

After crossing a stone bridge over a deep gully serving as a kind of moat, the "western courtyard" complex looms large with its rectangular extent being 105 meters from east to west and 180 meters from north to south. With only a single south-facing gate, colored red, the Hongmen Bao or "Red Gate Fortress" complex is strikingly impregnable because of its encircling brick-faced wall, which rises eight meters on the outside but only four meters on the inside.

Built between 1739 and 1793, a time of great prosperity during the Qing dynasty, Hongmen Bao has a relatively simple layout: a single 3.6-meter-wide north–south lane is crossed by three east–west lanes,

Opposite:
Each of the narrow side lanes is entered through a richly multitiered ornamented gate.

Above left:
This carved wooden horizontal member extends beyond the balcony it supports.

Above right:
Separated by roughly triangular-shaped dripping tiles, the circular tile ends are molded with protective totem-like animal faces.

Right:
Tucked into a narrow alley, this grand niche for the Earth God is made of stone to mimic a building constructed of wood.

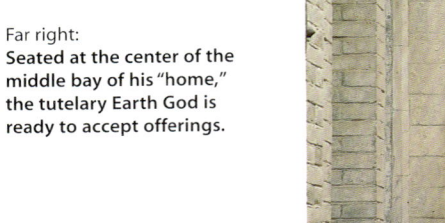

Far right:
Seated at the center of the middle bay of his "home," the tutelary Earth God is ready to accept offerings.

A craftsmen prepares new wooden carvings to replace those that are damaged.

an auspicious shape that mimics the form of the Chinese character for Wang 王, the family's surname. Set within this alignment are twenty-seven symmetrical courtyard units of various sizes. With encircling walls, courtyards within courtyards, and numerous gates, the Wang family manor fits well with the terrain, offering at once protection from external threats and security for the extended family within.

According to Wang family legend, the layout of Hongmen Bao represents an auspicious dragon: the red gate represents its head; the two wells located at both the eastern and western ends of the lowest row are its eyes; the south to north lane represents the dragon's body with the narrow lanes along the sides its claws; the luxuriant cypress towering above the fort in the rear is its tail. Throughout the courtyards of the Wang family manor, stone, brick, and woodcarvings, artistic and symbolic treatments of roof ridges, window frames, pillar bases, timber joints, and wall screens are especially noteworthy.

262　China's Fine Heritage Houses

Far left:
Clay chimneys throughout the Wang family manor are capped with pyramidal-shaped roofs with *faux* tile coverings.

Left:
Moral tales are among the most common themes of ornamentation throughout the Wang manor. Here, carved in bas-relief on the base of a column is a tableau portraying the well-known tale of filial piety in which a daughter-in-law provides nourishment of breast milk for her mother-in-law.

Below:
This polychrome woodblock print tells the same tale of filial piety shown above in the stone carving, of a devoted daughter-in-law suckling her toothless mother-in-law.

The restoration of the impressive Wang family manor began only in 1996. The initial challenge was the relocation of 212 households who had occupied its sumptuous spaces as squatters over the previous several decades, cluttering the courtyards and structures with the ephemera of everyday life and contributing to significant damage to woodwork and ornamentation. Teams of architects, engineers, and craftsmen then set out to clear the complex of damaged and decayed wood as well as disintegrated clay bricks and tiles. As part of the restoration process, some three million new bricks had to be fashioned of local clay in adjacent kilns and 3500 cubic meters of wood had to be obtained in order to overcome the accumulated decay of nearly two centuries of family and national vicissitudes.

Today, major efforts are being made to introduce those with the surname Wang anywhere in the world to the architectural magnificence of the Wang family manor in Shanxi, to have them learn of their noble background, mercantile acumen, and intelligence, but also to display to them the consequences of human failings. Moreover, there is optimism throughout Shanxi that the extensive renovation of the Wang manor complex and other historically significant residences, temples, and pagodas, as well as the establishment of sites noted for their natural scenery, will bring both tourists and ultimately prosperity again to the province. Shanxi is best known today for dirty coal-mining and industrial pollution. Yet, it seems likely that the richness of its architectural and historical treasures and its flourishing merchant and banking enterprises in which Shanxi merchants played such a dynamic role will contribute to increasing its recognition as an important center of culture.

The Manor of a Bean Curd Maker

WALLED CITY RESIDENCES
Fan Family Courtyard, Pingyao, Shanxi Province

Walking the lanes of Pingyao at daybreak, before the activity of old residents and newly arrived tourists infuse the town with an energizing hustle and bustle, is like traveling back several centuries in both time and place. There are only a few towns in China that provide the feel for the glories of yesterday, even the distant past, especially with intact gray walls surrounding it and old streets within. Built largely during the seventeenth through nineteenth centuries by merchants and Chinese-style bankers who aspired to a courtly lifestyle, Pingyao over the past century and a half, however, fell into a decrepit backwater status before resurging to prominence in 1997 as a UNESCO World Heritage Site. In less than a decade, some six million visitors are now arriving each year, forcing some to grapple with the unintended consequences of tourism, the negative impact of large numbers of people on a fragile cultural landscape.

Stagnation, more than actual intent, led to the preservation of Pingyao's network of narrow streets and lanes, along which there are some 3800 Ming- and Qing-era structures, with nearly 500 reasonably intact. Even a cursory glance suggests that most buildings were quite gracious in scale and ornamentation, constructed with substantial quantities of expensive wood, stone, and brick. As the twentieth century neared its end, most dwellings, especially, had fallen into a state of dilapidation. Most were shabby relics of past glory whose current occupants were living under difficult circumstances quite different from the lives of the affluent owners who built and occupied the houses in centuries past.

A look back at the source of the town's wealth is in order. Situated on a high, rather barren plateau with limited arable land and a dry, harsh climate, Shanxi province always has had a reputation as a difficult place to make a living. However, the location of the province midway between the imperial capitals of Beijing and Xian brought with it relatively easy access to the outside world by way of its north to south flowing rivers and old-style trunk post roads that crisscrossed the region. During the fifteenth and sixteenth centuries, especially, Shanxi merchants, called Jin Shang, came to dominate various commodity markets, including dyestuff, salt, iron, cotton, silk, and tea, especially in towns along the border with Russia but also in large cities in coastal China.

With increasing wealth by the beginning of the nineteenth century, the long-distance transport of silver cash loomed as an increasingly important concern. Pingyao merchants, basing their business acumen on the loyalty of kinsmen, introduced "paper notes" called *piao* that could be redeemed for cash at *piao hao* or "exchange shops"—in effect, nascent banks and forerunners of a modern finance system—as pay-to-the-bearer certificates. As a result, long-distance remittances were safe, loans could be made, and deposits accumulated by individuals whose lives depended on their mobility.

In Pingyao, all the main *piao hao* were attached to merchant shops, which were actually sumptuous courtyard structures with both business and living functions. Among the largest was Rishengchang, once merely a dyestuff store, which at its peak had 40 branches throughout China, each staffed by loyal individuals from Pingyao. It is said that by the middle of the nineteenth century, of the 51 traditional banks in China, 43 were owned by Shanxi natives, with those from Pingyao operating 22, all of them benefiting from a close relationship with the Qing imperial court, which also had a need to transfer funds around the country. However, by the later half of the nineteenth century, not only had Western-style banks begun to be established in China's major cities that

Above:
Surrounding Pingyao, the battered and crenellated walls, which also include projecting terraces, date from the early Ming dynasty.

Above right:
Depicted here as a roughly rectangular plan, this late nineteenth-century map of walled Pingyao depicts buildings and walls in elevation view so that they appear to be laying flat.

Below right:
As with any old Chinese town or city, buildings are low and horizontal.

Walled City Residences

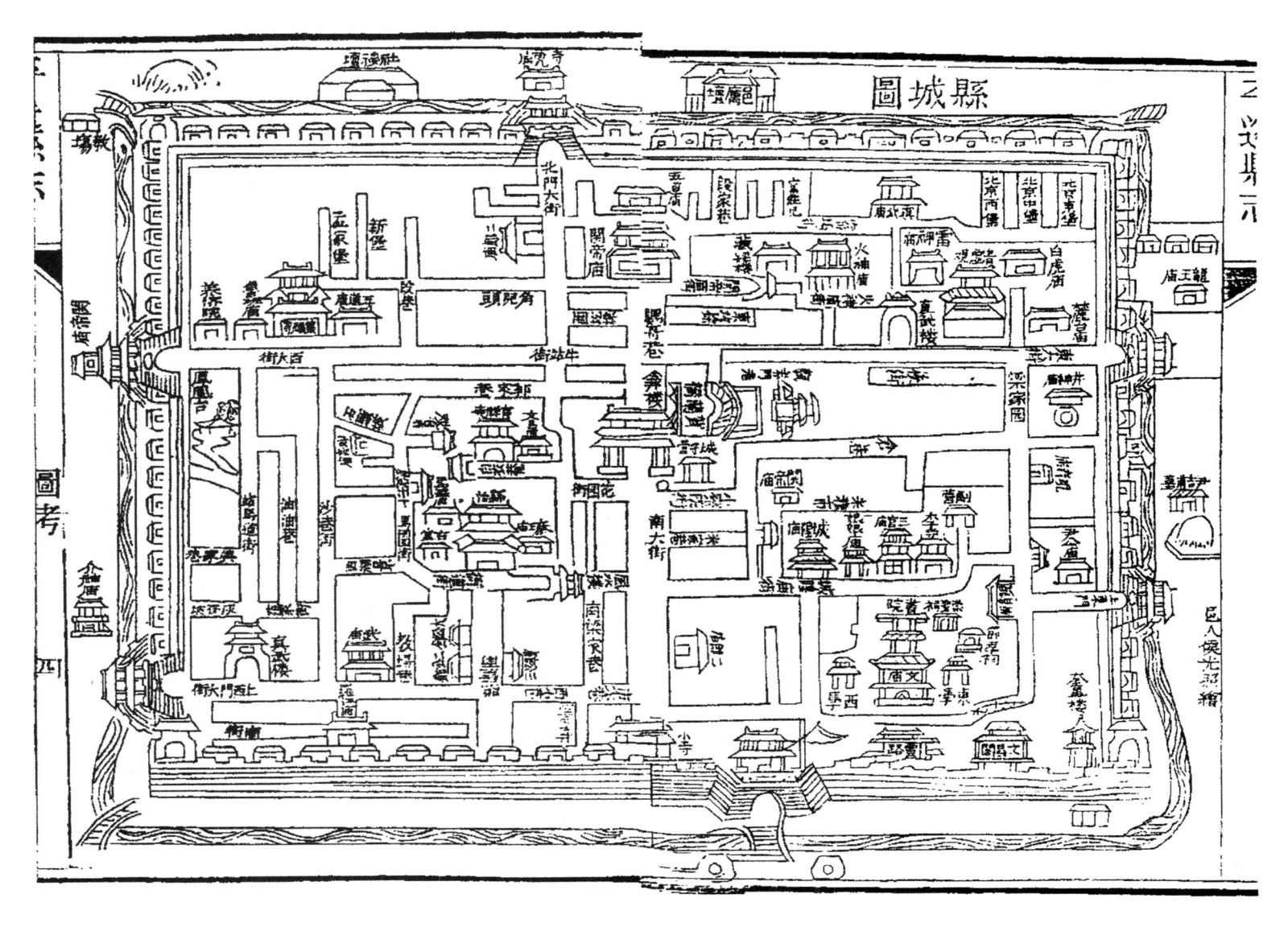

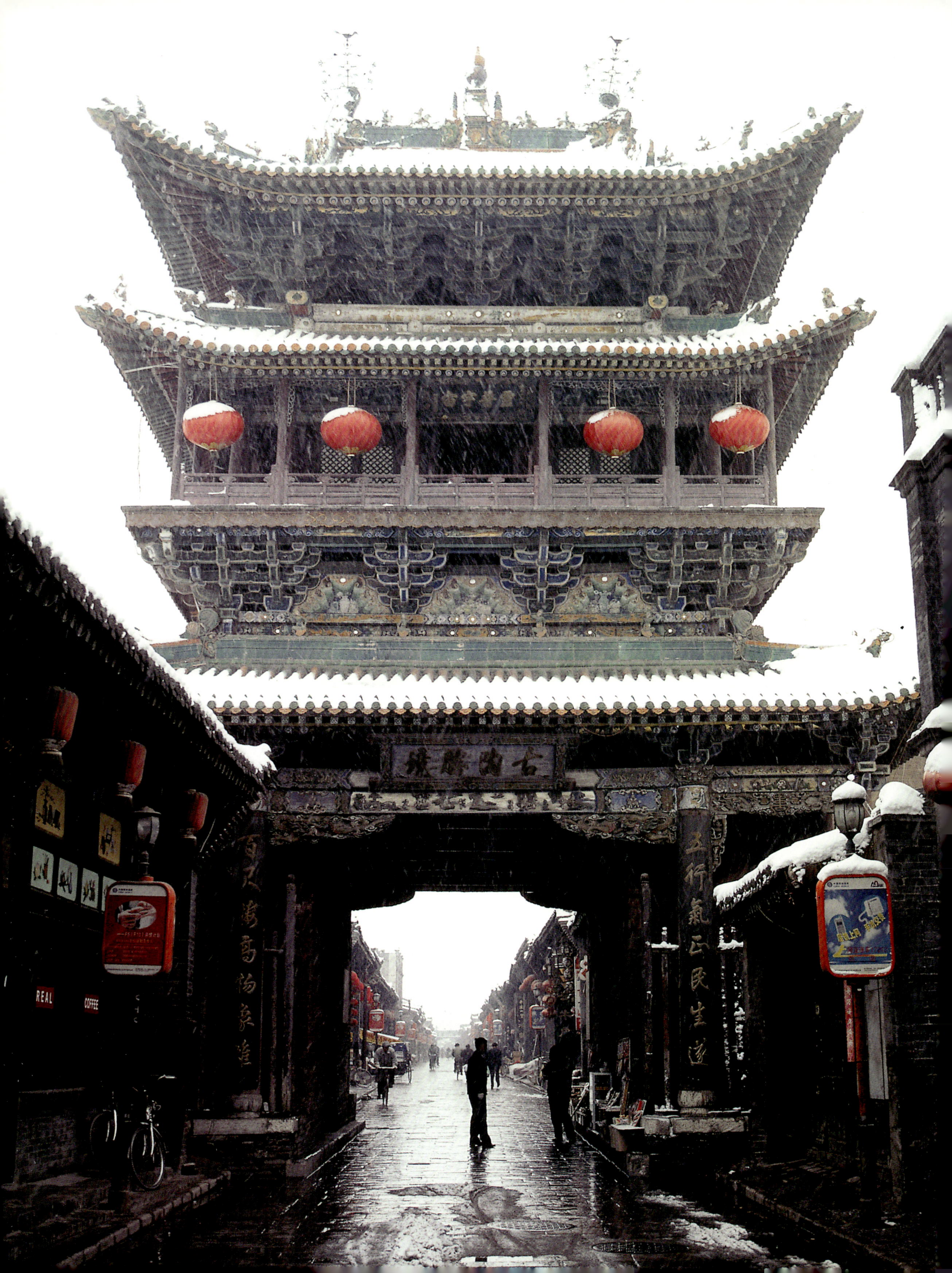
古陶勝境
REAL
COFFEE

Left:
Some 18.5 meters in height, the imposing Shi Lou or "Market Tower" is located at the center of Pingyao with the major north–south road passing through it.

Right:
Perspective view of the Fan family house shows an elongated series of structures surrounding two narrow courtyards.

Below:
As depicted in this Qing-dynasty drawing of Pingyao's principal landmarks, the tall Market Tower structure had adjacent to it the town's most important well, the "Golden Well."

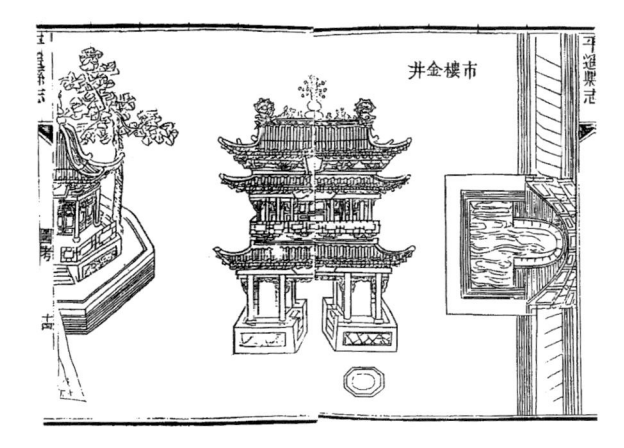

siphoned off resources from the traditional *piao hao*, but the Qing court itself was in rapid decline. By the end of the first decade of the twentieth century, the wealth of Shanxi merchants and "traditional bankers" indeed had evaporated. For the most part, many of these once prosperous businessmen retreated into the seclusion and safety of their magnificent houses in Pingyao, where old houses were left standing without being modernized, even in states of utter disrepair, while, unlike in other Chinese cities, the streets remained unwidened.

Pingyao is said to have "4 avenues, 8 streets, and 72 winding lanes": the four broad avenues lead to Pingyao's main gates, each allowing two carriages to pass easily; the narrower eight streets were lined with shops, pawnshops, *piao hao*, temples, and schools, most of which had residences associated with them; but it was in the quietude of the lanes, each unpaved and only 1.5–2 meters wide, where a distinctive type of quadrangular building was built.

Shanxi-style *siheyuan* are similar to the classical form found in Beijing in that they, too, express the spatial elements of enclosure, axiality, symmetry, and hierarchy, but in style and ornamentation those of Pingyao are nonetheless strikingly distinctive. The most obvious differences include very high walls all around, an imposing gate at the center of the lane-side exterior wall, elongated narrow courtyards, single-slope inward-facing rooflines on the side or wing structures, with the main structure in the rear having a flat roof and built to look like a series of elegant caves in the countryside.

The Fan residence, situated along South Lane, epitomizes both these similar and diverging features. Sited so that the overall plan of the residence "sits north and faces south," it includes a pair of nearly equal-sized open courtyards, which are separated from each other by a massive utilitarian structure whose scale exceeds that of other structures in the residence. Both the exterior gate, with its superimposed "hood," and the gateway leading from the first courtyard to the second are imposing and richly ornamented. Each of the two pairs of wing rooms is three *jian* in width with very high back walls from which a single sloped roof drops to lower walls fronting the courtyards. Unlike *siheyuan* dwellings in Beijing, these side buildings do not have columns supporting their extended eaves and thus no apparent verandah. The main structure at the back, called *zhengfang*, which is five *jian* wide, was constructed and ornamented so as to emphasize the broader three *jian* set of rooms.

This rear structure, with its arcuate windows, clearly mimics cave-like dwellings found widely in the loessial rural areas of Shanxi and neighboring provinces. Built in a style known as *guyao*, each is a set of freestanding structures that imitate subterranean dwellings in terms of the appearance of their façades but also in their overall dimensions and in the use of vaulted arches that carry the weight of a substantial overburden of earth. The end walls serve as piers that help contain the lateral thrust of the interior arches as well as bear the substantial volumes of earth that are piled in the voids above the vaulted

Walled City Residences   267

Left:
Passers-by are dwarfed by the imposing doorway and the projection above it that leads into the Fan family quadrangle.

Right:
View from the first courtyard through a grand "flowery gate" that leads into the transitional building before opening into the second courtyard. On each side of the doorway is a niche for a Door or Gate God.

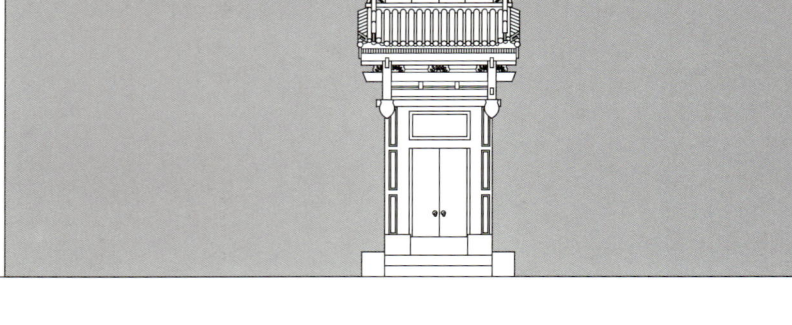

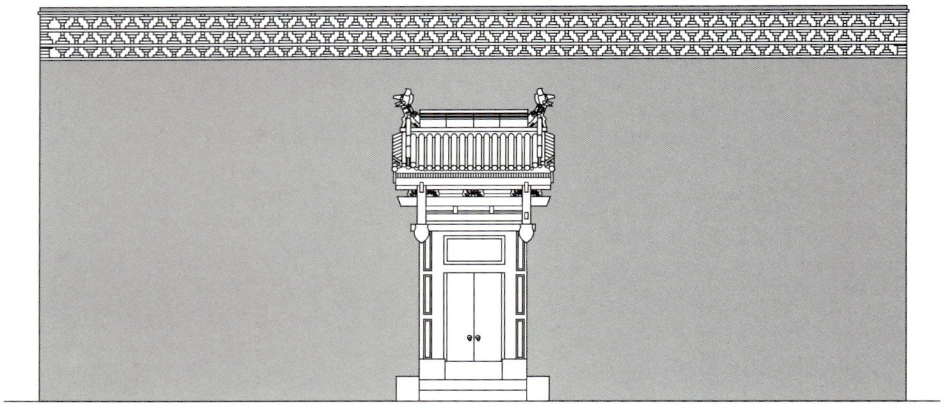

Above:
Shown in an elevation drawing, the façade and its entryway are simple and symmetrical in design.

Right:
Each of the complementary structures, except for the middle transitional building, is constructed as a three-bay module.

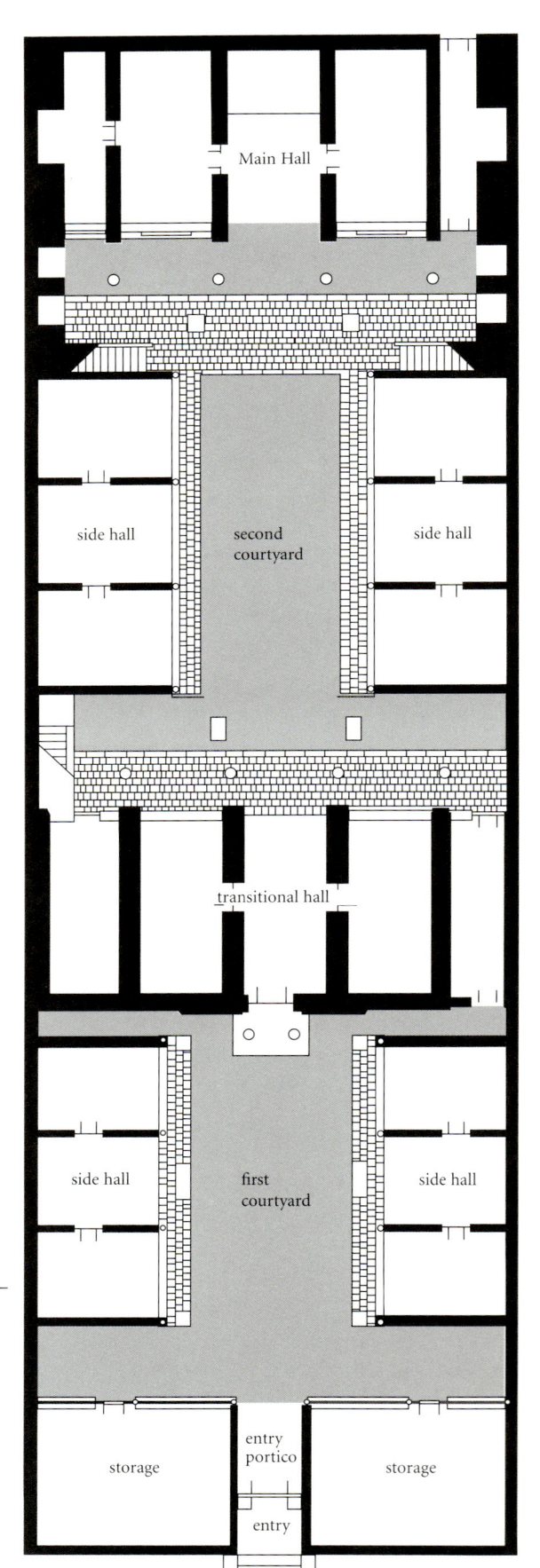

268 China's Fine Heritage Houses

Far left:
Detail of one of a pair of carved stone niches to hold a Door or Gate God.

Left:
Once inside the transitional building, it is clear that the passageway mimics the arcuate shape of a cave.

Walled City Residences 269

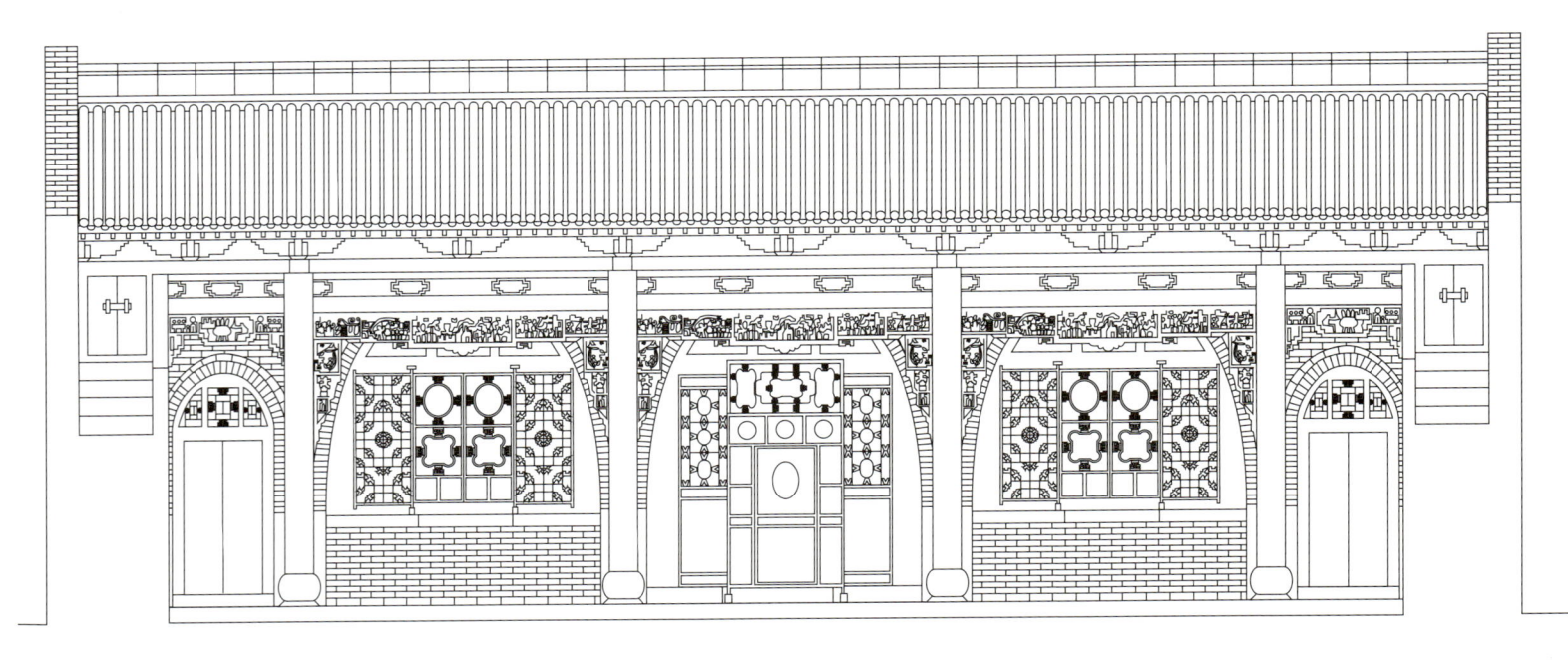

Above:
Elevation drawing of the symmetrical main building at the end of the second courtyard.

Below:
Detail of the entry to the main building. Framed between a pair of columns, the scene is one of richly ornamented wooden and stone carvings.

Far left:
The lattice frames comprising the façade of the entryway depict four bats, representing a homophonous relationship with the word for "good fortune," surrounding an open circle representing "longevity."

Left:
The type of carved figure that once sat upon the top of this stone post is no longer recalled, having been smashed some thirty years ago during the Cultural Revolution.

Below:
Adjacent to the rear building are stairs leading to a flat roof, a space used to catch the breeze in the evening and, perhaps, even provide a cool place to sleep on a sultry summer night.

structures and which constitute a thick, insulating roof that helps keep the occupants warm in winter.

As visitors pass through the open spaces and encounter the structures alongside them, the Fan residence has the ambience and intimacy of a rural village of subterranean cave-like dwellings even as one is aware of being in a well-structured courtyard with substantial quality workmanship. Windows and doors are made of wooden lattice designs, and carved ornamentation is found on most vertical and horizontal building members. *Guyao* preserve the positive attributes of cave dwellings while eliminating some of their negative points. In terms of thermal performance, the substantial earth, stone, and brick walls on three sides and on the roof as well as the earth beneath provide excellent insulation from severe cold in winter and heat in summer, at the same time retaining heat generated within during the winter. Moreover, air circulation is typically better within urban *siheyuan* dwellings of this type than in those built into the earth below ground.

In 1997, the United Nations named Pingyao a World Heritage Site because of its intact wall, streetscapes, and thousands of old buildings, but there is still insufficient money to carry out a full restoration. Suffering from decades of neglect and abuse, once stately residences became dilapidated, all too often stripped of their ornamentation by thieves out to make a little money or sold by families in need of cash. Crowded with its narrow unpaved dusty lanes, lack of plumbing, poor sewage treatment, and other infrastructure accepted elsewhere as essential, Pingyao is not a convenient place to live for many residents. Nonetheless, in half a decade, many residents of Pingyao have come to value their architectural

Walled City Residences

and cultural patrimony and have set out to begin the restoration of the town. Numerous inns, restaurants, and shops have opened in restored old buildings, many of which have updated plumbing, heating, and electricity, and others even have added high-speed Internet connections. Living with the past has not been easy even though visitors find the juxtaposition of old and new rather charming.

Yet, even casual visitors notice that all too often conservation work has been rushed and slapdash, with roughly hewn wooden pieces substituting for those that were elegant, and sometimes just a quick paint job instead of sealing old pillars with layers of cloth, horsehair, and then a final coat of lacquer. In trying to balance the needs of preservation with the requirements of modern life, authorities have been attempting since 2002 to move nearly half of the town's 47,000 population to a new nearby area where government offices, schools, factories, and hospitals already have relocated. Some argue that reducing the resident population to perhaps 25,000 will ravage the vibrant life that makes Pingyao so interesting to visit, while others see the reduction as critical in "saving" the city from erosion from within. Yet, it is the crush of visitors, not the long-suffering residents, who are aggravating long-standing problems relating to sewage and garbage disposal, inadequate electric power supply, and internal transport. Along many of the dusty lanes, block-like structures built during the first fifty years after 1949 are being demolished, leaving in their wake vast vacant spaces that neither invoke the past nor hint of what the future might bring. Some residents want to save at least the façade of their old homes as well as the courtyards within, but lack the resources to modernize the interiors to meet current needs. Few who appreciate old buildings desire to maintain old lifestyles, especially inadequate bathing and cooking facilities. The challenge is to preserve in the process some sense of Pingyao as a living settlement and not simply as a hollow monument. The next five years will likely set the direction for Pingyao. The question as to whether Pingyao and its remarkably intact urban landscape will be overwhelmed by unappreciative visitors who tolerate poor quality restoration or become a model for successful historic preservation is yet to be determined.

Tian Yuan Kui, a Traditional Inn

Along the main street of Pingyao, called Ming-Qing Street because of the predominance of old structures, including an imposing market tower, are a number of the town's finest *kezhan* or traditional-style inns. Tian Yuan Kui, one of the first to open in Pingyao, is a unique family-owned *kezhan* that exudes China's past although fitted with many modern amenities. Built as an inn during the reign of the Qianlong emperor at the end of eighteenth century, Tian Yuan Kui is at the beginning of the twenty-first century a symbol of reasonably sensitive restoration, and has been joined by scores of other inns.

Along the street, especially after dusk, red candles glisten through the façade. One enters the front door into a large rectangular room with high square tables and benches for eight, the so-called Eight Immortals tables or *Baxian zhuo*, where both candlelight and the sounds of traditional music change the mood quickly for the visitor. Mr and Mrs Cheng, the resident owners, are always present to welcome visitors, help them choose food, and offer suggestions as to what to see. Throughout the room, traditional arts enhance the atmosphere, such as the lattice windows with red paper cutouts or hanging paintings.

Just outside the back of the main room is an L-shaped narrow courtyard with a spirit wall and rustic seating for tea. Each of the generous rooms is fitted with a traditional-style brick bed, called a *kang*, which once was connected to a stove in order to be warmed by radiant heat. Today, each bed is piled high with soft comforters and pillows and heat comes from pipes through which circulating hot water moves. A bathroom, shower, and air conditioning provide services needed by many urban visitors for their comfort. Several inns of this type are spread throughout Pingyao, with most being smaller and simpler. A few larger hotels have been opened to accommodate those wanting more amenities.

Set for tea and light snacks in the Tian Yuan Kui inn, this Eight Immortals table or *Baxian zhuo* provides bench seating for eight.

Left:
Behind the large room fronting the street is an L-shaped narrow courtyard with a screen wall and rustic seating, a place to relax and have tea. Emblazoned on the wall is the character *fu*, meaning "good fortune."

Below left and right:
Window ornaments include red papercuts depicting pairs of "joy bringing magpies," a "doubled happiness" character, and five plum blossoms that represent the "five good fortunes." Together they represent an especially felicitous wish for a newly married couple enjoying their wedding banquet.

Walled City Residences 273

CAVE DWELLINGS OF THE NORTH
Subterranean Adaptations, Henan, Shaanxi, and Shanxi Provinces

Below:
The sloping entryway and the extent of excavated side rooms are clearly shown in this perspective drawing.

Bottom:
A village of sunken courtyard *yaodong* in Henan province presents a pockmarked landscape of geometrical indentations, each the home of a rural family.

Throughout the tawny-colored loessial uplands that stretch through the provinces of Shanxi and Henan in north China to Shaanxi and Gansu in northwestern China, below-ground caves, sometimes called subterranean dwellings or earth-sheltered housing, provide homes for some forty million Chinese. Cave dwellings are found in adjacent areas of Hebei, Qinghai, Inner Mongolia, Ningxia, and as far away as Xinjiang. Called *yaodong* or simply *yao*, meaning recessed cavities or holes in the loessial earth, this type of "building" sometimes also describes structures of stone, brick, or tamped earth built at grade level—above ground—that mimic underground forms in terms of appearance and basic character. Exquisite examples of these were shown in earlier sections.

Loessial soil, or simply loess and known in Chinese as "yellow earth," is finely textured windblown silt, which has been transported by strong and steady northwestern winds from the Gobi Desert and Mongolian uplands over thousands of years into the topographically rugged and semi-arid middle reaches of the Huang He or Yellow River. Here the loess has blanketed the region with soil depths between 50 and 200 meters. Loess possesses physical and chemical properties that have made it an optimal building medium in an environment with only limited possibilities. While the soil is rather dense, it is also quite soft, generally uniform in composition, and free of stones so that it can be cut into easily with simple tools. A cement-like crust some 20 centimeters thick forms on excavated surfaces as the surface soil dries out. A region of strong annual temperature changes, with summer temperatures often exceeding 35° C while those of winter drop below 0° C, the area is also quite dry. Once covered with grasses and dense forests and a productive cradle of Chinese agrarian civilization, virtually all of the loessial uplands have been dry and denuded for at least two millennia because of climatic change and deforestation due to accelerating firewood collection, charcoal-making, land reclamation, and brick-making.

As the availability of timber declined and without the economic wherewithal to bring in building materials from outside the region, Chinese peasants for centuries came to dig into the soil to make their underground abodes just as prehistoric peoples with much less technology had done earlier. Subterranean dwellings seen today, however, are hardly primitive caves. They have evolved in structure and plan to represent a significant dwelling type that is remarkably cool in summer and warm in winter because of the conservation of heat by the thick and solid earth "roof" above and the surrounding "walls." The use of

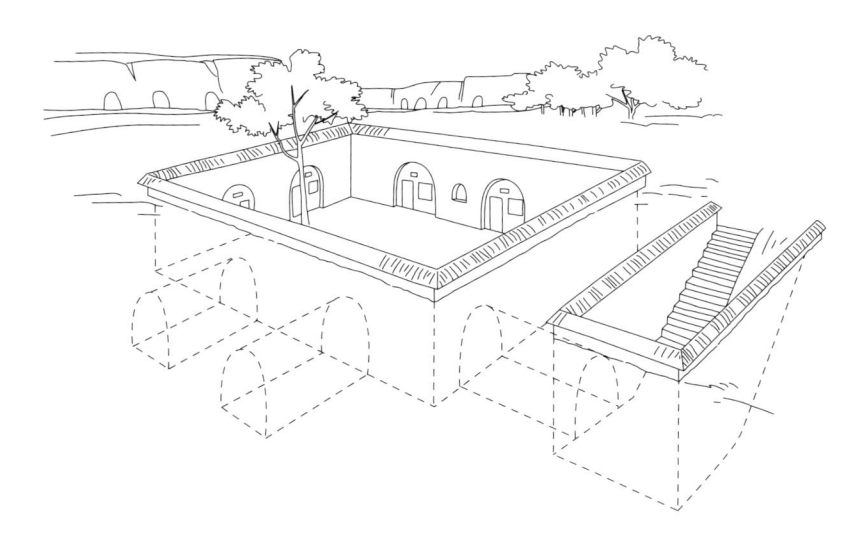

Above:
In southern Shanxi, villages sometimes include both above-ground and below-ground dwellings.

Left:
Newly dug cliffside-type cave dwellings in southern Shanxi, dug horizontally into the slopes of elongated ravines, are here faced with brick surfaces that have been painted white.

Cave Dwellings of the North

Using the irregular topography of a narrow valley, this village includes cliffside cave dwellings at many levels, which are then connected via earthen ramps.

the term "cave" is not meant to be disparaging but simply to express the product of hollowing out space inside the earth. While caves are "dwellings," they are not "houses" even though most are "homes." The *structure* of cave dwellings differs from other Chinese dwellings in that there is no three-dimensional external form built to create internal space. Rather, subterranean "structures" acquire identity from their internal form instead of their external design. Internal volumetric space, in effect, precedes structure, although there clearly is a complementary relationship between these building elements. Space is actually created without consuming the materials needed to fashion it. Excavated soils then can be used for other building purposes, such as leveling the site or for raising tamped earthen walls around a courtyard.

Site selection is the most critical decision made by those constructing a *yaodong*. Topographic conditions, surface and underground drainage, the specific chemical and structural nature of the local soil, in addition to the seasonal passage of the sun and the impact of other natural elements on the dwelling site, all must also be carefully considered. These factors collectively contribute to decisions made concerning the ratios of height, width, and depth as well as the nature of the structural arch and enclosing façade.

Three general types of *yaodong* can be differentiated: cliffside *yaodong*, sunken courtyard *yaodong*, and surface *yaodong*. Sometimes these types are mixed and sometimes they are combined with common above-ground buildings. Cliffside-type cave dwellings (*kaoya shi yaodong* or *kaoshan shi yaodong*) are dug horizontally into the slopes of elongated ravines and usually follow the irregularity of the topography. Jagged lines of cliffside dwellings usually are found cut into south faces of slopes so that each dwelling will benefit from the light and heat brought by the winter sun, a seasonal condition favored in the construction of above-ground dwellings elsewhere in northern China. If a slope face is high and stable, it is possible to place a number of stepped or terraced levels of cliffside structures staggered one above the other. Owners of a *yaodong* must remain vigilant to slumping of the soil due to gravity or erosion by rain since, if the *yaodong* is not maintained properly, its natural structural qualities weaken and it may have to be abandoned before it collapses.

Cave dwellings usually have an elliptical shape to the façade, although semicircular, parabolic, flat, and even pointed configurations also are seen widely. Side walls are vertical for perhaps two meters before arching upwards to form a ceiling. Excavated walls of *yaodong* that are to be inhabited are normally coated with a plaster of loess or loess and lime to slow the drying and flaking of the interior. Papering the walls with newspapers, colorful posters, and photographs is a relatively recent innovation that at once brightens the living area and also protects the walls from absorbing condensed moisture. Usually the floor of subterranean dwellings is simply earth that has been compacted to a brick-like quality. While supplementary support of the interior walls/roof is uncommon, the façade normally is strengthened with adobe, fired bricks, or tamped earth to support door and window frames that are hewn or hand-planed. Some are wide at the opening and then narrow as depth increases while others have a constricted entry but a flared interior. Broad openings certainly facilitate the entry of both light and air, but there is a trade off in a substantial loss of heat during the winter. Where

Far left:
Showing the tattered remnants of calligraphic couplets pasted at the New Year, this entryway leads to a brick-walled courtyard at the front of a cliffside-type dwelling in northern Henan.

Left:
Brickwork and wooden doors mark the entrance to one recessed room of this cliffside dwelling in northern Henan.

Below:
Viewed from above, the severe erosion of the soil walls of this sunken courtyard dwelling in northern Henan is apparent.

Cave Dwellings of the North 277

protection from cold winds is the critical factor that must be addressed, a narrow entry will sometimes be created even at the expense of diminishing natural lighting and ventilation to less than optimal levels. While the height of the longitudinal section of most cliffside dwellings is uniform, some are higher in front and lower in the rear. Cave "rooms" generally do not exceed a depth of 10 meters into a hillside, although some do reach 20 meters.

Excavating a cave is normally a slow process. This is not only because farmers do the work themselves but also because prolonging the pace provides time for the slow drying out of the soil, a condition necessary to maintain its stability. The best time for excavation is when the soil is moderately moist but not wet, perhaps several weeks after a rain. Only common farm tools such as mattocks, crude shovels, and baskets are used. Burrowing normally begins from above, at the location of the arched ceiling, and proceeds down to floor level. Excavation often begins a meter or so above grade level in order for the soil that is removed to be placed outside to form a level terrace at the entry of the cave or for some of the soil to be formed into adobe bricks or pounded into a frame in order to build a wall. A cave approximately six meters deep, three meters high, and three meters wide takes roughly forty days to excavate, with an additional three or so months necessary for the cave to cure or dry out completely before occupancy. With proper maintenance, subterranean dwellings dug into earth can be used for several generations but when neglected typically begin to break down through settling and eventual collapse. Individual *yaodong* chambers are sometimes interlinked to form a dwelling with many rooms, including sitting rooms, bedrooms, kitchens, stables, and storage areas—all separated from neighboring cave dwellings by walls around a courtyard, which contain a kitchen garden as well as a summer stove, pigpen, and small storage buildings.

Sunken courtyard-style subterranean dwellings (*xiachen shi yaodong, aoting yaodong* or *dixia tianjingyuan yaodong*) are found principally in the mesa-like loessial plateau in western Henan, southern Shanxi, and nearby portions of Shaanxi province. Here, peasants traditionally excavated large pits of varying sizes to depths of at least six meters below

Right:
Partially built above ground, this three-bay brick dwelling mimics cave structures in appearance and form.

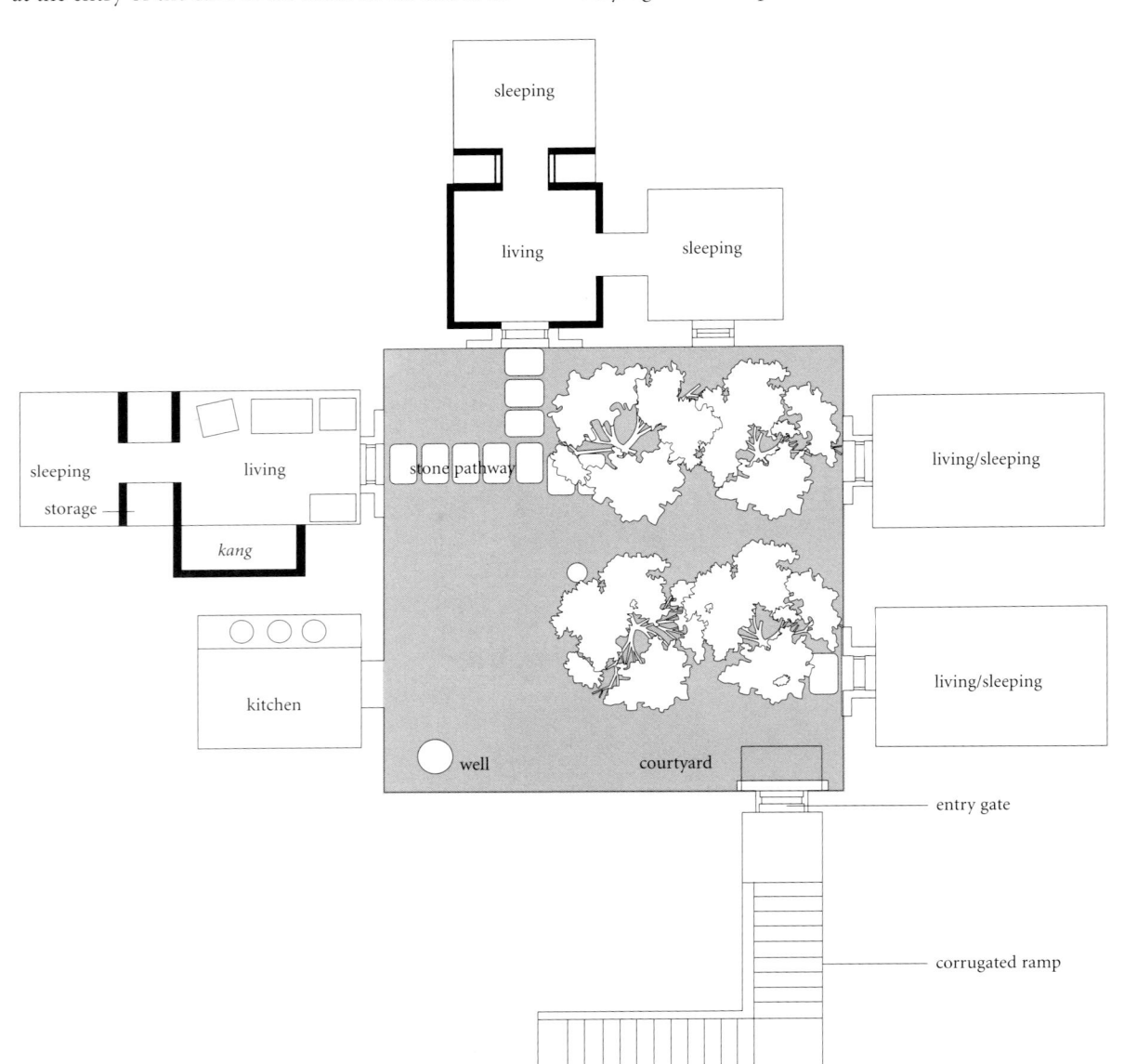

Left:
In plan view, a sunken courtyard dwelling reveals a north–south orientation as well as side-to-side symmetry.

Right:
This couple stands in front of the main room of their sunken courtyard dwelling in northern Henan. Apparent also is a summer stove outside the kitchen that complements one inside used during the winter.

grade. When viewed from the air, the bleak landscape appears pockmarked, a condition accentuated by the shadows of the winter sun. Square sunken courtyard shapes, sometimes reaching 81 square meters in size, are most common, but there also are rectangular and L-shaped ones.

The section and perspective views reveal that each pit forms a recessed courtyard whose four perpendicular side walls provide flat surfaces into which one, two, or three *yaodong* are dug. Entry from grade level is via a ramp or stairs sliced into the soil either along the southern or southwest sides of a sunken courtyard. Inclined passageways either run along a straight line or include right angle turns in order to lessen the gradient of the slope because of the need to move farm equipment, draft animals, and harvested crops to be stored. Oriented to the cardinal directions, cave chambers are normally dug into all four walls, which are left natural or are finished with a plastered lime surface. Chambers along the southern, north-facing wall are normally used only for storage and as a privy related to the nearby presence of stabled animals.

Viewed from inside, the exterior window only admits a small amount of light into the cave.

Since only one sunken wall surface can provide a southern exposure, this face usually becomes the location of the main chambers of the dwelling with bed and sitting rooms for parents and grandparents. Only during the early summer when sun angles are highest, however, does direct sunlight reach into this face. In winter, when the sun is low above the horizon and the daylight period short, the depth of the courtyard effectively shades all of the excavated space except for portions of the south-facing wall, a decided disadvantage. Living space for other family members is dug as needed into the east and west side walls. Large *kang* that serve as bed and sitting areas are common features of *yaodong* throughout northern China. Usually located along an outer wall, *kang* are built in so as to be connected to at least two of the walls as well as associated stoves. Shallow alcoves and lateral indentations for storage are dug into the receding sides of caves with newspapers and posters affixed to the walls to reduce flaking.

With all of these elements, the sunken courtyard becomes a "walled" courtyard compound with a significant outdoor living space open to the sky that is reminiscent of traditional northern courtyard houses. While the limited amounts of rain or snow that fall in these semiarid areas are not a major problem, blowing dust and dirt present some difficulties. As a result, low parapets of stone, brick, or tile are frequently laid along the upper edge of the excavated opening of better dwellings in order to impede the dropping or blowing of earth into the courtyard.

Within the sunken courtyard itself, it is common to find a tree or two, a trellis to support vegetable vines, a shallow well, a drywell-type drain, as well as a covered cistern in which to store water. Cooking during summer, when there is no need to warm the *kang* or introduce heat into the cool interior, takes place outside using portable clay braziers. In winter, however, stoves, burning wood or plant stalks, maintain warmth inside and are connected to the *kang*.

A village of sunken courtyard-style cave dwellings presents a landscape of large indentations that is generally quite orderly. Nearby level land *above* the village dwellings is actually tilled and planted. Special attention must be paid to keeping vegetation away from the upper lip of a sunken courtyard in order to reduce the penetration of roots into the ground beneath that might draw moisture deep into the ground and lead to a deterioration of the stability of the perpendicular walls. The surface areas between the sunken courtyards of a village provide abundant expanses to meet seasonal agricultural needs such as threshing grain and storing hay.

Some *yaodong* are semi-subterranean with only a portion of the dwelling actually embedded within the earth. In these cases, stone, adobe, or fired brick is used to construct a building that fronts the excavated chambers, becoming in effect an extended interior part of the underground space. How such structures are added depends principally on the angle of the hill slope, resulting in all or part of each of three sides and the roof being cut into the earth.

Cave-like structures that are freestanding rather than partially or completely excavated below ground, can be seen throughout the loessial region. Above-ground cave-like dwellings, called *guyao* or "aligned *yao*," imitate subterranean dwellings not only in terms of the appearance of their façades but also in their overall dimensions and in the use of vaulted arches that carry the weight of a substantial overburden of earth. They are usually rectangular in shape and comprise at least three adjacent arch-shaped units, the vaults of which are created using either stone, fired brick, or adobe brick as voussoirs placed continuously in semicircular or pointed sections. Chinese architects refer to this unique building form as "earth-sheltered architecture" (*yantu jianzhu* or *futu jianzhu*) in recognition of the thick layer of insulating earth used to cap them. The surrounding walls of *guyao* appear to differ little from common load-bearing walls seen throughout China that support the roof. With *guyao*, however, the massive outer walls enclose interior space but do not directly support roof timbers and a roof surface. Instead, the side walls serve as piers that help contain the lateral thrust of the interior arches as well as bear the substantial volumes of earth that are piled in the voids above the vaulted structures and that therefore themselves constitute an insulating roof and side wall mass.

Large numbers of exquisite cave-like dwellings and even *guyao* are found in the cities, towns, and villages of Henan, Shanxi, and Shaanxi provinces. Serving as a deliberate choice even for upper-class dwellings, they comprise simple courtyard complexes as well as extensive manors or estates. Several complexes of below-ground and above-ground dwellings have been discussed in earlier sections. Above-ground cave-like *guyao* preserve the positive attributes of *yaodong* while eliminating some of their negative aspects. In terms of their thermal performance, the substantial earth, stone, and brick walls on three sides and on the roof as well as the earth beneath provide excellent insulation from severe cold in winter and intense heat in summer. Air circulation is typically better within dwellings adjacent to courtyards above ground than in those built into the earth below ground. In some manors of the rich, there is the ambience and intimacy of a rural village of cave dwellings, which is enhanced by expensive ornamental treatment of wood, stone, and brick that is not usually found in the often poor villages of the loessial plateau.

Cave dwellings represent a positive adaptation to environmental conditions in that they creatively utilize an abundantly available resource—soil—by effectively capitalizing on the thermal qualities of the earth—warm in winter and cool in summer—and by ingeniously exploiting terrain that normally would not be suitable for housing. In a semi-arid region in which wood and brush for cooking fuel are themselves strikingly scarce, the reduction in the need for wooden building materials is fortunate. When the outside temperature during July and August is above 36° C, four to six meters below ground inside cave dwellings, the temperature is a relatively comfortable 14° to 16° C. During January and February, when above-ground temperatures drop to their lowest, interior temperatures below ground are still between 14° C and 16° C depending on the location in the dwelling. Temperature ranges throughout the day are similarly rather stable, a condition that is best appreciated late at night when outside temperatures in the region typically plummet. These numbers are especially striking when compared with those inside surface dwellings in north China. Powerful earthquakes, however, have brought periodic devastation to those living in subterranean dwellings in the loessial uplands, which unfortunately lie along an active seismic belt. Between 1920 and 1934, perhaps as many as a million people died in collapsing *yaodong* and other dwellings in the loessial region.

In the eyes of many, *yaodong*—cave dwellings—are equated with poverty and limited resources. It is not surprising then, that as farmers have more cash income, more and more are abandoning their caves, sometimes even filling the indentations and leveling the earth, and building above-ground dwellings. This effort to make progress, however, is made difficult by the fact that the new houses are neither as warm in winter nor as cool in summer as the old. They are nonetheless better ventilated than nearby subterranean dwellings. Major efforts are being made by Chinese architects to address the shortcomings of *yaodong*—limited interior light, inadequate ventilation, and high humidity levels—in order to meet the escalating housing needs of villagers.

Below:
A sunken courtyard, not surprisingly, helps to keep in check the movements of animals, providing in effect a pen that restrains them. Here, in what serves as a veritable barnyard, pigs are allowed to range freely outside their pen in the crude cave in the rear. Nearby, although not seen, is a cow. Chickens, on the other hand, are penned in an adjacent cave with a gate fashioned of branches. Fuel wood that has been scavenged in nearby hills is stacked here and there.

BIBLIOGRAPHY

Comprehensive bibliographies concerning Chinese houses can be found in other publications by the author.

Balderstone, Susan and William Logan, "Vietnamese Dwellings: Tradition, Resilience, and Change," in Ronald G. Knapp (ed.), *Asia's Old Dwellings: Tradition, Resilience, and Change*, Hong Kong and New York: Oxford University Press, 2003, pp. 135–57.

Beech, Hannah, "Appetite for Destruction: A Historic Neighborhood—and Architect I. M. Pei's Family Home—Fall Victim to Shanghai's Building Boom," *Time Asia*, 157(9), March 5, 2001.

Berliner, Nancy Zeng, *Chinese Folk Art: The Small Skills of Carving Insects*, Boston: Little, Brown, 1986.

_____, "Sheltering the Past: The Preservation of China's Old Dwellings," in Ronald G. Knapp and Kai-Yin Lo (eds.), *House Home Family: Living and Being Chinese*, Honolulu: University of Hawai'i Press and New York: China Institute in America, 2005, pp. 204–20.

_____, *Yin Yu Tang: The Architecture and Daily Life of a Chinese House*, Boston: Tuttle Publishing, 2003.

Bray, Francesca, "The Inner Quarters: Oppression or Freedom?" in Ronald G. Knapp and Kai-Yin Lo (eds.), *House Home Family: Living and Being Chinese*, Honolulu: University of Hawai'i Press and New York: China Institute in America, 2005, pp. 258–79.

_____, *Technology and Gender: Fabrics of Power in Late Imperial China*, Berkeley: University of California Press, 1997.

Bruun, Ole, *Fengshui in China: Geomantic Divination between State Orthodoxy and Popular Religion*, Honolulu: University of Hawai'i Press, 2003.

Chavannes, Edouard (trans. Elaine S. Atwood), *The Five Happinesses: Symbolism in Chinese Popular Art*, New York: Weatherhill, 1973; originally published as "De l'expression des voeux dans l'art populaire chinois," *Journal Asiatique*, series 9, vol. 18, September–October 1901.

Chen Chi-lu (Chen Qilu) et al. (eds.), *Zhongguo chuantong nianhua yishu tezhan zhuanji* (The Art of the Traditional Chinese New Year Print), Taipei: Guoli zhongyang tushuguan, 1992.

Flath, James, *The Cult of Happiness: Nianhua, Art and History in Rural North China*, Vancouver: University of British Columbia Press, 2004.

_____, "Reading the Text of the Home: Domestic Ritual Configuration through Print," in Ronald G. Knapp and Kai-Yin Lo (eds.), *House Home Family: Living and Being Chinese*, Honolulu: University of Hawai'i Press and New York: China Institute in America, 2005, pp. 324–47.

Gong Kai (ed.), *Huizhou gu jianzhu congshu* (Ancient Architecture in Huizhou Series): *Tangyue* (Tangyue Village), 1993; *Xiaoqi* (Xiaoqi Village), 2001; *Yuliang* (Yuliang Village), 1998; *Zhanqi* (Zhanqi Village), 1996; *Zhifeng* (Zhifeng Village), 1999, Nanjing: Dongnan daxue chubanshe.

Handler, Sarah, *Ming Furniture in the Light of Chinese Architecture*, Berkeley: Ten Speed Press, 2005.

Ho Puay-peng, "Ancestral Halls: Family, Lineage, and Ritual," in Ronald G. Knapp and Kai-Yin Lo (eds.), *House Home Family: Living and Being Chinese*, Honolulu: University of Hawai'i Press and New York: China Institute in America, 2005, pp. 294–323.

_____, "Brocaded Beams and Shuttle Columns: Early Vernacular Architecture in Southern Anhui Province," *Orientations*, 35(2), 2004, pp. 104–10.

_____, "China's Vernacular Architecture," in Ronald G. Knapp (ed.), *Asia's Old Dwellings: Tradition, Resilience, and Change*, Hong Kong and New York: Oxford University Press, 2003, pp. 319–46.

_____, *The Living Building: Vernacular Environments of South China*, Hong Kong: The Chinese University of Hong Kong, Department of Architecture, 1995.

_____, "Preservation Versus Profit: Recent Developments in Village Tourism in China," in Nezar Alsayyad (ed.), *Tradition: Maintaining Identity in the Face of Change*, Traditional Dwellings and Settlements Working Paper Series, Center for Environmental Design Research, University of California, Berkeley, vol. 138, 2000, pp. 28–53.

_____, "Rethinking Chinese Villages," *Orientations*, 32(3), 2001, pp. 115–19.

Hommel, Rudolf, *China at Work*, New York: John Day, 1937.

Knapp, Ronald G., "At Home in China: Domain of Propriety, Repository of Heritage," in Kai-Yin Lo and Puay-peng Ho (eds.), *Living Heritage: Vernacular Environment in China/Gucheng jinxi: Zhongguo minjian shenghuo fangshi*, bilingual edition, Hong Kong: Yungmingtang, 1999a, pp. 16–37.

_____, *China's Living Houses: Folk Beliefs, Symbols, and Household Ornamentation*, Honolulu: University of Hawai'i Press, 1999b.

_____, *China's Old Dwellings*, Honolulu: University of Hawai'i Press, 2000.

_____, *China's Traditional Rural Architecture: A Cultural Geography of the Common House*, Honolulu: University of Hawai'i Press, 1986.

_____, *China's Vernacular Architecture: House Form and Culture*, Honolulu: University of Hawai'i Press, 1989.

Knapp, Ronald G. (ed.), *Asia's Old Dwellings: Tradition, Resilience, and Change*, Hong Kong and New York: Oxford University Press, 2003.

Knapp, Ronald G. and Kai-Yin Lo (eds.), *House Home Family: Living and Being Chinese*, Honolulu: University of Hawai'i Press and New York: China Institute in America, 2005.

Knapp, Ronald G. and Shen Dongqi, "Changing Village Landscapes," in Ronald G. Knapp (ed.), *Chinese Landscapes: The Village as Place*, Honolulu: University of Hawai'i Press, 1992, pp. 47–72.

Lee Chien-lang (Li Qianlang), *Taiwan gu jianzhu tujie shidian* (Illustrated Encyclopedia of Old Architecture in Taiwan), Taibei: Yuanliu chuban shiye gufen youxian gongsi, 2003.

Lee Chien-lang (Li Qianlang) and Yu Yiping, *Guji rumen* (Primer for Heritage Sites), Taibei: Yuanliu chuban gongsi, 1999.

Lee Sang-hae, "Traditional Korean Settlements and Dwellings," in Ronald G. Knapp (ed.), *Asia's Old Dwellings: Tradition, Resilience, and Change*, Hong Kong and New York: Oxford University Press, 2003, pp. 373–90.

Li Qiuxiang, *Zhongguo cunju* (Chinese Villages), Beijing: Baihua wenyi chubanshe, 2002.

Liang Ssu-ch'eng (Liang Sicheng) (ed. Wilma Fairbank), *A Pictorial History of Chinese Architecture: A Study of the Development of Its Structural System and the Evolution of Its Types*, Cambridge: Massachusetts Institute of Technology (MIT) Press, 1984.

Liu Dunzhen, *Zhongguo zhuzhai gaishuo* (Introduction to Chinese Dwellings), Beijing: Jianzhu gongcheng chubanshe, 1957.

Liu Xin, *In One's Own Shadow: An Ethnographic Account of the Condition of Post-Reform Rural China*, Berkeley: University of California Press, 2000.

Lo, Kai-Yin, "Traditional Chinese Architecture and Furniture: A Cultural Interpretation," in Ronald G. Knapp and Kai-Yin Lo (eds.), *House Home Family: Living and Being Chinese*, Honolulu: University of Hawai'i Press and New York: China Institute in America, 2005, pp. 160–203.

Lo, Kai-Yin and Puay-peng Ho (eds.), *Living Heritage: Vernacular Environment in China/Gucheng jinxi: Zhongguo minjian shenghuo fangshi*, bilingual edition, Hong Kong: Yungmingtang, 1999.

Lu Yuanding and Lu Qi, *Zhongguo minju zhuangshi zhuangxiu yishu* (Art of the Ornamentation and Decoration of China's Vernacular Dwellings), Shanghai: Shanghai kexue jishu chubanshe, 1992.

Lu Yuanding and Yang Gusheng (eds.), *Minju jianzhu* (The Architecture of Vernacular Dwellings), part 5 of *Zhongguo meishu quanji* (Complete Collection of China's Arts), Beijing: Zhongguo jianzhu gongye chubanshe, 1988.

_____, *Zhongguo minju jianzhu* (The Architecture of China's Vernacular Dwellings), Guangzhou: Huanan ligong daxue chubanshe, 2003.

Lung, David Ping-Yee, *Chinese Traditional Vernacular Architecture*, bilingual edition, Hong Kong: Regional Council, 1991.

March, Andrew, "An Appreciation of Chinese Geomancy," *Journal of Asian Studies*, 27, 1968, pp. 253–67.

Matsuda Naonori, "Japan's Traditional Houses: The Significance of Spatial Conceptions," in Ronald G. Knapp (ed.), *Asia's Old Dwellings: Tradition, Resilience, and Change*, Hong Kong and New York: Oxford University Press, 2003, pp. 285–318.

Oakes, Tim, "The Village as Theme Park: Mimesis and Authenticity in Chinese Tourism," in Tim Oakes and Louisa Schein (eds.), *Translocal China: Linkages, Identities and the Reimagining of Space*, London: Routledge, 2005.

Po Sung-nien (Bo Songnian) and David Johnson, *Domesticated Deities and Auspicious Emblems: The Iconography of Everyday Life in Village China*, Berkeley: Chinese Popular Culture Project, 1992.

Ruan Xing, "Pile-built Dwellings in Ethnic Southern China: Type, Myth, and Heterogeneity," in Ronald G. Knapp (ed.), *Asia's Old Dwellings: Tradition, Resilience, and Change*, 2003, pp. 347–72.

Ruitenbeek, Klaas, *Building and Carpentry in Late Imperial China: A Study of the Fifteenth Century Carpenter's Manual Lu Ban Jing*, Leiden: E. J. Brill, 1993.

Spence, Jonathan, *Mao Zedong*, New York: Viking Books, 1999.

Steinhardt, Nancy Shatzman, "The House: An Introduction," in Ronald G. Knapp and Kai-Yin Lo (eds.), *House Home Family: Living and Being Chinese*, Honolulu: University of Hawai'i Press and New York: China Institute in America, 2005, pp. 12–35.

Steinhardt, Nancy Shatzman (ed.), Fu Xinian, Liu Xujie, Pan Guxi, Guo Daiheng, Qiao Yun, and Sun Dazhang, *Chinese Architecture*, New Haven: Yale University Press, 2002.

Sun Dazhang, *Zhongguo minju yanjiu* (Research on China's Vernacular Dwellings), Beijing: Zhongguo jianzhu gongye chubanshe, 2004.

Tuan, Yi-fu, "Traditional: What Does It Mean?" in Jean-Paul Bourdier and Nezar Alsayyad (eds.), *Dwellings, Settlements, and Tradition: Cross-Cultural Perspectives*, Lanham, MD: University Press of America, 1989, pp. 27–34.

Waley, Arthur (trans.), *The Way and Its Power: A Study of the Tao Te Ching and Its Place in Chinese Thought*, New York: Grove Press, 1958.

Wang Qijun, *Minjian zhuzhai jianzhu* (Vernacular Dwellings), Bilingual edition, Wien and New York: Springer, 2000.

_____, *Zhongguo minjian zhuzhai jianzhu* (Architecture of China's Vernacular Architecture), Beijing: Jixie gongye chubanshe, 2003.

Wu, Nelson, *Chinese and Indian Architecture: The City of Man, the Mountain of God, and the Realm of the Immortals*, New York: George Braziller, 1963.

INDEX

Note: Numbers in italic refer to illustrations.

Adobe bricks, 37, 40, *40*, *42*, *212*, *213*, *214*
Alcove bed, 53–4, 78, *78*, *79*, *139*, *153*, *175*, *217*, *222*, *244*, *245*
Altar table (*Shenlong anzhuo*), 136, 162, *182*, 214–15
Amulets: defensive charms, *47*, *48*, 60–1, *63*, 65, 76, *198*, *261*; neutralizing charms; summoning good fortune, 60–1, *73*, *84*, *85*, 90, *90*, *172–3*, 196, 198, *270*; stabilizing a home, 62–5; use by carpenters and bricklayers, 60–1, 62–3
Ancestral Hall, 72–6, 134–6, 171, *188*, 196–7, *214*, *222*; Baolun Ge (Pavilion of Precious Encomiums), 68, *158*, 165
Ancestral shrine (*shenkan*), 72, 76, 214–15, *214*, *222*, 225
Anhui, *2*, *12*, *13*, *32–3*, 45; Ancestral Hall, 68; auspicious symbols, *85*, *89*; Baolun Ge (Pavilion of Precious Encomiums), 68, *158*; Cheng Zhi Tang (Hall of Inheriting Ambitions), 166–75; *fengshui*, 57; Main Hall, *73*; Ming-period houses, 156–65; protective amulets, *65*; Yuan period houses, *174–5*
Animals, symbolism of: bat, 85–6, *85*, *86*, *239*; bird, *273*; butterfly, 85–6, *85*, *86*, *87*; carp, 88, *88*, 94; crane, 87; deer, 87; dragon, 109; duck, 94; fish, *85*, 88, *88*, 94, *96*, geese, 94; lion, 111; magpie, 94; monkey, 88; owl, *47*, *48*; phoenix, 85, 176, 181; rooster, 84, *84*; spider, 91; tiger, 62, 65, 85–6; tortoise, 87; *wudu* (five noxious or poisonous creatures), 64, *85*, *86*
Auspicious calligraphy, 60–1, *61*, *62*, *63*, 69, *69*, 76, 81, 82, *82*, *83*, *85*, *89*, 94, *193*, *206*
Auspicious symbols, 61, *62*, *63*, *78*, *84*, *85*, *94*, *96*; good fortune, 60–1, *73*, *84*, 84–95, *85*, *172–3*, *196*, *198*, *234*, *239*, *250*, *270*, *273*; harmony at home, 62–5, 68–70, *69*, 72, 80–1, 94–5, 95–7, *234*, *274*; longevity, 86–8, *87*, 91, *101*
Azevedo, Jerry: *61*

Bagua, *see* Eight Trigrams
Bamboo: use of in making walls, 37, *43*
Baolun Ge (Pavilion of Precious Encomiums), 68, *158*, 165
Baxian, *see* Eight Immortals
Baxian zhuo, *see* Eight Immortals table
Bay (*jian*), divisions of structural space, 30–1, *30*, *31*
Bazi (the "eight characters" signifying year, month, day, and hour of birth), 196
Bedrooms, 71, 77, 78–9, *78*, *79*, 115, 138, *139*, *150*, *153*, 162–3, *175*, 216, *217*, *222*, 225, 242–5
Beds, *see* Alcove bed; Platform bed
Beijing, *20*, *24*; auspicious symbols, *86*, *87*, *88*; courtyard houses, 22; Door Gods, 66; lattice, 44, 77
Berliner, Nancy, 55
Bray, Francesca, 68–9, 94
Breaking ground, 59
Brick, *see* Adobe brick; Kiln-dried brick
Brick-making, 40, *41*
Bridges, *45*, *51*, *121*, *125*, *127*, 261
Building magic and sorcery, 59–61
Building module (*jian*), 30–1, 34

Canal town housing, 120–31, 132–9
Cao family manor, Shanxi, 87
Carpenters, 35–6, 59–61, *59*
Carpenter's handbooks and manuals, 35
Cave dwellings (*yaodong*), 274–81; Henan, 22, 146–55, *146*, *147*, *149*, *274*; Shanxi, 261, 267, 271, *275*
Changchun She (Studio of Everlasting Spring), 165
Charms, *see* Amulets
Chengkan, Anhui, 156–65
Cheng Zhi Tang (Hall of Inheriting Ambition), Anhui, *2*, *4*, *12*, *13*, *32–3*, 166–75; auspicious symbols, 85; furniture, *74–5*; Main Hall, *73*, *74–5*
Chuandixia village, Beijing, *20*, *34*, 112–19
Chuandou (pillars-and-transverse-tie beam wooden structural framework), 34–5, *34*, *35*, 36
Circular dwellings, *see* Round dwellings
Climate and dwellings, 15–16, 21, 27, 31, 51, 112–14, 274
Coffins: storage of, 179, *183*
Columns-and-beams construction (*tailiang*), 34–5, *34*, 37

Column bases, 37
Confucius (Kong family manor), Shandong, 27
Courtyard houses, 20–9; Beijing *siheyuan*, *20*, 21, 28, 69, 100–11; cave dwellings, *277*, *281*; early portrayals, *16*, *21*; floor plan of, *28*; mountain style, 21–2, *114*, 115–17, *116*; northern, *20*, *21*, 22, *23*, *25*, *28*, 69, 100–11, *148*, *155*, *254*, *255*, *259*, *267*; restoration, 107–11; southern, *22*, *23*, *136*, *141*, *145*, *160*, *162*, *171*, *172–3*, *180*, *191*, *195*, *197*, *199*, *204*, *206*, *207*, *212*, *236*, *241*, *242*
Courtyards, 20–9, *see also* Skywell
Cultural Revolution, *see* Great Proletarian Cultural Revolution
Curtain walls, 31, 37–8

Daoji (Shitao), 8, *9*
Daojing ("inverting mirror"), 63, *63*
Deng Xiaoping: boyhood home, 37, 240–7
De Xing Tang (To Promote Virtue Hall), Guangdong, 192–8
Didactic narratives, 95–7
Dingcun, Shanxi, *254*, *255*, 255
Door Gods (*menshen*), 64, 66, *81*, 116, *117*, *193*, *201*
Doubled happiness (*shuangxi*), 91, *91*, *273*

Earth God (*Tudi gong*) shrine, 59, 60, *60*, 65, *262*, *269*
Earthen dwellings (*tulou*), 176–83, 184–91
Earth-sheltered housing, *see* Cave dwellings
Eight Immortals (*Baxian*), *89*, *92*, *93*, *174*, *206*
Eight Immortals table (*Baxian zhuo*), 76, 92–5, *92*, 215, *227*, *272*
Eight Trigrams (*Bagua*), 60, *61*, 63–5, *65*
Ellsworth, Robert H., 165
Emolument (*lu*), 88, *88*
Encircling Dragons (*Weilongwu*), Guangdong, 192–201
Entrances and entryways, 105, *111*, *118–19*, *154–5*, *157*, *160*, *161*, *163*, *164*, *167*, *176*, *177*, *178*, *179*, *192–3*, *201*, *203*, *205*, *222*, *237*, *248*, *251*, *257*, *260*, *268*, *269*, *277*, *279*
Environmental awareness, 51, *see also* Climate and dwellings
Ethnic minority dwellings, 17, *43*, *46–7*

Fan family residence, Shanxi, *22, 25, 37*
Feng family residence, Sichuan, *2, 4,* 228–9, 232, 234–9
Fengshui (geomancy), 16, 56–8; application of, *58*, 196; compass, 58, *58*; optimal, *55, 56–7*; ritual, 59–61; schools of, 58
Filial piety (*xiao*), 95–7, *96, 97, 263*
Fired brick, *see* Kiln-dried bricks
Fire pit, 215, *216*, 225
"Fish pond room," *171*
"Five generations under one roof" (*Wushi tongtang*), 68
Flath, James, 80
Floor plans, 24–6, *25, 28, 31, 68*; Beijing *siheyuan, 100, 101*; cave dwelling, *278*; Deng Xiaoping's boyhood home, *243*; Encircling Dragons (*Weilongwu*), *194, 196–7*; Fan family house, *268*; Liu Shaoqi's boyhood home, *221*; Ma family residence, *235*; Man Chung-luen residence, 202–9; manor, *149*; Mao Zedong's boyhood home, *210*; merchant's residence, *134, 170*; Ming-dynasty dwelling, *160, 160, 254*; northern, *31*; round dwellings, *190*; scholar's study, *70, 140* ; southern, *31*; Wang family manor, *258*
Forbidden City, 100
Foundations: tamping of, *31*
Four Treasures of the Studio (*wen fang si bao*), 142, *144*, 156
Fu (good fortune, blessings), *73*, 84, 85–7, *85, 91, 172–3, 179, 196, 239, 273*
Fujian: circular dwellings, *18–19*, 184–91; courtyard dwellings, 22; Earth God shrine, *60*; fortresses, 176–83, 184–91; Fu Yu Lou (Fortune in Abundance Tower), 176–83, *191*; graves, 58; roof styles, *46, 48*; Ru Sheng Lou (Like a Sheng Tower), *191*; screen wall, *66*; Zhen Cheng Lou (Inspiring Success Tower), 184–90
Fu lu shou (wealth, official position, and longevity), *see* Stellar triad
Fu Yu Lou (Fortune in Abundance Tower), Fujian, 176–83; perspective view, *46*; screen wall, *66*

Gardens, 102, 120, *253*
Gate Gods, *see* Door Gods (*menshen*)
Gates, *see* Entrances and entryways
Gendered space, 4, 25–6, 68–71, *68, 69, 70*, 78, 166, 168
Geomancy, *see Fengshui*
Glass, *206,*
Good Fortune, *see Fu* (good fortune)
Graves (*yinzhai*): as residences, 56, *58*, 179
Great Proletarian Cultural Revolution, 76, 111, 116, *118–19*, 153, *211*, 214, 217, 220, 224, 232, 241, 252, *253*
Green Vine Studio, Shaoxing, *6*, 140–5
Guangdong: amulets, auspicious symbols, *85, 89, 91*; De Xing Tang (To Promote Virtue Hall),192–8; Encircling Dragons (*Weilongwu*), 192–201; Main Hall, *73*; Ning'an Lu *weilongwu*, 198–201

Guangxi Zhuang Autonomous Region, *41*

Hakka (Kejia) dwellings, 184–91, 192–201
Hangtu (tamped earth construction), 37–9, *38, 39*
Happiness, *see Fu* (good fortune)
Hemudu Neolithic site, Zhejiang, *36*
Henan: cave dwellings; 13, *13*, 146–55; courtyard houses, 146–55; Kang family manor, 146–55; lattice, *44, 148*; screen wall, *66*
Hexes, *see* Amulets
Hierarchy, 21, 25, 68, 191, 195
Hipped roof style, *46*
Historic preservation issues, *10–11, 13*, 23, 107–11, 120, 165, 209, 263, 272
Hommel, Rudolf, 37
Homophonous auspicious associations, 84–6, *86, 87,* 95, 105
Hongcun, Anhui, 166–75
Hong Kong: Man Chung-luen residence, 202–9
Ho Puay-peng, 15, 72
Horses' head walls (*matouqiang*), 45–6, *45, 46, 128, 138, 159*
House-building ritual, 59–61
Huaguang Tower, Sichuan, 228, *230, 231*
Hui [Huizhou] culture, Anhui, 156–9
Hunan: adobe brick, *42*; Main Hall, *72*; walls, *42*
Hutong (Beijing lanes and neighborhoods), *24*, 107–8

Imperial City (*Zijin Cheng*), *see* Forbidden City

Jian (building module), *see* Bay
Jiangnan, 120–45, 156; *see also* Anhui, Jiangsu, Zhejiang
Jiangsu: auspicious symbols, *90*; beds, *53–4*; canal houses, *51*, 120, *121–5, 123–7*; lattice, *46*; roof profile, *45, 46*
Jiang Taigong zai ci ("Jiang Taigong is here"), 60
Jiangxi, 184, 198, 241; *fengshui, 57*; roof profile, *45*
Johnson, David, 84
Joinery, 36, 37, *241*

Kang (heated brick bed), 40, *78, 71, 77*, 80, 115, *115*, 272
Kang Baiwan residence, Henan, 146–55
Kang family manor, Henan, 13, *13*, 146–55; academy, *67*; alcove bed, *79*; courtyard, *28*; lattice, *44*; moon gate, *26–7*; roof profile, *45, 47*; screen wall, *66*
Kang Yingkui residence, Henan, 153
Kejia, *see* Hakka dwellings
Kiln-dried bricks, 40–1, *40*
Kitchen, 85, 93, *138,* 196, 208, *208,* 215, *216, 224, 226*
Kitchen God, *see* Stove God [*Zaojun*]
Kong (Confucius) family manor, Shandong, *27*
Langzhong, Sichuan, *24, 25,* 228–39

Lao She, 107, 111
Laowu Ge (earliest Ming-period private residence still standing), Anhui, 4, *4–5*
Lattice: doors, *22, 23, 44, 137, 174, 180, 181, 206, 234, 239, 269, 270*; screens, *66, 77*; windows, *44, 77, 117, 125, 137, 141, 144, 145, 162, 162, 163, 174, 243, 259, 269, 270*
Liang Sicheng, 31
Literati gardens, *see* Gardens
Liu Chong, *112*
Liu Shaoqi: boyhood home, 220–7
Liu Wencai residence, Sichuan, 153
Liu, Xin, 70
Longevity (*shou*), 86–8, *87*, 91, *101*
Lu Ban (patron of carpenters), 60–1
Lu Ban jing (Lu Ban Manual), 61, 62, *63, 65,* 248
Lu Xun: boyhood home, *130*, 131, *131*
Luzhi watertown, Jiangsu, 120–4, *121, 122–3, 132–9*

Ma family residence, Sichuan, *91,* 228–35
Main Hall, *32–3,* 70, 71, 72–6, *72, 73, 74–5, 178, 236, 238, 239, 243;* Beijing *siheyuan, 103, 104, 105,* 106–7; Encircling Dragon (*weilongwu*), *196;* farmhouse, 214–15, *214, 222, 225, 243,* 246; merchant's residence, *134–5, 137, 208;* Ming-dynasty dwelling, *161;* ritual space, 72–6; Qing-dynasty dwelling, 134–6, *135,* 205–6
Man Chung-luen residence, Hong Kong, 202–9
Mao Dun: boyhood residence, *131*
Mao Zedong: boyhood home, *42,* 210–19
March, Andrew, 58
Matouqiang, see Horses' head walls
Mei Lanfang residence, Beijing, 100–7; courtyard, *77;* lattice, *77*
Men, see Entrances and entryways
Menshen, see Door Gods
Mica: as glazing in windows, *233*
Ming-dynasty houses, 24, 46, 140–5, 156–65, *254, 255, 255*
Mirrors: as amulets, 63–4, *65*
Moon gate, *26–7, 130, 141 142, 208*
Moral tales, 95–7
Mortise-and-tenon joinery, 36, 37, *241*
Mou Erhei residence, Shandong, 153
Mulan, 140

Nanxun watertown, Zhejiang, 120,
New Year celebrations, 76, 80–3, *80, 81, 82, 83*
Nianhua (New Year pictures), 80–3, *81, 82, 83*
Ning'an Lu *weilongwu,* Guangdong, 198–201

Open spaces, *see* Courtyards, Skywells
Opera stages, *124,* 130
Orientation, 56–8, 106, 112, 115, 132, 228

Paifang (archway), 241
Pillars-and-transverse-tie beam wooden

Index **285**

structural framework (*chuandou*), 34–5, *34*, *35*, *37*, *229*
Pingyao, Shanxi, *22*, *25*, 264–73; auspicious symbols, *94*; lattice, *44*
Plants, symbolism of: chrysanthemum, 87; citron, 88, *88*, *91*; cypress, 87; fungus, 87; grape, 95; hibiscus, 84; lotus, 94, 95, *150*; melon, 95; narcissus, 94; orchid, 94; peach, 88, *88*; peony, 84; pine, 87, *87*; pomegranate, 88, *88*, *91*, 95; wisteria, 94
Platform bed (*ta*), *139*
Posterity (male offspring), 88, *88*, *91*, 94, 95, *150*, 254
Po Sung-nien, 84
Pottery ornamentation, 205
Powell, Robert, 4, *4–5*, *158–9*
Prince Gong's manor, Beijing, 102–3
Protective amulets, *62*, *63*, *64*, *65*
Puns, *see* Visual puns

Qiao family manor, Shanxi, 248–55
Qiao Zhongchang, *16–7*, 17
Qing-dynasty houses, 24, 100–6, 112–19, 124, 132–9, 146–56, *157*, 166–75, 176–83, 184–91, 192–201, 202–9, 210–19, 220–7, 228–39, 240–7, 248–55, 256–63, 264–73
Qing Teng Shu Wu, *see* Green Vine Studio

Raising the ridgepole (*shangliang*), 60–1, *61*
Rebus, 94
Resisting stones, *see* Taishan stones
Restored or renovated houses, *10–11*, 13, 23, 107–11
Ridgepole: raising of (*shangliang*), 60–1, *61*
Ritual: house-building, 59–61, *59*, *61*
Roof materials: clay tiles, 49–50; mud composition, 48–9; thatch, 49; wood and stone shingles, 50
Roof shapes and profiles, 45–7, *45*, *46*, *47*, *114*, *117*, *124*, *128*, *136*, *155*, *166*, *168–9*, *176–7*, *183*, *186*, *188*, *200*, *202*, *203*, *211*, *229*, *247*; *see also* Horses' head walls
Roof tiles: making of, *40*, *48*, *49*
Round dwellings, *18–19*, 184–91, *185–91*
Ruan Yisan, 120
Ruitenbeek, Klaas, 61
Ru Sheng Lou (Like a Sheng Tower), Fujian, 189, 191, *191*

Screen wall (*yingbi* and *zhaobi*), 64, 66; Beijing *siheyuan*, 102; canal-side, *132*, *133*; manor, *148*
Shaanxi: cave dwellings, 274; courtyard houses, 22, *25*
Shandong: auspicious symbols, *96*
Shangliang, *see* Raising the ridgepole
Shanxi: auspicious symbols, *86*, *89*, *94*, *95*; cave dwellings, 261, 267, 271, *275*; courtyard houses, 22, *25*, *28–9*; *kang* (brick bed), *77*; lattice, *44*, *77*; Main Hall, *73*; Ming houses, 254–5; moon gate, *26–7*; Pingyao homes, 264–73; Taishan stones, *64*; Wang family manor, *28–9*, *37*, 256–63

Shaoxing watertown, Zhejiang, 120, *130*, 131, *131*, 140–4
Shen Benren residence, Jiangsu, 131
Shen family residence, Jiangsu: roof profile, *46*, 132–9
Shenkan, *see* Ancestral shrine
Shilou (Market Tower), Shanxi, *266*, 267
Sichuan, 228–39, 240–7; bamboo walls, 43; lanes, *24*; courtyard houses, *25*; Deng Xiaoping, boyhood home, *37*, 240–7; Main Hall, *71*, 72; roof profile, *47*, *229*
Sihelou (two-story modern courtyard-style dwelling), 109
Siheyuan (traditional Beijing courtyard house), *20*, *21*, *28*, *69*, 100–11, *see also* Courtyard houses
Skywell (*tianjing*), 20–9, *25*, *42*, *136*, *160*, *160*, *162*, *163*, *166*, *171*, *172–3*, *175*, *195*, *197*, *214*, *217*, *225*
Spirit walls, *see* Screen walls
Steinhardt, Nancy Shatzman, 17, 58
Stellar Triad, *32–3*, *90*, *90*, 95, *149*, *150*
Stone: column bases, *37*, *193*, *201*; ornamentation, *37*, *171*, *200*; walls, *37*, *42*, *43*, *114*, *115*, *176*
Stone masons, 59
Stove God (Zaojun), 80, *80*, *216*, *226*
Study (library), 68, *70*, *136*, *152*, *202*, *225*; Beijing *siheyuan*, *106*; private school, *67*, *131*; scholar's study, *70*, 140–5, *144*
Subterranean dwellings, *see* Cave dwellings
Sumptuary regulations (code), 100
Su Shi (Su Dongpo), *16–17*, 17

Ta (low platform for sitting or reclining), *see* Platform bed
Tai Fu Tai (Daifu Di), Hong Kong, 202–9
Tailiang (columns-and-beams wooden structural framework), 34–5, *34*
Taishan shi gandang ("This stone dares to resist"), *see* Taishan stones
Taishan stones, 63–4, *64*, 248
Taiwan: Main Hall, *76*; roof styles, 48
Tamped earth construction (*hangtu*), 37–9, *38*, *39*, *184*
Thatch, 49
Three Living Gods of Wealth, 150, *150*
Tiangong kaiwu (The Creations of Nature and Man), *40*, *48*, *50*
Tianguan cifu ("Tianguan (the heavenly official) grants fortune"), *127*, 128
Tianjing (abbreviated courtyard), *see* Skywell
Tian Yuan Kui Inn, Shanxi, 273–4
Tiles: making of, *40*, *48*, *49*
Timber framework types, 31, 34–6
Timber walls, 44
Tombs, *see* Graves
Tongli watertown, Jiangsu, 120
Tourism, 116–17, 120, 123, 125, 130–1, 184, 218, 226, 230, 236, 247, 248, 255
Tradition: meaning of, 14
Tuan, Yi-Fu, 15
Tudi Gong (tutelary deity), *see* Earth God
Tulou (earthen dwellings), 176–83, 184–91

Twenty-four Paragons of Filial Piety (*Ershisi xiao*), 96, *96*, *97*

UNESCO World Heritage Site, 120, 236, 264, 271

Vernacular architecture, 13–16,
Visual puns, 84, 88, *96*

Walls: bamboo, 43; brick, 40–1; sorghum and corn stalks, 43; stone, *37*, 43; tamped earth, *37* 38, *39*, *186*, *187*; timber 44
Wang family manor, Shanxi, *28–9*, *37*, 256–63; auspicious symbols, *89*; *kang* (brick bed), *77*; Main Hall, *73*; moon gate, *26–7*; protective amulets, *65*
Washstand, *53–4*, *139*, *224*
Wattle and daub, 37
Well, *142*, *145*
Wen fang si bao, *see* Four Treasures of the Studio
Windows, *163*, *206*, *280*, *see also* Lattice
Women and household space, *see* Gendered space
Wu, Nelson, 20,
Wudu (Five noxious creatures), 64
Wu Fang Ting, Anhui, *158–9*, 165
Wufu (Five good fortunes), 86, *85*
Wuzhen watertown, Zhejiang, 120, *126*, *127–31*, *129*

Xiao (filial piety), 95–7
Xiao family residence, Jiangsu, *126*
Xitang watertown, Zhejiang, 120
Xu family residence (Yu Yan Tang), Jiangsu, *127*
Xu Wei, 4, *6*; Green Vine Studio, 140–5

Yan Yi Tang (Swallow's Wing Hall), Anhui, 156–65; auspicious symbols, *90*
Yang, male principle, *see* Yin–yang
Yaodong, *see* Cave dwellings
Yin, female principle, *see* Yin–yang
Yingbi, also *zhaobi*, *see* Screen wall
Yin–yang (complementary opposites): interaction of, 54, 56, 195, *see also Fengshui*
Yinzhai (an abode for the dead), *see* Graves
Yuan-dynasty houses, *164–5*, 165
Yunnan, 43

Zaojun, *see* Stove God
Zhang Daoling (Zhang Tianshi), 62, *62*
Zhaobi (also *yingbi*), *see* Screen wall
Zhejiang: auspicious symbols, *85*, *86*, *87*, *90*; bamboo, *43*; breaking ground, *59*; canal houses, *51*, 120, *127–31*, *127*, *128–9*, *130–1*; Xu Wei's Green Vine Studio, 140–5; Hemudu Neolithic site, *36*; joinery, *36*; protective amulets, *62*, *64*, *65*; roof profile, *45*; Taishan stones, *64*
Zhen Cheng Lou (Inspiring Success Tower), *18–19*, 19
Zhong Kui (formidable demon queller), *64*
Zhouzhuang, Jiangsu, 120, 124–7, *124–5*

ACKNOWLEDGMENTS

In the course of nearly forty years researching China's rural material culture, I have accumulated enormous debts to scholars, generalists, administrators, and ordinary villagers who have helped me understand and write about what is clearly one of the world's outstanding architectural traditions. In spite of increasing amounts of written material and after increasing visitation to China by foreigners, China's extraordinary architectural heritage is still not as well known as it should be.

Eric Oey's invitation to bring Chinese houses into focus in a lavishly illustrated large-format book written for a general audience has provided both an opportunity and a challenge. While selecting a "representative" sample of some twenty houses across a country as large as the United States has been daunting, this book has provided an occasion to discuss individual houses within the broader context of Chinese life and history in a way never attempted before.

After coming up with a shortlist of possible houses, I sought out additional recommendations from friends and acquaintances all over the world to insure that I had not overlooked any house that best epitomizes China. Among those who quickly offered opinions and guidance were Daniel B. Abramson, Nancy Berliner, Pai Ling Chen, Jeff Cody, Christopher Cooke, Lynne DiStefano, Fu Chao-ching, Guo Qinghua, Feng Jin, Gong Kai, Sarah Handler, Patrick Hase, Puay-peng Ho, Hsia Chu-joe, Hsu Min-fu, Huang Juzheng, Tess Johnston, Elizabeth Knight, Richard Latham, Hoyin Lee, Elizabeth Leppman, Andrew I-kang Li, Kai-Yin Lo, David Lung, F. Nuttaphol Ma, Meg Maggio, Nancy Steinhardt, Ruan Xing, Hsing-yuan Tsao, Joseph C. Wang, Wang Qijun, James L. Watson, Bill Wu, Alex Ya-ning Yen, Zhou Bihua, and Zhu Chengliang. All of their leads and suggestions were followed up, but in the end many variables contributed to my selection of houses to be featured. Some of those who offered advice may be surprised about some of the houses chosen, yet I hope that they too will encounter here houses that are new to them. The final decisions were mine alone.

It was my good fortune that Periplus/Tuttle selected A. Chester Ong to do the photography for this book. We worked well as a team, traveling twice together to China. My sense of how each house was to be presented aligned well with his ability to capture light even when there was darkness and to compose what appeared ordinary in order to bring out its beauty. It was always my task to negotiate permission to photograph when householders, administrators, and security personnel would rather that we not shoot. Thus, special appreciation is owed those families who opened their homes and permitted us to intrude on their daily life as well as administrators of several historic sites who gave us unprecedented permission to photograph whatever we thought necessary.

Special thanks are due two individuals who generously allowed us to use original artwork: Robert Powell, architect-writer-artist permitted the use of two of his remarkable watercolors of buildings in Chengkan village, Anhui. These had been painted for the China Heritage Arts Foundation (CHAF), set up by Robert Ellsworth, the New York Asian art dealer and collector, to promote architectural conservation in China. The assistance of Elizabeth Knight, editor of *Orientations Magazine*, in making these arrangements is much appreciated. Wang Qijun, prolific author of books on Chinese vernacular architecture in Chinese, took time out of a very busy schedule to draw the plan and perspective view of the Mei Lanfang residence.

Several institutions generously provided valuable art images from their collections: the Nelson-Atkins Museum of Art; the Smithsonian, Freer Gallery of Art and Arthur M. Sackler Gallery; and the British Museum. Kathleen Ryor's original translation of Xu Wei's poetry adds a valuable touch to that section. Craig Dietrich's advice on many of the essays was invaluable.

Jonathan Spence's willingness to write a Foreword for *Chinese Houses* is deeply appreciated. His generous words will help bring greater attention to the rich and fascinating subject of China's domestic architectural heritage, which has been sadly understudied by historians and others as a vector for understanding broader issues of Chinese culture and history.

Since its conception, this book has undergone a number of significant conceptual changes and has taken shape via the efforts of individuals on three continents. No one has played a greater role in shaping the book than Noor Azlina Yunus, Senior Editor at Tuttle/Periplus in Malaysia. With no other editor I have worked has it been possible in real-time via email to make decisions page by page in terms of content and design. Azlina's sense of style, wit, and guidance have been significant factors in giving shape to *Chinese Houses* in a time frame that often was 24/7. I owe her a great debt. Her assistant Yong Yoke Lian has ably met every electronic and design challenge we have encountered. Tan Hong Yew's ability to turn rough sketches into fine drawings adds an important dimension to the book. Much appreciation is owed Holger Jacobs, working in London, for creating a design that weaves words, photographs, drawings, and artwork into an effective narrative.

The list below acknowledges the sources of all illustrations not taken by Chester Ong.

a=above; b=below; c=center; l=left; r=right
4–5 Robert Powell, *Interior Perspective of Lao Wu Ge in Spring*, Xixinan Village, watercolor on paper, height 74 cm, width 92 cm, 2003. Collection of the artist.
9 Daoji (1641–c. 1717), "The Peach Blossom Spring," section of a handscroll, ink and colors on paper, height 9 7/8 in. Used with the permission of the Freer Gallery of Art, Smithsonian Institution, Washington, DC: Purchase, F1957.4.
16–17 Qiao Zhongchang, "Su Shi's Second Poem on the Red Cliff, handscroll, ink on

paper, 11.6 in. x 18 ft. 8. in. Northern Song dynasty, 1123. Used with the permission of Nelson-Atkins Museum of Art in Kansas City, Missouri (accession number F80-5).
18 "Circular House, Inhabited by the Members of One Clan," William Elliot Griffis, *China's Story in Myth, Legend, Art, and Animals*, Boston: Houghton Mifflin, 1911.
19 *Yongding tulou* (Yongding Earth Buildings), Fuzhou: Fujian renmin chubanshe, 1990.
21 Zhongguo kexueyuan tumu jianzhu yanjiusuo and Qinghua daxue jianzhuxi (joint eds.), *Zhongguo jianzhu* (Chinese Architecture), Beijing: Wenwu chubanshe, 1957.
23b Adapted from Huang Weijuan et al., *Min Yue Minzhai* (China Vernacular Dwelling [sic]: Fujian and Guangdong Provinces), Tianjin: Tianjin kexue jishu chubanshe, 1992.
25a Zhang Bitian and Liu Zhenya, *Shaanxi minju* (Vernacular Dwellings of Shaanxi), Beijing: Zhongguo jianzhu gongye chubanshe, 1993.
31a Ernest F. Borst-Smith, *Mandarin & Missionary in Cathay*, London: Seeley, 1917.
31c John Thomson, *Through China with a Camera*, Westminster: Constable, 1898.
35a, 1984; **39b**, 1984; **41a**, 1984; **41b**, 1994; **43a**, 1986; **43c**, 1994; **47c**, 2000; **49al**, 1987; **49ar**, 1988; **59a**, 1988; **61b**, 1990; **64al**, 1990; **65al**, 1987; **65br**, 1987; **84b**, 2001; **87c**, 1987; **95**, 2003 Photographs by Ronald G. Knapp.
36b Yang Hongxun, "Hemudu yizhi mugou shuijing jianding ji caoqi mugou gongyi kaocha" (Identification of the Timber Structure Well at the Hemudu Site and Inspection of the Technology of Early Timber Structure), *Keji wenji* (Collection on the History of Science and Technology), vol. 5, 1980.
38; **58a** *Er ya* (Examples of Refined Usage), juan 2, 6b.
39a "Building a Wall of Pisé de terre at Kuling," Rudolf Hommel, *China at Work*, New York: John Day, 1937.
40al; **40ar**; **48** Song Yingxing, *Tiangong kaiwu* (The Creations of Nature and Man), Shanghai: Huatong shuju, 1930.
51; **71a** Mrs Archibald Little, *Intimate China: The Chinese as I Have Seen Them*, London: Hutchinson, 1899.
54 *Gengzhi Tu*. Image 35866. © Copyright The Trustees of The British Museum.
55 Shang Guo, "Zhongguo fengshui geju de goucheng, shengtai huanjing yu jingguan" (Patterns of China's Fengshui: Formation, Ecological Environments, and Landscapes), in Wang Qiheng (ed.), *Fengshui lilun yanjiu* (Research of Fengshui Theory), Tianjin: Tianjin daxue chubanshe, 1992.
57b; **endpapers** Gong Kai, *Zhifeng, Huizhou gu jianzhu congshu* (Zhifeng Village, Ancient Architecture in Huizhou Series), Nanjing: Dongnan daxue chubanshe, 1999.
58b Ernst Boerschmann, *Baukunst und Landschaft in China* (Architecture and Landscape in China), Berlin: Verlag von Ernst Wasmuth A. G., 1923.
59b; **63l**; **63a**; **64b**; **248bl**; **138l** *Huitu Lu Ban Jing* (Illustrated *Lu Ban Jing*), c. 1600.
61ar Photograph by J. Azevedo.
62; **80**; **96**; **150c** Collection of Ronald G. Knapp.
68b; **70a**; **70b**; **78**; **171b**; **226a** Wu Youru, *Wu Youru huabao* (Treasury of Wu Youru's Drawings), Shanghai: Biyuan huishe, 1916.
69b Adapted from a drawing by Pan An.
71b Arthur Henderson Smith, *Chinese Characteristics*, New York: Fleming H. Revell, 1894.
91b Pan Lusheng, *Zhongguo minsu jianzhi tuji* (Collection of Chinese Folk Papercut Patterns), Beijing: Beijing gongyi meishu chubanshe, 1992.
92a Qiao Jitang, *Zhongguo jixiang wu* (Chinese Auspicious Elements), Tianjin: Tianjin renmin chubanshe, 1990.
92b W. A. P Martin, *A Cycle of Cathay: or, China, South and North*, New York: Fleming H. Revell, 1897.
96b *Ershisi xiao guobao tu—fu: wuni buxiao baoying tu* (Illustrations of the Twenty-four Paragons of Filiality—Appendix: Illustrations of Retribution for Unfilial Acts), Chengdu: Chengdu wenshu yuan, 1993.
97 Collection of Nancy Berliner.
100; **103a** Original drawings by Wang Qijun.
107 Kate Buss, *Studies in Chinese Drama*, NY: Jonathon Cape & Harrison, 1930.
112 Original drawing by Liu Chong.
114a Adapted from *Mentougou wenwu zhi* (Records of Mentougou's Heritage), Beijing: Yanshan chubanshe, 2001.
115b Adapted from Itō Tsuneharu, *Hokushi Mokyo no jukyo* (Houses of North China, Mongolia, and Xinjiang), Tokyo: Kobundo, 1943.
121b; **128a** Adapted from Joseph C. Wang, "Zhouzhuang, Jiangsu: A Historic Market Town," in Ronald G. Knapp (ed.), *Chinese Landscapes: The Village as Place*, Honolulu, University of Hawai'i Press, 1992. Original drawings by Men-chou Liu.
146; **149**; **169**; **170a**; **170b**; **234–5**; **250**; **253**; **254a**; **254c** Adapted from Wang Zhili (chief ed.), *Zhongguo chuantong minju jianzhu* (Chinese Traditional Architecture of Residence [sic]), Jinan: Shandong kexue jishu chubanshe, 1994.
147a Wen Zhong, *Zui e shijia Kang Baiwan* (Despicable Kang Baiwan Family), Zhengzhou: Henan renmin chubanshe, 1979.
156; **160a** Adapted from Yin Yongda, "Huizhou Chengkan gu cun ji Ming zhai diaocha" (Investigation of the Old Village and Ming Dwellings in Chengkan, Huizhou), in Lu Yuanding (ed.), *Zhongguo chuangtong minju yu wenhua* (China's Traditional Vernacular Dwellings and Culture), vol. 4, 1993.
157a Luo Laiping, "Chengkan gu cun," unpublished manuscript, 1999.
158–9 Robert Powell, *Street Elevation of Wu Fang Ting*, watercolor on paper, ht 75 cm, width 191 cm, 2003. Collection of the artist.
178a; **180a**; **187a**; **190a**; **190b** Adapted from original drawings by Huang Hanmin.
194 Adapted from an unpublished drawing of De Xing Tang.
199a; **201a** Adapted from Lu Yuanding and Wei Yanjun, *Guangdong minju* (Vernacular Dwellings of Guangdong), Beijing: Zhongguo jianzhu gongye chubanshe, 1990.
202bl; **208a** Adapted from Measured Drawings Collection, Department of Architecture, University of Hong Kong.
203b; **221b** Adapted from an unpublished floor plan.
210 Adapted from Liu Dunzhen, *Zhongguo zhuzhai gaishuo* (Introduction to Chinese Dwellings), Beijing: Jianzhu gongye chubanshe, 1957.
211b *Mao zhuxi Shaoshan jiuju* (Chairman Mao's Former Residence Shaoshan), poster designed by Xu Zhaohai, published by Hunan renmin chubanshe, October 1974. Print no. 8109.948. From the Leiden University International Institute of Social History Stefan R. Landsberger Collection. http://www.iisg.nl/~landsberger
213b; **215b** Hunan sheng Shaoshan guanliju (ed.), *Qingxi Shaoshan* (Shaoshan Sentiments), Changsha: Hunan renmin chubanshe, 2004.
240; **243a** Adapted from Ji Fuzheng, unpublished conference paper.
241a File photo used with the permission of China Features, Beijing.
256; **258** Adapted from a brochure.
263b Chen Chi-lu (Chen Qilu), et al. (eds.), *Zhongguo chuantong nianhua yishu tezhan zhuanji* (The Art of the Traditional Chinese New Year Print), Taipei: National Central Library, 1992.
265; **267l** *Pingyao xianzhi* (Gazetteer of Pingyao), 1883.
267r; **268r**; **268b**; **270a** Song Kun, *Pingyao gu cheng yu minju* (The Old City and Houses of Pingyao), Tianjin: Tianjin daxue chubanshe, 2000.
274a; **276b**; **279a** Adapted from Hou Jiyao et al., *Yaodong minju* (Vernacular Cave Dwellings), Beijing: Zhongguo jianzhu gongye chubanshe, 1989.
274b Wulf Diether Graf zu Castell, *Chinaflug*, Berlin: Atlantis-Verlag, 1938.
278 Adapted from an original drawing by Paul Sun, in Ronald G. Knapp, *China's Old Dwellings*, University of Hawai'i Press, 2000.